A Local Habitation

OTHER BOOKS BY THE SAME AUTHOR

POETRY
Stranger to Europe : Poems 1939–49. Cape Town: A.A. Balkema, 1952.
Stranger to Europe, with Additional Poems. Cape Town: A.A. Balkema, 1960
South of the Zambesi: Poems from South Africa. Illustrated by John Lawrence. London and New York: Abelard-Schuman, 1966.
On First Seeing Florence. Grahamstown: New Coin, 1968.
Selected Poems. Johannesburg: Ad. Donker, 1975.
Songs and Ballads, published with *Today Is Not Different* by Patrick Cullinan in Mantis Poets, edited by Jack Cope, Cape Town: David Philip, 1978.
Pilgrimage to Dias Cross: A Narrative Poem. With woodcuts and engravings by Cecil Skotnes. Cape Town: David Philip, 1987.
Selected Poems, with Additional Poems. Johannesburg: Ad. Donker, 1989.

PLAYS
The Dam: A Play in Three Acts. Cape Town: A.A. Balkema, 1953.
The Dove Returns: A Play in Three Acts. London: Fortune Press, 1956.
Cape Charade, or Kaatjie Kekkelbek. Cape Town: A.A. Balkema, 1968.
Take Root or Die. Cape Town: A.A. Balkema, 1970.
Richard Gush of Salem. Cape Town: Maskew Miller, 1982.
Demea: A Play. Cape Town: David Philip, 1990.

AUTOBIOGRAPHY
Karoo Morning: An Autobiography 1918–35. Cape Town: David Philip, 1977.
Bursting World: An Autobiography 1936–45. Cape Town: David Philip, 1983.

OTHER PROSE
Tales from the Old Karoo. Johannesburg: Ad. Donker, 1989.
A Rackety Colt: The Adventures of Thomas Stubbs. Cape Town: Tafelberg, 1989.

EDITED WORKS
A Book of South African Verse. London: Oxford University Press, 1959.
When Boys Were Men: Extracts from South African Diaries, 1795–1870. Cape Town: Oxford University Press, 1969.
Plays from Near and Far: Twelve One-act Plays. With Tim Peacock. Cape Town: Maskew Miller, 1973.
The 1820 Settlers: An Illustrated Commentary. With John Benyon; captions by Eily Gledhill; pictures by Rex and Barbara Reynolds; design by Ken Robinson. Cape Town: Human & Rousseau, 1974.
A New Book of South African Verse. With Chris Mann. Cape Town: Oxford University Press, 1979.
Out of the African Ark. With David Butler; zoological descriptions by Carmen Welz. Johannesburg: Ad. Donker, 1988.
The Magic Tree: South African Stories in Verse. With Jeff Opland. Cape Town: Maskew Miller Longman, 1989.
South Africa: Landshapes, Landscapes, Manscapes. Photographs by Herman Potgieter. Cape Town: Struik Publishers, 1990.

GUY BUTLER

A Local Habitation

An Autobiography (1945–90)

DAVID PHILIP   CAPE TOWN   JOHANNESBURG

First published by David Philip Publishers (Pty) Ltd, 208 Werdmuller Centre, Newry Street, Claremont, Cape Province, South Africa

ISBN 0 86486 180 X

© Guy Butler 1991

All rights reserved

DTP conversion by CAPS of Cape Town

Printed by Creda Press (Pty) Ltd, Solan Road, Cape Town, South Africa

Contents

ACKNOWLEDGEMENTS *vii*
PROLOGUE *ix*
1 ENGLAND : JUNE 1945 1
2 ENTER MY ANCESTORS : JUNE–AUGUST 1945 12
3 OUT OF THE ARMY : SEPTEMBER 1945 20
4 OXFORD : OCTOBER 1945–JUNE 1946 29
5 HOME VISIT : JULY–SEPTEMBER 1946 44
6 OXFORD AND SWITZERLAND 1946–APRIL 1947 54
7 WELLINGTON SQUARE : MAY–DECEMBER 1947 67
8 FRANCE & ITALY IN THREE WEEKS : SUMMER 1947 74
9 HOME STRETCH : SEPTEMBER–DECEMBER 1947 85
10 WITS : JANUARY 1948–DECEMBER 1950 94
11 PLAYS : 1945– 107
12 A HOUSE AND TWO CHAIRS : 1951 119
13 EARLY POETRY : 1945–60 137
14 APPRENTICE PROFESSOR : 1952–61 160
15 HIGH CORNER : 1951– 174
16 EARLY PLAYWRITING : 1950–60 193
17 MORE POETRY : 1961– 202
18 WEST AFRICA : 1954–JANUARY 1955 216
19 PROFESSOR AT LARGE : 1958–78 232
20 LATER WRITINGS : 1962– 243
21 RESTORATION OF OLD HOUSES : 1952– 256
22 EASTERN CAPE HISTORY, DIARIES & PLAYS : 1952– 263
23 THE POPLARS : 1946–74 274
24 MONUMENTS AND FESTIVALS : 1959– 296
EPILOGUE 309

FOR JEAN

Acknowledgements

As with the previous volumes of this autobiography, my deepest debt is to my wife Jean, and on many counts: for keeping letters, cuttings and photographs, for enriching this narrative with her own recollections, for clarifying obscurities, and for helping me through the protracted process of its completion.

I am also most grateful to my sisters, Joan Butler, Dorothy Murray, Christine Moys, and my brother, Professor Jeffrey Butler; to my lifelong friends and cousins, John Biggs, Godfrey Collett and their wives; and to my English relatives, particularly Guy Stringer, C.B.E.

Next to my family and relatives my chief debt is to my alma mater, Rhodes University. Three vice-chancellors, Dr Thomas Alty, Dr J.M. Hyslop and Dr Derek Henderson, have all treated me with patience and generosity, as have my academic colleagues over some forty years. The staff of the English Department has been consistently helpful, and I wish to record my special gratitude to its present Head, Professor Malvern van Wyk Smith. The brevity of the accounts of projects in which I took a leading part has been dictated by limited space. None would have come to fruition without broad support from countless unmentioned friends. I must also thank the many good students whose questions and answers have made my career as a teacher infinitely rewarding.

For help with illustrations my chief debt is to Barbara and Rex Reynolds; also the National English Literary Museum, the Cory Library for Historical Research of Rhodes University, the Library of the University of the Witwatersrand, Cecil Skotnes, Ronald Philip, Robert Brooks, Sue Imrie Ross, Sirion Robertson and John Lawrence.

This book depends heavily on the recollections of others as well as my own. The following have either provided me with information, narratives or anecdotes, or commented upon portions of the text.

Lionel Abrahams, David Bunyan, Prof. Peter Bayley, The Rt. Rev. B.B. Burnett, The Very Rev. Roy Barker, Jack Cope, Rob and Sue Clarence, Murray Carlin, Peggy Corbett, Marge Clouts, K.T. Cremer, Athol Fugard, The Rev. Charles Hooper C.R., Ruth Harnett, Daphne Levens, Douglas Livingstone, Sister E.M. Lantry, Prof. Don Maclennan, Roy Macnab, Prof. M.M. Mahood, Dr Dooley and Audrey Muller, David and Marie Philip, Rex and Barbara Reynolds, David Raeburn, Prof. Michael Roberts, Sipho

Sepamla, Peter se Puma, Brian Stanion, Prof. Malvern van Wyk Smith, David Wright, Dr Ron and Lois Wylde.

I am particularly indebted to the National English Literary Museum, the Cory Library for Historical Research, the University of Durham (for Plomer correspondence), and the University of the Witwatersrand.

ILLUSTRATIONS

The illustrations with the text are by the author unless otherwise specified. Those without captions are doodles, usually made during committee meetings.

For the numbered illustrations between pages 66-7 and 262-3, grateful acknowledgements are made to the following photographers and sources:

Guy Stringer 1; Ursula Brown 4; David Raeburn 5; University of the Witwatersrand 6; Roy Macnab 7; Community of the Resurrection 8; Anne Fischer, Cape Town (from National Theatre Organisation) 9; National Theatre Organisation 11; Cape Archives 12; Rex Reynolds 13, 36, 37, 38, 39, 40, 43; Sirion Robertson 14; David Wright 15; Douglas Glass, London, 16; Hope Eglington 17; Katherine Young (from Alan Paton) 18; Marge Clouts 19; Jack Cope 20; Pictone Studios, Hillbrow (from University of the Witwatersrand) 21; N.E.L.M. 22, 28; Ruth Harnett 23; Jim White (from Stephen Gray) 24; Stuart McColl, Durban, 25; Ruphin Coudyzer (from Ad. Donker) 27; Lionel Abrahams 29; Peggy Nairn 31; Jane Plotz 32; PACT, Pretoria, 41, 42; Hepburn & Jeanes, Grahamstown (from 1820 Foundation) 45, 46; David Goldblatt (from *Evening Post* and 1820 Foundation) 47; Susan Imrie Ross, Grahamstown (from 1820 Foundation) 48; 1820 Foundation 49, 50, 51; *Eastern Province Herald* 44, 52; Joan Butler 54, 55, 56.

Prologue

The first volume of this autobiography, *Karoo Morning 1918–35* (267 pages) ambled at a leisurely pace through my childhood and school education in Cradock in the Karoo.

The second, *Bursting World 1936–45* (300 pages), took me through my first four-year spell of student life at Rhodes University, my falling in love with Jean Satchwell and marriage to her in 1940, my first brief spell of teaching, and five years in the army – in South Africa, the Middle East, and Italy. It ended with my landing in Britain during May 1945 to help with the repatriation of South African prisoners of war. I went in the confident expectation that the war would soon be over, I would be joined by Jean and I would take up a scholarship at a British university.

Both these volumes attempted to deal with my growth from stage to stage, from year to year, in an historical progression. But clearly the pace could not go on – 567 pages to cover 27 years averages 21 pages per annum. To take the story to my retirement at 65 at this rate would need another 798 pages, a prospect which neither my publisher nor I could contemplate. For this reason alone a change in pace and method was essential. In fact the length of this volume has been determined less by simple sums like the above than by the shape my life has taken.

After my spell in Britain (May 1945 to December 1947) I spent three years at the University of the Witwatersrand (January 1948 to December 1950). These six years (1945–1950) were seminal and I could have recorded three times as much upon them as is printed here.

In 1951 I came to Rhodes University, Grahamstown, to a senior lectureship. Grahamstown held a particular magic for us, as those who have read *Bursting World* will appreciate. At the end of 1951 several things happened in rapid succession, including the acquisition of a commodious ruin, 122 High Street, which in due course we called High Corner. At the same time I became a professor.

The first portion of this book, dealing with the Oxford and Wits years, completes the account of my *wanderjahre* begun in *Bursting World*, and places me back in home territory, the Eastern Cape.

Certainly my life underwent a major change at the end of 1951. Professors are not entirely themselves. Their interest as persons decreases because they are now public personages. Much of their time is spent on committees whose function is to pick the brains of individuals without giving them credit. Committees can also make mistakes for which no one individual can be held accountable. Professors are of course allowed to be cranky, but they usually serve their disciplines and their universities rather than themselves.

The attempt at an historical biography changes after 1952 into a series of memoirs of particular activities. I have tried to present my life by teasing it out into the main strands from which it seems to have been woven, so that the reader will not be confused by the complex entanglement of interests. In any single day I may split my time and attention between my family, teaching, writing poetry, house restoration, politics and committee work. I have devoted separate chapters to what I think are the most important or interesting. The advantage of this for the reader is clear. If he is not interested in restoring old houses, or the origins of the Grahamstown Festival, or my passion for poetry, he can skim or skip until he finds something congenial.

It is a pleasant irony that the title of this book should have been provided by William Shakespeare, the main academic, dramatic and poetic interest of my entire career, to whom, in this volume, I pay virtually no attention at all.

The poet's eye, in a fine frenzy rolling,
Doth glance from heaven to earth, from earth to heaven;
And, as imagination bodies forth
The forms of things unknown, the poet's pen
Turns them to shapes, and gives to airy nothing
A local habitation and a name.
(Misummer Night's Dream V.i)

This book has been written at High Corner, our home since 1951, and it is to my wife Jean that it is dedicated.

1 June 1945

England

London, June 1945. I am still in uniform, with the triangular green-and-yellow flash of the 6th South African Armoured Division on my shoulder below my three pips. Twenty-seven years old, I am being entertained by my uncle, Norman Butler, and his daughter Pam. It is my first visit. I am to sleep on a stretcher to be erected later in this small room full of Victorian furniture.

Pam is petite and looks startlingly like my Aunt Eliza of Cradock must have looked at that age. She and her fiancé are planning to emigrate from bomb-battered London to New Zealand.

'Why not South Africa? You'll find quite a clan of Butler relatives there – descendants of James, Charles and Emma.'

She shrugs her shoulders, saying simply, 'We don't like your racial legislation.'

'We hope it will change for the better,' I say.

At this point the grandfather clock behind her father's tall-backed chair chimes the half-hour. It is almost the twin of the clock we had at The Poplars, Bree Street, Cradock, but looks finer – not surprising in a family whose founding-father, Philip, had been a clockmaker. It is over six feet tall, with a large enamel dial in rotating sections, with stars, sun and moon painted upon them – an astronomical clock. At fifteen-minute intervals it reminded Uncle Norman, and all within the house, that time flies; for that is the motto painted on its face: *Tempus fugit.*

I had flown to England from Italy on 26 May 1945, with General Poole, under rather odd circumstances, and was posted to the South African p.o.w. Repatriation Unit in Brighton, which didn't really want me. The war in the West was virtually over, although not in the East. I was to be kept on strength until my demobilisation on 8 September. Being in an army when there's a war on is bad enough but to remain on the payroll for five months afterwards when there is no real work whatsoever, merely because you need a dole to keep you alive until you start your second spell at a university, is a test of character which I don't think I passed! Time did not fly; it dragged. It might have flown if only Jean, my wife, could have joined me, but the waiting-lists for berths from South Africa to England were long.

2 ENGLAND

I shall not weary the reader with those five months in limbo except for a few items in which I found themes important to my career. They were not so clear to me then as they are now.

Uncle Norman's clock punctuated the pleasant evening. What I found a little unsettling was its habit of starting a gentle muttering to itself well before striking each quarter, as if its Quaker conscience were bracing itself for that little routine but important task which lay ahead. Uncle Norman and Pam were quite used to it, of course; but its insistence on its presence I found a little unnerving – particularly when Uncle Norman rather haltingly referred to his late wife's repeated illnesses, recoveries, relapses, escapes from death's door, and final lingering death. To strike nine then, on cue, seemed uncalled for.

I was on the stretcher by ten, but I could not sleep. Ali London sank slowly into a deep silence except for a few late cabs and the timepieces. There seemed to be a sinister collusion among the clocks, to strike not together but in deliberate sequence, so that the announcement of midnight consisted of at least forty-eight strokes on bells of different weight. The tolling of bells outside and telling of time from towers under the sky would have been tolerable but for this conscientious timepiece at the head of my stretcher. In addition to its chime, I had to listen to its slow mechanical pulse. The mill of my weary but unwilling wakeful mind had plenty of grist to grind.

It was the first time I had been in a private home since leaving South Africa in April 1943. The house was packed with reminders of my father's people. Uncle Norman's acceptance of me had been open and unquestioning. It was the first step in a slow rediscovery of the web and woof of the family, uncles and aunts, husbands and wives, brothers and sisters, parents and children, which wars assault so efficiently and tear to shreds on all sorts of holy pretexts. It made me dimly aware how tattered I was.

The clock was making up its mind again. I switched on the light, propped myself up as best I could and re-read an incomplete letter to Jean, begun three days before in Brighton.

'This Brighton is a drab place. The beach is bum, no sand, nothing but shingles; as for the waves, they don't deserve the name, they are too weak to break, they merely collapse; and the sun never shines for more than an hour at a stretch. The evenings are interminably dreary. It only gets dark at ten and I'm sick of sitting in the mess alone, reading, or of going along the beach front, pubcrawling. Last night I went out with Chris Ballenden, ex 12th Company, Italy. We sat in 'The Star of the Garter' drinking ale. On one of the rafters was written, "He who is tired of Brighton is tired of life." Old campaigners, snorting into our tankards, we knew of similar sentiments expressed about more interesting places: "See Naples and die."

Stonehenge, from the east

'So we have come up to London, but even the heart of the Empire has failed to produce the excitement I experienced when landing at Taranto, or even at Tewfik. I've seen the Ritz, but no angels dining there; I've been to Berkeley Square, but it has no nightingales. I did find the parks beautiful, and the buildings round Parliament, the Abbey and Whitehall. The massive bomb damage round St Paul's is less impressive than the triumphant building itself. It seems to deserve its survival. And so do all the people I met, particularly Uncle Norman Butler and his daughter. They are simply marvellous – controlled, quiet and humorous.

'You ask whether I have made up my mind about which university I plan to go to and what course I shall take. I wish I could give an answer. The war has thrown my career into the melting-pot. What do I really want to do? English? Maybe. I have a longstanding affair with it. History? Ditto. Fine Art? Well, that's what I would have gone for if there'd been any money in the family – painting or even sculpture. I took myself off to Salisbury to see that slender cathedral which Constable painted. It is marvellous, at a distance, stone that looks like lace. Then I took a bus to Stonehenge – how utterly different. Salisbury spire aspiring to heaven, and this contrasting circle a magnificent open sun-and-moon dial of massive stones set in green grass.'

Old Tempus Fugit struck two. And I stopped writing, switched off and tried to sleep; but just as I was drifting off, the chuntering started up again. Before the quarter had chimed I switched on the light to add:

'P.S. I forgot to mention Education. And Anthropology. Seriously. Sir James Frazer's *The Golden Bough* is wonderful.'

I switched off the light once more, but sleep was banned by the heavy thud of the pendulum.

At three-thirty, when the half-hour had finished chiming, I arose and opened the clock's mahogany case, gently seized the pendulum, and stopped it. In five minutes I was asleep.

I awoke in the early light, confused, to see a strange figure in a brown dressing-gown towering above me. He was very distressed.

'The clock has stopped, the clock has stopped!' he lamented.

'Yes, Uncle Norman, I am afraid I stopped it.'

'But why did you do that? It has never stopped since I moved into this house – fifty-six years.'

I apologised, and explained my difficulty in getting to sleep. He could accept my arguments rationally, but all through breakfast he remained upset. It was as if this soldier had brought the chaos of war into his house. I offered to restart it, but he shook his head. 'I must get the watchmaker,' he said.

Walking the next morning near Bush House, Pam quietly recounted one or two of her experiences during the blitz, particularly of flying bombs. She'd had a much tougher war than I.

Back at Brighton, I received a telegram from my mother's brother, George Stringer of Oulton Cross, Stone, Staffs, informing me that his son, Major Guy Stringer, was in Brighton, staying at the Hotel Dudley.

Major Guy Stringer. My mother, Alice, had not given me his rank, only that he had been with General Orde Wingate's Chindits in Burma for four years, and that he had been wounded in action. I had forgotten when he was born. So I went, wondering, to the hotel, where I found a note which read:

'Dear Cousin, I'm down on the beach below this road. I am fair-headed and wearing a white sweater. I am with – provided she will stay – a smashing fair-haired girl. Do come down. Yours aye, Guy Stringer.'

This gave me the impression that the major was a bit of a roué, probably about 35. He turned out to be eleven years younger: fair, stocky, full of nonsense, and very struck on the girl. He must have been a good soldier to be a major at 24. We found that, beyond the common interests of family and war experiences, we shared a zest for the ridiculous, the pathetic and the theatrical.

That evening at the Metropole we baptised our infant friendship by total immersion in beer. He was soon regaling me with the comic highlights of the campaign in Burma.

That meeting with Guy was crucial. Having found him so congenial, I set about meeting other English relatives with greater confidence; and I had begun one of the best series of friendships of my life.

A letter came from Grantchester Road, Cambridge, from Alice's widowed sister, May Daniel – whom I remembered vaguely from a visit she had paid to The Poplars in the mid 'thirties. Her letter reminded me of her husband, Uncle Dan, who had taken me to our tennis court one wintry evening to put me wise to the southern constellations, and to modern poetry. The Daniels were then living in Italy, at Rapallo, where he occasionally met an American poet, called Pound, with the unlikely name of Ezra. My uncle considered excessive the poetic licence which the poet Pound took in his translations of the Latin poet Sextus Propertius. Having heard that I was writing verse, he expressed the hope that I would learn to write in regular metres before I wrote so-called free verse. Free from what?

And now I was in Brighton, with all the time in the world, trying to knock into shape a collection of poems, in both regular and free verse, for submission to Messrs Faber and Faber. It mattered more to me than I dared to admit to anyone, except Jean.

I had no difficulty in recognising Aunt May on the Cambridge platform. For several days she gently but firmly introduced me to the architectural beauties of Cambridge. She took me into the quadrangle of Gonville and Caius, where her brother Harold had been a student, through a gateway which was evidence that at last classical architectural influences were being felt among Shakespeare's contemporaries. She pointed to Newnham, where her tragic sister, Janet, had been for one year. It was at Newnham, she explained, that Janet had met Frances Higham, whom she had introduced to her brother George. It seemed to her a foregone conclusion that I was going to Cambridge. When I told her that I could not make up my mind until I had seen Oxford, she smiled and said, 'That's Alice, I suppose. She always favoured Oxford with its dreaming spires. I do hope you come here though.' She urged me to visit Oxford as soon as possible. Time was important.

She wrote a charming letter to her sister Alice at The Poplars, saying that I looked well, but that I was rather vague. No doubt I needed a little time to find my bearings, but I must not shilly-shally too long between Oxford and Cambridge.

Shilly-shally is exactly what I did; not merely between Oxford and Cambridge, but between subjects: English, History, Anthropology, Education, Medicine, and even Fine Art.

One of my handicaps was the lack of anyone with whom to discuss these problems. Another was my incompetence at managing my own life. For five years I had obeyed orders. Each day had been shaped by routines and instructions not of my making. My whole life had been communal: particularly during the last two years, I had lived much at secondhand, identifying with the boredom, the crises, the victories of regiment, brigade, division, army and the Allies. In so far as I had had an interior, individual life, it had been that of sufferer, victim, spectator, sometimes jester or fool. Decisions had been few and far between.

But now the army was abandoning me to my own devices. The Repatriation Unit never found out what Special Service I was supposed to render.

On 25 June I wrote to Jean: 'If you can get a passage soon enough you'll be able to help me choose between Medicine, History, English, Education, Anthropology, Fine Art and Carpentry. I have not yet decided between Oxford or Cambridge or got myself accepted by a college. I'm told the matter is quite urgent now, so I shall dash off, make up my mind on a course, and which place I want to go to, and find a house for us in which to live.'

In the midst of these uncertainties I abandoned the idea of Medicine: five-and-a-half years of sweat in a new discipline on a budget so small that Jean (although more than willing) would have to work full-time, would delay intolerably what we had both expressed as our greatest need: to set up house and start a family. I also lost interest in Education. There were only three serious contenders left: English, History and Anthropology.

Aunt May invited me to Cambridge again. She brought me a little closer to earth. Had I made up my mind? Which was it to be? She then discovered, with some alarm, that I was hovering between three disciplines. She sensibly set about introducing me to such proponents of them as she knew.

It was good to meet Eric Walker, whose *History of South Africa* I had read and enjoyed. He explained what reading history at Cambridge involved. He was sure I'd not regret it. He might be able to secure me a place at his college, but time was running out.

As for Anthropology, of the many talents now needed was an aptitude for languages which had not yet been reduced to writing. I was no good at learning languages and suspected that Jean would not enjoy life in a tent or hut preparing meals consisting of bananas, cassava or yams. Anthropology was out.

'What about English?' asked May.

'If I decide on English,' I said, 'I shall go to Oxford.'

'But why?'

Because I was firmly convinced that the Cambridge School was dominated by F.R. Leavis, and F.R. Leavis was a fundamentalist critic who looked no further than the words on the page. I was prepared to be vehement about Leavis.

So the choice was History at Cambridge or English at Oxford. She made me promise to go to Oxford as soon as possible and make up my mind.

Having done her best for me she took me to relax in the Fitzwilliam Museum. Had she but known it, this revived my nostalgia for the Fine Arts.

I had no kind relative in Oxford to show me around, no one who knew anyone in any of the colleges. So I had to try to get in, all by myself.

The approach to Oxford by rail is not impressive. Had I not caught a glimpse of some spires between an electric pylon and a gasometer, I might have thought it was another town like Reading. Nor was the walk from the station any better.

I was among a jungle of buses on Gloucester Green when a captain of Royal Army Supply Corps, who had served in Italy, cried, 'Hullo, Springbok, you look lost.'

When he heard I had come to arrange about getting into Oxford, he looked rather surprised.

'You mean you have not yet found yourself a college?'

'I can find all the colleges,' I said. 'I can read a map.'

'Haven't you got a letter of introduction to anyone?'

'No.'

'Then how do you expect to get in?'

It was all very puzzling. How could my entire future depend on the lack of an introduction to the head or Fellow of a college? I had a good record, testimonials, and a scolarship.

'I know the system seems crazy, but it does work,' he said apologetically. 'Surely you know some old Oxonians?'

'I know several, but they are all in South Africa, or in Italy. I have been introduced to Eric Walker of Cambridge, who said he might manage to get me into his college.'

'Well, old chap, settle for Cambridge. A pity, but it's not a bad place, you know.'

I strolled around the heart of Oxford for an hour, asking early risers where the Registrar or Headquarters of the University was. Not a soul knew. The nearest one dear old gentleman got was the University Press and the University Church.

To prove to her that I was trying to make up my mind, I sent Aunt May a picture postcard of the spire of St Mary the Virgin, the University Church, saying that I thought it the loveliest thing I had seen outside Italy.

I had told Jean that the rejection of my poems by Faber and Faber would switch me off literature, which would mean History at Cambridge. Back in Brighton I found my manuscript, with a letter of rejection. My verse was a little oldfashioned, it said, and there was a glut of war poetry, but I might try the Hogarth Press. So that settled it. I must abandon Literature, espouse History, and go to Cambridge, where, thanks to my dear Aunt May, I did know someone.

But I found, to my annoyance, that Faber's decision did not put me off writing poetry. I re-read my rejected typescript. I knew I would go on struggling with words until I died, even if I never got into print. One of the reasons why the poems were not more compelling was, perhaps, my minimal contact with poetry during the last five years. Maybe I needed a spell of saturation in literature.

Then I would groan, feeling the weight of my years. By my age Keats had written all his marvellous poetry, Milton had completed the 'Nativity Ode' at 21, and Roy Campbell had published *The Flaming Terrapin*. Here was I, hovering between Europe and Africa, and between Pound and the

Romantics, and strangely, stubbornly determined to hover until I found on what axis I could move; but I would not move merely because of a new fashion or on another man's manifesto. Much as I enjoyed and admired the poetry of Pound, Auden, and MacNeice, I did not feel I belonged in that spectrum; nor with a new group round Henry Treece called the Apocalypse. Eliot, yes, in parts; W.B. Yeats, yes, from about 'Easter 1916'. But to feel an affinity was one thing; to find one's own voice was another.

Meanwhile Aunt May had received my postcard and deduced that I had opted for English, but that, however much I might like the spire of St Mary the Virgin, I had not found myself a college. She wrote to Frances, her brother George's wife, in some distress about Alice's dithering son. What on earth was to be done about him? Then Frances recalled a happy accident but for which I might never have got into Oxford at all.

Frances was the daughter of a lion-headed Anglican priest called Higham, who had been in charge of Wynberg parish in the Cape during the Anglo–Boer War. Her spinster sister, Maud, was keeping house for the white-maned old lion in a cottage in Stone, close to Oulton Cross.

In 1936 Uncle George had taken his family plus Maudie Higham on a holiday to a seaside resort in Wales. The neighbouring house was occupied by a reading party of students under the eye of a classics don from Oxford. One day there was a knock at the door. It was the Oxford don asking whether, by any chance, there was a Miss Maud Higham there? Yes, there was: Aunt Maudie.

'Ah, how odd. You see, my name is also Higham. So the postman made an excusable error.'

The postman's error led to an acquaintance sufficient to be presumed upon in a crisis. Aunt Frances wrote to Tom Higham of Trinity, informing him of her nephew-by-marriage's bomb-happy indecisiveness, and also to me, instructing me firmly to write to Higham, asking for an appointment, and to accept whatever advice he gave me.

I duly received an invitation to coffee at Trinity and met the University Orator. He was distant and gentle, and clearly in doubt about what was best to do. Trinity, he said, was full – had been for weeks. He had phoned one or two other colleges, where the story was the same. After quizzing me a little, he said: 'There's just a chance that the Indian Institute may be able to help you. I have a friend there who knows better than most of us how to place late and unusual applications.' I had a glimpse of myself sitting in a waiting-room with chaps in turbans and tarbooshes.

Higham's friend at the Indian Institute was courteous and businesslike, asking me a host of questions, jotting down the answers.

'I think we'll try B.N.C.,' he smiled. 'The Principal, Stallybrass, likes South Africans.'

From what I could deduce from one end of the ensuing conversation,

The Old Quadrangle of Brasenose College, with the dome of the Radcliffe Library and the spire of St Mary's beyond, in 1805, by J.M.W. Turner.

the Principal of B.N.C. – whatever that acronym meant – wanted to know what my academic record was. This was rattled off to him. It sounded quite impressive, even to me. My economic status followed, then a pause. Would I need accommodation in college? No, I was married. What subject? English. An appointment was made and I left, giving thanks. Once outside, I asked someone what B.N.C. stood for.

'Brasenose College,' he said.

'Where is it?'

'Why, just around the corner.'

And there it was on the Radcliffe Square, in the heart of Oxford, with the spire of St Mary the Virgin perpetually on view. I began to feel better.

The omens were good.

I was interviewed by a large man with a round face and very thick spectacles, the Principal, Dr Stallybrass, usually known as Sonners. (I heard subsequently that his father's name had been Sonnenschein. He had changed it to his mother's name at the same time and for the same reason as the British royal family had changed theirs.)

Sonners said he would require certified copies of my certificates and any testimonials I might have. He accepted me provisionally. He would see me again in October, when Michaelmas Term started. In the meantime I should see a person whose name I have forgotten, in the English faculty.

He was the opposite of Sonners in every way: small, narrow-faced and sharp. I was asked what degree I intended enrolling for. Many Oxford and Cambridge dons in the years immediately after the war regarded a higher degree as a pretentious Germanic fad which had unfortunately infected American universities, with the result that that continent was sending over droves of earnest young men in search of B.Litts or doctorates. Oxbridge, short of fighting them on the beaches, did everything it could to discourage the invasion.

When I said that my brain had been pretty idle for five years and that I had forgotten almost everything I had ever learnt, my interviewer nodded approval and almost smiled. When I said I wished to enrol for the English Honours degree he became quite affable.

'I'm so glad,' he said. 'For a moment I feared you might follow the example of our pot-hunting American friends.'

I was upset to hear that B.N.C. was a hearty college and that one of the reasons why Sonners liked South Africans was for their assumed sporting prowess. In those days I did look like a front-row forward.

I had no one to advise me about accommodation, such as the married Rhodes Scholars might have had, and the house-agents, because they had very little to offer and many takers, were not in the least helpful. After three days of increasing confusion, I took a semi-detached house with a small garden: kitchen and living-room downstairs, two bedrooms upstairs, fully furnished, in a good neighbourhood, Five Mile Drive, available from 1 September until 31 January. It was rather far out of town, but I had provided a roof over our heads from which we had three months to look around for something else.

I returned to Brighton with a sense of achievement. With the goodnatured assistance of many, I had made some crucial decisions and arrangements. Most important, I had decided to read English. I had chosen a university and committed myself to it; I had been accepted by a college, I had enrolled for a degree and I had found a house in which to live. All these matters were settled.

I would be demobilised on 8 September and take my final army leave in a direction still to be decided. I would become a university student again on 14 October 1945.

All I had to do was kill the intervening time, until Jean arrived by ship. I was confident that we would be together before the Oxford term started.

2   June–August 1945

Enter My Ancestors

Among the crowds of South African p.o.w.s in Brighton suddenly a face would seem familiar, filling my mind with my childhood and youth among people and homes and landscapes belonging together, particularly my farming cousins from the Karoo. They were mostly captured at Tobruk in June 1942.

And here was my cousin Godfrey Collett, staring at the fresh fruit in a Brighton shop window, in company with his fiancée's brother, David Bladen. What one says on such occasions often seems ridiculously inadequate. Our eyes met.

'Hullo, Guy. I'm wondering whether the two shillings and sixpence price tag on that tray of peaches is for the whole tray or a single peach.'

Later I heard his account of being tried for sabotage and being sent to a detention barracks in East Prussia; later still the saga of a winter march, just ahead of the Russians, lasting four months through 750 miles of snow.

And here is John Biggs, my close friend since the age of 5, telling me of a zigzag march as long – about ten or fifteen miles a day on secondary roads, spending each night in a big barn.

'One night in Poland I was woken by the bitter cold. I had hung my boots above my head by their laces. I felt for them. They knocked together. They'd frozen hard and rang like bells. So I took them down and tucked them into the straw beside me, to unfreeze them. Other chaps had to slit theirs at the back to get them on. Their feet were so bruised that blood oozed out at the heels on to the snow.'

'The Russki p.o.w.s marched with us, unprotected by the Geneva Convention. Most of them had no boots, only rags round their feet. The guards kicked them when they fell. We gave them what we could. I gave my spare pair of boots to a barefooted Russian.'

All this grimness was relayed in the unemotional gentle voice of someone who had come through it.

All three of us – Godfrey, John and I – had a common ancestor in John Collett of Grassridge in the Eastern Cape.

'My boy, I want to put you wise about your ancestors. Your dear mother and the aunts have probably told you a lot of lies about them.'

Thus Guy Stringer's father, Alice's brother Uncle George, from his hearth at Oulton Cross, near Stone, Staffordshire.

Twenty-four hours previously I had alighted on Stone platform, on the lookout for a man known to me only in family fables – and recognised him without difficulty: short, very erect, high colour, a close-trimmed moustache, grizzled hair (with a cow's-lick very like my own) and blue eyes. As he moved toward me I noticed he walked with slightly splayed feet, like Alice, like myself. His gestures, too, immediately signalled that he was Alice's brother; but unlike her, he was deliberate in everything he did.

His wife Frances was not deliberate. Indeed, she once confided to my sister Joan, 'If I didn't wind George up he'd stop.' Highly intellectual and hyperactive, her Higham nose and slightly protruding eyes gave her a hawklike, watchful look. If she detected any errors of fact in our uncle–nephew conversations she would come swooping down, spot-on target, and put the record straight. During her erudite and rhetorical displays, George would stuff his pipe carefully with Three Nuns tobacco; then, when she had returned to her lookout, he would start up again with slightly more emphasis and even greater deliberation. It was after our fifth or sixth meal that he managed to see me alone.

I had very little interest in my ancestors. True, I was aware of a host of funny, charming or moving stories about various relatives, but it had never occurred to me to ask how true or false they were. I had observed that my mother and aunts had a way of sometimes stopping short, leaving three or four dashes or asterisks in their narratives, for our adolescent minds to fill with whatever romantic or lurid invention we wished.

'You have no doubt been told that you are descended from an illustrious Captain Lucky who died heroically at Waterloo.'

Yes, I did recall the unusual name, 'How unlucky to have been Captain Lucky!', I had punned when Alice first mentioned his early death.

'Well, here he is.'

I looked at a charming, slightly primitive painting of a gentleman in a red coat. Under a black triangular hat his face was smiling, gentle, refined.

'Lie number one: he wasn't a captain; he was a sergeant-major in the Northampton Militia. Lie number two: he did not die of wounds on the field of Waterloo, but of the terrible dysentery on the south coast of England. He was in charge of one of the Martello towers there, part of the anti-invasion measures against old Boney. He's buried in the churchyard at Rye. You might go and see if you can find his grave, my boy. Although the inscription on the stone was transcribed about a century ago it seems to have disappeared. I've tried and had no luck.'

It was important to Uncle George to be as exact as possible about the past, and to pass on to others some knowledge of Staffordshire and the neighbouring counties. He spent his entire month's petrol ration showing me bits of England which might mean something to me. Armed with a picnic lunch and with Ordnance Survey maps we set out. He pointed out Watling Street's Roman directness in contrast to the twistings and turnings of those ancient English roads made, according to G.K. Chesterton, by reeling English drunkards.

Through lovely summer lanes we felt our way towards Shrewsbury. We stopped at the old Roman ford across the Severn, and there, on the greensward, took tea. Two swans slid by, white and Spenserian under the grey-green shadows of oaks. Uncle George talked of Shrewsbury and Sir Philip Sidney, and of an important battle there resulting in the death of Hotspur. He spoke, too, of A.E. Housman's 'Shropshire Lad' and pointed out Wenlock Edge.

He took me to the ruins of the old Roman city of Uriconium, a little way beyond a parish church. The caretaker was a grizzled old guardsman, an Anglo–Boer War veteran with a high Roman nose. One massive portion of the wall about fifteen feet high remained standing. For the rest, little was visible but foundations, a little mosaic, and the sites of the inevitable baths and the inevitable forum.

Unfortunately our guide was not good at ceramics. He committed several howlers about the origins of Samian and other ware in the little museum and he made the mistake of persisting in his errors even after Uncle George (who was a director of New Hall Pottery, and very knowledgeable about such things) had corrected him. This may have accounted for the final exchange between them.

As we were threading our way through the wicket gate, Uncle George pointed with his shooting-stick to a large abandoned block of stone, battered and lichen-grown, but with definite signs of carving on it suggesting a gargoyle or large corbel.

'Is that Roman?' he asked.

'That', sniffed the guide, 'is modern trash: Norman.'

Uncle George's love of facts about people and places, his familiarity with landscapes, and his sense of belonging to and being possessed by his country was so natural, so easy. When almost a decade later I became fascinated by the letters and diaries of the British settlers on the Eastern Cape frontier, I'd find myself, map in hand, trying to locate a place where a diary entry had been made or a house had once stood, or deciphering a tombstone in an old graveyard, or the weal of an old wagon road. When, sometimes, I take people to a site, I think of him and his son Guy, who has the same passion for places. They feel about them as they do about friends. 'You really must see so-and-so.'

Uncle George was responsible for instigating my first piece of ancestral research. I took a lonely bus ride from Brighton to Rye to look for Captain Lucky's grave. It was a glorious day and the bus was in no hurry, pausing at several villages where it was possible to down a pint or two between stages. Through all my responses to the changing views and villages the captain/sergeant-major drew ever closer to me. Who, my dear sergeant-major ancestor, first gave you the bogus commission of captain? Who paid for your tombstone? Why, my dear fellow, did you volunteer? How many children did you leave your widow to raise? From which of them am I descended?

He could answer none of these questions. By the time I stepped off the bus at Rye, I was saying: 'Unlucky Sergeant-major Lucky, how lucky I am to be looking for your grave, not rotting in the military cemetery at Castiglione dei Pepoli, or in the sands of El Alamein.'

Leaning on headstone after stone, inspecting illegible inscriptions and obliterated dates, I moved irregularly among mottled shadows under the trees. I sat down on a horizontal slab, so weathered that no trace of a letter could be seen beneath the green, grey and orange circles of lichen. I ran my fingertips over the surface to see if I could find any remnant of the legend by braille. Nothing. So I stopped moving my hand and still kept my eyes shut.

Nothing. Not even the awareness of nothing. No one to be aware. Like sudden absolute sleep.

I came to, startled, confused. Where was I? How long had I been away? Where had I been? My eyes picked up the inscription beneath the dial of the church clock: 'For our time is a very shadow that passes away.' *Tempus fugit* again. I looked at my watch, took lightning stock of myself. I was in the graveyard of the church at Rye, looking for someone without whom I would never have been.

According to Uncle George, my Lucky ancestor's tombstone had sported a quotation from Shakespeare (*Othello* V.ii) not the Bible; unusual, perhaps, in the 18th century, but beautifully apt for a sergeant-major:

nothing extenuate
Nor set down aught in malice.

Who but a hero could have such courage, to invite people so to 'Speak of me as I am'?

I did not find his grave, but I was glad I had looked for it. I returned to Brighton feeling a little less lost.

Then came a series of blows.

On 26 July 1945 I had been profoundly disturbed by the results of the British general election, the sweeping victory of Labour (393) over the Conservatives (189). I was not opposed to Labour; it was the rejection of Churchill that hurt. While I realised that I understood little of British politics, I thought a system that could so discard its heroes callous if not brutal.

Roosevelt dead, Hitler and Mussolini dead, Churchill out. The only survivor of the wartime Titans was Stalin. The contemporary world caught up with me. I began to permit certain events, which I had censored as too painful to contemplate, to impinge on me. Chief of these were the revelations of the Nazi death camps. What kind of a creature was man that he could commit such acts? War was horrible enough, but deliberate, methodical genocide, the conscientious gassing of millions of Jews in the name of the German race, this was surely a horror new to creation; and nothing in my socialist theories could account for it. There was no economic or class explanation for Buchenwald. Did one have to recover an older world view which accepted the reality of a monstrous evil power? I began having nightmares out of Hieronymus Bosch. I felt defiled.

Not very long after the election results, on 6 August came the atomic bomb on Hiroshima, followed by another bomb three days later on Nagasaki. I could accept no excuse for this. We should have told the Japs that we had such a weapon and given a demonstration of its power by bombing small unoccupied islands. If that had not produced the desired effect, then we might have used the weapon. What destroyed any moral case we had was the dropping of the second bomb before the Japs had time to react to the first. This seemed a bully's brutal display of power.

If the revelations of the death camps provided a grisly justification for our war against Hitler, the way we had used the bomb deprived us of our moral credibility. Yet how far were we, the ordinary people, white, black or yellow, responsible for these horrors? Whatever the answer to that difficult question, we were all members of the same species.

So deep was my disgust that I no longer wanted to be part of the human race. A creature that could do such things and at the same time dream up proud utopias was insanely self-deluded, hopelessly self-condemned. I hankered for a 'universe set in another key'. The night was suffocating and entire, and in a dark hole I cried for some other air to breathe, some other way to be. For weeks on end I poured my disgust and anguish on to paper, or rather I let them spill and splash, torrents of words at which I sometimes glance only to become aware that nothing I have written has come near encompassing that darkness. It clung to me for years, periodically surfacing like the Kraken, but not dying.

V.J. Day, 15 August, was not a good day for me. Yes, one could rejoice that the war was over and that millions of soldiers would be going home. But was it a victory? We may have beaten the Germans and the Japs, but had we won the war? It was in this depressed state that I received a letter from Jean saying that her booking had fallen through; she was back at square one. Brighton was suddenly utterly intolerable.

If I had known my English relatives better, I could have gone to stay with them for a week and recovered my sense of human worth. On impulse, I decided to visit Durham. Why Durham? Because it was far away. Because

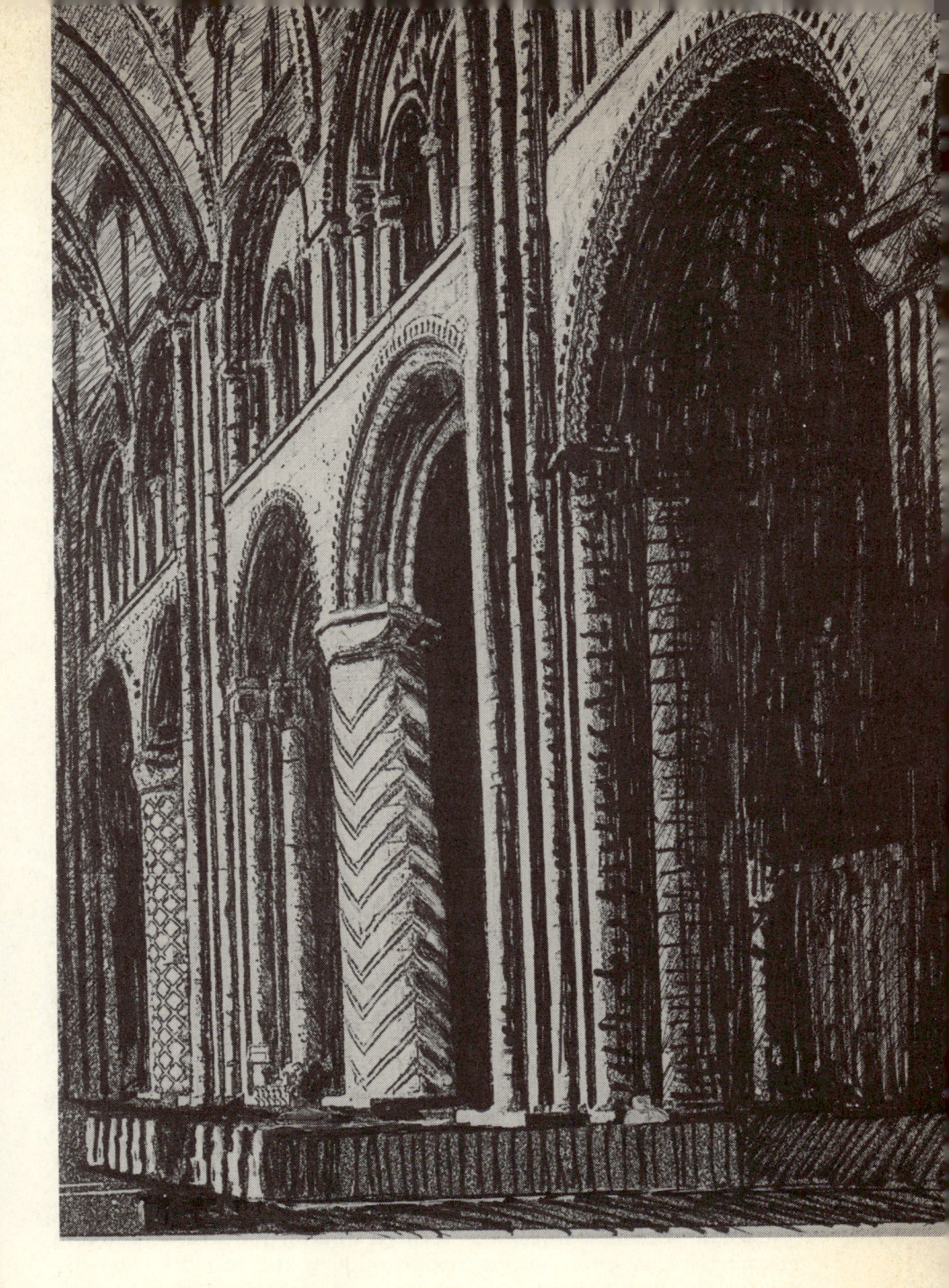

The Nave, Durham Cathedral

I'd seen pictures of the cathedral nave (Norman of course, 'modern trash'); I'd seen them when I was an innocent 18-year-old mad about art and western civilisation.

As lonely as only a soldier in a strange land can be, guidebook in hand, I drifted between the great stone cylinders of that stupendous nave acknowledging the genius who had given them their strong and various herringbone hatchings. A party of German p.o.w. officers came in on a guided tour, enemies of three months ago, looking at one of the churches their airforce had left intact.

There was one handsome young man about my age, whose eager head movements showed that he was impressed and determined to miss nothing. Our routes separated. A little later as I entered the cloisters for the second time, I ran across them again. My friend was in the rear. As he reached the corner, he dropped to one knee, but there was no effigy or crucifix in view. I then saw that he was taking a sighting along one of the dressed stone courses in the ancient masonry, to see whether it was still level after all its obedient centuries of simply standing there. Apparently it was. He rose, shaking his head in admiring disbelief. An architect, I suspect.

Seeing my interest, he exclaimed in his best English: 'Vunderful!'

'Ja!' I said, in my best German.

From the top of the tower there were fine views of the landscape, and closer at hand the U-turning river, the bridge and the town.

Very close, so close one felt one could lob a penny into it, was a cloister of a different kind: the prison yard in which even then the prisoners were walking round and round in a circle, just as in that study by Van Gogh.

On the return to Brighton I watched rooks in the fields and seagulls on the beach. If one had to be cursed into existence at all, would it not have been better to be a simple creature like a bird, or even a stubborn growing thing, a windy gorse bush on a chalk cliff, a lichen plant on a weathered tombstone?

Then Lizeen Lantry, whom I had got to know in Italy, arrived bubbling with joy. She had none of my anguish. The war was over and she was going home to Ireland, the holy land of Ireland. But first she would spend a week or so in London, visiting her sisters.

We went striding over the downs near Brighton, picking our way between abandoned pill-boxes, skirting barbed-wire entanglements, talking of this and that, happy to be together. Before leaving for Ireland she said, 'Why don't you come and visit us now? We're simple folk, but what we have you'll be welcome to.'

At last news came that Jean had secured a berth. She had secured it in characteristic manner, seizing opportunity by the forelock. She discovered that the man whose teeth she was X-raying was head of the

Union–Castle Line in Johannesburg. Having placed the uncomfortable sections of film in his mouth she commanded him to secure her a berth to England immediately. The patient shook his head and pointed towards his mouth, indicating that he would reply when the X-raying was over. Jean said that the matter did not call for discussion. All he had to do was to nod assent, otherwise he'd be there for a very long time. He showed signs of stubbornness, whereupon Jean said that while he was making up his mind about one berth he'd better add another for her friend, Welly, who needed to get to Sherborne to marry her sailor fiancé before Christmas. The head of the Union–Castle Line nodded sadly, twice.

But the ship which would bring her, the s.s. *Drottingholm*, would not dock at Liverpool until 23 October – almost two months ahead.

This was a cruel blow. I had spent much time happily speculating where Jean and I might spend my final army leave before the Oxford term began on 14 October. Now all these plans vanished into thin air. And such travelling together would have to wait until the end of term, in mid-winter.

3   September 1945

Out of the Army

How I got through my final weeks in the army I do not know. I recall being given some clothing-coupons to buy civilian clothes. I have always been hopeless about clothes, and after five years in uniform I could be excused for not being sartorially conscious. The young man who served me was not helpful. Back at my billet I donned my new identity and did not quite recognise what I saw in the mirror, but I went round to a friend to take her to a show. She could not believe what she saw. She could not believe I had with serious intent bought those pin-stripe trousers and she hoped I did not expect her to appear in public with me got up like a comic turn. Why hadn't I bought a bowler and umbrella while I was about it? I returned to my billet, got back into my army clothes and felt much better.

The time for my demobilisation leave was drawing near. All the dreams of spending it with Jean were now vain. Where should I go? What should I do? I was determined to get out of England, but where to? Wales? Scotland? Ireland? Ireland.

I had fancied going to the Emerald Island at some stage, not for family reasons, although I was pleased that William Yeats's second name was Butler. As far as I knew, our branch of the enormous clan had left Ireland in the mid-seventeenth century. Ireland, or one or two fragments of it, had become part of the landscaping of my mind: the Dublin of James Joyce and the west coast of J.M. Synge. It had achieved a less literary dimension through Lizeen.

I wrote to Lizeen, asking if she was serious about the invitation or was that all just blarney about Killarney and Kate Kearney?

Before leaving Brighton I went to the quartermaster, who was selling surplus stores. I came away with two boxes of South African canned peaches. I left the Unit without a handshake from anyone except the quartermaster, whom I hardly knew. So ended my military career.

I arrived in Oxford with very little kit indeed. The taxi-driver who took me out to 73 Five Mile Drive was friendly enough and helped me get the canned peaches into the house. Alone in the house I had a sudden yearning to sample those peaches but I couldn't find anything with which to prise open a tin. So I walked to the bus-stop and waited for a bus. There

I drew up a list which was headed: claw hammer, screwdriver, tin opener.

I bought a bicycle, a load of logs, some coal and anthracite for the boiler. I looked at the unkempt little garden, and I contemplated the sluggish movements of one unhappy fish in the diminutive pond and wondered if it would survive the coming winter. In a vacant field opposite was a squad of German p.o.w.s. They worked hard. They laughed sometimes. They had company.

Then I received a letter from Lizeen, whose mother would be delighted to have me as her guest at Faha for ten days from 17 September.

In mid-September 1945 I took a train from Dublin to Killarney. It took the best part of a day. On the station stood Lizeen 'tall as a Grenadier', laughing as always, next to her brother Diarmuid, huge and goodnatured but at present not a little worried because his beautiful horse had slipped on the wet tarmac and maybe hurt his knees.

We jogged slowly along in the jaunting car, through the evening, up hills and lanes to secure from the ruins of Aghadoe a view of the lakes of Killarney and the isle of Innisfallen. Beyond these the mountains were hidden under fog and mist. The River Loune runs swiftly under old stone bridges among endless trees. Diarmuid, when not giving the folklore and history of every natural feature, questioned me about the world I came from. He was curious for news about any country in the wide world.

We arrived at Faha farm at dusk and met Mama, the widow Deborah Lantry, her daughter Anna, and Mikeen, her youngest son. Faha had a large central living-room which went right up to the slates. Ground-floor rooms led off it, left and right, and a ladder to reach two dormer rooms on either side above them. One was for the daughters, one for the sons. The house's heart was a huge open hearth burning peat. It had an elaborate wrought-iron crane from which hung a variety of cauldrons and pots. The furniture was simple, the pictures few and holy. Mama presided over the ham and eggs. She was alert and a wonderful talker. I felt at home immediately.

'The Irish are very family conscious,' I wrote that night. 'They will talk at length about a group of O'Connells or O'Donoghues. They talked of their two sisters in London and also of brother Tom, a member of the Palestine police, killed at the blowing up of the King David Hotel. This is the big tragedy of their lives, I think. And then they talk about the life of the countryside. Diarmuid is amazed at the prices paid for horses at Ballbridge recently.'

Looking back, I think the quite unexpected access of sheer happiness which I enjoyed at Faha sprang from the living presence there of something essential to me: a family alive and breathing in a building to which they gave the name home. Below the life of Faha lay the life of The Poplars, of Vrede, of Katkop, of Ons Hoek, all places where individuals knew they were accepted without question, where they belonged, individually and together in families. Antennae of my nature which had been pulled in for years emerged from the dark shell. The end of the war and the removal of my uniform was like shedding a metal carapace.

Half of each day was spent sightseeing on bicycles, the rest working on Faha farm.

'Have huge meal of mutton, cabbage and spuds, then apples and cream until tight as a drum. Then with Diarmuid and Mikeen to spend the rest of the evening until almost dark, getting the hay into the shed . . . Everybody has read the article on the death of the singer John McCormack in the Dublin paper which I had brought. Mama and Anna eat their supper before milking the cows. Supper is bread, scones, butter, jam and tea. Then we sit around the peat fire and talk about everything under the sun and the moon: gulli-gulli men in Alexandria, conjurers at Irish fairs, the old schoolmaster whose wife travelled so much, African superstitions, baboons, snakes, and the war. Already we are distancing the war by anecdote. Oxford and London seem a million miles away, this morning a thousand years ago. Yet nothing has happened, just an effortless forgetting.'

A day later:

'Sun setting, purple dusk and rain against the pale west. Above the trees round Beaufort Bridge, ten thousand crows rising and falling, circling and wheeling at different altitudes before settling for the night. The River Loune grey and cold-looking. As we cycle up the road with its walls of trees on either side, suddenly the wind strikes out and rain comes. We race to the pub for shelter and spend an hour gathering all the talk, which is often witty or droll. A voice says, "That Captain O'Neill would be about a second cousin of mine." Another chips in, "Och, that wouldn't make you a lance-corporal!" One hears adjectives being used as J.M. Synge's Arran islanders must have used them, "He has a fierce memory." What a phrase!

'On our way home the air is luminous with moonlight diffused behind broken clouds. When it emerges it pours quicksilver on the rough surface of the rain-wet boreen and glints on the leaves of the scrub oaks. The only sound is of water in the ditches draining away from the quiet hills and bogs.'

Later still:

One day Lizeen and I cycled into Killarney. A stiff autumn wind churned among the turning copper-beeches on the edge of the lake, whose surface alternated between sunless slate and coruscating silver paper. Warm enough in our battle dress, we dismounted when we had had enough of the wind, and looked about us and talked.

Knowing my interests in history, Lizeen answered my every question with a fine melancholy and righteous tone stemming from Ireland's immemorial martyrdom at the hands of the English. That she had just spent five years serving on the side of these villains did not seem to disturb her. From a hilltop above their Faha farmhouse she had pointed out all their neighbours to me, every second one seeming to be of Scots or English descent: so that her plotted-and-pieced landscape, her beautiful garden of Eden, was spoilt by serpents she called 'planters' or 'black-Protestants'. It was as if part of her homecoming was a happy, half-serious recovery of ancient local prejudices.

Leaning across our saddles we stared at the ruins of a fine country house on the shores of the lake.

'Burnt by the Black-and-Tans in the time of The Troubles,' she said sadly. So when in Killarney itself I paused before a rather striking small granite statue of a mourning woman with veiled head, standing upon a base whose inscription was in impenetrable Erse, I was not surprised to hear her say, 'Mother Ireland grieving over the deaths of her sons murdered by the English.'

She was more accurate when it came to giving names to the trees, the shrubs, the wayside flowers – names familiar from one's reading, now given shape and colour and texture for the first time.

Diarmuid, by contrast, took his Irish history with a pinch or two of fact. Two days later when it was his turn to show me the sights, he stopped opposite the same ruins on the edge of the lake.

'Now there's an interesting thing. In the times before the other Great War, the Lord Kenmare was giving the big hunt-ball. A vain young female left a sconce of candles burning before her looking-glass. She also left the window open and a breeze came across the lake and blew the curtain into the candle flame. A loving couple on the lawn saw the start of it, but the flames got a grip so quickly nothing could save the place.'

So much for the Black-and-Tans. And in Killarney, among other sites, he showed me the little granite statue of a mourning woman. 'I'm fond of her now,' he said. 'Mother Ireland, lamenting the death of the four Kerry poets.'

Who were the Kerry poets? To my shame I knew only of William Allingham. This delighted Diarmuid and when I started reciting 'The Abbot of Innisfallen awoke ere dawn of day', he cried, 'Innisfallen! But surely we must take you there.' Which he did, rowing across the lake to the ruins of the abbey rising out of the grass among the trees.

Thursday was the 'treshing'. Early in the morning Mama and Anna were busy preparing the huge simple midday meal of spuds, cabbage, ham and porter. I waited with Diarmuid and Mikeen, holding our pitchforks with which we presented arms to the tractor driver as he passed, trundling the huge oblong box of the peregrinating threshing-machine behind him. Yesterday at McCrackens, tomorrow O'Neills, today here; and so for a month from farm to farm.

Behind the tractor came the other neighbours. And who should they be? The very 'planters' and 'black-Protestants' whose proximity had triggered off Lizeen's melancholy rhetoric two days before.

It was a relaxed and friendly gathering. I enjoyed standing on the top of the stack with Mikeen and pitching the sheaves to the fellow feeding them into the trembling, deafeningly noisy machine, or later, intermittently sneezing, building the new stack from the golden hay. The haze, the rhythmical movements and the dumbness imposed by the noise produced a near-hypnotic state in which I relived a similar immersion in this final ritual of harvest.

Italy had provided a most memorable rite of Ceres, goddess of corn and peace. Somewhere south of Chiusi, when the First City/Cape Town Highlanders were mauled in that Etruscan city in that haunted summer landscape where, harvesting stalled by battles, the corn was already overdue for reaping and heavy showers were already flattening patches of field after field.

I was fairly far forward in the battle zone, visiting a company headquarters of the Wits/De la Rey Regiment. The men had been in the line for a long spell and were dog-tired, so that the shelter of the large farmhouse and its outbuildings was welcome. But they could not have come at a worse time for the farmer. As our three-ton trucks pulled into the farmyard, so did a bullock cart laden with sheaves, the last of the harvest reaped that day, right there among the forward troops, almost in no-man's-land.

The farmer and the company commander had 'words'. Could not the trucks be parked on one side, so that the bullock cart could get to the stack of sheaves? And could they not leave a space clear for the threshing-machine which would be coming soon?

The first request would be granted, but the implications of the second were grave. A threshing-machine? Now? Here? Didn't the fool know there was a war on? wondered the company commander.

Yes, the farmer knew, indeed he knew. Two days ago it was the Tedeschi and now – but was there not, perhaps, a farmer among the soldiers to whom he could explain?

The company commander was a farmer himself and said so. But his duty now was to look after his men and they needed sleep, good, sound sleep.

Well then, did the commander not understand, could he not see, that the corn had to be brought in and had to be kept dry? Didn't he realise that there was rain about? Yes, the company commander admitted, but the corn was stacked and safe from rain.

Please, said the farmer, there is only one threshing-machine in all this area, it goes on a route and one has to take one's turn or miss it; and it was already behind schedule – because of the soldiers, the Tedeschi and now the Inglese ...

'When will it come?'

'Maybe tonight, maybe tomorrow.'

The company commander reluctantly kept a space near the stacks free of trucks for the threshing-machine.

It came, pulled by a tractor, about ten o'clock that night. Most of the tired company were deep asleep, including the company commander. I was awake, talking to my fellow information officer. A fair-sized moon had come up and shone from a damp sky. We saw the farmer cross the yard and help the driver position the machine.

'Do they intend threshing now?' we asked.

'We must,' said the driver. 'We must use the moon.'

'The soldiers are very tired,' I said.

'We too are very tired, but the corn ...'

'Can't you wait for another hour or two? It will be better to wait.'

It was not impossible that some brittle-nerved soldier, particularly one who had been through the Western Desert, might spray the threshing-machine with his tommy-gun. The bitter men who had reaped their crop in no-man's-land were prepared to run that risk. And so they started threshing and we went back to our brandy and our talk.

This company of the Wits/De la Rey Regiment had a high proportion of young men of farming stock. Some of them, hearing the sound of the machine, groaned, rolled over and drifted back into dreaming of harvesting at home. One or two peered out of their windows or tents at the silhouettes' purposeful movements under the moon.

First one then another quietly crossed the yard to the stack. Above the drumming of the machine came good-natured cries in soldier's Italian. Before long all the Italians were off the job, resting, drinking wine, watching their sheaves being efficiently fed into the machine. And the young soldiers handling the sheaves with familiarity, rhythmically building the haystack, were driven happily lunatic by the sanity of what they were doing.

It was all over by three in the morning. The tractor pulled its lumbering box away. I fell asleep, not realising that I had witnessed a rite of Ceres, goddess of corn. I had had the experience but missed most of the meaning.

The 'treshing' in which I took part in Ireland and did not merely watch, revealed a little more. A man who is subsequently doomed to spend his life at a desk will recall with peculiar intensity moments when his body was happily engaged in physical work, especially team-work, of a kind whose significance is both ancient and contemporary.

As memorable as the wielding of the pitchfork was the break for the midday meal – Mama's expert swinging of the settlecrane from the open peat fire – the unhitching of the large pots of potatoes and cabbage, the cheerful heaping of large platters with steaming food, the plates on the scrubbed table-top, the faces and forearms recently washed of dust and sweat at the well, and the relaxed talk of men who knew each other and their neighbourhood.

Anna had lost her bucket down the well. I made a wire anchor hook, attached it to a rope and retrieved the bucket, with another, lost several months before. After this miracle of ingenuity had been praised by Mama, Lizeen and I walked up to the top field to say goodbye. We could hear the threshing-machine roaring quietly down at the Cliffords'. We saw the beloved Diarmuid on top of a rick against the evening sky.

Mama was very tired. After a chicken supper Diarmuid, Lizeen and I went down for the last time to 'The Beaufort Arms' and drank whisky until eleven, and followed the unpredictable hare of Irish conversation dodging this way and that, always escaping the boring hound-packs of rational expectation. 'Leaning over Beaufort Bridge one day – the time of the Moving Bog – I see a man come floating down, and him hoeing a ridge of potatoes – and a smashing fine crop he had too.'

Asked in the County Home who the father of her baby might be, the hedge-woman replied, 'He had a brown-painted bicycle.'

We returned singing Irish and South African songs. Diarmuid's favourite song was 'The lark in the clear air'.

I was woken by Lizeen at first light, the first birdsongs stirring outside in the low mist.

I caught the Dublin train at ten.

Thirty-seven years after that first visit in July 1981 business called me to Ireland. I took the opportunity to visit one or two sites linked with W.B. Yeats and to make a sentimental journey to Killarney. I was accompanied by two of my ex-students, Rob and Sue Clarence, in their car. Rob drove and Sue looked after the picnic basket while I guided the tour. I wrote copious letters home to Jean. The following extracts about Faha seem to belong here:

Much has changed in thirty-seven years. Ireland has been re-housed. The countryside is sprinkled with new, rather characterless homes, such as you might find anywhere in the West. The pub at Beaufort where Diarmuid and Lizeen and I used to take a couple of jars, now seemed a seedy place without charm. It was packed with depressed-looking regulars who scowled at our bringing a female into the place. I had forgotten how to reach Faha, so I asked the pubkeeper.

'Faha? Nobody there. It's in ruins. No roof.'
'Where could I find Diarmuid Lantry?'
'Diarmuid is dead, years ago.'
'Dead?'

'Yes.'
'And his younger brother, Mikeen?'
'Dead too. Peritonitis, in Dublin.'
'And the mother, Deborah?'
'Dead. Go and see the ruins if you must.'

(As Jean and I had recently heard from Lizeen, we knew that she was still alive.)

He drew a very inadequate map on a scrap of brown paper. I felt sad beyond belief and would have given up the search after the first three of four blind alleys, but Rob and Sue were hot on the scent. Eventually three miles farther on we were led up a long unused boreen to Faha by a loquacious and articulate teenager.

Faha was indeed in ruins: the slates and thatch gone, only a few skew roof-timbers against the grey skies; thistles, elder and bracken growing inside and outside all the rooms; all timbers of doors and windows gone, the apertures blind and gaping, likewise the little row of outbuildings where Diarmuid's horses had been stabled; and the neat yard where the threshing-machine had pulled in and where the haystack had stood was now nothing but rubbish and weeds. The only part intact was an addition, a tasteless room with steel windows, built where the entrance to the living-room from the yard had been. Its concrete floor had been cast over the well-head. But it was the disarray of the roofing timbers that hurt me most. That seemed to be the devil's final touch.

It reminded me of the ruined pergola pillars and beams of my own childhood home, The Poplars, Bree Street, Cradock, when the great floods of 1974 had burst the banks of the Great Fish River and destroyed many of the houses in the old town.

I was overcome with a desolate outrage, an anger at change and at death. In 1945 Faha had been such a neat and living place, belonging happily in its fields and hedges. And where was the family I'd seen living in it?

A house is so perishable a thing: its surfaces, its flesh and skin take to blemish and decay so quickly and it is painful to witness it. Once the roof has gone completely, once all signs of furnishings, timber and plaster have disappeared, once its walls have been stripped to the stone and picked clean by the weather, the ruin of a house may become bearable, even beautiful, like a skeleton of white bones. One does not feel its humanity, its association with individual lives any longer. It is being metamorphosed into history, architecture, archaeology. But during this betwixt-and-between stage it is like a friendless body crying out for burial.

The 'dreaming spires' of Oxford from Wytham Woods (from a watercolour in 'Campaign for Oxford' calendar, 1991)

4 October 1945–June 1946

Oxford

After heady Ireland my first term at Oxford in October 1945 was a sobering experience.

At B.N.C. I found a note instructing me to present myself at the house of Mr Brett-Smith in Norham Gardens and that Mr Brian Stanion would be my tutorial companion.

Brian was tall, with black curly hair, and goodlooking. He was five years my junior and had recently been demobilised from the Royal Navy. It was his second spell at Oxford. Having won a scholarship from Manchester Grammar School, he had come up to B.N.C. in October 1941 to read History, leaving in June to join the navy. He had not found History entirely to his taste, particularly the palaeographical problem presented by medieval documents, so when he returned to Oxford after three years in the Atlantic, the Arctic and the Mediterranean, he switched to English. However, he retained an affectionate recollection of one of his History dons, Billy Pantin of Oriel, who was always in carpet slippers, tiptoeing between the piles of books which turned his study floor into a miniature Manhattan, and who 'really believed that the fact which he was chasing through those tottering skyscrapers of words was important to civilisation'.

Brett-Smith was a charming pink-faced man who struck us as incredibly old. He blushed whenever he had to correct my lapses in English usage which betrayed my uncultivated origins. 'We call it The House, not Christ Church College.' While most other colleges were called by the first element in their names – Magdalen, Queen's, Trinity, etc., and some abbreviated like Univ, or turned into an acronym like B.N.C., only people from outer darkness would refer to 'New College' as 'New'.

Subsequently Brian and I compared the impressions we had made on each other. 'I felt cheered that my companion was neither of the alternatives which I had expected. You were not a boring, striving grammar-school boy like myself, nor were you a public-school boy who would have been interesting but not relaxed (I would have had to prove myself). South Africans were then socially neutral. It was like meeting a Spaniard, or an American, or somebody from another service. You were not part of the undergraduate scene as I knew it.'

It was through Brian that I became aware of the deep social cleavage between the products of the two English school systems, and of the north–south tension. 'England's wealth is created in the north and spent in the south, which gives itself airs and graces, and sneers at the north.' Also his approach to the war was somewhat different from my own.

'Why did you go into the navy?' I asked him.

'Well, it couldn't be the army. Whenever my family relations met in my childhood, sooner or later the women would start keening over Sid who was gassed at Ypres, or Tim who was killed at Passchendaele. So the infantry was out. As for the air force, in 1943–4 the death rate among bomber pilots was discouragingly high. The navy seemed safest.'

But his account of the cold, cramped life in the small ships made me realise how unrestricted my army life had been, a happy-go-lucky Cook's Tour by comparison.

Like all the friends I made in Oxford, he raised a particular question. He recalls the occasion vividly.

'We were walking down Norham Gardens after a tutorial with Brett-Smith. Just before we got to Banbury Road, I asked you, 'Are you going back to your semi-fascist dominion?'

'Why semi?' you asked, smiling. I liked this, because it showed you'd considered the implications and were prepared to go back because of some thoughtful commitment.'

John Bryson of Balliol was my language tutor, an elegant man of languid physical demeanour but quick intellect. He managed to make Barnett and me feel that, important as it was for us to be word-perfect at construing *Beowulf*, it was more important for him to be word-perfect at *The Times* crossword puzzle and to finish it before the tutorial was over. I can't recall him ever confusing his slight irritations over his puzzle's cruxes with those occasioned by our inability to solve the Anglo–Saxon cruxes which had floored Klaeber, Wrenn and other philologists.

As neither of my tutors was attached to B.N.C., I found it difficult to develop any sense of belonging to the college whose position I had so much admired, but I took occasional meals there and a beer or two in the buttery, developing a nodding acquaintance with the inhabitants and with the porters.

Work was heavy going. Rain water and desert sand seemed to have got into my brain and rusted and jammed the works. It was not that I got bored; it was the inefficiency of my memory and the slowness of my wit. In 'The Turf' tavern I overheard a couple of youngsters just up from Winchester chatting about Cyril Connolly's editorial policy for *Horizon*. What was *Horizon*? Astounded by their genuine sophistication and convinced of my own authentic ignorance, I wondered what I was doing in the place.

73 Five Mile Drive, that distant house all to myself, told on my nerves, the more so since my experience of the family life at Faha. A spell of grey

weather made Oxford seem suffocating, England gloomy, everything desolate.

One morning I woke up with the opening trumpet theme of Tchaikovsky's Italian Caprice ringing in my head, brilliant and bright, in ridiculous contrast to everything else inside and outside me. I decided I must hear the whole piece, and at once. I went into Acutt's music shop in the High and asked whether I might listen to a recording of it. They did not usually allow this, but stretched a point for an ex-serviceman.

It transported me back to the olive terraces near Lucca, in the sparkling early spring of 1945. We had been resting there after months in the mud and snow of the Apeninnes. The simple removal from the world of rock and ice and the threat of death into the world of cultivation, almond blossom and spring growth had released the springs of song in me. The great baroque-faced villa in which brigade headquarters was billeted had a glass floor in part of its hall, under which rushed the clear waters of a powerful perennial fountain pouring from the living rock of the hill against which the great white gable was set. Not only had I experienced a burst of lyrical writing, but the bright air seemed to draw song out of everyone. Usually morose people whistled while they worked. Everyone who had an instrument played it. A marvellous moustached major, Van der Riet, (later a general), sang as he strummed his guitar, with deadpan mock-heroic solemnity, of the epic fight between Abdul Abulbul Amir, the Turk, and his Russian rival, Ivan Skavinsky Skovar.

It seemed that even army headquarters had suffered from spring fever. It had opened the Lucca Opera House and put an opera company into it. It was one of my duties to fill it with soldiers. That had been when the Italian Caprice had first impinged on me, ringing piercing sweet from someone's radio, out of a high window of the villa: light, joy, vigour, song.

In an abstracted state, I thanked the Acutt's shop assistant and explained that I did not think I would take the records yet. High on Tchai, I turned toward the entrance. Miraculously the sun seemed to have come out.

The next moment my head encountered a hard surface, there were a cracking and a splintering, and several cries of alarm. I had walked straight into the closed plateglass door, which now lay in large sheet-ice fragments about me. An attendant pulled me away from the jagged hole in which I stood and inspected me for cuts. Dazed, I listened to a tirade from the manager. I assured him that I was not drunk, had not done it deliberately, and that, if his insurance policy did not cover such accidents, I would approach the army and see whether they would help him.

Having left my address I escaped into the High and went down towards the Cornmarket, humiliated, disoriented, and not knowing what to do next. It was in this condition that I heard someone say, 'What the hell are you doing in Oxford?'

It was Frank Hauser, Italy again. In June or July 1944, as liaison officer to an anti-aircraft regiment converted to infantry, operating on our flank in the Monte Albano area, Frank had shared a tent with me for four or five days. We had got on well. The front was comparatively quiet and we had had time to talk about what interested us, literature, the theatre, music. And there he was, grinning, his chin pulled slightly in, his forehead tilted forward.

'I've just walked through a plateglass door,' I said.

'Bully for you,' he replied, as though I had done something only slightly unusual. 'Let's have some coffee.'

Frank was back at his old college, The House. Although he had been granted a wartime degree in English before going off to the Middle East, he had decided to come back and do the full Schools. I found this reassuring as I had decided to do something similar. He had also come back because Oxford was full of theatrical life of amazing variety, to which he introduced me.

At long last, on 23 October 1945, the s.s. *Drottingholm* docked at Liverpool, and Jean joined me in Oxford. Settling down together after years of separation in a rented house on the perimeter of the city in winter proved to be a difficult adjustment for both of us. I spent most of my days at lectures or in libraries in the town. Jean had to fill hers at 73 Five Mile Drive, an unfriendly house in an alien neighbourhood.

Sometimes I brought friends from other colleges for tea, whom Jean entertained, showing considerable ingenuity in variations on canned peaches. Years later friends confessed that they did not cycle or bus all that way to Five Mile Drive to enjoy my company, or to taste Jean's teas, but simply to be near her. Bachelors all, they were as starved of female company as I had been. There was an ex-wing-commander who said he was suffering from TB, a complaint about which radiographers are well informed. He would happily spend hours telling Jean about his lungs.

'Lungs my foot!' I snorted.

Then Ian Maclaren wrote. Could he visit us? I'd last seen him in 1941 or '42, at his 21st-birthday party. He had seconded to the British army and lost both legs on a mine in Normandy. With him came a doctor friend who was helping him over the initial difficulties. I can still hear the struggle up and down those steep, twisted stairs, and Mac descending with a bugger-you-I'm-fine grin on his face.

Jean continued to hunt for digs closer to town. It was desperately difficult. We had learnt that hot baths were one of the few ways of getting warm in England. This meant turning down a possibility in Walton Street, where hot water was available 'all day Sunday and Wednesday afternoons'. How would we maintain our warmth or cleanliness the other five and a half days?

The Cadena café was a great meeting-place for coffee. A completely strange girl in a fur coat got up from her table and crossed to ours saying, 'Excuse me, but you simply must be Jeffrey Butler's brother. It's more the voice than the looks.'

She was Pat Penwill, née Mackay, from Johannesburg. Before her marriage she had spent a holiday with the Van Rensburgs of Waaiplaats in the Cradock district, to improve her Afrikaans, and there she had met Jeffrey. So she had seen him more recently than I had. She joined our table. Our accommodation problem came up soon enough. She was about to go to live in Nettlebed prior to having her baby. Her present perch was a single, large ground-floor room in 5 Beaumont Street. Could we contemplate living in one room? Breakfast supplied, no cooking or kitchen facilities, no happy homemaking, but snug and central. If we took it, we would have to go out for lunch and supper, which could be costly.

We inspected the room and took it. Suddenly the clouds seemed to lift.

One room in Beaumont Street in the heart of Oxford proved heaven after that entire house far out at Five Mile Drive. Mrs Manning, our landlady, was a dear soul and gave us a good breakfast. For the rest we picked up starchy meals in British restaurants, and sometimes a so-called Chinese meal in a place called 'The Stowaway', down a murky lane off the High; or, if we were feeling reckless, at 'The Angel', where there were ancient waiters in dress suits as ancient and crumpled as themselves. This place, supposedly the first coffeehouse in England, is now a co-op.

Over Christmas we spent ten days at Seddlescombe with Elise, a friend of Peggy, Jean's sister. There was an Englishman there called Massey Hicks who, hearing that I was a South African, thought that a safe opening conversational gambit would be:

'I suppose you play rugger?'

To which I replied, 'No, I write poetry.'

This brief exchange struck him as hilarious. He never forgot it. It slipped my mind. A relative of his relayed it to me in 1979. Indeed, I remember little of Christmas except cheerful warmth and seeing the front of Battle Abbey, and liking it.

The snow had an intoxicating effect on Jean's New Zealand friend, Fay Gerrard. She and their lodger, Des Henwood, a South African Rhodes Scholar, enjoyed a fine snow fight in Museum Road, then, having made peace, turned their white salvoes on to the dons as they pedalled past in gowns and mortarboards along Parks Road. Des and John Gerrard used to take a big Wedgwood jug to 'The Lamb and Flag' for a quart of cider. The Gerrards were so fond of that public-house that I painted a watercolour of it for them.

Our colonial innocence and outlandish customs would break surface every so often. Brian Armitage, a Rhodesian, held his wedding reception in B.N.C. dining-hall. Before midnight the emblazoned portraits of founders and benefactors adorning the walls witnessed simultaneously at opposite ends of the hall, for the bridegroom a Zulu war-song-and-dance routine to the footstamping and handclapping of 'Ai-zika-zimba-zimba-zimba, Ai-zika-zimba-zimba-zay'; and for the bride the Maori Haka, an ancient warcry now a welcome, with yells and big arm gestures, hands thrust above the head, mouths open and tongues stuck out as far as possible.

5 Beaumont Street was next door to the Playhouse theatre. At that time it housed a versatile repertory company which put on important plays that a total ignoramus like myself needed to see, at prices we could afford. We were too poor to frequent pubs much, least of all the enormous Randolph Hotel, our near neighbour. Jean began to make more friends, particularly with wives of other ex-servicemen. And she immediately set about looking for a job.

Her first interview was for a junior post at the Taylorian Institute. This would have suited very well, being almost opposite number 5, but she was not optimistic, having been told that the library dealt in French, Italian and other modern languages. Perhaps there were non-linguistic jobs.

She was thrown slightly off balance by the first question:

'Have you a head for heights?'

'I've been in an aeroplane,' she replied.

'Ah yes, but have you been up a ladder?'

'Cleaning windows you mean? No.'

'Putting books back on shelves,' he said, gesturing. Jean's large eyes followed the waving hand.

'I see what you mean. I'd cope.'

'Good! Now, Mrs Butler, how many languages do you speak?'

'English,' she said.

'Ah. You read a little French, perhaps? No? German? No? Italian? No? Spanish? No? ... Surely you must have some command of some other language?'

'Latin?'

'Very little use to the Taylorian. We're modern languages, you know.'

'Afrikaans?'

'Afrikaans! Well, well, well!' he beamed. 'We've been waiting for years for someone who knows Afrikaans. And I'm sure you'd be happy to take French and German classes while learning the job.'

'For thirty-five shillings a week?' exploded Jean. 'To climb step ladders, speak Afrikaans, and learn German and French? For thirty-five shillings a week? No thanks.'

She then applied for, and got, a cataloguing job in the library of the Forestry department. No one explained what she was supposed to do so she worked by guess and by God, and spent much time chatting to another confused cataloguer, Mr Dibbs.

Mr Dibbs was an actor of bit parts at the Playhouse. Whenever he had a part in a play he discussed with her the challenges it presented. When we went to opening nights his first entry would be hailed by Jean with a cry of 'There's Mr Dibbs!' And we saved our applause at the curtain calls for the entrance of the extras. He was very grateful for such acknowledgments of his talents.

Jean felt her own talents could be better employed, and watched the papers. Before long she was walking down St Giles to the X-ray department of the Radcliffe Infirmary. It was not a happy place but she made some excellent friends among the para-medics there.

In addition to friends from the Radcliffe and their friends, mostly undergraduates, we struck up a friendship with another denizen of number 5 called Neil, a tall Etonian who'd spent such a boring war in India, my dear, but was full of the most helpful tips about matters of life and death in post-war England, like the best booze buys. There was, for instance, an Algerian wine, dirt cheap, believe it or not, Algerian my dear, but a perfectly adequate base for a student punch. He adored Jean. He was most helpful to her, for instance, in the matter of curtain-lining.

'Simple, my dear, how many yards do you need?'

Jean told him.

'Plain white do?'

'Anything, Neil.'

'Well, dear, if you promise you won't tell – neither of you is superstitious or fussy?' We shook our heads. Reassured, he whispered: 'Shrouds ... shrouds. As many as you like.'

We were temporarily taken aback.

'*New* shrouds. I mean to say, I'd *never* have offered secondhand ones! You wonder where I get them? Promise you won't tell? My dear mother, during the blitz you know, had to run some sort of emergency mortuary. Fortunately there were not as many dead as expected. She's been discreetly dealing in shrouds to selected living ever since.'

It was through Neil that we met Basil and Alan. We had witnessed Kenneth Tynan's attempts to get himself seen by walking down the Broad, dressed in gold waistcoat and a purple suit. He tried so hard and he succeeded so well. Basil and Alan managed to be seen without even trying. They did not have to work at being surprising, they simply were, in dress, in speech and in behaviour. Nothing they wore, said, or did was for anyone's benefit but their own. Their faces presented a perpetual look of slight surprise at the evidence all around them that the universe was going to pot, but it would not do to betray one's irritation too much to hoi polloi. Their failure in this last heroic attempt was one of the reasons why they were noticed.

The strangest conversations we ever shared were at one of Neil's parties, after a vac. Basil and Alan were present. What was surprising about it was the utter matter-of-factness with which their adventures were recounted, at most a slight irritation, a moment's pettishness, that was all. Jean's contributions, incredulous, outraged, delighted, were not allowed to disturb the even tenor of their cosmic boredom.

Jean (to Alan): 'Where did you spend your vac?'
Alan: 'In Ireland.'
Jean (to Basil): 'And you?'
Basil: 'In gaol.'
Jean: 'Gaol?'
Basil: 'Yes, my dear, such a bore.'
Jean: 'But why?'
Basil: 'A beastly magistrate in Bristol sent me there.'
Jean: 'But what had you done?'
Basil: 'I did nothing. A constable arrested me.'
Jean: 'But why?'
Basil: 'My Triumph had an argument with a traffic-light and the constable thought that improper and held me responsible.'
Alan: 'Basil's Triumphs are always having arguments with traffic-lights.'
Basil: 'Always? Don't be silly. Always!'
Alan: 'The Beak did give you a warning last time, you know.'
Basil: 'But a month, my dear fellow, and without the option!'
Jean: 'What did you do in gaol? Pick oakum?'
Basil: 'Oakum! My dear, where have you spent your life? Picking oakum went out with the Flood!'
Jean: 'Well, what did you do?'

Basil did not reply, sulking ever so slightly at being harried over a past grief. Alan, the sneak, whispered audibly for all to hear: 'He sewed mailbags.'

'You, Alan,' said Basil, with a high moral tone, 'should keep off the subject of mail.' (To Jean) 'My dear, they don't let you get many letters in gaol, you know, not during the first month. One a week. Not that I was looking forward to letters from home. Having to write to me when I am in gaol always does ghastly things to my father's style. So when the warder came in with five letters in his fist like a poker hand, I had to pick one, blindfold, as it were. And who was it from? Him!'

He pointed at Alan, who looked out of the window.
Basil: 'From Ireland.'
Alan was not hearing.
Basil: 'A postcard.'

Alan turned round and faced his accuser.

'Be fair, Basil. A coloured postcard. I spent several minutes choosing it.'

Basil: 'Of a hotel. In Killarney. With an illiterate X marking his hotel window. And the briefest of messages on the space provided:

'Stone walls do not a prison make.
But how are the iron bars?
Having a gorgeous time.'

Much of my spare time in Trinity term was spent on the river. My rowing career, like my previous sporting ventures brief and inglorious, was the most pleasurable of all. 'When I rowed at Oxford' sounds impressive, particularly if followed by a lyrical description of the Thames beyond Iffley Lock, down past Sandford on a spring day, and eight blades in perfect unison snatching circles into the mirror surface, the shell slipping past as one rides forward on the mobile seat for the next hypnotically timed stroke. I had dreams that I might recapture in words that mixture of extreme physical exertion and rhythm which transmutes eight young men and a slight cox into one of the more beautiful expressions of body-and-mind.

It is aways something of a comedown to have to admit that this apotheosis was vouchsafed to me as number five in the Brasenose College Third Eight, whose hefty crew was dismissed patronisingly in the college magazine as 'mostly rugger players in for a lark, not serious rowing men'. In fact we did extremely well in Torpids, achieving a bump each day and only missing an over-bump by a few feet in the final race.

The Third Eight did contain a high percentage of 'colonials', all ex-servicemen who lacked, perhaps, a proper respect for the finer points of rowing lore, and the even more important law of the river. We had mastered only one or two fragments of sacred knowledge which all Englishmen imbibe with their mothers' milk. I don't know whether what follows is lore or law. If you travel up the Thames it changes its name and becomes the Isis after Iffley Lock. I do not know where it recovers from this identity crisis but I suspect at Folly Bridge. Certainly by the time it reaches the complex of locks, canals and railway lines behind Worcester College, it is, officially at least, the Thames once more. Notices at the locks unequivocally direct barges to the Thames, not Isis. I've seen them. But I am assured by dons that the Isis continues upstream at least up to Godstow and 'The Trout' inn. The notices are an irrelevant impertinence committed by the Thames River Authority. However, the undisputed Isis between Iffley Lock and Folly Bridge has a peculiar dog-leg, if not exactly a zig-zag, at least a zig, which is known as the Gut. It was no doubt discovered in ancient times by early rowing-men (King Canute perhaps, in his canoe?) that it was in the interests of good racing to abandon the universal rule and cut straight across the Gut, and row the rest of the race

B.N.C. Third Eight (from an old snapshot)

towards Folly Bridge in midstream or on the right-hand bank. This breaking of all rules is known as the Rule of the River.

It is assumed that this unusual arrangement is common knowledge to rowing-men, and by any of the population of England who aspire to handle craft on that part of the Thames called the Isis. There is no notice at Iffley Lock or Folly Bridge to inform the public of this irregularity. It would be redundant. The English learn and accept innumerable illogical 'laws' by osmosis. Their idiosyncratic spelling demonstrates this, surely.

Our cox was a delightful Irishman, Wilson (who weighed less than most coxes because he had left an entire leg behind on a recent battlefield). He explained many mysteries of law and lore to us, for which we were immensely grateful, not least for the note of irony that sometimes crept into his voice.

One gorgeous day – it must have been a public holiday or a Saturday – Wilson was replaced by a short, slim, dark, peppery fellow called Genders, an Englishman proper, who did not, I suspect, appreciate that his crew were uncouth men from the world's perimeters.

What we lacked in finesse we made up for in weight and enthusiasm, so that, provided no one caught a crab, we could get that eight moving lickety-split. Genders was appalled by the barbarous zest of our start and brought us to a halt. He told us to feather our oars properly, and together to keep in time and not to splash 'like sticks of bombs going off in the sea'. We pulled away demurely. 'That's better,' he said.

One of the great symbolical and moral features of rowing is the crew's total trust in the cox. You have absolutely no idea of what lies ahead, what swans, eights, canoes, punts, locks, you might encounter. After a while, unless you are 'stroke', you hardly notice your cox either; you notice the shoulders and spine of the man in front of you, you get into the rhythm, into the groove if you like. Groove is a good metaphor for an eight and when all in that narrow groove move together it is more than satisfying. The more you forget yourself, the more you find yourself liberated.

Well, we were just bordering on this happy near-oblivion when our cox shouted, quite loudly but without much anxiety:

'Fore!'

Isn't that a verbal signal reserved for golfers? I wondered, pulling my wrists into my solar-plexus. Another two strokes and Genders repeated the cry, at screaming pitch.

'Fore!!'

Then, 'Hold her all!' he yelled. We jammed our blades into the water and, amid much splashing, felt the prow connect with another craft, heard a woman shout and a young child cry.

Slowly our fellow mortals in this near-disaster drifted into view. They were in a punt, a large, pleasant-faced but very angry lady, in a floral dress and a big hat, and her two sons or nephews. The punt-pole was being recovered for her by another punt-party.

The accident had occurred in the Gut.

'Why don't you look where you're going?' demanded the woman.

'Madam,' replied Genders, courteous but icy, 'do you not know the Rule of the River?'

'I know my left hand from my right hand!' she retorted. 'Which you don't!'

Genders cast his eyes helplessly to heaven and decided this was a case of invincible ignorance.

'Steady all,' he commanded.

His opponent, now erect, her punt-pole recovered, had not done with him yet.

'I hope you lose next year too!' she cried.

That we, the B.N.C. Third Eight, had been mistaken for the Dark Blue Eight destined for the duel lower down the Isis/Thames was amusing enough, but it was Genders's next remark that we really enjoyed.

'What,' he cried to the world, 'what can you expect with a Labour government in power?'

We were not coxed by Genders again. I believe he became a bishop in Barbados.

Our wives – most in that eight were married men – used to watch our efforts, somewhat gingerly cycling along the towpath, avoiding those reckless old rowing-coaches (frequently clerics) who, well into their forties or fifties, pedal along that treacherous towpath at high speed, their eyes glued to the eight they are training, yelling through a megaphone, never looking at the path, with their old college scarves trailing like meteors from their scrawny necks.

But when the madness of Eights Week came, our wives caught the fever and yelled, and ran, and triumphed with us. Jean so lived through the heroic efforts of the B.N.C. Third Eight that she finds it hard to believe we were not the team that met Cambridge a few weeks later.

One other memory. After a gorgeous row down beyond Sandford, while pulling the eight back over the rollers at Iffley Lock, someone suggested we stop for a while and stroll into the village in order to look at Iffley church.

I took to that church, so chunky, strong, simple. There is something in a Norman dog-tooth doorway that I find more satisfying than most Gothic arches. Iffley's west door with the signs of the zodiac, the heavenly calendar of stars and seasonal labours, left a firm fingerprint on my mind at a time when the great civilisation which preceded ours, the medieval, was challenging the humanist assumptions of progress and the inevitable benefits of science on which I had been nurtured. I was engrossed in Chaucer, Langland and the Gawain poet.

Years later, in 1980, Jean and I spent several months in Beechwood Flats at Iffley. Sometimes, after a day's work in the Bodleian, I would walk along the towpath and Jean would set out from Beechwood and we would meet somewhere near the locks. We would watch the eights exercising. It was all perfectly nostalgic. The only new note came from the female coxes shrieking orders at docile masculine rowers. It was perhaps an omen of the impending premiership of Margaret Thatcher.

One Saturday, wearing dark-blue rosettes, we trooped down to the Thames with a million others to watch the Oxford–Cambridge boat race from somewhere near Hammersmith Bridge. The day was rather foggy. The air was resonant with loudspeakers. Most of the people around us were wearing light-blue rosettes, including an aggressive Cockney woman and her 7-year-old son, who had also brought a flag to wave. We heard the starting detonation and presently discerned the two eights approaching, one clearly ahead of the other. My heart sank. Poor old Oxford, losing for the umpteenth time in succession. But I was wrong. Two Cambridge men standing near me could not believe their eyes. As the shells passed under the bridge the Dark Blues were about two lengths ahead.

'Still, it's a cinch,' said one. 'Our boys haven't started pulling yet.' The narrow craft slipped into the fog like two sleek foxes followed by a variety of motor launches, rather like the rabble of a hunt.

Then the loudspeaker on the bridge gave the news. The Dark Blues had won! The little boy broke into tears. His mother put an arm round him and said, 'Never mind, dearie, Cambridge came second.'

One day towards the end of Hilary term, Guy Stringer had appeared out of the blue. He had married and had come to invite us to spend ten days with them on Castle Farm, Watchfield, where they were living while he attended a course at the Military College near Faringdon. He had decided to become a professional soldier. So, in due course, we took a bus to Faringdon, where Guy met us at 'The Crown' in a 1927 A-model Ford.

Mary was taller than Guy, as Jean is taller than I am, which made Jean cry, 'Why do tall girls like short men and short men like tall girls?' She handed Mary her offering, a pair of nylons and one of our tins of peaches.

It was cold that April at Castle Farm. Mary had a difficult time cooking on a three-ring Florence stove, but the results were triumphs of ingenuity over limited resources. There was no central heating. We bathed in a tin tub supplied with water from two buckets, one hot, one cold. We gathered vegetables from the patch Guy had cultivated – notably broadbeans, which Jean had never seen growing before: 'They're like babies lying in their cots, they live in little furry nests.'

Guy had inherited Uncle George's liking for places where men had left indelible fingerprints on the landscape. He was expert at organising expeditions to places he had found interesting, or expected might be so, and never disappointed us. So that in subsequent years during periods of leave, I have had places to revisit, places to introduce to others as one introduces old friends, with a fair confidence that they will take to each other. Some of the best of these visits have been 'trips down Memory Lane' for the four of us.

For instance that simple, enormous, grey tithe barn at Great Coxwell, its vast plain roof of Cotswold stone tiles absorbing sun and rejecting rain for centuries, whole quarries held up by a dry, time-frozen, delicate forest of rough-hewn timbers, marching down the nave of the dark interior, bay after bay, back into the early 14th century.

Once Guy stopped his old A-model Ford on high ground, and said,

'Now, old man, this hill is named after one of the merriest monarchs. Which?'

Such a quiz was frequent and I did my best.

'Charles the Second?'

'No, try again.'

British dynasties seemed short on merry monarchs.

'Prinny? Henry the Eighth?'

'No. Both too fat. Give up?'
'Yes.'
'Old King Cole.'
This brought in Jean and Mary, who solemnly recovered the words of the nursery rhyme from their childhood. I looked over the quiet copse-studded hillside and found it hard to imagine three fiddlers accompanying that merry old king tooting away on his pipe. So did Jean, who said she would prefer Nat King Cole and started singing 'I haven't time for the waiting game'.

After Castle Farm we spent a week in Aunt May's house in Grantchester Road, Cambridge. We walked down to Grantchester, enjoying the Backs with flamboyant touches of yellow provided by daffodils, and that juxtaposition of old stone and brick with lawn and tree which is less common in Oxford. Jean wondered how on earth I could have chosen Oxford. But what street in Cambridge could compare with the High, or St Giles, and what spire with St Mary's?

We were planning a little party at Beaumont Street and invited the boys from Pemmy. They had expanded beyond the nucleus of my tutorial companions. Hugh Arnold said he was sorry, but he had a date in London that weekend. Jean urged him to cancel it, or postpone it, and not to be such a stick-in-the-mud. With a slight blush he said: 'Couldn't really.' It was quite by chance that we heard some time later that he'd been summoned to the Palace to be decorated for his part in the Saint Nazaire raid. It was the sort of English reticence that we could not quite understand but admired greatly.

In mid-1946 the Commonwealth staged an enormous victory parade in London. The South African contingent was flown over in air force Dakotas. As many participants intended staying on in Britain for various reasons, there were empty seats on the return flights. These were made available to South African ex-servicemen who had not yet been home. When Jean heard of the opportunity she proposed that I should apply for a seat. When I demurred, she started making arrangements on my behalf. She would follow as soon as possible by sea. She set to work and secured a berth for herself on the *Carnarvon Castle*.

We had struck up a warm friendship with Desmond Stutchbury and his wife Norah, who had survived the most appalling experiences in Japanese internment camps and were recuperating in Oxford before returning to duty in the Colonial Service in Malaya. On the eve of my departure for South Africa we spent a long summer evening with them.

The French doors of their lovely large room opened on to still lawns and tall windless elms. The account which Desmond and Norah gave of their survival on little but hope and great love moved us deeply. The next day their presences accompanied me all the way to Cairo, where, sitting in the garden of the Almaza barracks, I wrote a poem 'Letter to Desmond and Norah Stutchbury'. The closing stanzas give some idea of the impact they had on me. They had no time for my doom-laden talk.

> ... *nor did you think*
> *Europe's end would be 'death and madness',*
> *Were short with singers of infinite sadness*
> *Whose robes are purple and black, untouched by gold or pink.*
> *You brought me the birth of another year,*
> *Awoke a wish in me to return to myself, and live.*

It was, I think, a thank-you letter disguised in verse.

Some years later I was waiting for a bus on Sogot's Corner, Johannesburg, reading the *Rand Daily Mail*. It contained a brief account of Norah's assassination by guerrillas while going to join her husband near Kuala Lumpur. I found her death so difficult to accept that I remained sitting there for a long time while buses came and went. I thought of that long summer evening, the open French doors and the still trees, and of Jean and me listening to the story of their love in a Japanese internment camp.

5   July–September 1946

Home Visit

Early on a June morning in 1946 at Princess Gate, Hyde Park, while waiting for transport to the SAAF Dakotas at Blackhurst aerodrome, I was approached by a handsome young naval lieutenant called Roy Macnab, who introduced himself to me. Roy says I seemed 'rather detached and casual; maybe it was too early in the morning or I was too sensitive'. Roy is not the only one to have found me standoffish, although that is not how I saw myself. Unfortunately we were put in different Dakotas. Roy was unhappy with his flight as 'every one seemed to be drinking and I was afraid the crew were too'. His was delayed in Cairo, where he wrote in his hotel garden what proved to be his most anthologised poem, 'El Alamein Revisited'. My own state of mind – political disillusionment, qualified by a belief in individual loyalties and loves – was finding expression in the poem I wrote for the Stutchburys, in another Cairo garden.

Up to that point in the five-day flight to Pretoria my mind was still tuned into Europe and the Mediterranean world, but from Cairo onwards we were over Africa, horizon after horizon, vast, raw, bleak and inhuman in its scale. The great Nile itself – 'a copper hot cobra asleep on the Delta' – was now a single thread of yellow silk in Saharan infinities of sand. Some time after Khartoum it turned into a slender interminable snake doubling back upon itself in figures-of-eight and essing through marshes and swamps so vast that they might effortlessly swallow up France and Spain.

It was over the Sud that our pilot did the first of several 'dives towards the deck', looking for sights to relieve the boredom of his passengers. For some time we sailed over fields of tall reeds, how tall became apparent only when we saw a Lilliputian man poling a toy dug-out between two towering walls of grass. Then nothing for another half hour, until at last some dozing hippos and basking crocodiles, half in, half out of the silver-streaked water. Our pilot kindly circled over them. They slid into the water with a kind of slow contempt, as though shrugging off a childish nuisance.

Two days farther south we flew low over the outstretched grass plains round Lake Rukwa, stampeding herds of thousands of zebra and wildebeeste, the hoof of each hurtling animal exploding in a tiny dust puff as it hit the earth. Then the pilot pulled up high to look for elephant. When he first spotted them, the herd seemed like a single rough-skinned grey tick on the gold pelt of the savannah below. The plane came circling down, first from behind, then from the flanks, teasing them into separate, magnificent beasts afflicted by a mounting terror until they stampeded in a single-minded panic-impelled course, like a dozen express trains thundering simultaneously down adjacent parallel tracks. Magnificent! What silly games we play with the brute creatures.

A few hours later on the shallow shores of another lake, we were amazed to see an enormous pearly-white shield composed of a million wading flamingoes. Then we watched its progressive disintegration from one edge skywards into a coarse white dust of birds which changed to gorgeous pink as the underside of their wings became visible.

That evening we spent in Salisbury (now Harare). There was a great reunion of friends, ex-army and old Rhodians. It was held at the club, again another and quite alien world of trim-clipped hedges and velvet lawns, cane and striped canvas chairs and tall African waiters in white ankle-length coats, their red fezzes accentuating their height.

The only friend I recall clearly was Robert Fynn, who had been one of our group at Rhodes in 1937–8. As a Rhodes Scholar he had spent the years 1939–43 doing Medicine at Oxford. He had been in the Oxford hospital wards during Sir Alexander Fleming's discovery of penicillin, and witnessed Professor H.W. Florey's development of its possibilities. I was particularly interested in penicillin because we had reason to believe that generous doses of it had saved my brother Jeffrey's life.

From Salisbury southwards the views from the air began to change. The face of earth showed more and more evidence of having been tampered with. Roads, railways, ploughed fields and villages all increased in frequency as the plane approached Pretoria.

We landed at Waterkloof. I'd been away since early 1943. It was now well into 1946. There was no welcome of any kind. A cold wind was blowing across the tawny highveld grass, wonderful to watch. I was torn by a sickening mixture of feelings. What was Pretoria to me? – this administrative capital, this concentration of military installations, Australian bluegum trees and South American jacarandas?

The South African street scenes were familiar enough, the separate facilities for whites and blacks and the park benches with 'Europeans Only' notices on them, but one now looked at them with the knowledge that the friends one had made in England would not have taken them for granted.

If absence had not made my heart grow fonder of the Transvaal it had certainly sharpened my appetite for the Karoo. I began to feel easier in an S.A.R. railway compartment of varnished teak upholstered in green leather. I looked forward to waking early next morning surrounded by the silhouettes of the mountains of the upper Fish River valley familiar since my childhood.

At last I reached The Poplars and the blessed familiarity of my parents and my sister Joan. The old building itself was unchanged, solid and simple, on the corner of Church and Bree streets, Cradock.

But the joy of homecoming was mixed with the personal anxieties of its occupants. Joan was between careers. She was leaving school-teaching to train as a housing superintendent. As always she was a kindly and shrewd observer of those closest to her. Without her help I doubt if I should have understood what was happening to our parents and indeed to all of us. All our worlds were changing.

The Poplars was far too large for Alice and Ernest, particularly now that the children came home so seldom. What was there to attract them to Cradock? And when Dad sold the *Midland News,* the parental loneliness increased; there were more empty hours to fill, particularly for Alice.

Dad was occupied enough converting the old garages and outbuildings into a smaller house for themselves. He had plans to divide the old Poplars into two flats, an idea which shocked me but which would generate useful income for a retired man without a pension scheme. Ernest had a project to occupy his hands. But what of Alice, the sociable one? Suddenly there were no calls on her time to write the social columns for the *Midland News* – reports of weddings, the show, the church fêtes – or to maintain the contacts with people, which she so enjoyed. And all her children were so far away that she seldom saw them.

Alice and Ernest were already cherishing a dream, to buy a seaside plot and build upon it, at Kenton-on-Sea on the crest of the first range of sand-dunes. It had an excellent view of the estuary and the sweeping coast towards Kwaaihoek and the Dias Cross. As soon as the alterations at The Poplars were complete, Ernest would start to build a simple seaside house out of cement blocks, with six bedrooms, one for themselves and one for each of their children.

But the main sources of anxiety at The Poplars were the post-war difficulties of their children, particularly Jeffrey the youngest. He was back at Rhodes. Joan had watched his homecoming.

Not only was Jeff the apple of Ernest's eye, the youngest, the gay spark, always in and out of scrapes. He had come back maimed, his left arm off at the shoulder, his right hand crippled and his face scarred with shrapnel. But what was left of him was his own. He was now a totally independent young man. He had got home before the war's end on 1 November 1944. What was there for a convalescing returned soldier to do in Cradock? Most of his like-minded local contemporaries were still at the front, in Italy, or in the SAAF or RAF, or 'in the bag' in Polish coal mines, or dead. Shrapnel splinters were still emerging from his wounds through little festering sores. The nerves in his stump gave him periodic hell. He would crack loud jokes about not being able to *handle* his artificial arm (ha-ha).

While grateful for assurance and affection, he missed the camaraderie of his own age group. His surviving hand went septic and he had to return to the Military Hospital at Voortrekkerhoogte for some weeks. When he returned to The Poplars, father and son had words about his fondness for alcohol. Jeffrey was adamant. He was not going to pretend to have inherited his father's inhibitions about strong drink. So his stay at home had been truncated and he had gone back to Rhodes in March 1945, where he could go out on a slightly bigger town with many more ex-servicemen, and where his uncoordinated homecomings need cause no grief to his teetotal Papa.

In Cradock Ernest sought out another ex-serviceman, a crony of Jeff's, and stuttered out a homily on the danger to one's self, one's family and society of the demon drink. This I know is so because twenty years later, during a seaside holiday, a sober and successful man had made a blushing point of telling me of it. 'I was going to pieces and I knew I was going to pieces. And your old man had the guts quietly to tell me – me, a conquering hero – the truth. He's dead now and I can't thank him. So I'm telling you.' It was my turn to look out to sea and blink and swallow. Ernest's shade was suddenly uncomfortably close.

There was not much in Cradock for me either. I read some Freud which did me no good at all. I knew that I was harbouring a great unjust Oedipal resentment of my father. Everything would have been so much easier for all of us if he had been more of a man of the world or had not given us such demanding super-egos. Like Jeffrey, I needed company of my own generation, so after a dutiful ten days I too decided to go to Rhodes.

The first thing I saw from the window of my room in College House was Jeff, strolling up South Street with a girl. He was not wearing his artificial arm, and the empty sleeve flapped free. With his remaining hand, whose movements were slightly odd, he was gesticulating, using the large gestures of our mother Alice. His form had filled out and he seemed happy. So did the lovely girl with him. She was fair, sported a lively ponytail and was wearing a track suit. This costume made it possible for me to identify her as Val de la Harpe, who was a good athlete. I had last seen Jeff two years ago in July 1944, sitting on the edge of his bed in a Naples military hospital, keeping the rest of the ward in fits of laughter with his wisecracks.

We drank affectionately and pleasantly enough in 'The Vic', swopping the news.

I was vaguely aware that a grizzled ex-serviceman of 1914–18 vintage had moved up and was standing on Jeff's left-hand side. Suddenly Jeff's voice rose in a fury.

'No, I won't have another bloody drink, thank you!' And he turned his back on the man and cried, 'Come, let's go!'

'What's up?' I asked, out in the street.

'Sympathy! I can't stand people getting a kick out of what happened to me.'

Among those interested in literature were Murray Carlin and a girl called June Carey Hobson, both of whom had published poems which appealed to me. I found myself expatiating at length on the subject of South African writing in English to the literary editors of the student papers, particularly Norman Addleson and Herbert Kretzmer, editors of the *Rhodes Outlook*. In August the *Outlook* published an article by June Hobson, 'Where do we go from here?' which expressed the dreads and aspirations of would-be South African writers immediately after the war.

'English-speaking South Africa is, one way and another, a country without a voice. We can't express our political opinions in the press without censorship – a censorship which nominally does not exist. We haven't a literature. Incredibly enough, we haven't even a literary periodical of any discrimination where the standard of our creative work can be improved by intelligent criticism ... As a result all our young writers of any ambition are forced either to migrate overseas or have all their work published there, so that they tend to lose their national identity. Those who remain either keep the silence of desperation, or give in to necessity and find their channels of expression in the *Outspan* or others of its kind. Under these circumstances we, as a nation, have no standards culturally speaking by which to live.'

How radically this scene has changed will become apparent later in this book.

The student Left in 1946 was small, incisive and articulate, many of them influenced by the Professor of Sociology, James Irving. After serving an apprenticeship to Scots trade-unionism and research at Cambridge, James had spent some years in China. He was a travelled man who had read all Balzac and was never too quick on the draw with his Marx or Durkheim. Among the students there were Hamish Dickie-Clarke, Brian Taylor, John Rex and Dave Brokensha, all destined for chairs in sociology or anthropology in Britain, Ireland or the U.S.A. And there were others, enlightened 'liberals' with a lingering devotion to the old gospel, such as Calvin Cook and Rodney Davenport. All these were urging yes to the question 'Shall we throw our doors open to blacks?'

The Right was to find its leader in an ex-RAF pilot, tall, friendly and efficient, his face still shining with fresh scars of plastic surgery: Ian D. Smith, future Rhodesian Prime Minister.

I took part in whatever discussions were going, finding myself exasperated at my inability to give more than lukewarm support for the socialist ideologies which in my view depended on over-optimistic assumptions about human nature. As an information officer I had preached the hopeful social gospel to the troops. It assumed that most men were reasonable by nature, that intelligent self-interest would work for social justice and that men would rather serve each other as brothers and comrades within the logical structures of a socialist state than compete with each other in a jungle of capitalism. But I had lost much of my faith in the social gospel, not because its economic theories were questionable, but because it did not address itself to the real questions about man which the war in its concluding stages had posed for me. The gas chambers, the concentration camps, the dropping of the atom bomb and other atrocities had destroyed for me the 19th-century progressive vision of man on which Marxism is based. The notion that mass class movements, with their dependence on party organisers and party rhetoric, could be relied on to produce just and peaceloving societies struck me as simpleminded. Man in the mass as a merely political animal was something horrifying to me. Nuremburg rallies, victory parades, May Day celebrations, and broadcasts to the nation were all suspect.

Filled with such pessimism I went for lonely walks. One afternoon I was caught in a gloomy hailstorm on a hillside above the town. When I got back I started a poem ('After Ten Years') to which I kept returning during the rest of my stay.

What about the Christianity that had always been a kind of last stronghold (or funk hole?) in times of moral crisis? 'I'd lost my faith' as the saying goes. I was in the position of many Westerners, secularised, deprived of the cosmic consolations of nature or religion, encapsulated in time, reduced to the routines of industrial cities and deprived of the dimensions of height and depth.

I was utterly graceless in my religious disillusionment. I heard that my friend and bestman, Bill Burnett, who had married Sheila Trollip, was now at St Paul's Theological College. I had seen his former half-section Wilf MacRobert in Pretoria. Like me the war had undermined Wilf's religion and when he came out of the navy he abandoned his intention of entering the church. It was good seeing Bill and Sheila again and hearing something of Bill's escape from the p.o.w. cage and his life in the Abruzzi, cared for by the Italians for months. He knew I had seen Wilf and asked me how he had looked. According to Sheila, I replied: 'He had the hangdog look of someone who was being prayed for.'

I was sleeping badly. At intervals, mostly at night, I worked away at the poem with which I hoped to pull my disintegrating self together.

Jean was due to disembark at Port Elizabeth from the *Carnarvon Castle*. She would take the train up to Cradock, where we would rendezvous before proceeding to Johannesburg. Having thumbed a lift the previous afternoon, I rose in time to meet her on the Cradock platform early next morning, in my hand a spray of scarlet erythrina plucked in Grahamstown. It was still dark and the air was sharp with frost. She looked very warm and beautiful in the lit compartment with her golden plait round her head. Since her first visit to The Poplars in 1938 she had been a favourite with my mother. My father said she was the best publicity agent any man could have.

After a day or two with them we took the railway bus to Queenstown *en route* for Engcobo in the Transkei to visit Dr Murray Satchwell, Jean's brother, then in his first practice. Jean recalls a menu at the Hexagon Hotel, Queenstown, which could not fail to impress people accustomed to starchy and stodgy meals in the postwar British restaurants of Oxford. There was a choice of four different meats, and we tried them all.

We were not impressed by the lifestyle of the whites in Transkei whom we observed at the Engcobo Hotel. The men all gathered in the bar and the women in the ladies' lounge. Occasionally a man would send the Indian waiter to 'go and see if my wife wants another drink'. We were by now used to civilised English pubs.

On the way back, surrounded by the grandeur of the mountainous Karoo, I tried to reconstruct, from Deneys Reitz's *Commando*, General Smuts's movements almost half a century earlier.

At The Poplars we found that Jeffrey had returned from Rhodes. A message had come from Graaff-Reinet indicating that our grandmother wished to see her grandsons. So it was decided that Jean, having seen me, her in-laws and her brother, should continue to Johannesburg to visit her parents and her sister Peggy. I would join her after seeing a few of my Karoo relatives.

I shall not recount here the wintry adventures which Jeff and I endured hitch-hiking to Graaff-Reinet across the Wapadsberg. They deserve leisurely treatment if only because the hitch took over twenty-four hours instead of the anticipated three. When at last we reached our hosts the Booysens, our knapsacks were searched by the police. They suspected us of being hoboes responsible for breaking into a barber shop in Cradock and making off with quantities of razor blades and Brylcreem!

We were advised that we were expected to visit Grannie as soon as possible. We washed, brushed our hair and put on our best behaviour as if we were 8-year-olds, for we both reverenced not only Grannie but also Aunt Mary who was looking after her.

And there sat Annie Letitia, as neat as ever, with a crocheted shawl over her shoulders, her hands on the arms of the same bentwood rocking-chair, and standing behind her was Aunt Mary, smiling, contained, posed as in a Victorian daguerrotype.

Grannie raised her hands towards me and as I stepped forward to kiss her on the cheek, she grasped me firmly by the forearms and held me for a moment. Mary embraced me, gently pecked me on the cheek and then held me at arm's length saying, 'Let me look at you.' She scrutinised my face, and then turned to Jeffrey. What did she see in us I wonder – two soldier grandsons of her dear pacifist father?

Conversation was difficult as Grannie was deaf and her questions were

Teebus and Koffiebus in the Karoo

so devastatingly direct. How long had I been married? Why had I not produced a son? A Butler great-grandson would please her. As for the war, one thing she was sure about: the Gestapo (*Gest*-a-po) were a wicked lot and we had done well to fight them. Of Jeffrey she asked, 'Does it hurt still?'

Annie Letitia had seen her menfolk – grandfather, father, uncles, brothers, sons and grandsons go to fight in various wars in the Amatolas, Basutoland, the Orange Free State, Transvaal, German South West Africa, East Africa, Flanders, Egypt and Italy. So she had a large and deep perspective into which to fit us. It was not a political one.

With Mary it was different. Up till ten years ago she had been almost a third parent in The Poplars' household. If we had been through exile and *wanderjahre* since, so had she. Her career as the Florence Nightingale of the Cradock location had ended most distressingly in a complex crisis where she had been caught in the crossfire between white bureaucracy and rising black nationalism. She had resigned from the location dispensary and left her beloved Cradock for a mission station in the alien northern Transvaal. But now she was here with her mother, to help her until she no longer needed human help of any kind. She said little. Mary seldom made occasions for speech. Our times are in His hand. If there was anything important to be said by her she would be given the occasion to say it.

Our next stop was Vrede. Vrede is one of the permanently important places in my mental landscape. I had my first schooling there and enjoyed non-parental affection of a rare kind, countless childhood adventures among mountains and flats on a farm where interesting things were always being done, such as bush being cleared for new lands, sheep-shearing, harvesting, and above all, dam-building – particularly a big dam up the valley towards Botha's Hoop.

I visited the walled graveyard to pay my respects to Uncle Frank's grave. I had not been to Vrede since his funeral in 1936 when the success of his still incomplete dam had been in doubt. Indeed the financial strain it imposed had been such that there was talk of bankruptcy. Now the dam was full of water and the prophets of doom confounded. Throughout the war years the farm had been run by Aunt Flo, Uncle Boy Vorster and Denys. John had returned to it in August 1945. It was almost exactly a year since I had seen him in Brighton.

After Vrede I visited Katkop and its Collett families, also part of the permanent landscape of my being. Those places got inside me as a small boy and have never let go their hold. Words can never do them justice.

There was the silhouette of Rhebokberg and the tree-lined course of the Great Fish River, the dam, the poplar bush and the lands. And more important, there they were, Uncle Norman and Aunt Gladys of Katkop, with the same gentle strength, the same lack of pretence, the authenticity of good people.

They had had to endure the long years since the fall of Tobruk with three of their four sons, Neville, Godfrey and Keith, as prisoners-of-war. Now they daily counted their blessings. All three sons were safely back home, each finding his feet on a separate farm.

Godfrey was farming at Terminus. He had arrived home on 4 August 1945, and married Joan Bladen on 9 October at St Peter's Church, Cradock. It was at The Poplars that she had dressed for her wedding.

The young couple were living in the old stone house (now a shed for tractors and trucks) then called Terminus. They were building the first part of a new house which would in time take the old name of Katkop. Godfrey was busy subduing the farm to his will and Joan was preparing for the coming of their first child. Allocation of priorities presented difficulties. There was the question of a cradle but they were very short of funds. When was Godfrey going to put his mind to it?

He showed me what woodworking tools he had and some rough-sawn boards cut from the Katkop poplar bush. These enchanted me – maybe as a small boy I had climbed that tree. So, to a design which Joan had learnt to appreciate while nursing at Groote Schuur Hospital, Cape Town, I made the framework of a canvas cradle in which in turn Elizabeth, Judy, Hugh, Alan, Philip and Charlotte were to spend their first months. The latest bulletin is that it has been of use for Judy's children too. I never did a better couple of days' work in my life.

6 October 1946–April 1947

Oxford and Switzerland

After the Karoo I joined Jean again at Ons Hoek, Tyrwhitt Avenue, Johannesburg, where our wedding reception had been held six years before. Jean had secured a *locum* with Doctors Krige, Charlton, Craib and Osler. She was happy among her old friends and earning the money we needed very badly.

Jean and I had a difficult decision to make. It was now October 1946 and I was due to write Schools either in June 1947 about eight months ahead, or in December (an option open to ex-servicemen) fourteen months ahead. After her recent experience Jean dreaded another English winter (and what a winter that of 1946–7 turned out to be!). After much agonising we decided that I would go alone and that if I decided to take the November option, Jean would join me in Oxford in May in the spring.

We were also worried about my future career. I had a very open mind about it, almost as open as my mind had been in mid-1945 about what course I should take, or which university I should attend. As before, I knew that I could always fall back on teaching, but I cherished no burning professional ambition, merely a love of the arts in general, and poetry and the theatre in particular. It is important to state that an academic career was not among the possibilities I considered at this point.

I wanted to get back to St John's College, Johannesburg, where I had taught briefly and happily in 1940. I visited it and warmed to the place immediately. There were many old friends in the common-room. The buildings were as beautiful as ever and so was the view towards the Magaliesberg.

I had a very pleasant interview with the headmaster, Nobby Clarke. Was there any possibility of rejoining the staff from which I had resigned almost three years before? If I wrote Schools in July '47 I would be available in August or September; if I wrote in November I'd be free in January '48. Nobby could not commit himself but he expressed interest in the possibility.

I had looked at the salary scales of teachers and at the cost of living, and particularly at the prices of houses and accommodation. An appointment at St John's would be a proposition only if I could be given one of the staff houses. At this Nobby shook his head. There was absolutely no possibility.

This was most depressing. Jean and I wanted to set up house and start a family.

One evening Jean and I went to a dance at the Orange Grove Hotel with some friends. In the company was Ruth Weinbren, who held a junior teaching post at Wits. (She subsequently became Professor Nevo at the Hebrew University of Jerusalem.) On the way home I started cursing society for the poor salaries it paid to schoolmasters. What on earth was I going to do when I finished at Oxford? The regulations of South African departments of education are such that I would not be able to get a permanent post without a qualification known as the University Education Diploma. Without this my choice of schools would be limited to the so-called private ones like St John's, and St John's had no living accommodation to offer me.

Memory is an odd thing. I can recall exactly where Ruth made a suggestion that was to change the course of my life. The car was coming down Munro Drive.

'Haven't you ever thought of university teaching?'

'Who me? No.'

'Well, lecturers do get a little more than schoolmasters. And I think there's going to be a vacancy at Wits before long. Would you like to meet the head of department, Professor Greig?'

So she arranged for me to meet the man who was to have a profound influence on my life.

After questioning me as to my interests he said he would certainly like to receive an application from me. I was to watch the columns of *The Times Educational Supplement* as there might well be a vacancy within a year. I began looking at universities in an unfamiliar way.

Shortly after my return to Oxford on 15 October, I attended a peculiarly memorable symphony concert conducted by Sir Thomas Beecham in the Sheldonian. It was my first experience of the inside of that Wren building, of that conductor, and of Sibelius's Second Symphony. And as I came away there was a placard outside Blackwell's announcing the suicide of Hermann Goering, head of the Luftwaffe, found guilty at the Nuremburg War Criminal trials.

I worked hard. It was the term in which Helen Gardner lectured on John Donne. I was impressed by both. Her exposition of 'A Nocturnal upon St Lucie's day' coincided with my mood and prepared me for the winter ahead.

When Bryson went on leave I was sent off to a female don who had been a lexicographer with the *Oxford English Dictionary*. I was told that she lived in the lower depths of a house in North Oxford; that she had birds' nests in her hair, had never been seen in anything but red carpet slippers, could not speak unless she had a cigarette dangling from her lower lip, and was the world authority on all English words beginning with *str* (or was it *stu*?). This last attribute meant that a difficult tutorial on 'Sir Orfeo' or 'The Owl and the Nightingale' might suddenly turn into a full and fascinating excursion into the lexicography of a word beginning with *str* (or was it *stu*?).

Lies, lies, lies, male chauvinist lies. No birds' nests, only a vague Strewel Peter effect; and the red slippers were seen only four times in an entire term. I concede the cigarette. She managed to smoke it until the ash was at least an inch long before it fell and smudged her serge or woollen front. But I waited in vain for the display of lexicographical pyrotechnics. She was one of several blue-stockings I have known who soon made me forget 'the he and she'. A delightful person.

J.B. Leishman continued as my literature tutor. Once a week for two years, in a book-lined room in Bardwell Court, he listened to Arnold, Barnett and Butler reading their essays. What can one say of this big angular man, intensely shy, beetle-browed, in ancient tweed jacket and baggy plus-fours, his lips compressed on a pipe the size of a saxophone, which stubbornly refused to smoulder? He smoked a box of matches each tutorial. There was no doubt about his learning, intelligence and perception, and his concentration on whatever we were reading. One could hear his forehead crack like ice into a frown when one was being more than usually simple-minded, and one could see when he was pleased. But his comments, when spoken, were painfully brief and frequently incomprehensible; when written they were all but indecipherable. And yet I consider him to have been a good tutor, I suppose because he managed to suggest the high seriousness of literature and of all art.

I knew those of his Rilke translations already in print. Fond as I was of Yeats, I found the richness in Rilke irresistible. Also congenial to me were Rilke's prophetic claims for a new mode of being to be mediated by art, claims which I found particularly appealing during the times when I could forget the awful implications of Hiroshima, Buchenwald and Yalta.

Occasionally Leishman would let fall a comment which betrayed his own growing pessimism about the future. After a weekend in London among the dilletanti, literati, superficial know-alls and whizz-kid reviewers for the then-growing Sunday papers, he cried: 'There was once an assured place for the writer and the reader. Now both are increasingly at the mercy of these middle-men of letters. They and the publishers are calling the tune.'

On another occasion, angered by I cannot recall what sign of growing barbarism in what paper, he said, 'Do you know Yeats's *Curse of Cromwell?*' 'No,' I said. 'Read it,' he said, 'aloud.' And then he intoned the final stanza.

I came on a great house in the middle of the night,
Its open lighted doorway and its windows all alight,

J.B. Leishman (sketched during a tutorial)

>   And all my friends were there and made me welcome too;
>   But I woke in an old ruin that the winds howled through;
>   And when I pay attention I must out and walk
>   Among the dogs and horses that understand my talk.
>   O what of that, O what of that,
>   What is there left to say?

In 1948, safe in a job at last, I wrote thanking him for all he had done for me. He wrote back:

'I am happy to know that you feel I have been of some help to you during a critical time. I often feel that, except in purely practical matters, one can only really help others involuntarily, and that if one has done so it is, as it were, because one has been used for that purpose – or, at most, because one has been able to allow oneself to be so used. I greatly enjoyed our association and was very sorry that it came to its end so soon. It was also a regret to me that I never met your wife – one day perhaps, when you both visit England again, I shall have that pleasure.' (He was to meet Jean in 1954.)

'I am very glad to know that you are happy in your work and that you are finding it possible to live, as it were, vertically as well as horizontally. Of all modern writers I think Rilke would help you most: no other has so profound a sense of what he called "das Einige des Lebens und des Todes".'

John Barnett tells me that he met him, years later, striding alone through Wytham Woods or across Shotover. 'Barnett,' he said, 'do you not feel that the world is getting colder?' And in 1954, when I visited him in Bardwell Road, he kept saying: 'Read Musil's *The Death of Virgil.*'

There was in him no betrayal of the great Renaissance vision of man. Tragic, noble and beautiful were epithets he could still use without irony.

When I heard that, walking alone in the Alps, wandering from the path to gather flowers, he had slipped and fallen a thousand feet to his death among rocks and ice, I was appalled; and then I rejoiced at the awful appropriateness. For all his learning and sensibility, Leishman was an elemental man.

What was I to do during the coming vacation? That was a question I did not address with sufficient urgency in the autumn of 1946.

Several friends were going off on skiing parties to Switzerland. The idea did not appeal to me, but what else was there to do? Over the festive season 5 Beaumont Street would be empty. Even Mrs Manning and her daughter Barbara would be visiting her relatives at Swindon for most of the time. When at last I took the decision, all the Oxford skiing parties (organised by the National Union of Students) were fully subscribed, so I joined a students' tour organised from London.

I prepared for Switzerland in a rush, my visa arriving two days before departure. I secured a sufficiency of traveller's cheques, which I deposited with my passport in my impenetrable hiding-place, beneath the paper lining of the right-hand top drawer of my dressing-table. I was excited and also abstracted, making my first effective acquaintance with Wordsworth's *The Prelude: The History of a Poet's Mind.* J.B. Leishman was great on Wordsworth.

I booked into a small hotel near Waterloo Station from which I was due to catch the boat train early next morning. I was already in bed when it occurred to me that I had better check to see whether I had everything I needed. Yes, all was there – except the passport and traveller's cheques!

I flung on my clothes, hurtled down an escalator into the underground, surfaced like a bubble and burst through the barriers at Paddington just in time to catch the last train that would be of any use to me – to Didcot. From Didcot to Oxford is fourteen miles. I would solve that problem when I got to Didcot. I would thumb a lift or steal a policeman's bicycle, but I would manage.

It was drizzling liquid ice on Didcot platform. Fortunately for me there was one taxicab waiting in vain for someone supposed to be on my train. He was very happy to take me to Oxford.

I knocked up Mrs Manning, who eventually shouted in terror without opening the door, 'Is it the police?' as though her house was about to be searched for contraband.

'No, it's me, Guy. I've left my passport.'

She opened the door. I had never seen her in a mob cap and scarlet dressing-gown before.

Back at Didcot I waited for about an hour and a half for the next train to London, a milk train that stopped at sidings I had never noticed before.

Dizzy with lack of sleep, frozen to the bone, I had some difficulty in waking the porter back at the hotel in London. He was more philosophical than Mrs Manning. He gave me a knowing leer and chuckled, 'Ah well, boys will be boys!'

The journey to Switzerland was interesting, the ski-hut warm, the scenery astounding and, for a man whose mountain iconography has been etched by the dry Karoo, utterly alien. The Alps, being folded mountains, may evoke the jagged mountains of the Western Cape but never the Karoo mountains, over some of which I had recently trudged, never.

The key figure in the party was Hans, our Swiss student coach and guide, German-speaking, blond, blue-eyed and beautiful, and moving on his skis with the confidence of a hawk in the air. He spoke English well. There was a certain tension in him owing to the fact that he was cursed, he said, with imagination, unlike most of his fellow Swiss. He recited Schiller with a soft abstracted air. His opposite pole was provided by Jacques, a volatile Frenchman who spoke with shoulders, hands, shrugs, headshakings, all moving in syncopation with the sing-song of his voice. Between these two continental extremes we, the Anglo–Saxons, kept the even tenor of our ways; 'we' being a very young official from the Foreign Office, a chartered accountant on leave from India, three Scots students who spoke little but pungently, some robust boys from Birmingham, and myself. Alas, 'we' could not disclaim the Rook sisters, both in their thirties, huge, vacant and voluble, given to rhapsodising in girlish voices. Walt Disney was 'delicious' and the sliced carrots 'so clever'. They were so exasperating to the Foreign Office official, who was concerned for his country's good name, that he took Hans on one side and explained in his suavest manner that not all English women were as large and silly as these two.

As for skiing, I was not very quick at learning the rudiments. Even the Rook girls were quicker – but they had been skiing before. I was not comfortable about the way they used to vie to pick me up whenever I fell.

Some time in the second week I became reckless and gave myself over to gravity and a long slope, like a mystic allowing himself to fall into the Everlasting Arms. For a few seconds I experienced the ecstasy of speed, my face like a pink hatchet cleaving the cold blue air. I cannot describe what happened next because I do not know. Half buried in snow, my nose full of ice crystals, I found myself trying to untie myself, a complicated knot of limbs, skis and ski-sticks. The pain was not as bad as the humiliation. Sweet little Swiss girls of 4 slid slowly by on one ski while beastly little Swiss boys simply hissed past, flying backwards.

A severely twisted ankle confined me to the chalet. It was a happy accident. But for it, though I might have learnt to ski, I would not have written certain poems and a piece of prose which marked a significant advance in my writing.

Towards the end of our stay, my ankle being better, I joined the rest of humanity again and went down on the ski-lift into Davos, where we spent a convivial evening round a table, spiking small cubes of bread on long forks and plunging them into a crock containing a simmering fondue of cheese and white wine. We all tried to learn a complicated French country dance from Jacques in the snowy street, 'Sur le pont d'Avignon'.

Back in Oxford I had to decide whether I would sit my Schools in June or December. Having spent most of the three months' vacation of 1946 on the trip to South Africa I was in need of time to read. I wrote to Jean. If she could join me in the spring we could have the whole summer together. 'The winter would be over and done, flowers would appear on the earth, and the voice of the dove be heard in the land.'

England was entering one of the bitterest winters on record. The snow fell thick at frequent intervals, making gloomier the short spells of daylight under a sagging sky so cold that no thaw could set in.

Bitterly cold as it was, some February days were bright. The freezing for weeks on end of Port Meadow and the canals released an unexpected joy. Young and old took to their skates. After my recent experiences with skis in Switzerland, I didn't even try to learn to skate but would walk gingerly along the ice-clad towpath, watching, thinking of Breughel's paintings, seeing the sun setting in the west over Wytham Woods, glinting on the meadow which flung the light upwards like a mirror. People appeared alternatively dark and then bright, according to their relationship to the light; and there was the fine definition of tree shapes:

I love to see, when leaves depart,
The bare anatomy arrive,
Winter, the paragon of art
That kills all forms of thought and feeling
Save what is pure and will survive.

Brian Stanion and I, wrapped up like Laplanders, attended a good series of lectures on the Romantics – or was it Yeats? – by C.M. Bowra, and a lively production of W.H. Auden's *The Ascent of F6* at the Playhouse. I found the mountain/mother equation even less convincing in production than in reading. T.S. Eliot lectured in Pusey House on the proposed ecumenical Church of South India. I went, not because I was so interested in the attempts to re-unite a fragmented church, but out of curiosity to see a great poet. The place was crowded with dons and clerics. Eliot was not an impressive speaker but I recall an interesting metaphor. The weight of Christian mission work in India was borne by several churches, each of which had its own traditional strength. To attempt to unite them might be dangerous – like trying to transfer the weight of a bridge which is supported on several small arches on to one big arch.

I was introduced to the Joyce Carys who lived in a large house almost opposite one of the entrances to the University Parks. This was my first acquaintance with a real English writer. I knew little of his work at this time, only *The Case for African Freedom*, I think.

If only I had read then *The Horse's Mouth*, my whole writing career might have been different. The comic triumph of the creative spirit over failure and over fashion might have shaken me out of the gloom which still hung with intermittent bright periods over my spirit. Cary's hero, Gulley Jimson, suffered from an old-fashioned obsession with the grand heroic picture, the great allegorical statement on a wall or large canvas, and could not comprehend a world in which such magnanimous painting was not only no longer in fashion but ridiculous. I felt an affinity with him. Was not my labour on a long poem a similar folly?

So almost a decade before I met Gulley I had met his creator.

Joyce sat in a bright, large room alive with books and pictures, an extraordinarily positive and hopeful presence in a sad, cold season.

The restrictions on heating were severe. At one time no room in all England could be warmed by electricity without the permission of the Home Secretary unless it contained a nursing mother, an invalid, or an over-80. The heartless younger Fellows of one college, which had two octogenarian dons, cried, 'Eureka! At last we have a use for them. We can hire them out by the hour to sit in rooms which need heating.'

There were moments of light relief. 'Snow shovelled off the roof of a College was seen to descend on the head of its Principal,', reported the *Oxford Magazine*. There was also ammunition for the radically righteous: 'Undergraduates in another College observed with disfavour how the roof of the Master's lodgings was the only one from which the snow had melted.'

Mrs Manning's landlord had instructed her to give notice to a number of her tenants, including me. Jean was due in five weeks' time so the hunt for somewhere to live began all over again. There seemed to be nothing available. Eventually I found a place in Wellington Square, a flat consisting of one spacious room under the slates with a large window looking on to the treetops of the square. There was a small landing over the stairwell, provided with a sink of neolithic earthenware, some shelves made by Heath Robinson and a small gas stove by Beatrix Potter. I decided to take it.

In term-time colleges provided overseas students with a social context. Vacations, by contrast, could be a miserable and friendless vacuum. I had learnt from my tardiness about booking for Switzerland and made a special trip to London with three or four friends to be interviewed or 'vetted' by Lady Frances Rider and Miss MacDonald of the Isles, who arranged holidays with hospitable people for lonely students. They did their best to meet the wishes of both visitors and hosts. Where would I like to go? Scotland and the West country, I said; and to Scotland and the West country I duly went, spending a memorable week in a home in each. Both families had been tragically involved in the war and had offered to host students, preferably ex-servicemen.

The journey from Glasgow to Tayinloan on the Bight of Kintyre was a wonderful experience – down the Clyde, shedding the dockyards, moving into island-scattered waters, then approaching the small port of Tarbert, where an older, slower rhythm seemed to take over. The ancient bus rattled south down the west coast of the peninsula, close to the sea from which the bare, heathy country rose steeply to what seemed like a plateau. There were very few trees and the farms lay far apart.

The house itself did have some trees, but for all that it looked bare. The hospitality staggered me. Yet not only was the mother of the house harassed by two adolescent boys, wild with freedom after a term at one of the great English public schools, but the laird was on crutches, a casualty of Dunkirk. Blonde, big, handsome, he was still struggling to accustom himself to a leg lost high in the thigh. The walls of the passage bore those trophies so dear to sportsmen – cups, shields, photographs and an oar with the names of the victorious eight painted upon its blade. We ate porridge out of beechen bowls, served by the laird himself, with salt, not sugar.

Bruce, my Australian co-guest, was also from Oxford. He had been in the Royal Australian Air Force and his forehead showed signs of plastic surgery. We were not congenial. Although he was doing P.P.E. he seemed to know far more about English Literature than I did. He was sharp, with an incredible memory. I thought we might find common ground if he had any feeling for the presumably wide open spaces of his country. Yes, he came from a farming family. In fact he was heir-apparent to one of the greatest sheep-runs (or series of runs) in South Australia. They had so many sheep and had to pay so few men to handle them that they were the envy of all. This achievement was the result of a careful time-and-motion study of every single operation on the ranch and the cunning use of fences and sheep-dogs. I thought of the farms I knew in the Karoo and wondered how life would change there if all black and coloured labourers became as costly as whites were in Australia when organised into unions. Sooner or later there would be an agricultural revolution in South Africa. It would destroy the world I had known where almost all large farms were owned by whites, where all labour was poorly paid, whether coloured or black, and where there were no unions.

Bruce was highly critical of almost everything in Britain. His Oxford tutor was an old-fashioned economist who did not keep up with the relevant journals. They had better men at the University of Sydney. I became dimly aware that he had come to Britain filled with practical, exploitable expectations. He wanted to go back and run more sheep with even fewer men; or, having learnt something more about investments, to play the stock market with greater skill. He felt he was getting nowhere.

The third day we all went on an outing up to the hills, to dip sheep. It was a very leisurely ritual, an important occasion for the laird and his crofters, if that is what they were still called. His maimed but handsome form had to be lifted into the saddle, and the solicitude in the craggy faces of the oldish men was striking. Very little was said. There was a sharp wind, and the heath pulsed on either side of the path.

Eventually we reached a small stone pen, very like a South African kraal, with three or four shepherds waiting. A slow, laconic exchange of greetings took place in which it was quite clear that the man dismounting from the horse was recognising, and being recognised by, his own people.

Before the dipping began we gathered in the shelter of the stone wall, and whisky was passed slowly from hand to hand and savoured with an unashamed smack of the lips. Then followed nutty bread, and meat grilled over an open flame. No one hurried. If any creature was restive, it was the odd sheep.

There were almost more men than sheep. Each sheep was manhandled individually and given as much attention as a human baby. Even so the dipping did not take very long.

After it was over there was more passing of the flask, and more slow talking, and then the leisurely straggle back to the distant house, which resembled a strong cube of granite on the open plain below.

The day in the saddle had been a strain, and the laird was not at supper. At breakfast I volunteered how much I had enjoyed the dipping. I asked whether there were shepherds who lived up on the hills all year, and had those old men been there in his father's time? Before an answer was possible, Bruce launched into how many minutes it would have taken one Australian man and two dogs to dip those two hundred and twenty-six sheep: certainly not an hour, let alone a whole precious day. You did, however, have to construct a fenced approach to the dipping-tank, and the dogs had to be trained to frighten the sheep into a sort of controlled stampede so that they leapt into the water and immersed themselves thoroughly. Scots sheep-farmers would do well to visit a big sheep run in Australia ...

The laird put his spoon down alongside his untouched porridge and, grabbing his crutch, swung himself out of his own dining-room. His wife followed him. Bruce looked surprised. We ate in silence for some time.

'Did I say something wrong?'

'You don't tell your host he doesn't know how to run his own farm. Yesterday was more than a dipping – it was a ritual get-together, an ancient custom.'

'Rituals and customs are the death of this country,' said Bruce.

He left that afternoon. I walked down to the bus-stop with him. He turned his sharp mind on me and my country, politely but firmly calling me a romantic liberal. Neither is a swear-word in my vocabulary. 'You want both the comforting reassurance of traditions and the material benefits of capitalism. Can they be reconciled with any show of justice? In South Africa, for instance, is the wealth of the mines being used to provide material benefits for all on an equitable basis? Whose traditions are being nurtured, the whites' or the blacks'?'

To all of which I had no answer, except to say that new civilisations which resulted from the clash and blending of two or more existing cultures were slow in coming into being, like modern Europe itself. Australia, New Zealand, the United States, were all lucky, unilingual ex-colonies, where the indigenous populations had been small and weak and easily reduced to military and cultural impotence. South Africa was altogether different. If he wanted to make comparisons, let him imagine an Australian aborigine population of forty million. It would be a long time before the shape of South African culture emerged.

'You take long views,' he said, laughing.

'Short views can be short-sighted.'

'A long view on the dipping of sheep spells death to the wool industry. Artificial fibres are here to stay.'

'Would you Australians have developed that dipping system with a man and two dogs if labour had been plentiful and cheap?'

The debate dried up while we waited for the bus. We looked towards the sea, the Irish Channel, the Atlantic. In a very different tone of voice he said: 'My mother is Scots. Do you know an old Scots ballad about the Four Marys? It's been going through my head all morning.'

'Yes,' I said.

There was Mary Seaton and Mary Beeton
And Mary Carmichael and me.

'That's right,' he nodded and, looking away, continued: 'You remember what Mary Morrison said on the scaffold?'
So I said:

O little did my mither ken,
The day she cradled me,
The lands I was to travel in
Or the death I was to dee.

'That's it,' he said. 'When I think how our host got up from the table and grabbed that bloody crutch, I can die of shame.'

I stayed on for two more days, reading in the garden in the early spring sunlight with daffodils flopping from side to side under a naked beech-tree, the bare fields stretching beyond to expanses of empty sea. I struck no common vein to explore with husband and wife, who, I imagine, were exploring strange worlds of love and anguish. Some wounds continue bleeding although the surface scars are healed. All over the world there were millions of men and women getting used to the differences the war had made to their bodies and their minds.

When I told my liberal Oxford friends that I was to spend part of my vac in Budleigh Salterton they laughed. What was funny about Budleigh Salterton, I asked.
'It's music hall shorthand for retired colonels, Blimps and Pooh-Bahs of the British Empire.'
The couple in Budleigh were not a fit target for music-hall jokes. They had lost their only son in the RAF. For years they took in as many as four students at a time. On this occasion all were South Africans.
We went for wonderful walks in the broken country and all along the edge of red-coloured cliffs; we visited Exeter Cathedral, and Nether Stowey, where Coleridge was born.
When the others went golfing, I had some time to myself.
On two or three occasions I went down to the shore to talk to the fishermen making lobster pots out of willow withies, big-boned men with craggy faces, black hair and very blue eyes. The old Celtic stream ran clear in them. One day, sheltering from the sharp wind by the sea wall, I asked my companion what he thought of two ageing Saxon officers, erect and vigorous, their pink faces, white hair and whiskers thrust cheerfully into the wind as they promenaded with vigour along the sea-front. There was a long pause. When the reply came it was circuitous and took courteous account of my African origins.
'I hear that ivory hunters in Africa all dream of finding the elephants'

graveyard. When an elephant feels death coming, he makes for a particular place in a far-off forest, and lays his bones amongst the bones of his kind. Well, about a hundred years ago Budleigh Salterton became the graveyard of the bull elephants of the British Empire.'

I laughed.

'They don't belong here,' he continued. 'They just come here to die.'

I waited, knowing there was more to come.

'If you go to Budleigh churchyard and look at the old, old gravestones, you'll see who belongs in this place.'

With a toss of his head towards his fellow fishermen, he added: 'All our families are there.'

They felt deeply that some bones belonged better in Budleigh churchyard than some others. I did not see myself among the bull elephants of the Empire seeking to lay my bones in Budleigh. Yet I was part of that same exercise, a by-product of British Imperial expansion in the late 18th century. Had anyone asked me where my bones would lie, I would have shrugged.

'Somewhere in Africa of course.'

1 St Mary the Virgin from Brasenose Lane.

2 Guy Butler and Guy Stringer meet outside the Dudley Hotel, Hove, 1945.

3 The novice skier, Davos, 1945.

4 Jean and Guy near Lucca, 1947.

5 *Agamemnon* by Aeschylus, Christ Church, Oxford, 1947.

6 Prof. J.Y.T. Greig, Head of the Department of English, University of the Witwatersrand.

7 Roy Macnab as an Oxford student.

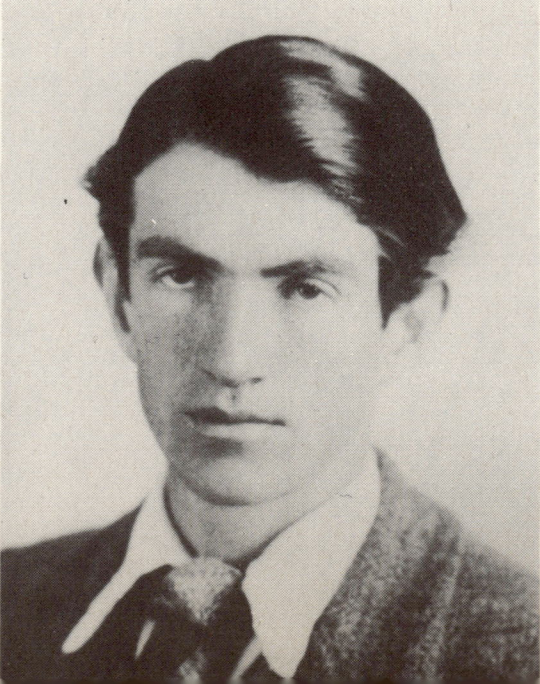

8 Father Trevor Huddleston leading a procession of witness, Sophiatown, 1947.

9 *The Dam*, 1952. Noelle Ahrenson as Katrina, Gerrit Wessels as Kaspar.

11 *The Dove Returns*, 1955. Aubrey Louw as Sergeant Hime, Leonard Graham as Victor Maycock.

12 The Messenger's Cottage (1814) under thatch with a second storey added to the Club in 1862.

13 The Messenger's Cottage, 122 High Street, bought by Jean Butler, 1952, and named High Corner.

14 Rhodes University Tower through the Drostdy Arch.

15 David Wright. 16 Roy Campbell. 17 Charles Eglington.
18 Alan Paton. 19 Sydney Clouts. 20 Jack Cope.

21 At the Wits Conference on South African Literature in 1956, Guy Butler, William Plomer, and Uys Krige. 22 Ruth Miller

23 Ruth Harnett. 24 Stephen Gray. 25 Douglas Livingstone.
27 Sipho Sepamla. 28 Es'kia Mphahlele. 29 Lionel Abrahams.

30 Athol Fugard, Richard Rive and Don Maclennan at Olive Schreiner's tomb.

31 Jean holding Patrick, with her parents, Kathleen and Leslie Satchwell, on her left, and Guy's parents, Alice and Ernest Butler, on his right, 1953.

32 Jean and Guy Butler, 1953.

33 Jean with Jane, David and Patrick, 1958.

34 Guy, Christopher, Jean and David at the opening of the Little Theatre, Stutterheim, 1971.

7   May–December 1947

Wellington Square

On May morning 1947 Jean and I rose early to celebrate her return. Standing on Magdalen Bridge we tilted our listening faces towards the choir singing in the dawn from the top of the beautiful tower. But the thundering transport lorries had already started rolling through Oxford in a continuous stream. We came away with a phrase of treble song from the sky, and a glimpse of white surplices teased by the wind.

We had moved into 11 Wellington Square. Jean could see its good points – the space and the wide view over the treetops – but also its handicaps. For instance, the three flights of stairs and the remote bathroom to be shared by the entire populace of the building: the Naval Commander, the Optometrist, *et al.* The ancient linoleum floor was of a dreary grey which, every here and there, showed hints of underlying green. Jean started scrubbing it at once, with a cake of bath soap, a mixing-bowl and a nailbrush, at which point Anne Welsh popped in. Wrenching her thoughts from Kant and Keynes to kitchen logistics, she asked Jean to make a cup of tea for her, she'd be back in five minutes. She returned with a bucket, a huge scrubbing-brush for floors and some special powder designed to clean ancient lino in a jiffy.

Furnishing the place was fun. I acquired an old army-issue folding-table for ten shillings, which fitted perfectly into the dormer-window recess over which Jean draped her favourite green woollen blanket. For the rest of the year I wrote my essays and tried to write my poems on that soft surface whose colour matched the lighter leaves in the treetops of the square.

It was a hard time for young wives learning how to entertain. A ration of one egg per week made cake-baking a difficult art to learn from scratch. Our first cake-baking session did not promise well. It was a disastrous flop, thin as a Marie biscuit and rather hard. She put it on the shelf over the banisters and withdrew to her bed. I was due to dash out to a lecture. While I was struggling into my vast army greatcoat on the small landing, a sleeve swept the cake and its plate into the stairwell. I had instant visions of it cleaving the bald pate of the Naval Commander or the wig of the Optometrist and I was infinitely relieved to hear the sharp sound of china splintering on tile. When I reached the bottom of the stairs I was confronted by an interesting sight. All the other tenants were looking at the splintered plate lying at various distances from the cake. The cake itself had survived the fall intact.

I took the débris upstairs. Jean was not amused. 'What did you bring that for?' she exclaimed. 'It'll be marvellous in a trifle,' I said comfortingly.

Nothing daunted, Jean tried again, to make a cake for the Stringers' first visit, and did much better. The cake rose adequately over three-quarters of its circumference. The final quarter presented a mysterious trough or depression. She decided to camouflage this with an extra-thick layer of cream, giving me instructions to keep this portion uncut and out of circulation. But we all had good appetites and Guy Stringer had just returned from soccer with an extra edge to his. So after a fine initial slice or two he found himself presented with some airless heavy material.

'I say,' he said, 'what caused the collapse in the west wing?'

Unexpected metaphors of this kind were one of the delights of his company.

All streets have lives of their own, and what brief sojourner can capture anything so various, so composite? By the time the tops of the trees in the square reached the level of the slates, our level, they had won a green victory for themselves and for us over the cold and earthy season of spring 1947.

We never saw our lyrical milkman but heard him in the early mornings before the traffic could drown his voice. A young, strong, uninhibited tenor he had, and his favourite song was from the musical, 'Oklahoma':

Oh, what a beautiful mornin',
Oh, what a beautiful day.
I've got a wonderful feelin'
Everythin's goin' my way.

I have always liked people who make music in the streets. Years later in the winter of 1954, in Nuffield Foundation House in Bayswater, London, frozen and miserable, my work going badly, with a difficult baby to handle, the snow dirty, the world sleazy, Jean and I would hear them come – our three musical musketeers: trombone, banjo and saxophone, thrumming, blaring, wailing their aggressive desolation up the pavement, *not* line abreast but line ahead, in the order I have given. They were exactly behind each other, balancing as on a tightrope on the very edge of the kerb, all in black suits and bowler hats, in perfect step, to their great uncompromising signature tune: 'The Happy Wanderer'. I could never resist them. I'd get up, open the French-window and go out into the cold to watch them assault that empty, quiet street. Visually the scene was a cross between a Lowry painting and a picture from Picasso's blue period, but in their stoic desolation they were prophetic of that miserable Irishman Samuel Beckett, so much so that, when *Waiting for Godot* was performed, it was no news to me. I'd fling down a coin, which was caught with great dignity and the minimum of movement in the banjo-player's bowler. In that length of Leinster Gardens they had only one other regular fan, a Nigerian, as sun-starved as I was, who would come through his balcony doors to acknowledge them.

How different was the organ-grinder who used to shuffle in rags and misery round Wellington Square in the summer of 1947! He made no music. He turned a handle that ground out some sounds. Still, I would throw coins to him.

When Jean left 5 Beaumont Street she had discarded a lot of old junk, including the turquoise straw hat which she had worn jauntily for our wedding. When she felt sufficiently settled in at 11 Wellington Square, she invited our old landlady at number 5, Mrs Manning, and her daughter Barbara, to tea. To our surprise Mrs Manning swept in wearing Jean's wedding-hat! She hoped Jean did not mind the liberty, but it was just too good to throw away and it did suit her, didn't it?

It did.

The hurdy-gurdy started up in the square and I opened the window to fling a customary copper.

'Oh dear no, Mr Butler, you mustn't do that!' remonstrated Mrs Manning. 'He's not a deserving case. He owns property, he does.'

My casting of copper largesse puzzled Jean, particularly when there was not even the pretext of a beggar. This self-indulgence took place when we were out walking beside the canals at the back of Worcester College. The sight of any smooth, unbroken sheet of water in the semi-desert of my childhood had always been an irresistible invitation to find a flat pebble and skim it, bouncing it off the surface, leaving a series of diminishing silver rings before it expended its impetus and sank. But as the Oxford towpaths were bare of such flat pebbles I would use pennies, large copper coins then about the size of a South African one-rand piece. Jean insists that the bottom of that stretch of the canal is lined with copper sequins.

Those walks! All the way up to Port Meadow, to 'The Perch' or 'The Trout', watching and hearing swans take off or come in to land like flying-boats, and the swish and snatch of oars in the water. We'd go and return by any of a dozen routes.

Coming or going, as like as not we'd see Winston Churchill, no longer Prime Minister, complete with cigar and bulldog, sitting on the park wall next to the scarlet pillar-box where St John's Street joins Wellington Square. He seemed to like that pitch, where he could button-hole people who came to post letters and tell them with a growl that he was not Mr Churchill's double, but that Mr Churchill was his double. His wife kept a boarding establishment in one of the houses near the pillar-box and I suspect she got a bit tired of having the great man about the house all day. In her lobby was a large frame containing two seemingly identical

photographs.
Beneath the first was the inscription:

Q: Is this Mr Winston Churchill of 10 Downing Street?
A: No, it is Mr Arthur Bigglestick of 29 Wellington Square.

Beneath the second was the inscription:

Q: Is this Mr Arthur Bigglestick of 29 Wellington Square?
A: No, it is Mr Winston Churchill of 10 Downing Street.

We spent a long weekend with Guy and Mary Stringer at the Military College at Faringdon. Their first baby, Prudence, had arrived and we were green with envy. I recall a long walk with Guy through mist on an open stretch of country. Through the silvery blindness we heard the sound of bagpipes. 'That'll be Captain MacLeod. Whenever he's had more of England than he can stomach he plays the pipes.' We continued walking in silence until the piper's shape appeared as an ethereal silhouette in the mist, then we stopped and listened with the respect of men at a cenotaph: 'The Flowers of the Forest.' O heart, O human heart.

When the time came for us to leave, Guy drove us to an old Romano–British site on the southern slopes of the Wiltshire Downs and told us that if we walked uphill for a while we'd hit the Ridgeway itself.

It is wonderful to walk in early spring on the immemorial Ridgeway, with crops coming up on either side of the hedgerows that define a path that has been in continual use for three thousand years or more. A mortal young man notes these interesting facts when walking with his mortal young wife, but they are less important than the always-changing, immediate emotional field that he and she generate between them. I do not think I have visited Britain since then without visiting the Vale of the White Horse and walking a portion of the Ridgeway with Jean. It is one of our special places.

We were happy in Wellington Square.

Some time in May, throwing financial caution to the winds, we went in a large party to the B.N.C. Commemoration Ball.

With a fashionable band from London working hard, the traditional lashings of strawberries and cream and the frequent popping of champagne corks, the evening rolled on happily past midnight into the small hours. Among the stragglers were ourselves. Fay Gerrard went singing home to Museum Road barefoot, swinging her shoes by their straps. Her husband John took a solemn view of her behaviour and sent her round next morning to all the other members of the party to apologise for her wantonness.

One of our more serious games was job-hunting. An application for a lectureship at the University of Natal having fallen through, we kept our

Standing stones: 'Wayland's Smithy', the Ridgeway

eyes skinned for the Wits vacancy. It took a long time to appear, during which Jean found me several wonderful jobs in romantic places. For instance, one was at Raffles College, Singapore. I told her the war had destroyed the world of Somerset Maugham for ever and that Malaysia was going to be a nasty place for some time.

Then the news came that Peggy, Jean's elder sister, was to be married and that her husband-to-be would be in London for a spell. Bert Nairn was a somewhat surprising choice of partner, a Scots mining-engineer who had done so well on the stock exchange that he could retire while in his mid-forties. He was visiting London to take one of his four sons to see a Harley Street specialist and wrote inviting us up to London to spend a few days with him at the Dorchester Hotel. I was extremely reluctant to accept.

'Why?' asked Jean, baffled at missing the only chance that would ever come our way to stay in a star-studded hotel.

'Broke,' I said. 'We're just too poor!'

'But Bert will pay for everything.'

'No, he won't.'

'What won't he pay for?'

'The tips. And those waiters and other flunkeys will accept nothing less than a fiver each.'

'Nonsense!'

'I'm telling you! For their vacations, they all go grouse shooting, or play roulette in Monte Carlo.'

Nevertheless we went. Not by train. Bertie wouldn't think of allowing us to travel by train. A black limousine that took up one side of Wellington Square pulled up and a chauffeur as smart and glossy as his car rang our bell. My nerves almost snapped at this early stage. My clothes and equipment – particularly my cardboard suitcase – were not *en suite* with this splendid Rolls.

It was worse disembarking under the *porte couchère* at the Dorchester Hotel, where elegant porters in green uniforms and cockaded hats (who never handled anyone but Dukes, film stars, ambassadors, and multimillionaires) took charge of us and, alas, our baggage.

I noticed one of these gentlemen handling my suitcase as if it contained a polecat. True, it was cardboard and torn at one of the hinges; but I should have seen to it that no portion of any garment escaped through that tear. A pink-striped pyjama leg was trailing behind it, all up the entrance steps and across the hall carpet into the lift.

Jean hugely enjoyed our stay. The double room was vast and beautiful, and Bertie had filled it with five thousand sweetpeas and other spring flowers. They looked and smelt lovely, but they gave me hayfever.

At a decent hour in the morning, heralded by a discreet knock, a waiter in impeccable black and white pushed in a mahogany trolley with our breakfast upon it. The food itself was under a large silver dish-cover. We thanked him, he bowed and left.

We leapt out of bed, slipped on our gowns and, licking our lips, approached the trolley. Jean removed the cover with a great flourish, to reveal two diminutive slices of fried bread supporting a quarter rasher of bacon apiece. Post-war austerity was apparent even at the Dorchester, London.

8   Summer 1947

France and Italy in Three Weeks

I had promised to take Jean to Italy. It was a deep-sworn oath, repeated once a week in my wartime letters to her, starting from Gravina in Puglia in May 1944 and ending in a villa outside Turin in June 1945.

Our companions were George and Ursula Brown. Our plan of campaign was simple and cheap. We would make the long journeys by train or bus and explore certain chosen regions more closely by bicycle. We'd sleep either in youth hostels or under the open canopy of heaven. We each took a change of clothes and a macintosh of some kind. At the Army and Navy Stores George and I equipped ourselves with wide-brimmed seamen's hats like late medieval helmets, of a strident yellow colour.

The foreign currency allowed us was very small. George had a few illegal dollars stashed away. I decided to put my wartime bartering experience to good use. I loaded up with tins of coffee to flog on the French and Italian black-markets. The commissariat was further inflated by the special diet which the doctor had prescribed for my incipient ulcer, which we called Oscar. He was like an extra juvenile member of the party. He had to be fed on baby foods and maizena – fortunately not difficult to prepare, but what a chore and a bore, particularly for Jean.

We took the train to Basingstoke, to catch the boat train to Southampton. But alas, at Basingstoke the bikes of the Butlers were missing. I spoke to an official called Mr Morgan, who took note of our distress and assured us that the bikes would reach Southampton early next morning.

There we got digs with a seaman's wife. The house was adorned with hideously beautiful *objets* from all ports of the world.

The next morning we went to the station to pick up our bikes but, maugre Mr Morgan, they were not there. This was most frustrating – but we made the most of it by spending the day in Winchester. 'Fine nave. Norman transept. Tombs of Waynflete, Wykeham, Fox, Cardinal Beaufort. Could not find Miss Jane Austen's.'

My bike had arrived, but not Jean's. It did not arrive the next day either, so the ever-patient Browns killed another day with us in the New Forest. 'Pass a pub called "The Angry Cheese". See *Queen Mary* now joined by

Queen Elizabeth in docks at distance. Queenly indeed. Also hundreds of swans in the rush-grown estuaries of the river. Back in Southampton – still no bike for Jean. So we buy a second-hand bike plus carrier for eight pounds fourteen shillings. In the late afternoon to the docks'. The tickets (to Rouen) were three pounds three shillings each and for the bikes we were charged nineteen shillings each to Le Havre.

We had trouble getting the bikes off the ship and into France. The fact that the number stamped on Jean's newly acquired bicycle did not correspond with the number on our papers aroused continental suspicions. Ursula, who had been to school in Switzerland expressly to learn French, tried to assuage the bureaucracy but failed. It was practical George who solved the problem. His French wasn't as good, but his francs leapt the language barrier.

However, this delay meant that we lost the train to Rouen and Paris, the next being four hours ahead, at 12.10. Unwisely we decided to cycle to Rouen. Mile after mile after mile over very bumpy cobbled roads and long, winding hills. At eleven we made tea. 'The countryside asserts itself. The heat is terrific so we put on our yellow hats, and look like a circus act. Labourers scything grass with slow immemorial rhythms. Bull behind fence in orchard, in corner of which I find, right next to me, a grave with a Gerry helmet on it. Suddenly the idyll snaps. On and on and on, all feeling the heat and hating the hills. At Lillebon we pass an old Roman amphitheatre. On and On. It is clear that the girls are suffering cruelly, so we stop an overloaded bus with a mountain of luggage on its roof ...

'Rouen lovely from the hills: many spires; broad Seine; ships; hills beyond, all in heavy heat haze. As we draw into it we see the devastating bomb damage. The vast cathedral, with the cast-iron spire, is gutted.

'The arrangements at the youth hostel are elementary. Showers, of which we had dreamt, are non-existent. George and I washed under a pump. I am halfway through my ablutions, peering through the soapsuds streaming out of my hair, when I notice a girl next to me, in nothing but black knickers. She explains (I think) that the pump must serve everyone. I stare but who cares?'

We decided to travel by train to Paris and from Paris to Avignon. We had been advised of a fine youth hostel up in the hills at Les Baux, from where we could find our way through Van Gogh landscapes to Arles. At Arles we would again take the train to Rapallo and then explore the Portofino–Santa Margharita area on our bikes, and so on.

We got to Paris about mid-morning and decided first to get ourselves tickets for a night journey from the Gare de Lyon to Avignon, hand over our bikes and then explore Paris on foot and by bus or taxi. This meant crossing Paris. We were all new to French traffic and its legendary terrors. We examined a street map of the great city and decided on the simplest route from the Gare St Lazare to the Gare de Lyon.

'Keep close behind me,' I say to Jean as we launch ourselves into the stream, holding close to the bank, out of the main currents. Wide tree-lined streets. Magnificent vistas. George and Ursula ahead, Jean and I following.

Jean was clinging closely to the line of the kerb, looking up periodically to see if my yellow fisherman's macintosh was visible, ringing her bicycle bell without intermission, and trusting in God. The plan worked well until we got to a vast and Dantesque circle, or rather whirlpool, of vehicles misnamed the Place de la Concorde.

Ahead, a fierce little uniformed man on a box, standing very erect, blew a piercing note on a whistle and started gesticulating like a marionette. The whole pattern of the maelstrom changed in instant sympathy. It almost seemed to go into reverse. This had the effect of cutting me off from Jean. Appalled, I was aware that her bicycle bell was now mute. Into what infernal sidestream had she been sucked or whirled by the change in the direction of the traffic? In haste I pulled my bike up on to the kerb, leant it against a lamp standard, then clambered up on to its saddle to get an aerial view of the scene. I felt like a sailor aloft in the crow's nest, looking for a beloved passenger overboard in the high seas. At last, far round the other side of the circle, I saw her white hat, still moving but very slowly.

When I caught up with her she was immobile beside her bicycle, its bell silent, a very beautiful girl stranded on the shores of an insane whirlpool of internal-combustion engines.

Slowly, together we found our way to the Gare de Lyon, bought tickets, shed our bikes and spent several wonderful hours mainly in the Louvre and at Notre Dame, which was my first experience of French Gothic.

We managed to catch the 8.30 p.m. and arrived at Avignon at 7.30 a.m. on Saturday 26 July 1947. I think it was the worst train journey of my life. All Paris was crammed into that train, heading for the Riviera. Big as those coaches were, they were crowded as I had never thought possible. We four, with luggage, had to share one seat between us. At any one time three of us were standing. By midnight, however, George and I had slowly established about five feet of standing space in the gritty corridor, on which we made a 'bed' out of one of the small tents, and Jean and Ursula took it in turn to sleep.

Ursula stoically took charge of the smallest child of a family of four, who joined us about midnight. The parents leant against the bunks, swaying like zombies. By this time George was squatting on his parachute bag in the corridor while I was conducting a broken conversation with a simply marvellous French youth of about 18 who claimed to have been in the Maquis. He made many apparently hilarious jokes (he laughed fit to kill himself, driving Morpheus into the loo) about booby-traps for the Boches, and Maydays with the Muscovites.

The Papal Palace at Avignon

It was insufferably hot. At every stop – and there were not many – people would stampede from the train, with any container they had, to whatever tap could be found on the naked platform. I never stood a chance because I could not bring myself to fight with the women who crashed whatever rudimentary queue might form near the tap. As the seconds slipped by, discipline would collapse and there would be a circular scrum round the pipe, with more water running to waste than got into the mugs, water-bags or soda-water bottles.

I was getting really anxious, as Jean's need for fluid seemed urgent. The engine made premonitory noises; so, despairing, I turned for our coach, which was towards the back of the train. But the French boy, seizing my two bottles, cried out, 'Leeve eet to moi!'; then dropping to his knees at the back of the mêlée round the tap, he started burrowing his way through the thicket of male and female ankles and calves ahead of him. 'Maquis, for sure,' I thought, making for our coach. The sky was black and huge, the night vast, the lamps few and far between.

The train pulled out, without my friend. I felt contrite.

Still, a young chap with that *esprit* would have no difficulty with life. It would be nothing to him to wait on a bare platform for a few hours for the next train, with those two soda-water bottles intended for his Anglais comrades' *jolies femmes*. Chivalry was not dead.

Nor was nerve.

A good ten minutes after we'd left and were hurtling through blackness, we were startled by a banging on our window. There he was, grinning and

The bridge at Avignon

clinging to the outside of the coach with the bottles full of water, which he handed to George and me.

What follows is mostly extracted from my diary of the time:

Day is creeping up. Between bouts of dozing I see a clear sky paling and southern trees in dark silhouette, and then stone houses with tile roofs, tiles as worn and old as the weathered stones. Then the sun a violent red, flickering behind a grille of poplars. First glimpse of the Papal Palace at Avignon very white in the early sun. We get out, dizzy with sleeplessness. Our young French friend has disappeared. Was he real? How real is anything in this early light? Real enough. We discover that not all the bikes have arrived. This time George's and Ursula's are missing; not ours, thank Heaven!

We find our way to a youth hostel on an island in the Rhône. Shower. Breakfast. Do a first sketch of the Palace from the front of the Auberge. Try to sleep. Jean asleep. Flies. Cicadas making a noise like a steel scraper on a large tin pan. Can't sleep. An axe's sound has a battle to cut through the air, so heavy is it with humidity and heat. I read some *Paradise Lost* Book II. Also heavy and hot. So calm even the poplar leaves are immobile. The shadows very intense.

At intervals I have heard, through the heat, a flute, I think. Beautiful. Or is it a clarinet? I walk along the river bank. Both flute and clarinet. Incredible. Interweaving.

Later that evening they walk in, the instruments, in the hands of two students from Liverpool; also a very pale-faced American reading philosophy at the Sorbonne. We talk Sartre. But I can't take Sartre too seriously. Man does laugh, enjoy himself and rejoice sometimes. Flute and clarinet over the water through the poplar shadows. No nausea in that, no guilt. Just given, free. The Grace of God. Sleep.

The next morning I do a sketch of the bridge.

The Browns' bicycles have arrived at last. Leave Avignon about 7 p.m. Sunday. Ride halfway round old city under battlements, then down avenue to Château Renard and take a short cut to St Rémy, where, with the moon on our faces, we drink beer and consult our maps. We push on through the dark in which we get a glimpse of the Roman ruins. Rocks look gaunt in pale light of the moon; pine-trees pitch black. Devious s-bends. 'Ideal for brigands,' observes Jean. The road is now so steep that we dismount and push our bicycles for the final three kilometres.

The air has changed. We have reached the escarpment of the Alpilles, high and desolate with wind-hollowed rock-faces. In the distance we hear the flute and the clarinet, so know where our friends are. The music stops and we move in silence, reaching the auberge at about ten. Nice clean place. Sleep well.

Up before the rest are stirring. Take a walk around. The South, the Midi. Walk to the top, look down on olive groves, grove upon grove from the cliff's edge. The cicadas' high throb beats skyward from below, over the ruined château and the empty tower of the Saracens. And in the distance the Camargue, and beyond, the sea.

Spend much of the day on the steps of the open-air calvary in the Piazza. It is the cool shadow of the trees, not piety, which places us here. There is a 12th-century church opposite. While I draw it, Jean sits beside me reading *So Many Loves*.

The next day we are there again in the square, in the shadows of trees splashed thick on the white gravel, the cicadas shouting from high rocks. By ten o'clock the sky is already acquiring the blue-purple tint of intense heat.

Through the changing evening light all four of us walk up to the château and the high ruins, look down on the olive groves and almond orchards of the Val des Fontaines and the blue-grey-purple of the wind-eroded cliff face. A lone falcon cuts slow arcs round a crag stabbing the pale sky. Pink light slowly deepens to red, red to purple, while darkness rises from the valleys like water filling wells. Everything below is saturated in shadow, while we four stroll and pause to stare at caves, ruined walls, old battlements, odd stones hewn for forgotten purposes.

Yes, we talk – of America and Russia, the giants to East and to West, and we are earnest enough. But I think of young couples who walked here perturbed in the aftermath of Troy's fall, or appalled by Athenian deaths in Syracusan quarries, certainly all the great campaigns, civil broils and

Les Baux

assassinations of Rome must once have broken as startling news over this acropolis. There is no need to take either the present or the past too seriously.

Jean and I go off and stand for some seconds in an empty doorway looking at purple hills rising into the dulled scarlet of the west. No Spenglerian overtones are called for as our hands and lips touch. We turn back and cross the bare plateau to the edge of the cliff, where we lie on our backs and stare at the Great Bear. No Marxist totem either. I show Jean how to find the Pole Star. The moon is towards full. In place of cicadas screaming there are crickets chirping. And the scent of sun-dried grass and herbs, not heavy but very fine as in parts of the Western Desert, as in much of the Karoo.

It is ten years since we first met. We lean over an old stone wall under an interminable sky. We are acutely aware of the sacrifice the war has demanded of us. We were married in 1940 and now, seven fragmented years later, we are still unlocated, still disoriented and homeless.

We retraced our steps through the old gate with weathered armorial bearings, past the fine stonework of the falling 16th and 17th century houses. Over one doorway, or mantle, I read: *Post Tenebrem Lux.* After darkness, light. Perhaps our dark years of wandering would soon be over.

From Les Baux we cycled down to Arles in early-morning light. For once the landscape lived up to the image Van Gogh had given us, and everywhere I seemed to catch glimpses of my swashbuckling fanfaronading countryman, Roy Campbell – particularly in the ancient Roman

Les Baux

circus still used as a bull-ring. There were posters of a bull-fight on the walls. Roy Campbell claimed to have had a rather unusual view of the place – from aloft, between his own legs, having been tossed skywards by a bull.

With Ursula's help I tried to turn some of my contraband coffee into francs, but no one was interested. Coffee was plentiful in Arles. And Ursula said it was cheaper than in the U.K.

Inevitably we found ourselves cycling along a Rue van Gogh. Artists! We neglect them and we drive them mad when alive. Then, dead, we idolise them and walk and ride upon their upturned faces.

We get good seats in the train for Nice – passing through the flat lands at the estuary of the Rhône. But while it looks like the Karoo I see no wild white horses about which Roy Campbell writes so eloquently.

We spend the night trying to sleep in the waiting-room at Nice or on the platform. All feeling a bit low, too dispirited, too unkempt to venture into the famous city. I reassured my companions that our next stops in the Rapallo, Santa Margharita, Portofino area would make up for the Nice railway station. But I was wrong.

I thought our next memorable stop should be Viareggio. It had Shelley associations for me. Had not his drowned body been washed up there and burnt on a pyre built by Byron and others? The pine-woods of Viareggio turned out to be the worst pitch I could have chosen. I had never known the space under trees so dense with litter. There were more cigarette stubs than pine-needles, and enough packets, old newspapers and shoe-boxes to start a pulp mill. Beyond the trees, where the litter was marginally less, the sun was a flaming brand hurting the eyes, and the sea a surly quicksilver.

We found a comparatively clean piece of earth by fighting our way into the heart of a small colony of brambles, where we kicked an area clear of prickles. Unrolling our sleeping-bags, we lay down to doze just as all Italy started arriving there for its Sunday swim.

It was not the increased volume of happy southern voices which woke me. It was the uncanny sense that I was being stared at. I opened an eye.

Brownies. Little Italian girls in Brownies' hats. They stared dumb-founded at these mad English asleep in the brambles. They then started moving round us in a circle, first clockwise and then anti-clockwise. This was too much for George who leapt to his feet and flung his arms up with a loud shout of mingled Italian and Xhosa. *'Basta! Hamba! Tutta via.'* They fluttered away like a brood of Rhode Island Red chickens.

The brambly sleep in some small measure compensated for the suffocating train journey and the forest's filthy floor, as did our cycle ride towards Lucca. Periodically I would try to see the journey from Jean's or Ursula's or George's point of view. They suffered in silence or enjoyed what they could, while I re-entered and re-lived that portion of my life where the landscape had taken possession of my memory as only the plains and mountains of my boyhood had. They were as kindly sceptics obliged to go on a pilgrimage with a zealot. And my zeal was increasing with every mile that brought us closer to Florence. Who could fail to be entranced? And there would be a crescendo of interesting stages on the approaches. There would be – but it didn't happen like that at all.

The major experiences in depth had already been afforded us, at Avignon and at Les Baux, places new to all four of us where Jean and I had entered strange new landscapes together and at the same time. What followed was the easy comedy of four young people happily improvising each day through changing scenes and various villages and cities.

After Viareggio we cycled to the terraced hills which separate it from Lucca, and halfway up pitched camp under some olive trees opposite the ornamental iron gates of a beautiful country house with a baroque façade. I myself had lived in that house like a young lord in April 1945, when it had been 12th Brigade headquarters, riding about in my Jeep organising parties of soldiers for the opera in Lucca and writing poems like 'Cape Coloured Batman'. So, having washed and brushed up, I approached the gate and, explaining my interest to the majordomo, asked whether it would be possible to show my wife and friends the walled garden with the espaliered trees, and the glass-floored hallway with the fountain waters flowing beneath it. The answer was a curt no. Snubbed and saddened I turned my attention to the cottages farther up the road where I used to go in search of tomatoes. I was welcomed warmly at last, and totally embraced by ample Mama Badolino. I learnt the sad truth about the price of coffee in Italy. Marshall Aid had brought an end to food shortages. The poor British taxpayer was paying more than double the Italian price for his coffee. I had not only brought coals to Newcastle; I had smuggled contraband to a non-existent black-market.

I have one vivid recollection only of Pistoia – a baroque church, dilapidated, the yellow plaster peeling off. It had presumably been deconsecrated at some stage as it was now being used as a warehouse. The great door was ajar, letting a shaft of sunlight fall upon a mountain of golden grain. Well, Ceres and the Virgin are close kin. And on and on we pedalled, to Florence. We found accommodation on the south bank fairly close to the Ponte Vecchio, in a house in which Machiavelli had lived. My organisation of the sight-seeing was cut short by a septic throat which became quite excruciatingly painful before driving me into delirium.

I have no recollection of what happened during the next couple of days. Jean found her way to the Hotel Roma, where I had told her the staff had spoken English during the war. She had great difficulty explaining her problem, but she persisted until she was at last introduced to a perfectly charming young doctor who had no car and had to walk with her back to our lodgings. He inspected my infected throat and then walked another intolerable distance with Jean to a hospital, where he provided her with some antibiotic pills that proved extremely effective. When Jean asked what his services cost, he replied, 'It is free.' Apparently his family had been well treated by South African troops. Jean took his address and her mother sent him parcels of items difficult to obtain in Italy at that time.

This crisis over, we wished to extend our stay. But we had run short of money, and coffee had turned out to be a very soft currency. So we decided to sell our good black Raleigh and B.S.A. bicycles on any market, black or otherwise, that would give us a good price. The Italians turned up their aquiline noses at them. Black bicycles? Who but an undertaker's assistant would want a black bicycle? Red, green, silver, blue – yes. But black? We must be joking. And then their weight. Why do the British make their bikes like tanks or battleships? Twice the weight of any Italian bike. They found it incredible that we'd brought all this ugly metal across Europe to try to sell in Florence, Florence of all places!

We returned to England by train. It was fun going through the Florence–Bologna tunnel, at both ends of which I had watched our Sappers at work, repairing the damage done to it by the retreating Germans. As we emerged at the northern end, the scenes round Pian di Sette brought back the experiences of the winter of 1944 and the spring offensive of 1945. Ahead rose Monte Sole and its grim companion heights and to the left the sequence of Monte Stanco to Point 826, a front of a few square miles where twenty thousand South Africans had lived and fought for a few very long months.

The train moved slowly over the new bridge at Pian di Sette. Astride the parapet, a mason was sitting with a small hammer and chisel, giving the stone coping a final trimming. It was an Italian touch I shall not forget, that craftsman's concern for detail and finish.

Beyond him the crops were green in fields which I had seen only as snowy or muddy wastes. Grass grows quickly on a battlefield, so the saying goes, but there were circular and ovoid patches where the density or length of the stems was less – blemishes caused by the removal of the topsoil by high-explosive shells.

We had no difficulty at all with our bicycles on the return trip. They arrived quite safely. Unpacking my haversack in Wellington Square I found a tin of coffee.

9 Sept.–Dec. 1947

Home Stretch

No sooner had we returned to Oxford from France and Italy on 15 August 1947 than we were invited to spend a fortnight in a charming house in Woodstock rented by our friends the Newhams. We were to look after their two small children while the parents went on a much-needed holiday to Scotland and the Lakes. I was trying to get my head down to study for the impending ordeal of Schools. This was a trifle difficult as I was frequently called upon to play with the exasperatingly energetic Antony.

It was wonderful having Blenheim Park at hand in which to walk and wander. I have frequently been lucky in this way, finding for shorter or longer periods my front or my back door opening on to parks or botanical gardens, places where mankind has shown unusual artistic and practical love for the land. By employing a combination of his talents Man has created these, his largest works of art, so large that they cannot be seen from a single vantage point. One has to enter a masterpiece of landscape gardening and become part of it, a mobile, observed and observant figure in a scene both natural and artificial.

Guy Stringer recently gave me a copy of *Blenheim, Landscape for a Palace*, by James Bond and Kate Tiller, with a note of thanks for having introduced him to the park when he visited us at Woodstock in 1947.

Jean remembers Guy Stringer's visit well. While the three of us were walking in the park appreciating the cunning of Capability Brown, we offended the territorial sensibilities of other moving figures in the landscape, a herd of black-and-white cows that not merely glowered at us, but began to walk towards us in a manner distinctly threatening. Or was it just curiosity? While Guy and I were debating this point, Jean took to her heels. I caught a glimpse of her trying to scale the famous high stone-wall which surrounds the park and decided I ought to be on hand to help her over. We caught up with her in a bed of nettles on the Woodstock side of the wall. She was looking sadly at her bruised legs and cursing the cows for ruining a brand new pair of nylons, which at that time were virtually unobtainable. In spite of this, Blenheim Park, like the Ridgeway, has remained a special place for both of us.

A letter from the University of the Witwatersrand offering me a lecturership put an end to one of our great anxieties. I wrote to my parents, 'We are both very excited, but how or where we shall live we cannot imagine.

Flats are unobtainable.'

When the Newhams returned to Woodstock, we set off for the north, Jean to Newcastle to visit her grandmother for three or four days, and I to visit the Lakes. We planned to rendezvous in Keswick and to spend the remaining days together on the track of Wordsworth and his sister Dorothy, whose diaries Jean had discovered and delighted in.

I went equipped with a knapsack and, according to someone who met me amongst those mountains, dressed in old fawn corduroys and my oatmeal-coloured rowing-jersey. My tutor, J.B. Leishman, had urged me to give my brain a rest, to get out into the open and walk. Pointing his pipe at me, he intoned:

Enough of science and of art!
Close up those barren leaves!
Come forth, and bring with you a heart
That watches and receives.

But as usual I was incapable of doing the thing properly. I took with me a small notebook of useful talismans and shibboleths such as the one above, which I might try to learn by heart against the approaching day of doom. I also tried to keep a diary, which I abandoned as soon as Jean rejoined me at Keswick. I quote from it:

We had parted company at Crewe, Jean for Newcastle and myself for the Lakes. At Wigan, a blind epileptic woman whose pale and empty eyes had stared at me for three hours, was helped from the train, to be taken off into a grim and grimy waste of red-brick houses built on the jig-system; but, provided she received kindness there, it would be heaven to her. Blindness could be an asset in Crewe.

From Kendall, 'with its small ruined castle on a knoll and traces of a moat', the train took me to Windermere, from where I bussed to Grasmere.

Lakes calmer than any I have ever seen: reflections in the water seem firmer than the objects reflected. Only in the midst of the smoke-grey image of a mountain, in the midst of the motionlessness of earth and heaven real and replica, one small rowing-boat, one oarsman moving, rhythmically twitching; leaving as wake a long sharp scar of silver straight as a glacier scratch on smooth granite.

After a vain attempt at finding lodgings, I landed up at a youth hostel outside Grasmere. In the slow twilight the trees drooped heavy below feathery clouds, sunset-touched. Stone walls and all grey things were darkened by their dampness. No wind and all water surfaces without one wrinkle, yet seldom out of the sound of running water.

After supper, down to the village. A half-moon the colour of a Jaffa orange. One of the scientifically minded youths worked out how many years it would take him to cycle to that moon and back. Two others debated the merits of Schnabel and Fischer as performers of Beethoven's piano concertos. I talked to a coal-chemist, a German Jew who had arrived in 1937. We agreed that there was not very much time left for man if he remained nation-locked. A red-headed boy was being perpetually witty, but at nobody's expense, so forgivable.

Friday. Up very early. Before breakfast I pace between the stone-walls of a narrow lane, back and forth, learning quotations for Schools, past a dray-horse, stationary, contemplative, perhaps still half asleep? In the fields, through a faint-purple mist haze, a dozen or so gulls were flapping and crying plaintively, and nearby, black, raucous and unmannerly, twa corbies waiting their fee. Apart from these ancient bird-cries, it was very quiet, and the mountains mist-veiled, but a veil used as if by a woman, not to hide but to enhance her mystery.

I left the Youth Hostel at 9.30, paused a second at Wordsworth's Tomb and Dove Cottage, but decided to save them so that Jean and I could enjoy them together.

Up the path to the west of Loughrigg Fell and down to Elterwater. I decided to follow the path up and along the Langdale Beck and make for the Stake Pass between the Scafell Pikes and Langdale Pikes.

Along stone walls not entirely unlike those built on the Eastern Cape farms a century ago, up to the sheep-fold. The hills on either side are drawing in, becoming accented, as is one's sense of isolation and liberation. In normal walking position there is no horizon, no sky visible, nothing but rock and bracken, bracken and rock. As I go along, gaining altitude, I learn quotations from Sir Thomas Browne.

'The night of Time far exceedeth the Day, and who knows when was the equinox? And every hour adds to that current arithmetic.'

A short, steep climb alongside a stream, noisy, white, gushing, splashing, tumbling over sharp black jumbles of rock. Laden with time and metaphor, deliberately I move upstream, contrary to it. But I envy that abandoned fluid, that current arithmetic that has cut these vast sculptures over which I crawl like an ant.

At the top of Stake Pass on the watershed, I lie on the deep, matted grass of a rounded hump of earth – one of many – left perhaps by a retreating glacier? A saucer of grass between the great peaks, not a single tree, no large rock, a few brown mountain sheep, silent, browsing far apart. No wind. Sun.

Shoulders aching, body weary, heart beating, lying on my back, I relax every muscle and even shut my eyes. No thoughts, no quotable quotes, aware of physical sensations only, the weight of body pressed skywards by the earth, but my heart was pulsing, particularly in my throat. In my ears was a sea-deep silence. There is no silence like that of mountains.

As I open my eyes, the sky is very blue. Life is very simple in that instant. Beyond metaphor, beyond the current arithmetic. Stillness absolute. Light steady and equal.

Then two clouds move into my field of vision and their rapid swirling motion puts a sudden end to these symbols of perpetual poise and stability. Now I stare into a vortex, into Einstein's spiral of worlds and systems and nebulae turning, wheeling, migrating through immeasurable space-time.

Reassuring for some reason, my map tells me that up to the right are the High White Stones. The High White Stones! Back into the world of magic, of words. I jerk my stiffening body erect.

I do not attempt to reach the High White Stones, but relax and let gravity pull me in an easy slow lope like a happy drunk staggering down the path along the Longstrath Beck. Waterfalls, sodden grass, Scafell at my back.

How aware I am of that mountain, almost uncomfortably so. Why? Am I influenced by Wordsworth's great peak that 'with measured motion like a living thing/Strode after [him]'?

No. Nor, after consideration, am I being haunted by Monte Cifalco and Monte Cairo towering above Monte Cassino in the moonlight. Mountains in German hands, overlooking our lines in 1944. They always seemed, day or night, to be over one or other shoulder. There is no such dread in the ghost that animates Scafell for me.

Four hawks, very high, mewing. The beck below, crystal water over white and pale-blue stones, is never silent. So on down to Stonethwaite and then to Longthwaite Youth Hostel.

My return to buildings and comfort and company is ambivalent. The few hours alone in these strange mountains have been an odd kind of homecoming. The landscape of my childhood so high and spacious, so empty, is that what has been breathing down my neck? Where in my childhood was a mountain world as moist as this? Not the Wapadsberg over which I had walked a year ago with my brother. More like the Hogsback, and yet not quite.

I walk through the village, glancing in desultory fashion at my notes, but English Literature can wait. I register the current arithmetic, of the autumnal red hips and haws and other berries and the few seasonal flowers lovelier for being late. The air is cool and my hands and face and lungs feel it. The year moves to its dénouement. It is past the equinox. Each night the water in the streams and becks will get colder and colder until they are stilled into ice. The hikers will become fewer, the hotels emptier until, under the laying on of hands by the snow, those to whom these valleys are home and these mountains familiars will be left to their private loves and their hates, escape from which will not be as easy as it is now.

I really do wonder just how Wordsworthian these people are or ever have been. The tripper, like myself, is likely to be a fanciful fool. His comments on the scenery are inexpert, cliché-ridden and gross. He knows nothing of the local sanctities or current fears. He relies merely on a four-and-six-penny map, a tourist guide and some literary gossip.

And yet there is this hunger of the imagination that will not rest satisfied with mere appearances, that must select, reject, combine, make a picture, a scene, set a man or an object in relationship to others, or in a landscape.

At this point the little diary dries up, unfortunately just before one of the most surprising and pleasant coincidences of that rich year occurred. This I have managed to recover from my memory and the memory of others.

The next morning I strolled down the valley in search of a bus route between Borrowdale and Keswick where I was due to meet Jean. I saw the figures of a girl and a young man standing at a bus stop with that look of maximum patience and minimal expectation which is the gift to humanity of country bus services. I joined them.

Suddenly I was recognised by the girl, Peggy Luscombe from Westbrook, a farm deep in the Camdeboo Mountains, Graaff-Reinet. I had last seen her in 1933, fourteen years previously, when she was perhaps 7 or 8 years old. Yet recognition was instant and certain.

And as soon as I recognised her I knew why that mountain, Scafell, had been teasing my memory. It bore a strange resemblance to Toorberg, whose dark-blue gable head rises at the back of Westbrook, the Luscombe homestead. Toorberg is the magic mountain of the Camdeboo range. Its fountains feed the fertile valley in which Vrede lies. Some of the streams in its valleys never dry up even in the severest droughts. It was good to recognise it as a piece of my permanent inner landscape.

It was during one of those droughts (Peggy thinks 1933) that the extended Biggs clan and their close friends decided to take a break from their scorched farms, where operations had been seared into immobility, and camp in the one place in the district where there was always water: the Deep Pool in the Toorberg foothills.

I suspect there were at least a dozen children present. Hour after hour the mountain stillness was broken by a small avalanche of children, splashing, diving, and laughing, and every so often a dignified adult would enter the sacred waters, a Triton among the minnows.

One night, as if the informal pilgrimage to Deep Pool had placated the angry water spirits, there was thunder among the mountains and then it started raining heavily. Long before daylight nearly all the menfolk had disappeared to get back to their soil. The stream that feeds the Deep Pool started swelling. 'We had to make a dash for it before the river cut us off completely,' writes Peggy. 'I remember very vividly the squelching walk home and being handed across the already swollen river by the big boys, John Biggs standing mid-stream, braced against a rock.'

And here was Peggy Luscombe who had grown up in Toorberg's shadow, beside me on this bus-stop in Borrowdale, Cumberland. With her was a young man whom I knew only slightly. I had met Michael Corbett as a subaltern in the Royal Natal Carbineers, somewhere south of Florence. He was now at Cambridge reading Law. He is now Chief Justice of South Africa.

As planned, Jean and I had rejoined each other at Keswick. She had enjoyed seeing her relatives, particularly her grandmother, close to her hundredth year, pious, gentle, bright-eyed, who had no complaints against life except that it was going on a bit longer than she wanted it to. All her generation had left the world years ago. She had mentioned this in her prayers, but God who had been good about other requests did not seem to hear this one. 'He's forgotten me,' she had said.

We bussed down to Cockermouth. It was difficult to imagine an orphaned boy, William Wordsworth, playing beside that very stream. Later, based at a pretty inn, in fitful sunlight, we explored the shores of slate-blue Buttermere and wind-ribbed Crummock Water; then to Dove Cottage, and Ambleside. We visited the great poet's grave in Grasmere churchyard. There were no other sightseers. A quiet, cool day, with some spells of sunlight spilling through the clouds. Aware of august and friendly presences we walked beside the lake, beneath the trees. We found a suntrap in the lee of an old stone-wall, where we lay on the grass, and Jean read Dorothy Wordworth's *Journal* aloud. And so back to Wellington Square.

I remember very little of that Michaelmas term. To get us accustomed to writing short answers under exam conditions Leishman gave us previous question papers, telling us to see what we could make of them in three hours. These he marked with discouraging rigour, adding pungent comments.

As for Bryson, he endured the *longueurs* of tutoring with polite stoicism. His beautifully furnished rooms in Balliol were an education in themselves. There was a gorgeous Sickert of the façade of a French cathedral whose diffused and sublimated gargoyles gazed unfocused over my shoulder as I struggled through Beowulf's wrestling-match with Grendel. During our trip to France I had been to Rouen and had paused amazed for some minutes in front of the cathedral, thinking not of Joan of Arc, or of the Earl of Warwick, not even of Madame Bovary, but of Sickert. At my next Anglo–Saxon tutorial I could not refrain from saying how much his picture had added to my enjoyment of the cathedral itself. Bryson looked at me with an unusual flicker of interest and referred to Wilde's *mot* about life imitating art.

Under the strain of the impending examination, old Oscar, my incipient ulcer, returned. I was put on a diet of white bread, coddled eggs, baby food, milk, and milk of magnesia. I was told to eat little and often; and indeed I found it essential to have a doorstop of white bread in the middle of the morning to avoid considerable discomfort. How, then, would I cope during the examinations?

The doctor gave me a letter which recommended that the examiners should allow me to leave the hall of the Examination Schools in order to consume a sandwich in the vestibule in the presence of the janitor.

We wrote our nine three-hour papers in five days: three hours in the morning, three hours in the afternoon, until the ordeal was over.

Some time during the strain of Schools an event occurred prophetic of things to come. Schools was more than an examination; it was a rite of passage into the great community of Oxford scholars. It was, therefore, proper that one should dress for it in regulation costume known as *subfusc*. And it was the duty of the invigilators to reprimand anyone who appeared improperly dressed for the occasion.

Moving like a long-legged fly upon the streams of silence between the rows of desks and chairs in the Examination Schools, Lord David Cecil was distressed to see a naked female calf twisted round the leg of a chair. He pondered the matter. The woman candidate was otherwise correctly dressed. He did not disturb her until the very end, when he said:

'It is my duty to point out to you that you are improperly dressed.'

The young lady responded, 'What is improper about my dress?'

'You should be wearing black stockings.'

'Stockings, my lord, are a bourgeois convention.'

I did not enjoy my viva-voce exam. There they sat, the Olympians, variously jovial, mercurial, saturnine. I recognised most of them: Leishman, of course, who according to a good convention, would ask no questions of his own candidates; C.S. Lewis, whose lectures I had attended assiduously; Lord David Cecil, Frank Hauser's tutor; J.R.R. Tolkien, C.L. Wrenn, Hugo Dyson, and some whom I did not know.

'We enjoyed your papers, Mr Butler,' said the smiling chairman. 'Some of us would like you to expand a little on certain points you made in them.'

He nodded to the ogre on his left, who picked up what must have been one of my scripts.

'Mr Butler,' he said, 'in paper 5, question 3, your answer on Sir Thomas Browne – most lively – mm, yes, here we are – you quoted: "Mizraim is become mummy." Could you tell us who Mizraim was?'

'I suspect he was an ancient Egyptian, most likely a Pharaoh.'

'Quite,' he said. 'Any comment on mummy?'

'Egyptians preserved their great men by mummifying them.'

'Yes, of course. Had the word not, perhaps, acquired a medical meaning by Sir Thomas Browne's time?'

'Not that I am aware of,' I said, knowing I had missed something.

'Thank you, Mr Butler.' And he nodded to the chairman, who nodded to another ogre, a pink-faced one:

'Mr Butler, we particularly liked your answer on Wordsworth. You know the "Intimations Ode"? Of course you do, you quoted from it:

The soul that rises with us, our life's star,
Hath elsewhere had its setting and cometh from afar.

'Would you care to expand on what you said about this passage? You were clearly rushed for time.'

I did my best, but I'm poor on Plato.

'Mr Butler, someone at some time seems to have advised you to be cautious of too absolute and categorical an attitude in your statements. You have perhaps listened too well; your papers are full of such phrases as "in general", and "by and large". Particularly "by and large". What does "by and large" mean?'

'Roughly speaking,' I hazarded.

'Any idea of the origin of the phrase?'

'None,' I said.

'Has anyone?' asked the merciful chairman.

A lively little discussion then ensued among the Olympians on this interesting etymological point, in which the man at the stake was forgotten. I think it was Tolkien whose suggestion ultimately found general acceptance. The term was nautical: crowd on as much canvas as possible (large), and keep on course as closely as you can (by) ...

The torturers had done with me. There remained only the lantern-jawed hangman.

'Mr Butler: Milton. Please turn to *Paradise Regained*, Book X, lines Y-Z. Would you care to construe?'

I read it through once, tried, and failed. The syntax was not impenetrable Chinese, it was pure Latin; and anyone with a reasonable background in classics would have untied the knot.

I knew I was sunk.

'I think that will be all,' said the Chairman, then added, 'By the way, you're some sort of a foreigner, aren't you?'

'I'm a South African,' I said. I did not add, 'I don't regard myself as a foreigner. It is a shock to be considered as such.'

They were right of course, those dear dons, to withhold the First and to detect something foreign in me. Had I not already written a poem, one of my best, called 'Stranger to Europe'?

We returned to South Africa on the *Athlone Castle*. I remember very little about the voyage, except that I read and wrote a great deal of poetry. I also brooded about Europe, that ancestral, quarrelsome continent, which for the better part of five years had been my home. She had been lavish with experiences of all kinds, abounding in great and ancient cities, art and architecture, literature and learning, and culture in one of its older senses. And I brooded also on her relationship to southern Africa, the continent which had given me my life and early nurture, by comparison natural, raw and young, whose mother city was not yet three centuries old.

I also began writing an elegy for those South Africans in Italy and the Western Desert who would not return.

And I pondered on the sea and the Portuguese navigators who had first discovered South Africa. They were not looking for it but were looking for India. Africa was an enormous obstacle between the ancient civilisations of the East and West, something to be got around. And I read Fanshawe's translation of *The Lusiads*, a work which I had first heard of as a schoolboy in Louis C. Leipoldt's *Uit Drie Wêrelddele*, and in Roy Campbell's ominous Adamastor in "Rounding the Cape". Whilst I might have been voyaging away from Europe to Africa, from the northern to the southern hemisphere, I was also moving deeper and deeper into what has been a lifelong concern: the interdependence of those continents in me, an unconscious symbiosis and a conscious tension.

But when Jean and I saw Table Mountain riding the waves, with Lion's Head on one side and Devil's Peak on the other, our thoughts were neither epic nor elegiac, but lyrical. The day was calm and bright. Adamastor was far away, in the world of poetic fancy. We stepped ashore with high hopes, excited by the challenges and opportunities of entering on a professional career at last, and making a home.

10   Jan. 1948–Dec. 1950

Wits

My student days were now over. Living off scholarships and loans for soldiers was past. Life took on a different shape: one was no longer merely responsible to oneself and free to behave like Doctor Johnson – 'to survey mankind' (and anything else that caught one's attention) 'from China to Peru'. A job focuses the direction of one's thoughts and energies. I now had to earn money by teaching, by giving to the best of my ability what I had learnt from the lectures and dons at Oxford to students at Wits. I had a legal contract with an employer, the University of the Witwatersrand, and an experienced and wise boss, Professor J.Y.T. Greig. My salary was not princely. We would not have survived unless Jean had gone back to work as a radiographer.

    The nomadic aspect of student life was at last over. Jean and I were not going to live in digs; we had done with digs for ever. We were going to create a home. The Satchwells looked after us while we set about house-hunting. Always generous, they did more, they advanced Jean the deposit needed by the building society.

    Protected by a tall hedge, 243 Jan Smuts Avenue was set back from the busy road and below its level. It was an old building by Johannesburg standards, with high ceilings of pretty pressed-steel. The eastern side had a glassed-in porch, pleasant for sleeping in during the warm weather. The south-facing kitchen opened on to a tall stoep which overlooked the back vegetable and rose garden, the garage and the servant's rooms. At the end of the stoep was a study where I was destined to spend many brainstorming hours. The house's main attraction, however, was a large drawing-room with a deep bay-window looking on to the front lawn, which Jean soon flanked with zinnias, petunias and shaster daisies. While she chose pretty fabrics and made curtains and covered cushions in her spare time, I was happy at weekends with saw and hammer, installing long low bookshelves on two sides of the large sitting-room. Then came the pleasure of taking one's favourite books out of cartons and arranging them. Our little stock of furniture, some of which I had made at Spitzkop Camp in 1941, and which had been stored at Ons Hoek during our stay in Oxford, was supplemented by items Jean bought on sales. Mrs Satchwell lent and gave others, so much so that Mr Satchwell, on a visit to the young folk, raised his eyebrows and said, 'I'll have to nail every blooming stick at Ons Hoek to the floor!'

We joined the parish of St Martin's-in-the-Veld whose priest was a colourful outgoing character with a noisy preaching technique and a very limited range of ideas. One of the churchwardens was Ted Morse Jones. I was to get to know him better in future in Port Alfred, to which place he retired and became an exceptionally effective amateur historian. He was also a keen ornithologist.

There was no office to spare in the English department on the first-floor of the Wits Arts Block (where it still is), so I was allocated a study with Charles Hooper on the ground-floor, at the opposite end of the building among the sociologists. In a recent letter Charles reminded me of it: 'The room was revolting in every way — miles of bookshelf, no books, light wrong, canteen too near, too far from all English classes and our colleagues. You sat near the door and faced the window (and me) and I sat in front of the window facing you. You were the second creative writer to be put in with me. The first was Bob, who had put his head in a gas oven. I don't know what you did at your end. Bob, while alive, used to bash away at his novel.' I liked Charles and found him enormously helpful in finding my feet. It was through him that I met those members of the department to whom I was to feel closest: Sheila Macaulay and Meg Cross. Meg was a scholarly and perceptive critic of Eliot and Auden, Sheila excellent on the Jacobeans. And, of course, Charles himself. He, however, did not find me easy.

'You were aloof — perhaps that fear of getting into a coterie? We made limited contact, in the area of religion mainly. You appeared to avoid all peculiarly South African issues, yet were at the same time from the outward view aggressively South African — nobody was going to confuse G. Butler with any damn rooinek. It seemed over-emphatic to me, but then I hadn't had a spell of Oxford behind me. You seemed also to exist to some extent in the cocoon of your marriage. One was aware of reserves and reciprocated with reserve, I think.'

It is a pity we did not share that room longer.

It is only now, looking back, that I can see how important the Wits years were to me. I worked very hard at my job and at learning how to do it. Fortunately I found that I enjoyed the teaching situation. I liked most of my colleagues and liked nearly all my students. I discovered that the best way to get to know and enjoy a poem or a novel is to have to teach it.

I learned how to employ three teaching strategies. First, to read the work and what critics had said about it, to listen to one's colleagues who had taught it and write notes so that one could, if necessary, lecture on it. Second, to discuss it with students in small groups or seminars — students who have been given key questions in advance which they must be prepared to answer.

I also discovered that the seminar is a great trap for the teacher who wishes to be a guru or a leader of a little literary Oxford Group. The students say very little and think even less in such seminars. They sit at the guru's feet, adoring, absorbing. The adulation of the young is heady wine. But, properly conducted, there is nothing like a seminar. The teacher frequently comes away refreshed and enlightened, with his hope in the future strengthened by contact with young minds frequently brighter than his own.

The third and hardest teaching tool is marking students' written work, which must be set at frequent intervals. Opinions differ on how to do this. I favoured the Oxford method of meeting the student face to face, having the essay read aloud to me and discussed then and there. Others preferred to mark the essay with detailed comments, including reasons for the marks given and then allocating times for students to discuss their work.

Charles Hooper refers to the coteries that existed among members of the staff. Most English departments in South Africa at this time worked on the traditional Eng. Lit. model, with its heavy emphasis on literary history, biographical study of writers, dates of publication of literary turning-points, and very little detailed critical attention to the actual works in the traditional, established canon. A group of critics in Cambridge had demonstrated conclusively that the products of this type of literary study were incapable of answering simple questions on the meaning of poems whose praises they had parroted, let alone demonstrate how the much-lauded artistry of one poet differed from another. It seemed to me that they made out an unarguable case for close reading, for attention to the words on the page: the study of verbal technique – which as a would-be poet I found interesting and chastening. And I think most of the Wits English Department staff, even those of darkest Oxonian blue, accepted this and conscientiously conducted seminars based on the close analysis of poems or key passages from prose works. But the light-blue zealots went further. The literary text was autonomous. The words on the page contained everything that the reader needed to know for a proper reading and understanding of the work. The poet's biography might be interesting, as also the period he lived in, so too the zeitgeist which influenced him; but these were not necessary; indeed they were frequently a beguiling and time-wasting distraction from the proper business of the critic, which was with unique works of literature, not biography or history.

I had several difficulties with this approach. Certainly works of art have integrity, and some can be enjoyed and appreciated with little or no attention to biography or history or the zeitgeist. I can't even read a musical score, and can't describe what the sonata form is, yet I listen to music by the hour. And children and others love reciting or listening to poems they do not understand.

But for scholars to turn their backs on the genesis and origins of literary works struck me as simply unscholarly. For one thing the uniquely arranged sacred words on the page were not fixed in their connotations and unless one used a dictionary based on historical principles one could make serious mistakes in reading. For instance students today need to be told how the word 'gay' has acquired a new meaning since W.B. Yeats wrote of 'poets who are always gay'. If words, the very materials out of which poems are made, are products of dynamic social changes, works of art made up of words must also be seen as such, and some attempt be made to read them in the knowledge, as far as possible, of the differences between our age and the age that produced them. For instance studying the critics of Shakespeare frequently tells us more about the age which produced the critics than about Shakespeare. He is, as it were, a fixed point of reference, a mountain we look at through telescopes from various distances and points of the compass.

But my greatest difficulty with the light-blues, whose high-priest was F.R. Leavis, was the moral claims they made for literature. I knew with the rest of them the old debate about the moral purpose of literature, to teach and to delight, to teach delightfully, and so on. Of course. But is not to give delight in itself perhaps enough? Leavis was following Arnold. Religion was dead or dying, but man still needed texts to carry the accumulated wisdom of the race into the hearts and minds of men. And from this line of thought flowed the Great Tradition, a surrogate holy writ to be expounded by English departments.

The debate was taken very seriously by all of us. Greig organised a weekend seminar at which Professor Geoff Durrant from the University of Natal, *the* South African protagonist of the Cambridge School, was invited to address us, and very impressive he was. I can remember one exchange between us during discussion time.

'Guy, you are afraid that literature is taking, or might take, the place of religion.'

To which my reply was something like, 'Literature can't take the place of religion. They are different things. Very few writers and poets wrote with religious or profoundly moral intent. To use their works as religious texts is to place a burden on them which they were not intended to carry.'

So, while I was not against pointing out moral elements in literature, I could not find myself preaching with D.H. Lawrence that 'the novel can teach us how to live' – Lawrence of all people, whose gospel of personal salvation through sex has misled millions of unhappy men and women to expect from sex what sex alone is unable to supply.

Indeed, in my own heart-searchings on this, I had to confess that I believed that the proper emphasis in teaching literature, while not ducking the moral issue, should be on the special pleasures the works afforded. After all, I had had no high moral motives when I chose to study literature. I had chosen to do what I enjoyed doing. I believed that enjoying literature – like enjoying architecture or music or ballet – was a good in itself. People read or go to the theatre or to concerts to enjoy themselves. Great artists in all genres are great because they are givers of joy. And joy in my opinion is a higher category than morality, although it can comprise it. We are created in joy, and our destiny is nothing less than to enjoy God himself.

Before I had settled properly into my study, I found myself involved as stage manager to Phyllis Warner's production for the English department of J.P. Sartre's *The Flies*. Much of Sartre's agonised debate about identity, belonging, guilt and commitment leapt into life, particularly on the second night when the results of the 1948 election were coming through to us over radios in the dressing-rooms. That election! I had spent much of the previous day helping Jack Lewson ferry people to the polls. Artists and politicians were always at each other's throats for not being what the other thought they ought to be.

That is one of my abiding impressions of the Wits campus: lively debate and involvement of staff and students – at least in the Arts faculty. Engineering and commerce students might achieve numeracy but were classed as illiterates, which they were sometimes proud to be.

Before that election there was a small festival of experimental one-act plays in the Great Hall. Among them one or two were performed by blacks, with some rows of blacks in the small audience. It was a sort of brave venture which would soon become virtually impossible.

One play stuck in my mind: set in a crowded Sophiatown shack, it had affinities with O'Casey's *Juno and the Paycock*. It was about an heroic mother whose family breaks up in a rapid series of disasters. I was puzzled by the blacks in the audience. When the daughter confessed she was pregnant, they laughed. When news came that the husband was in gaol, they laughed. When the son was knifed in her presence, they laughed too. Why? The acting was not *that* bad. I was told that it was nervous laughter, laughter as a surrogate for tears of anguish. The action was too close to township experience. The whites in the audience were stricken with pity.

But open-minded as Wits was, there were very few blacks on the campus then.

I was, however, becoming increasingly aware of the townships, particularly through our contacts with the Community of the Resurrection, the Anglican religious order, and its services at the Church of Christ the King, Sophiatown, and St Benedict's Retreat House in Rosettenville. This was opposite St Peter's School, that great school for blacks which apartheid would soon destroy: a school that counts Es'kia Mphahlele among its alumni.

I had some contacts with the South African Institute of Race Relations. Both Quinton Whyte, the Director, and his successor, Fred van Wyk, had been at Rhodes with me in the mid-'thirties; so two interests came together when I got involved with Leon Gluckman's production of *Antony and Cleopatra*, which he produced to raise funds for the Institute.

Ex-servicemen of all types, from war theatres all over the world, were still present in large numbers on the Wits campus. This gave me, as one of the same breed, an easy entrée unusual among members of staff to part of student life. It was not unlike Oxford had been, where young dons in their twenties found themselves tutoring former wing-commanders and brigadiers in their early thirties. Add to this my involvement with plays whose casts and production teams are frequently an excellent blend of students and staff, and it comes as no surprise that I spent a great deal of my time having coffee or tea in the Students' Union, which was located in one of the temporary timber buildings on the lawns between the Arts Block and the Library.

I found teaching very enjoyable. Many of the tutorials were given in these timber huts. I was learning fast, but sometimes not fast enough. We had to drive the first-years through Prof. Greig's very useful language text, *Language at Work*. I had done three language papers at Oxford, but they were little use now. The modern linguistic approach was new to me. I had to unlearn so much to make sense of it. My students started with a clean slate. Further, most of the novels we had to teach were new to me – such as that modern masterpiece *Passage to India*.

Some of the students I recall vividly: Dan Jacobson, sitting in the front row on the aisle in the Anglo–Saxon class; Gillian Friedman playing the lead in *Lady Precious Stream* opposite David Zeffert in an enchanting production by Sheilagh Osborne; Lionel Abrahams, indomitable evidence then, as now, of intellect and courage; F.D. Sinclair, a slender-faced, fine poet who died young; Fred Langman, David Gillham, Trevor Whittock and Don Maclennan, who all became professors of English, and of course W.H.D. (Cake) Manson.

Although I had only glimpsed him, I recalled Cake vividly as one among a hundred other soldiers filing through the autumn woods for the second assault on Monte Stanco in Italy. He was now trying to be a cross between Hemingway and D.H. Lawrence. Christina van Heyningen thought very highly of him. I got to know him best through theatrical productions. He made a superb Bottom in *A Midsummer Night's Dream* and a memorable Menas the Pirate in *Antony and Cleopatra*.

He was addicted to shocking the bourgeoisie. Like Roy Campbell, he generated legends. For instance, it is said that he gatecrashed, with several friends in tow, a northern suburbs Christmas party. This dislocated the catering arrangements, to the distress of the hostess. Disappearing into the night for half an hour, Cake played Robin Hood, reappearing with a large roast turkey. He apologised to her for the few missing slices, but the people from whose house it came had already had their first course. Cake's chums loved such unconventional acts. Others did not. The hostess, for instance, declined a slice of the stolen bird. It would stick in her throat, she said.

As struggling fellow playwrights, Cake and I would in time come to sympathise with each other. We were both inclined to believe that plays should be written in poetry. He did not have my African bug. He died tragically in a motor-bike accident.

The Department of Nederlands/Afrikaans offered a crash course for members of staff who wished to learn, or brush up on, Afrikaans. This I joined and enjoyed. Before long I was given an oral exercise, a ten-minute talk to the class on Johannesburg. It went down well. With the guidance of Uys Krige and Charles Eglington I avidly read the new Afrikaans poets – the Louws, Elisabeth Eybers, Opperman, Ernst van Heerden and G.A. Watermeyer. My interest became known and I was invited to give a paper to the Johannesburg A.T.K.V., comparing Afrikaans with South African English poetry. In some respects they were similar, or they complemented each other. At that time the quantity of good poetry in Afrikaans far exceeded that in English. It struck me as little short of tragic that there should be so little contact between English and Afrikaans writers – a concern expressed in an article I wrote for *Vista* called 'South African Literature'. It also contained my first protest poem, 'The Underdogs'.

That number of *Vista*, published by the Students' Council of Cultural Societies, is worth glancing at, if only to get a flavour of life on the Wits campus in 1950. Among the contributors were H.C. Bosman, S.G. Millin, Lionel Abrahams, Uys Krige, Christina van Heyningen, Prof. Raymond Dart, Thelma Gutsche, Barney Simon, E.V. Hinwood (Fr. Bonaventure) and M.C. O'Dowd.

After the Nationalist Party's victory in 1948 many educationists became alarmed by their 'Christian National Education' policy. This was set out with devastating frankness in a pamphlet so entitled.

There was much that was unexceptionable and much that was understandable in the document. What frightened us was the elevation of the cultivation of the love of one's own (people, language, culture) to a prime and excluding principle. Every subject had to be taught from a Christian National standpoint in order to create what was essential for it to have, separate single-medium Afrikaans and English-speaking schools. The same principle would have to be applied to all language groups. Far more important, it provided one of the ideological excuses for the greatest of all Nationalist follies and crimes: the Bantu Education Act.

On this educational issue Christina van Heyningen and I were united. I found myself on the platform of the Selborne Hall in a symposium which included one of the main proponents of C.N.E., Professor Chris Coetzee of Potchefstroom. These Christian Nationalists were going to legislate all education into a monolithic master-plan of separate linguistic kraals. Like the 'thin-lipped Genevan ministers' of old, they were ready to lop off limbs that refused the proffered strait-jackets. I remember making a point of protesting against these protestants that would allow no room for protest and I found myself, with Christina, dashing about to address anti-C.N.E. meetings as far as Tweespruit in the Free State. I followed this up with an article in *Die Huisgenoot.*

Like many others I was still optimistic that the 1948 election results were a freak. After all, Smuts had actually polled more votes than the Malan/Havenga alliance. A book entitled *'n Halwe Eeu van Afrikaner Prestasie 1900–1950* contains an article by Professor Greig and myself on 'South African Literature in English', which is evidence of my copious reading in contemporary autobiography, travel, poetry, short story, novel. I hailed the short stories of Herman Charles Bosman and Nadine Gordimer, I pointed to the lack of strong national sentiments among English-speaking South Africans and to their writers' liberal stance on race. The writing of the draft of that article was, I suspect, my first attempt to formulate my ideas of the odd little minority species to which I belong and for whom I – no one else being foolhardy enough – have since become a sporadic and reluctant spokesman.

My concern for the literature of this English-language group naturally extended to what sort of education they were receiving, particularly in English, and I was happy to get involved in teachers' conferences organised by Professor Greig. At one of these I gave a paper entitled 'The Difficulties of Teaching a Non-indigenous Literature'. One of the many points I attempted to make was the need for the South African English child to encounter his environment in some of the literature he reads at school. English in schools was in danger of becoming the purveyor of an older Victorian culture from the northern hemisphere. Almost none of it was rooted in his present South African experience. History and geography, I maintained, were important to literature. It was after all one of literature's functions to heighten the child's awareness of the world, and the world presents itself to the child through local specifics. The point had been made before, but I must have made it more sharply. All sorts of people sat up and took notice. I was seen by some as a renegade Englishman preaching South African nationalism, in fact a covert Nat, or a parochial-minded nut, and certainly not in the Great Tradition. If many of the teaching establishments at all levels were against me, most of the writers were on my side. I found them writing to me out of the blue.

Again, in the educational field, Professor Greig persuaded me to mark Transvaal matriculation scripts. The pay was poor but the experience invaluable.

Greig as moderator for the Joint Matriculation Board had established beyond argument that the marking of the essays was subject to so many subjective factors as to make it a dubious indicator of students' ability. Correlations with other elements in the students' performance were unacceptably poor. Tests showed that different examiners diverged in the marks they allocated to the same scripts. If they marked the same essays after an interval of six months they did not correlate with themselves.

Greig introduced a sensible new system. A detailed memorandum was evolved defining what qualities were to be looked for and what errors or deficiencies penalised. Each essay was to be marked independently by two examiners. Provided their marks did not differ by more than ten per cent, the average was taken; otherwise the two markers appeared before the chief examiner, when each had to justify his mark.

It was a good but exacting system. For two years I laboured at it, my half-section being John O'Meara. We had much to talk about when not marking. Like me, John was an ex-serviceman, ex-airforce, who was gradually moving away from the extreme radical position which he had held during and immediately after the war. He had been on the executive committee of the Springbok Legion, an ex-soldiers' organisation which was led by men of the Left. He was no longer sure that the Soviet Union had all the answers. Our pilgrimages had followed similar courses, although I suspect that at that time he was already far less starry-eyed about the U.S.S.R. than I was. The U.S.S.R. had to invade Hungary and mow down students with tanks before it quite lost the nimbus of the New Jerusalem with which I had endowed it during the war. It is difficult to abandon a comforting delusion.

For 90 per cent of the scripts we were well within the ten per cent margin; but for the balance we would be as much as 20 per cent apart. John and I got to know each other well while earning what we called 'blood money'.

Sometimes the examiners set unforgivable topics such as 'A day in the country'. It fell to my lot to mark a large batch of 76 from a co-educational school along the Reef, which had organised a day's picnic to the Vaal Dam. I marked 70 accounts of that picnic and came away with a composite picture of a badly planned attempt to bring young urban minds into brief contact with the beauties of nature. They were unanimous in recalling that the soup was burnt. I was tempted to give those who did not write about the picnic A+ for originality. One could also hazard at the end of marking any large batch, 'Lucky kids to have that teacher', or 'Poor brats, suffering under an industrious dunce'.

One of my tasks was to take two evening classes a week for B.Comm. and part-time students. Many of these were older than usual, having been in the war. One was a chap almost my own age, an ex-Indian army type who, on demobilisation, had tried to turn himself into an engineer at Wits. He had not succeeded and was currently working on the mines while doing a Diploma in African Administration, later changed to B.A. part-time. While in India he had discovered he had a talent for, and an interest in, languages. He soon left the mines for the study of Linguistics and Bantu Languages at Wits. Len Lanham was to become a close friend and collaborator in many projects related to the study and teaching of English in Africa.

Another was an ageing African clergyman who, after failing English I for the third time, sought my advice. He wanted me to recommend a good dictionary. In some surprise I said, 'Do you mean to say that you have been trying to study English without a dictionary?'

'Oh, no, I have a dictionary.'

'Which dictionary?'

'The *Oxford Concise.*'

'Well, that should be adequate for first-year work. Why do you wish to change it?'

'I have lost confidence in it.'

I did not know how to restore his confidence in the *Oxford Concise*. But if the magic had drained out of its pages he had better switch to another. So I recommended *Chambers*. I looked at his essays more closely after that. They were really very bad. He needed a remedial course; perhaps he needed to start all over again. But how ever had he matriculated?

The medical students' English essays posed similar problems: how had they matriculated? In those days this noble profession still aspired to literacy. To prove that they were literate, aspirant doctors had to pass a simple enough test, to write a literate essay on any of a wide choice of topics. For this they were allowed, I think, two hours.

Every year there were some quite excellent offerings but the average was poor in style and content. The values exhibited made one wonder whether they would understand the meaning of the Hippocratic oath. To think that such moral cretins would soon be advisers to people in conditions of crisis disturbed me profoundly.

There were some astoundingly puzzling cases. One student wrote in the English of the American strip cartoons, actually placing the words of his different speakers in balloons. Another wrote simply: 'Sir, I am a forainger. I learn the facts. I don't spik English. Please pass me. I can't affort to stay another year.'

Pure Hyman Kaplan. Yet he had been at Medical School for years and years.

It was borne in on me that many disciplines are taught by and to people with an inadequate command of language; and that universities were prepared to (forced to?) compromise with Babel.

The English essay was dropped as a requirement shortly afterwards, and with it the pretence that the medical profession is literate. As one of them said recently to me, with sadness: 'We're just a lot of skilled plumbers. Few of us read anything sensible. Apart from our practices, our main intent is money, money, money. As for ethics – well, just look at the Biko case.'

If I have written this account of my years at Wits with any measure of accuracy, it ought to reflect a general wellbeing, much good fellowship, expansion of horizons and growth. I was about as happy as I have ever been. Why did I leave? I was not retrenched. I did not receive an offer I could not refuse. I was not subject to hints or pressures from my boss, nor from my colleagues. Jean and I were happy in 243 Jan Smuts Avenue, which we were unlikely to have bought if we had not intended staying in Johannesburg for a fair spell.

But there were things which both Jean and I disliked about Johannesburg. It was too big and imposed too many pressures. One of my difficulties sprang from my inability to say no to the demands of good causes and good people upon my time. I was becoming busier and busier and getting on more and more committees. Was my life to be a frenetic promoting of causes which I only partly understood, working in harness with people whom I never got to know? As for Jean, the prospect of bringing up a

Old milestone on Grahamstown–Cradock road.

young family in Johannesburg was not attractive. Looking ahead, she saw her days being spent in taxiing children to and from school, to and from friends, to and from games, ballet, birthdays; between which, there would be social teas and cocktail parties. No, thank you. A small town with good schools had much to recommend it. We had recently visited Pietermaritzburg, and liked the look of it; and there was Grahamstown, for which we both had a special affection, as well as for Rhodes University, where we had first met.

Besides, there were financial considerations. Though both of us were working, our combined salaries were barely enough to cover our expenses. Every so often I recalled Wally Mackenzie's words in Brighton: 'Remember, we have lost five years in the army, five years' seniority, five years' salary increments, five years' time in our professions.'

I started looking for senior lectureships. Two came up, one at Pietermaritzburg and one at Rhodes. The Rhodes offer came first and I took it.

But there were many who thought I was mad even to consider Rhodes. Those whose thinking equated size with quality I could dismiss. Because a university had twice as many students, it did not mean that it was twice as good. I could also dismiss those big-city enthusiasts who thought universities gained from being subjected to the perpetual pressure and stimulus of a metropolis; I could also grant that certain faculties – like medicine or engineering – needed big cities; but even the short period I had been at Wits made me wonder whether it was not the prisoner of a great Babylon called Jo'burg.

Friends would shrug and say: Perhaps Babylon is better than the backveld. That did not worry me either. A backvelder born, like myself, often has a stubborn belief that God made the country and man made the town. But the results of the 1948 election and the government which the backveld vote had put into power did give me some cause for reflection. No, my real hesitations came from the persistent rumours that Rhodes University was bankrupt and due for liquidation.

I was, however, partly reassured by news from Hugh Rose, an old Oxford friend who had taken up an appointment in Economics at Rhodes. The new Vice-Chancellor, Dr Thomas Alty, had come through his baptism of fire, which had been fiery indeed.

Alty had no sooner taken office in October 1948 than the bank informed him that it would not extend the university's overdraft beyond the end of the year. So his first task as Vice-Chancellor had been to tell the staff that their January cheques might not be paid. He felt that he had not been properly informed of the state of the university finances and that he was quite entitled to resign at once. One evening at the depth of the crisis, there was a knock at his door. Hugh and Vincent Grocott, brothers who owned the local bookshop and published *Grocott's Penny Mail*, having apologised for disturbing him, asked if they might be allowed to help;

then, even more apologetically, asked Alty to be kind enough to accept a cheque for 'a sum the like of which the Rhodes University accountant had not seen for some time'. This gesture acted as a catalyst. Alty put certain proposals to a properly penitent Council, and giving himself exceptional emergency powers, he grasped the nettle firmly and launched a successful campaign for funds. In a remarkably short time he steered his ship into clearer financial waters. He could now turn his mind to the legislation which would convert the University College into a fully-fledged university, and affiliate Fort Hare to it. On 22 April 1949 the Rhodes University Bill was passed and plans were laid to inaugurate the new university early in 1951.

11   1945–

Plays

My dramatic education owes a great deal to Oxford, to certain friendships, and to the fact that we lived almost next door to the Oxford Playhouse. Jean and I haunted the place. Its repertoire was excellent, as was the company.

The piece to which we kept returning in memory was O'Casey's *Juno and the Paycock*, with three Abbey Theatre actors in it – Francis Sullivan as Captain John Boyle, Norah Nicholson, who gave 'a fine, sensitive, living portrayal of Juno' and Larry Burns as Joxer. Joxer's 'The tide's out here' has become part of our family vocabulary when glasses need replenishing.

The offerings of the Playhouse were supplemented by a wide variety of student productions which varied greatly in quality.

Frank Hauser dropped in one day.

'Come with me to St Hugh's' (or was it St Anne's?). 'They're staging some bits and pieces. They'll be bloody awful, but there's one item I'm keen to see.'

The item consisted of two substantial excerpts from Kyd's *The Spanish Tragedy*, the second of which was an addition attributed to Ben Jonson, presenting the distraught Hieronymo's inability to master his grief, and his exposé of the limitations of art.

Hieronymo was spoken, not very well I thought, by a gangly large-eyed lantern-jawed undergraduate with an unbelievably lugubrious expression, more comic than tragic to my uneducated taste. But Frank disagreed. 'He'll go far,' he said. 'He's got a feel for the theatre. Of course he hammed it, but Elizabethan plays need to be hammed up a bit.'

The young man was Kenneth Tynan.

During the April vacation Jean and I went up to London by bus, making our base with Eileen Dalton, a friend of Peggy's who lived in a mews in Swiss Cottage. That evening we saw the Old Vic's production of *Henry IV, Part 1*, with Laurence Olivier as Hotspur and Ralph Richardson as Falstaff. I wrote to The Poplars: 'Nothing I have ever seen on stage or cinema can compare with it, particularly Richardson's performance. When he came forward to the edge of the stage and took the audience into his confidence on the question of honour, he shattered the invisible fourth wall which is supposed to divide audience from actors.' This raised a host of questions about the sanctity of accepted theatrical conventions.

During my visit to Rhodes in 1946 I spent some time on the fringes of a circle revolving round a handsome fellow dressed in the fragments of a naval uniform, Leon Gluckman. His father was Minister of Health in Smuts's cabinet. Just before meeting him I had seen and been very impressed by his production of Eugene O'Neill's *The Emperor Jones*. The sets had been designed by a fine-arts student Ronnie Philip, a pre-war friend of Jeff's, whom I knew and was to meet again in Johannesburg.

The Dramatic Society was already rehearsing its next production, another O'Neill play called *Where the Cross Is Made*. I spent hours at their rehearsals in the Old Great Hall – a wood-and-iron structure which went up in flames not very long after, some say due to an electrical fault. I do not find this suggestion surprising when I recall the spaghetti of wires with which the technical staff had draped the backstage area.

Leon's two chief supporters were Herbert Kretzmer, who in time became theatre critic on one of the big London papers, and Norman Addleson, who became a judge. Norman was the less mercurial but the wittier. He read everything, especially the *New Yorker*, and watched the world with large eyes which suggested both startled innocence and the ancient wisdom of the serpent. It was the beginning of a lifelong friendship which included effective collaboration to build a little theatre for Rhodes. If I recall correctly, the heroine and star of the show was a tall girl called Joy Hopwood. The production went down to Port Elizabeth for the Eastern Province Drama jamboree and in due course won the national competition. This encouraged Leon to think big. In 1947 he made history with a memorable production of *Murder in the Cathedral*, the success of which in Johannesburg convinced the Gluckmans, father and son, that Leon had talent enough to make a career in the theatre.

Before going to Johannesburg, the play had been staged in Grahamstown's Cathedral of St Michael and St George, a building not really designed for theatricals. Actors wishing to get from one side of the acting area to the other had to go outside and halfway round the Cathedral. Thus Norman Addleson, playing one of the Knights clad in full medieval armour, glittering and sinister, encountered a confused gentleman returning from a public bar. Alarmed as at an apparition, he turned in his tracks and ran screaming for help, with Norman in hot pursuit shouting 'I'm not a ghost! I'm from East London!'

During our stay at the Dorchester Hotel in London in 1947 with Jean's future brother-in-law Bertie Nairn, we were taken to the original 'Oklahoma'. This, and 'Annie, Get Your Gun' made us realise what delight American musicals could give. Their energy, their joyous zest, their colour, their lyrics all affirmed a capacity for happiness which the war years had all but stifled. A matinée performance of Webster's *The White Devil* was quite superb, with Robert Helpmann, the ballet dancer, as Flamineo and Margaret Rawlings as Vittoria. It moved me far more than *The Duchess of Malfi* at the Haymarket, in spite of a fine and frantic Ferdinand played by Gielgud, and a most moving Bosola by Cecil Trouncer.

The tortuous poetic and psychological excitements of Jacobean drama did not appeal to Bertie. He found me quite incomprehensible. He was the first man I had met who saw no place whatsoever for literature in the scheme of things. Laying a railway across a continent appealed to his imagination and one might possibly write about the romance of the great steam train. But I was not convinced that I could do for the South African Railways what Conrad had done for the British Merchant Navy.

Years later, chance meetings within a single day with a cross-section of our mining industry – a financier, an engineer, a mine captain, a shift boss, and a gardener who had worked nine years underground – made me realise that one of the great fields of human skill, courage and team-work had not found its voice. Mining has been reduced by a number of factors to an economic paradigm of exploitative capitalism. It can also be the material for a human drama of great power and creative achievement. The folklore, stories, jokes and songs, black and white, of the South African mines need to be gathered. Perhaps someone some day will write a book about them, something like *Nostromo*, only with much more attention to the men at the rockface.

I was still incapable of looking at any career apart from teaching, except as material for a book. Teaching, however, did differ from most other professions. I saw it simply as introducing the young to two forms of writing which I loved, fiction and history. I can see this now but could not then. When Bertie urged me to change courses, I wondered whether I had not gone hopelessly wrong somewhere, pursuing a fantasy which a good school and a big city would have knocked out of me years ago. I was getting nowhere as a writer. The raw fact was that no-one thought my poems worth publishing, yet the long poem in terza rima got longer and longer and more and more confused. It would not let go its hold on me.

Trinity Term, 1947, was most memorable for the variety and excellence of its theatrical offerings. In May the Playhouse presented *Hamlet*, a first for me. The lead was taken by Frank Shelley (who would in the distant future play the lead in one of my own plays, Andrew Geddes Bain in *Cape Charade*). The New Theatre gave us T.S. Eliot's *Murder in the Cathedral*. Although Mr Robert Speaight was 'unbelievably good' in the title role, the critic did not like the play and gave his reasons. 'Though Mr Eliot's drama has had a popular success both in and out of the Cathedral, it does not impress as suitable for the commercial theatre ... It is a notable work of poetic art, but not a great play. As drama it fails, mainly because it attempts to combine three incompatible dramatic methods – those of Greek tragedy, the Medieval miracle and the modern Shavian satire comedy.'

My own difficulties lay elsewhere. Twice I simply lost interest because I could not understand what Thomas à Becket was driving at in convoluted meditations about the relationship between action and suffering. And the chorus which spoke the powerful verse in well-drilled unison sounded dead to me.

I have never heard a Becket who could make those speeches convincing, but I was soon to see how a chorus could be brought to life.

A chorus needs to be broken up into at least three groups of individuals: those for the protagonist, those against, and the waverers; the lines must be allocated accordingly; and then significant movements must be found to accompany them. These movements can help to show the audience how a united group disintegrates into a confused crowd, to see them taking sides and to witness them visually presenting a solid front. The movement clarifies the meaning, and the division of the speeches gets rid of the peculiar hoot of many voices speaking in unison.

This articulation of the chorus was the chief reason for the success of David Raeburn's production for the Experimental Theatre Company of the *Agamemnon* of Aeschylus in the Louis MacNeice translation. Before the gigantic main figures entered, the chorus had communicated their dreadful unease to Jean and me in a way the chorus of *Murder in the Cathedral* had failed to do, although Eliot had given them the words with which to do it.

Jean and I watched the performance in a minor quadrangle of Christ Church, using an existing building to provide a stark classical façade. The Watchman, announcing the import of the blazing beacons, stood high on the parapet against the evening sky. I had read the play and brooded on it, and had come with appropriate piety to be educated. Instead I was astounded and came away with my views of the theatre and of mankind changed for ever. I was not alone in my enthusiasm. E.R. Dodds, the Professor of Greek, wrote to the student producer:

'My one criticism is that Clytemnestra, though clever, was not (except in the last scene) enough of a *grande dame*: at times she suggested a Parisian tart. But I have never seen so good a Watchman or so good a Herald; Cassandra was most moving, and I thought your handling of the choruses a brilliant success. I'm really grateful to you.'

In my reading of the play I had, of course, seen the significance of the red carpet which Clytemnestra causes to be rolled out as a welcoming gesture and moral trap for her returning husband Agamemnon; but to see that take place! And to see the fatally proud man step on it and walk up it into the house to his ordained death was chilling indeed! But to the experienced eye of Neville Coghill, it could have been better handled.

'I do not feel Clytemnestra was overwhelming enough ... more a Delilah than a Clytemnestra: chiefly a matter of her voice which didn't ring with majesty or give it that sense of quakingness in the pit of one's belly.

Agamemnon's voice was splendid, but his acting a little unimaginative. I did not get the effect of horror that was due to me when he stepped on to the carpet. I think it was a mistake to allow other actors (including the slave who put the carpet out) to walk upon it. I think the greatest care should be taken that NO ONE, not even Clytemnestra, should dare to tempt the Gods, all should skirt the edge and avoid putting a toe on it, except the destined victims. I feel this perhaps more strongly than you do; I think a thrill of horror should have been visible in the Chorus, a thrill of wicked joy in Clytemnestra, and a sudden movement of intuition from the huddled Cassandra, as if she could feel his foot touch the carpet even though she could not see it.'

I thought Daphne Levens's Cassandra superb. I had never seen prophetic insanity presented before and I had expected to find it interesting and perhaps quaint, to be accepted only with a willed rather than a willing suspension of disbelief. I found her agonised clairvoyance compellingly convincing.

Years later she invited Jean and me to have lunch with her to discuss this play and others. She was most interesting on the production of another great play with strong Greek elements, Milton's *Samson Agonistes*, produced in St Mary's Church by Kenneth Tynan. It was an artistic disaster and a scandalous success. As G.B.T. in the *Oxford Magazine* remarked: 'It is unfortunate when the producer of a play regards it as dull; still more so when he proceeds frankly to divert his audience with sideshows.' Tynan had attempted 'to enrich the dramatic conflict by protuberant symbolism intended to bring out ideas unfortunately neglected by the author'. Most remarkable of these was Samson's isolation on a Tower of Abstraction. This consisted of a box ladder on wheels, such as is used by the City of Oxford to replace street lights. This had pride of place in the beautiful Gothic nave, and on top of it stood the blind hero, foreshortened, his splendidly hairy legs more visible and impressive than his face. Up this ladder the temptress Delilah had to clamber towards him, in high heels, mouthing Miltonic cadences. Her beautiful legs were quivering with sheer terror. G.B.T. concluded his revue: 'When our main impression is of an ingenious director hampered by an obsolete script, it is time for him to show us a play he respects.' Indeed. Daphne Levens calls it one of the sensations of those years. 'Tynan himself was strapped to the roof of St Mary's in a harness with huge feathered wings which, by means of a cunningly placed electric fan, fluttered as he spoke. And he spoke all the best lines, including the final ones. Ken had Delilah's eight-inch-heeled sandals sent in from Portugal. What a superb publicist he always was! Do you remember the poster for *Samson?* Ten-foot boards facing the High in front of St Mary's, announcing in red cursive fascimile on an enormous sheet of modest white: "This space reserved for Ken Tynan." Well, R.I.P.'

Tynan appeared again that term shortly after the *Agamemnon*, in Antony

Besch's production for OUDS of *Love's Labour's Lost*. He played a lugubrious Holofernes, upstaging everybody. The Merton Gardens setting was charming.

On 4 December, in the middle of Examination Schools, that test of nervous and intellectual stamina, we gave ourselves a suitable lighthearted break. We went to see Donald Wolfit in *King Lear*. The production had been highly praised in the *Sunday Times*. John Bryson reviewed it for the *Oxford Magazine*.

'Mr Wolfit's Lear has received high praise: it is in some ways a remarkable performance. It is audible, it has size, and it is unashamedly theatrical in a way that is out of fashion. That's all right; one can act away like mad so long as the acting convinces, but there's a danger of monotony if you remain on the loud but limited range of the top note. Mr Wolfit starts fortissimo and he keeps it up till the storm scene, making a big thing of the end of Act I with the striking of the Fool and the two great curses on Goneril. He fails, I think, to ride the storm, and from Dover Cliff onwards he is mostly acting the foolish fond old man while before he had been nearly every inch a king.'

With this I could not agree. I found the storm scene as it ought to be, terrific and tremendous, and the interaction between King and Fool appropriately apocalyptic. Bryson took no note of the Fool. I did, however, agree with him about the rest of the cast.

'Part of the trouble is that Mr Wolfit demands so little from his supporting cast. His productions are one-man shows, and the secondary parts go for naught – which is a pity, for Shakespeare's minor characters offer wonderful opportunities without ever obscuring the central figure. His Cordelia is business-like, but she has little tenderness to offer in the awakening scene. Goneril and Regan are surely meant to be contrasted types of female villainy. They were played in an identical mood of strident cruelty which simply made for boredom.'

Bryson also indulged himself a little at the expense of the effects man in the orchestra pit who was trying to create the sound of the sea:

'We were worried by an extraordinary noise in the orchestra, like the sudden unpacking of food parcels from America, which quite drowned the description of Dover Cliff. As soon as Edgar had informed us that the tissue paper was really the "murmuring surge", the tide suddenly changed and the irritating noise set fair for France.'

At Wits, in 1948, as previously mentioned, I found myself involved as stage manager to Phyllis Warner's production for the English Department of J.P. Sartre's *The Flies*.

The sets were Mycenean, with tapering columns surmounted by heavy capitals, designed by Ronnie Philip. I helped to manufacture them and as usual I enjoyed getting to work with my hands and with machine tools.

We also built a ten-foot-tall effigy of Zeus, god of flies and death, with white eyes and blood-smeared cheeks. Our mixture of glue and papier-mâché was a disaster. It refused to dry and a fermenting process set in. So much so that by the end of the run the stage stank with as authentic a putrefaction as the text did, with images of pus, disease, unwashed bodies and dirty sheets. Soon the imagined Flies were matched by real ones, which settled indiscriminately on the rotting god and the exasperated actors.

I found the figure of Orestes most interesting, particularly his problems as an exile returning home to a country revelling in remorse for crimes of which he is innocent. Not that I regarded myself as entirely free of my own country's white guilt, far from it, but like Orestes in the play I knew of alternatives to Argos. I also knew of an Athens and a Corinth. Orestes does not have to take up the curse, but Argos is his own, whereas the other cities are not.

'Nobody is waiting for me anywhere. I wander from city to city, a stranger to all others and to myself, and the cities close again behind me like waters of a pool ... I want to be a man who belongs to a place, a man among comrades. Only consider. Even the slave bent beneath his load, dropping with fatigue and staring dully at the ground in front of him – why, even that poor slave can say he's in his town, as a tree is in a forest, or a leaf upon a tree. Argos is all around him, warm, compact, and comforting. Yes, Electra. I'd gladly be that slave and enjoy that feeling of drawing the city round me like a blanket and curling myself up in it.'

Maybe, but as the First Soldier remarked to me in the wings, in South African terms that slave would be a Sophiatown black. Would a white Orestes settle for that? If he wanted to, would he be allowed to? Only as a missionary, perhaps.

Later Orestes utters some heroic existential statements:

'Suddenly, out of the blue, freedom crashed down on me and swept me off my feet. Nature sprang back, my youth went with the wind, and I knew myself alone, utterly alone in the midst of this well-meaning little universe of yours.'

But nothing ever crashed down upon me. It struck me that Sartre was very ignorant about religious experience. No person with even superficial knowledge of the universe as mediated in either Greek or Hebrew religion would call it well-meaning or little. His Zeus talks pure Sorbonne. He may have been up Parnasse, but not Parnassus, let alone Oreb or Sinai. Errol Wilmot spoke the part beautifully, but the terrible action had no terrors for me. I thought of the *Agamemnon* I had seen in Oxford the year before.

But it certainly got us all talking. The Left liked its atheist anti-religious message, but rejected the emphasis on individual freedom of choice. The uninformed religious objected to it because a proud man was presented as the victim of an irrational god. The more enlightened tried to sift the chaff from the wheat: the religion under attack was not any that had ever been practised in the world. It was an eclectic fabrication for evoking and exorcising the guilts and dreads of a Paris under the Nazis. Orestes is a man of the Resistance called to purge Paris, France.

There was, however, one line which has come back to me time and time again: 'Human life begins on the far side of despair.'

I found myself more and more drawn to the theatre and spent much time watching rehearsals or working backstage. In 1949 my enthusiasm landed me in the hot seat of chairman of the University Players at Wits for two years. I don't know whether I made much of a contribution to the lively world of young players, but I do recall interminable negotiations about funds, and programmes, and adverts, and dates, and venues. It was a matter of life and death for the medical students to secure certain dates, and no others, for their run in the Wits Great Hall (of a dreary little piece called *Rope*).

The English Department provided the base for much of this activity. Prof. J.Y.T. Greig had the sense to encourage readings and performances of Elizabethan plays. For a few weeks every year a collapsible Elizabethan set was erected on the stage of the Great Hall. Here Sheila Macaulay, Charles Hooper and I mounted acted readings of excerpts from the set plays. It was in supervising these that I got my first introduction to the problems of play production. It was a revelation to find what laughs could be extracted from an unpromising text. Many critics had written off the comic subplot of *Doctor Faustus* as worthless, but with Michael O'Dowd (now of Anglo American) and Ted Hinwood (now Father Bonaventure) as Robin and Ralph it jumped into unexpected life, and its parody of the main plot became apparent. We also produced the trial scene from Webster's *The White Devil*. Vittoria Corombona was played by a spirited girl from Pretoria. Vittoria's lover and patron played by David Zeffert, now Professor, strode into the court with appropriate panache and proud contempt for the corrupt Bench.

In collaboration with the South African Institute of Race Relations, the English Department mounted perhaps its most ambitious production, *Antony and Cleopatra*. It was produced by Leon Gluckman. He was allowed what seemed to me an astronomical budget and given permission to employ, if he so wished, two professional actors for the leads, whom he had endless difficulty in finding. Lydia Lindeque, Uys Krige's wife, after a rehearsal or two went down with a brain infection; and a noble, greying-at-the-temples middle-aged Antony disappeared before her replacement was found. It seemed we were all set for an *Antony and Cleopatra* without the triple pillar of the world and his royal wench. Then a cheerful, ebullient young man with a good presence, profile and voice, called Philip Birkinshaw, was conjured out of the British Cultural Attaché's office, to play a somewhat young Antony to an even younger Cleopatra, a bouncing young girl called Vivienne Drummond.

My troubles started with the cutting, a buck which Leon had shrewdly passed on to a 'professional academic'. No Shakespeare play is really easy to cut and I spent an agonising time over it. Of course I got scolded by all sorts of people, according to each of whom one or other of my cuts removed an essential element from the work.

Christina van Heyningen's first objection to the production (there were four dozen others) was this wicked mutilation of the text. I said that to present an uncut version would kill the show. Audiences in London, let alone Johannesburg, would not take an uncut version. Could she give an example of an unforgivable excision? She chose Octavius's speech about Antony's stoic and noble behaviour after slaying Hirtius and Pansa, consuls. Apparently the portrayal of Antony's character depended 'upon browsing on the bark of trees' and 'drinking the stale of horses', without once losing his temper or condition.

But I leap ahead.

In addition to being Leon's consultant about cuts and the meaning of abstruse passages, I had two bit-parts to perform: the Fortune Teller and the Schoolmaster. Needless to say by the end of the run I was capable of making out a case for either of these roles as examples of Shakespeare's ability to create a complete character out of no more than half-a dozen or so lines.

I did not agree with all of Leon's production.

Special music was written for it by Spike Glasser. Ronnie Philip had devised a unit set, all curves, ramps and pyramids for Egypt, and columns, steps and rectangles for Rome. A wonderful electrical wizard called Harry Ligoff had brought in enough lighting equipment for a Ziegfeld Follies and the costumes were by an expensive Johannesburg couturier.

One of the best lessons I learnt from this production was from the opening. The orchestra struck up and Spike's music was sufficiently original to be attention-catching if not distracting. Then the curtain parted on a set which was a teasing piece of stage sculpture. The entire Egyptian portion of the cast processed across the stage, complete with ostrich-feather fans to cool the gypsy's lust. To judge by the red and gold sunset on the cyclorama it had been a torrid day in Alex and we were all in for a gaudy night. The audience's eyes and ears were so dazzled and humming that they did not notice the two Roman diplomats, Philo and Demetrius, nor did they hear the former's crucial opening speech. Harry Ligoff's lights failed to pick them out and no voice could have competed in volume with Spike's overture now building towards its climax. The first faint words we heard were:

Cleopatra: If it be love indeed, tell me how much.
Antony: There's beggary in the love that can be reckon'd.

'And let your fools', says Hamlet to the players, 'speak no more than is set down for them.' Many of the bright eye-and-ear- catching ideas and gimmicks of directors produce effects akin to the barren laughter which drowns the necessary business of the play.

It was not a good production. But I thought it better than another ambitious attempt, *Oedipus Rex*, with Johann Nel in the title role, produced by Taubie Kushlik. I was very much on the fringes of this, but sat in on one or two rehearsals. Taubie had strong and simple ideas about the theatre which work very well most of the time with most plays; but I don't think this old Greek piece was her glass of ouzo. I remember the actor who was, I think, playing Tiresias, approaching her during a break. 'Miss Kushlik,' he said, 'I don't quite understand the meaning of what I'm saying in this speech.' Taubie's response was easy. 'You sound fine, darling, why worry about meaning?'

I have already commented on the superbly articulated chorus of the student production of *Agamemnon* which I had seen in Oxford. They moved through intricate and meaningful patterns so that one witnessed a kind of dance of the mind in their anguished and ominous debates.

The Wits *Oedipus* chorus consisted of about twenty old men wearing cottonwool beards about as convincing as those of a toy-shop Father Christmas, and were all costumed from the same new bale of cloth. They came in one behind the other, hands on the waists in front, out of step, intoning like owls in poor unison. From where I sat they looked like a large silkworm with spastic peristalsis – a visual and aural disaster.

After the opening night Charles Hooper and I entered the departmental tearoom in full contemptuous spate, ridiculing the rave write-up in the *Mail*. We were unaware that Prof. I.D. MacCrone had entered five minutes before and pronounced the production to be superlative. The Chorus, he thought, was particularly impressive.

'So,' he scolded, 'you see fit to sneer at this great play?'

'We're not sneering, Professor,' I said. 'It's because the play is so great that we object to a production which shows no grasp of its meaning.'

'I,' said the Professor of Psychology, 'I know about Oedipus. And I found the production good.'

I did not dare to say that in this case literature might have prior claims to psychology, but he read my thoughts all right. For the rest of my stay at Wits he would send me American journals of Psychology flagged at articles psycho-analysing literary figures as though they were real people. The most ingenious of these proved for all time that Iago was a repressed homosexual in love with Othello.

In spite of this inauspicious start I came to respect and like Professor I.D. MacCrone, but not because of his literary insight.

On the suggestion of Leon Gluckman, I tried to adapt *Everyman* to black township life. It was a difficult and fascinating task. I have lost the draft script and cannot recall why we abandoned the venture. Since writing a one-act play as a student, I think it was my first attempt at dialogue.

The first full-length play I wrote, however, came as a complete surprise. As part of my reading programme for filling in important gaps in my basic Judaeo–Christian heritage, I decided to read the Apocrypha. I kept coming across stories or passages that were familiar, and thought in my humble way that the Protestant Bible was the poorer without them. Late one night I read the book of Judith and could not sleep again. What a story! What poetry!

I started writing at once. English poetic drama under the leadership of Eliot and Christopher Fry was very much the vogue and it was a poetic drama which I wrote: blank verse for most of the dialogue with ballad stanzas for the soldiers' choruses; the diction Jacobean, spiced with contemporary allusion and phrase. I enjoyed myself enormously. 'Judith' was the most extended piece of writing I had yet done. For a later radio production for the SABC I tinkered with it a little, but have never published it, nor written a play in that mode since.

A University Players' production of *A Midsummer Night's Dream* nearly ended in disaster for the actor playing Moonshine. For his dog he had been provided with a perfectly adequate spotted wooden dog on wheels, which he used at rehearsals. But he decided to make history on opening night with a *coup de théâtre*. He would surprise the producer, the audience and the critics with a real dog. He had no dog of his own, but like most campuses Wits had plenty of strays of undistinguished parentage and curious shape who were friendlily disposed towards students, forming rapid attachments to anyone who fed them. He found the largest and ugliest dog on campus and gave him a crash course in devotion by carrying slices of pink polony in his pocket for him. The dog would remain in faithful attendance until the last slice was disbursed and then go in search of another patron.

But Moonshine had forgotten an important detail which he would have discovered if only he had allowed himself one dress rehearsal. Just before his call on the opening night he found that his costume had no pocket for the polony. There was no time to sew one on, so he put it in his jock strap.

Well, his entry certainly created a stir. The dog was hailed by all the students in the audience. Even the producer, outraged at the liberty taken with her production, had to laugh. The dog loved it too, but was baffled by the reluctance of his master to disburse; so, with the talent of his kind, he started to sniff, inserting his long snout under Moonshine's tunic. Moonshine had to break up his lines to dismiss his hungry friend. In vain. The friend was now ravenous and decided to make a quick sneak-and-snatch dash for the hidden polony. Moonshine made a premature and painful exit.

There were other talented and picturesque young people about. As I have said, Gillian Friedman played an exquisite Lady Precious Stream opposite a fetching David Zeffert, under the brilliant direction of Sheilagh Osborne. Gillian's husband, the sombre large-eyed Gerry Becker, knew all Dylan Thomas off by heart. And then there were the Fine Arts people, like Cyril Fraden, who helped with the décor of one of the productions, and Christo Coetzee with another; and artistic ex-servicemen like Gordon Vorster, Cecil Skotnes and Larry Scully. Post-war Wits was bursting with talent.

12   1951

A House and Two Chairs

Jean and I could not travel to Grahamstown together. She had to stay behind until she could get a decent price for 243 Jan Smuts Avenue. What little capital we had was tied up in it. We would have to free it in order to buy another house for which I was to start looking, 'at least as nice as 243, with more rooms and a big garden'. I added: within easy walking distance of my work. I was heartily sick of having to take two municipal buses – and the better part of an hour – to get to work.

    I decided to break my train journey and spend a few days with Alice and Ernest at The Poplars, Cradock. They still needed to see their children as often as possible, but preferably only one or two at a time. During the train journey I had time to think over a Christmas holiday which the whole family had spent together a year before.

    Towards the end of 1949 we had been invited to spend Christmas with them in their newly completed seaside house at Kenton-on-Sea. They hoped all their children would make every effort to come as it would be wonderful if the entire family could be under one roof again. We agreed with alacrity.

    The idea appealed to all the Butler children and what could their spouses do but agree? So the holiday season 1949/50 saw us all together, having converged from north, east and west on 'Sunset View' at Kenton-on-Sea. It would be the first time the family had been together since 1938, at Dorothy's wedding: there was so much to catch up on – a whole decade, in fact. But we had all reckoned without Old Father Time, who had changed the 'mix' for ever. During the intervening years each of us had lived through a war, suffered various heartbreaks, broken through far horizons, grown away from our parents and away from each other: none of us realised how dividing these distances were.

    Starting with the youngest son, Jeffrey, then a teacher at Kingswood College, Grahamstown: he had married Val de la Harpe in 1947 and they came with Katie, their first-born, about a year old, in a carry-cot. Val found the furniture inadequate, and put Jeff on to making extra shelves. For the first time he started exploring what one arm and two legs can do in the carpentry line. Christine 'can still see him with his naked big toe hooked over the plank, the one arm sawing away', knocking up shelves for Val.

    Christine had married Rex Moys and they came a long distance from his teaching at Umveni in the Transkei, with three small children. She was worn out. She and Rex seldom emerged from the room they shared, which she said was badly designed. There was no fridge in the house so she 'used to swim across to the Langleys at Morningside to fetch the butter'.

Next, Guy, a lecturer from Wits, had married Jean in 1940 in Jo'burg. They had no children and were envious of those lucky enough to have them. Nevertheless they frequently went for long walks to get away from the noise and the nappies.

Next, Dorothy, who had married Bill Murray, a civil engineer, and they had come all the way from Robertson in the Western Cape with, I think, three children. Bill found the concentration of Butlers all but intolerable. 'Must you people all argue all the time?' Not that he was entirely muted himself.

Last, the eldest, our second mother, Joan. Joan had not married, but she had come with the news that she had received a proposal from someone she liked very much. Her siblings were keenly interested in her romance, but they were, as the saying goes, working hard at their marriages. They were finding that they had to work harder at them at Sunset View than anywhere else, and particularly at meal-times.

Vivid incidents recur to me, one of which I must record. I heard the circular saw snarling and rattling, snarling and rattling in the garage. There was Jeffrey, pushing planks past a naked blade with his one remaining hand, in which the tendon and bone structure had still not adjusted to the damage done by the same mortar bomb that had so mutilated the other arm that it had to be amputated. In the manner in which parents, seeing a child walking along a high wall, will restrain their panic, and wait speechless and breathless for the danger to pass, I restrained myself, went off and found Ernest, and exploded.

'You must be mad to let Jeffrey work the circular saw! And without a guard on the blade too! Can't you see what it'll mean if he damages that hand?'

Ernest went pale, said nothing, rose slowly and strolled to the shed housing the engine and switched it off. He affixed the guard over the blade and Jeff continued working. My solicitude was well meant, but wasted. Jeffrey was quite capable of looking after his remaining digits. He has built clap-board houses since. But I have had to abandon my jointing bench – because I was silly enough to work my own circular saw without a guard. That is another story.

But there were lighter moments. I had submitted a portion of my long terza-rima poem called *On First Seeing Florence* to the SABC for a poetry competition: it had won the prize, and been read over the air. Someone in Cradock, who had heard the announcement, congratulated Alice on this.

'What was the poem about?' she asked. 'What was it called?'

'Oh, something about his first meeting with some girl or other. Florence, I think.'

Then, after a pause and a straight look, 'I thought your son was married to a girl called Jean?'

One morning Alice asked me, 'Now son, where's this prize-winning poem of yours?'

I gave it to her. She read it in the kitchen while making her famous scones, muttering to herself – alternate lines from the poem and the recipe book. She read it several times, and came into tea with the flour-dusted typescript in her hand, frowning, puzzled. She sat down, and looked straight at me: 'And you mean to tell me that they gave *this* a prize? I can't understand a word of it.' Jeffrey admits to having enjoyed watching me being cut down to size. Dorothy says he burst out with a triumphant laugh, which puzzled Alice.

Not all was friction and rivalry. The siblings rallied to make Christmas what it ought to be – for the children's sake and for the grandparents': particularly Alice, who had come prepared with her box of ancient tinsel and baubles and the golden angel she had brought back from her visit to Nuremburg in 1934. Jeff and Val disappeared with an axe and, after a couple of hours, returned with a beautifully shaped young pine-tree on their roof-carrier, I suspected from the Grahamstown Mountain Drive. That bit of evergreen dressed in its glad-rags, radiant with candles lighting up the faces of the children, worked its immortal wonder. Early next morning some of us rowed across the calm river with Alice for Christmas Communion at the church of St David.

In an attempt to recover the old family feelings I think we all regressed, unconsciously trying to play no-longer-accepted roles. But it did not work. Jeffrey could not revert to the licensed family jester which he had once been: and he refused to be patronised by this insufferable Oxonian of a big brother. The in-laws found the sheer noise a strain, felt left out of the flow, so much so that they had no wish ever to repeat the experience of a holiday at Sunset View with the family en masse.

The parents' long-cherished dream of re-establishing The Poplars family magic by the seaside, even temporarily, had failed. Jeffrey thinks they made the not uncommon mistake of believing that the children would really want to see each other for more than three days per year – preferably fairly far apart. I'm not so sure. I think it was a matter of facilities and space, particularly after I had overheard a conversation in an S.A.R dining saloon between two oldish Afrikaner couples. They had both recently had similar sad experiences on the South Coast of Natal.

'It was not like that in the old days, when people gathered at the seaside in wagons.'

'But each family had its own wagon, and each wagon is a house with its own hearth.'

'You can only expect trouble if you ask two or more women to cook on the same fire.'

'That is so.'

When Alice and Ernest got back to Cradock, The Poplars must have seemed emptier than ever. Particularly as the children were moving even farther away.

In August 1950 Jeff and Val had left for Oxford, and Joan was planning to leave for England. Alice had prided herself on being a good mother in accepting the fact that young birds must leave the nest. In a letter to me she said, a little ruefully, 'It was a mistake to try to gather you all again when you yourselves were nesting.'

I had a good few days at The Poplars. The small-town quiet was what I needed. It was fun having my parents all to myself – leisurely talk about what I had been doing, what I hoped to do; gathering news of my sisters and brother; doing odd jobs in the workshop. There were also old friends to see, like Ted Diesel and Keith Cremer. It was only towards the end of my stay that the matter of the failed reunion at Sunset View came up.

'You are all too independent and self-willed,' Alice said with her little frown. It cleared up at once and she laughed: 'It's our own fault though, isn't it, Ernest? We bred them like that.'

She nurtured dreams for each of her children.

'A senior lecturer!' she exclaimed. 'After only three years as a lecturer! Well done, my boy!'

Then an hour later, after she'd walked round the garden: 'Would it be very silly of me to imagine you as a professor in, say, another six years?'

'I don't want to be a professor, Mother.'

'But why not?'

'It would mean research, and committees, and administration – all sorts of things that don't appeal to me.'

Married to a girl with whom I had fallen in love in these surroundings, I was returning to teach where I had been taught, serving under my old Professor, Peter Haworth, who was due to retire at the end of the year; working with my fellow senior lecturer Dr Ron Seary, who had taught me, tried and found me wanting in Anglo–Saxon, and who had introduced me to modern literature by lending me a smuggled, Paris-printed copy of the banned *Ulysses*. Junior to me was Alan Hall, recently returned from Wadham College, Oxford, who had been a clerk with me on 12th Brigade Headquarters in the Western Desert.

I stayed with the Halls, reading the books I would have to teach, and house-hunting. The latter was simple: there were no houses for sale and precious few to let.

At last Jean found a buyer for 243 Jan Smuts Avenue. The Halls agreed to have her as an additional p.g. This told hardest on Jean, who had enjoyed making 243 into a home.

As the housing situation remained static, we took a barely converted stable called 9a Somerset Street in the back garden of a row of old cottages which stood where the J.L.B. Smith Ichthyology Institute now stands. It had a little garden with a custard-apple tree. I used to get up before Jean, and do my morning meditation under it. I was using the contemplative method of St Ignatius Loyola. I achieved a rare measure of interior peace, which I needed after years of turmoil. I had no further academic ambitions: I wanted to settle down, make a home, start a family and, in due course, do some more writing. Occasionally I wondered if Uys Krige was doing anything about finding a publisher for my poems and when the result of the play competition would be announced. Jean spent more time looking for a house than I did. I was preoccupied with my new job in a department with different syllabuses; and the whole university was about to undergo a major change in status, from being a constituent college of the University of South Africa to an independent university.

On the morning of 10 March 1951 Rhodes University College was formally inaugurated as an independent university in its own right. I took part in the impressive procession from the Rhodes Arts Block, across the Drostdy grounds, through the Arch, down High Street, past the Cathedral and the City Hall into Commemoration Church, then the largest venue in the city. It was appropriately led by the Students' Representative Council, followed by representatives of other universities, South African and overseas, and our own Senate and Council. It was a very different procession from the Good Friday procession of Witness of the previous year in Johannesburg: but both were essentially affirmative. Since then the university processions I have taken part in have all been protests against an apartheid regime's interferences with academic freedom. Before very long our happy affiliation with Fort Hare would be terminated and the university's branch in Port Elizabeth killed off with the founding of the University of Port Elizabeth under Broederbond auspices. That Rhodes University procession down High Street was walking into a troubled academic future.

The inauguration was conducted with due pomp and ceremony, and the representatives of other universities made fine speeches welcoming us to the international academic brotherhood (from which we were subsequently excluded). The next day was marked by a service in the Cathedral. On the 12th the new university conducted its first graduation ceremony, conferring honorary degrees on four of its distinguished guests, two of whom I got to know, Keith Hancock and Basil Schonland, both subsequently knighted.

There was a grand garden party on the lawn in front of Drostdy Hall after this graduation, attended by many luminaries from other universities, among whom was Professor T.J. Haarhoff (Classics) of Wits. He buttonholed me and we chatted about this and that. Was I liking Rhodes? Was I missing Wits at all? Some people at Wits were missing me. I was glad to hear that. It would be sad if one had made no friends during those three happy years. Later in the afternoon Dr Alty asked me, 'What was Haarhoff talking to you about?' I told him.

Apart from the lack of a proper house we were settling pleasantly enough into Grahamstown, in which charming old-world customs still survived. Ladies in gloves and hats found their way down the lane to 9a Somerset Street, and left their calling-cards. Although we might attend Evensong at the Cathedral of St Michael and St George, for Mass we went down Somerset Street to St Mary and All Angels, the chapel of the Training College, still run by the Sisters of the Community of the Resurrection. We frequently followed in the wake of a crocodile of so-called coloured children from an orphanage in New Street run by the same sisterhood. The Training College girls sang loud and clear and the ritual was gratifyingly High Church. Whenever the sound of the angelus reached us during the week, we would pause in whatever we were doing.

And what weather in the world can beat the autumnal glow of much of May and early June in the City of the Saints?

Then what I had written caught up with me. I received a telegram saying that my play, *The Dam*, had won the first prize of five hundred pounds in the national playwriting competition. The play would be produced early in 1952 during the Van Riebeeck Tercentenary celebrations. I had barely received the news when the house agent ran me to earth in my study, beaming, saying that he could now offer me houses in a different bracket. Jean and I looked at his offerings in the higher bracket: none of them pleased either of us. The prize upset the even tenor of my contemplative days. Where might such an excursion into drama not lead?

In the second term I threw my inexperienced self into directing *Julius Caesar* in the open, in what is now the intermediate quadrangle between the Library and the Arts Block. It was my first production of anything, let alone a Shakespeare play, but my Wits experience proved invaluable.

One afternoon while I was absorbed in a rehearsal, a senior member of the administration, on his way home, paused beside me and remarked quite casually that he noticed I had not put in an application for the Chair of English. Was I not going to do so?

'No,' I said, surprised.

'Why not? My guess is you'd stand a good chance.'

I went back to my rehearsing. How on earth could I put in for it? I was not even sure whether I wanted to be a professor. I loved teaching – but could I honestly say I was fit to profess the subject? I was too young and too ignorant to occupy a Chair; and while I could become mildly mad about writing, I had never felt the same compulsion to undertake a piece of formal research. If I was proper professor material would I be wasting time producing this play? I was also inexperienced in the teaching of the vast subject, and in running a department. True, I had gathered, particularly from Professor J.Y.T. Greig, a few convictions and ideas which I would dearly have liked to see introduced at Rhodes, but I had no wish to be head of a department and a member of the University Senate: Senate, a body packed with senior and serious people who seemed not to have changed in all the years since I had been a student; some of whom still addressed me as though I were a student. Like most students and lecturers I enjoyed the privilege of having a Senate to grouse about. I did not fancy being one of them at all.

One day a Senator 'who loved the place' and whom I respected buttonholed me in the Arts Block. He said that it was my duty to apply and that, although literature was not his field, he was convinced (as others were) that I was the man for the job.

I walked home slowly from the Arts Block to 9a Somerset Street and told Jean. Jean did not need to deliberate on the matter: 'Apply,' was her view. Still uncertain, I consulted our house guest, sitting under the custard-apple tree. Dominic Whitnall, C.R., was on a short rest from Sophiatown, a sweet and gentle priest. He told me to pray about it and so would he. We would discuss it later that day. What praying I did I do not recall, but I remember his comments fairly well.

Clarity is not always possible in important choices. Certain people found decisions difficult because they had too many interests, all tugging for attention. It seemed that I was a good teacher; and that, as I was likely to spend my life doing what I was good at, I had a duty to use the talent God had given me. I had to be serious about my profession; I had to commit myself to it. That meant preparedness for greater responsibility.

Like my mother and father, he did not regard my writing interests as incompatible with a regular job. And I knew that, having married a wife and wanting children, I had little choice in the matter of a money-earning career. He continued: It was a little presumptuous to think that by applying I would be making a major decision. The choice of professor was not mine but that of the Senate's selection committee, approved by Council. My only decision at this stage was whether to let my name go forward or not.

With twenty-four hours to spare, I put in an application on 30 August. The matter was now in the lap of the gods. Anything less god-like than senate committees and university councils I cannot imagine.

As if the gods had decided to encourage us to stay in Grahamstown, we at last found a property which we liked: it was not on the market but would be in the near future. How did this information come our way? I needed to see a doctor about some minor complaint, so I went to the old consulting rooms of Dr Dru Drury. I was attended to by Doctor Ron Wylde.

When, in answer to a conversational question after consultation, I told him that we were happy enough in Grahamstown except that we could not find a house close to the university, he said:

'I don't think for a moment that it will suit a young couple, but this old wreck of a building on the corner will be on the market soon. It belonged to old Dr Drury; my partners and I don't need it for consulting-rooms. None of our wives want to live in it. You see, it's never been used as a dwelling – not since the end of the last century – when it was a Club. It will take a fortune to fix. So we've decided to put it up for auction. We think someone might buy it for the stand – it's a prize site, you must admit, on the corner of High and Somerset Streets.'

'Would it be possible to look over it?' I asked.

'Go ahead,' he said. 'As often as you like.'

We took him at his word. He provided us with a history of the old Club, which Dr Dru Drury had written. With each visit our interest grew. Built right on High Street, it had a frontage of 115 feet. The front entrance to 122 was the front door of an old but substantial three-roomed cottage, built in 1814. Under the iron of the roof were two dormer rooms, roughly lined with yellowwood, which might have been habitable when the building was thatched. A beautifully proportioned large room with a bay window on to High Street had been added some time before 1862.

This cottage by itself – provided we could get the dormer rooms into use – and add a bathroom and kitchen on the garden verandah – would make a living unit as large as 243 Jan Smuts Avenue; but it comprised less than half the total floor space of the property. Beyond the cottage's big room with the bay window lay another seven rooms, two of them of exceptional size and ceiling heights. At the point of transition the roof line leapt to accommodate a double storey.

In 1862 the property had been acquired by a syndicate of men who, arriving as boys in 1820, had made such a success of their lives that they felt keenly the want of a Club, that institution without which most 19th-century Englishmen of means and cultivation could not survive. They added a large and handsome drawing-room with fine, double swing-doors leading into the billiard room, which was almost as large. Off the billiard room was what had been a buttery. Upstairs, over the drawing-room, were four small bedrooms, 'for country members', reached by an outside timber staircase.

The cottage had been unified with the new building by the expedient of inserting doors. So, from the entrance lobby off High Street, one progressed through a succession of interleading rooms, all interesting. There were no passages, although the outside broad verandah, on to which several doors did open, helped to cope with this lack of communication.

Towards the end of the 19th century the Club had disappeared and the building had been run as a boarding-house. It was put up for auction in

'High Corner' property about 1823. The Messenger's House is at left lower corner, and the first gaol beyond it, also on the High Street. The second gaol (still in use during our early years there) is in the right foreground, partly completed. (From a painting by an unknown artist.)

1899. Dr Greathead had no need of the place, but attended the sale out of interest. He returned to his home on West Hill and told his wife he had bought it by accident. The accident was simple. The bidding was being led by a very determined butcher.

'We cannot', he explained to his wife, 'have the meat-filled window of a butcher shop next to the entrance of our surgery.'

Neither Dr Greathead nor his successor Dr Drury had found a proper use for the rambling place. They had done little to it. Dr Drury knocked down a portion of it (which old drawings show as extending into the garden) 'for exercise'.

For fifty years the rooms had stood empty or been used for a variety of purposes. Two cottage rooms had been a dispensary and office. In the big room with the bay window Mrs Dru Drury had held occasional regal tea parties. It was known as the rose room because of the wall-paper design. The large rooms had been lent to gay and dashing ladies like Mrs Florrie Streatfield for their violin lessons and dancing-classes; to the Girl Guides when driven indoors by rain; to others for art exhibitions and soirées of various kinds.

The upstairs rooms had long been abandoned, as the outside timber staircase was rotten and hazardous. The roof was leaking badly. Paraffin tins were placed on the floor upstairs under the leaks.

There was one lavatory on the entire property and a single colossal Victorian bath on cast-iron ball-and-claw feet, complete with a brass geyser, in what had been the buttery.

The garden had received no attention for years. In it was an old stone building with a sunken floor, which, we were told, had been the tanning pit of a saddler and soldier called Stubbs before the Club management had converted it into a cellar.

In the south-east corner of the erf were some old double-storey outbuildings, which the doctors were to retain as part of their consulting-rooms, together with a strip of land amounting to about a third of the original erf.

An early owner, probably Stubbs, had surrounded this whole erf by a high stone wall which had mellowed with time. On 'our' portion it was falling apart, or leaning inwards at a dangerous angle.

'You'll have to replace it,' said Jean.

'I'll prop it up,' I said. 'Buttresses.'

Jean and I were enchanted by the place. It could not have been closer to my work. The fact that it had been neglected for fifty years made it look ruinous. This would deter buyers, as would the lack of passages and a dozen other architectural disadvantages. But on our second or maybe third visit I found a partial answer to these problems: cut the rambling old barracks in half, turn the cottage into one unit with its entrance onto High Street and convert the 'club' into a handsome house, to be entered from the garden side, with a path leading to an existing gate in the old stone-wall onto Somerset Street.

I persuaded two old British artisans who worked for Andrew Carr, the building contractor, to inspect the building. 'I know about the rotten iron in the roof, and the falling gutters, and the peeling plaster, and the dangerous staircase, and the lack of plumbing, and the old electrical wiring. I want you to tell me about the foundations, the walls, the main timbers. Are her bones sound?'

I left them to it. Their verdict was clear.

'Keep water out of the walls and she will last for ever. We don't build like this any more.'

This opinion inclined us to put in a bid for the place. When the advertisement for the sale appeared in *Grocott's Mail* we decided that we could afford to go to three thousand pounds, but not a penny more. We waited impatiently for the day to arrive.

Then things took a series of giddy turns.

The news that I had applied for the chair leaked out. Jean was snubbed by the wife of a senior colleague at a cocktail party at which I was not present. He never smiled at me again. He was reported to have told the

Vice-Chancellor that, should I get the job, he would find it impossible to serve under me and asked Council if he could be released from serving his six-month notice. I wished I had not applied. I suspect this must have been after the Senate meeting of 18 October, at which the report of the selection committee recommending me to Council was approved. The matter still had to go to Council, which was due to meet early in November – shortly after the date set for the sale of 122 High Street.

Next came a big bolt from the blue: a longish telegram from the Registrar of the University of the Witwatersrand asking me to meet Professor J.M. Hyslop, Dean of the Faculty of Arts, at the King Edward Hotel in Port Elizabeth, to discuss the Chair of English at Wits.

Still car-less, I hitched down to Port Elizabeth for the interview. The Dean of the Wits Arts Faculty, a handsome, somewhat severe-faced Scot, had been sent to ascertain whether I was interested in the Wits' Chair or not: if I was they would recommend me to their Senate, which would meet shortly. He was speaking for the Arts Faculty only; he made that quite clear. He could not speak for Senate, let alone Council.

I told him what I believed the status of my application at Rhodes to be and he smiled. 'Things are often determined by the chance dates of committees,' he said. 'Are you interested?'

'Yes,' I said. 'I would be even more interested if the offer came from your Senate.'

As I had no lift back to Grahamstown, I took a bus to the old red-painted iron bridge over the Zwartkops River and stood there a long time, contemplating a choice of two professorial chairs and trying to thumb a lift back to Grahamstown.

A few weeks previously I had been a happy, contented young senior lecturer, practising meditation under a custard-apple tree. Now I was in turmoil. I took some comfort in the fact that the Wits offer would have broken into the quiet interregnum even if I had not put in for the Rhodes post. On the other hand, had I not put in for the Rhodes job, the Wits decision would have been a simple yes or no. Of course I was highly flattered and intrigued by the Wits approach.

Wits again, I mused. They must think I'm a man of steel to be capable of handling that high-powered and faction-torn staff. I was still musing at dusk when it came on to drizzle and I began to feel distinctly cold and dislocated. At last a van did pull up. The smiling driver said that I could see the cab was full, but I was welcome to sit in the back – on some coffins which he was taking to Grahamstown.

I am not superstitious, but I do respect the dead.

'Are they – er – in use?' I asked.

'No,' he smiled.

So, for the next two hours, swaying from side to side, I sat in the dark on a coffin in the back of a van. Many odd, uncertain journeys came into my mind: none more insistent than the journey in that ambulance – 'the meat wagon' – going down the line in June 1944 to find my brother Jeffrey, who had been very seriously wounded.

The Vice-Chancellor of Rhodes University, Dr Thomas Alty, wore round, metal-rimmed spectacles, perfectly centred on his pupils. This fact, taken together with a sharp narrow nose, a slightly receding chin and an impressively large cranium, gave him the appearance of an extremely alert and intelligent bird: which he was, of course.

He cocked his head ever so slightly on one side. 'Which job would you prefer?' he asked.

That was the question.

'The attractions of the Wits job are many,' I said. 'The staffing is large and the members very good, if quarrelsome.'

Alty intervened: 'The number of students is of course much greater.'

'Yes; but the staff–student ratio is much much better than here. I believe in small-group tuition. There is no other method for teaching English.'

He glanced down and then up.

'What else?'

'Wits has a theatre. You cannot teach Shakespeare or other drama without a theatre. Rhodes has nothing.'

He glanced down. It was some time before he looked up.

'What would keep you at Rhodes?' he asked.

'The prospect of small teaching groups and the hope of a theatre. I also happen to like this place. My wife and I want a family and Grahamstown would be a better place than Johannesburg for that.'

Then he said something which offended me. Years later, having learnt about the way academic jobs change hands in the U.S.A. and Canada, I understood what he was getting at.

'If Council offers you the chair here, will you use the offer as a lever to land the Wits job?'

On my dignity, I informed him that my impression was that I did not need the Rhodes offer at all 'to land the Wits job'. They had approached me, not I them.

'You are staking everything on an offer from the Wits Arts Faculty, remember; their Senate and Council have still to speak.'

In this extremity, I phoned John Greig in Johannesburg and asked his advice.

'Sit tight,' he said, 'and take the first hard offer.'

If Dominic Whitnall was right, that I had a responsibility to both my discipline and my career, I must be prepared to accept higher office however reluctant and hesitant I might be. It was a little like a prospective priest waiting for a call from God. The possibility of that call being back to Wits naturally brought our house-hunting to a halt. We did not attend the sale of 122 High Street at Ansley and Co.

The more I thought about the Wits job, the less I liked the idea. There I would inherit a staff, most of whom were my seniors, and several of whom held convictions with a fanatical fervour which I associated with religious and political extremists rather than academics. At Rhodes I would inherit a staff of one, Alan Hall, who was as bright as could be and no fanatic. I would have *carte blanche*, a free run.

Rhodes Council met on 2 November. The phone rang after eleven that night when I was nearly asleep. Jean answered. It was Dr Alty.

'Is that you, Mrs Butler? I thought you would like to know that Council has decided to offer your husband the Chair.'

The letter of appointment from the Registrar reached me on 5 November, Guy Fawkes day.

Guy Fawkes Guy, stick him in the eye,
Hang him on a lamppost and there let him die.

Perhaps I have been dangling from the academic lamppost ever since, my feet not quite as firmly in touch with reality as they might otherwise have been.

I accepted the Council's offer and sent a telegram to the Dean of Arts at Wits, as promised.

We had been so worried about which of the two Chairs I'd have to sit on that we had forgotten all about the sale of 122 High Street. What had happened? Who had bought it?

Jean went down to Ansley's Auctioneers. The bidding had gone up to two thousand seven hundred and fifty pounds, and stopped. This offer had been put to the doctors, who had declined to sell at that price.

We took another look at the commodious but impractical old ruin, the lovely but neglected garden with its ancient dangerously listing stone-wall and decided that, as we had felt we could go up to three thousand pounds when I was a Senior Lecturer, we could still go up to three thousand pounds now that I was a Professor. Jean should ask Ansley to make the doctors an offer of three thousand pounds.

But the doctors seemed in no hurry to sell. We waited in vain for news. So, after a week or more, Jean went to Ansley's. 'As I entered, Maurice Ansley rose from his desk and before he opened his mouth I knew that the answer was yes.'

'Would you mind going to Arthur Wheeldon, the attorney, and get it all in writing?'

'I'd love to,' she said.

When the offer had been signed and accepted, Jean said to the lawyer: 'To make it quite binding, shouldn't money change hands?'

Arthur Wheeldon smiled. 'You must come from Johannesburg.'

'That's right,' said Jean, writing out a cheque for one hundred pounds. This was in November 1951.

When news got about that we had bought 'the old ruin at the top of High Street for three thousand pounds', many thought we were mad, 'that the Chair had gone to Guy's head'. Others thought it shameful that innocent new arrivals should be taken for a ride by hard-headed locals. One such was Bob Kinkead-Weekes, then at the Grahamstown bar, who had been at B.N.C. with me at Oxford. He sought me out and found me in the big room, with a tape measure and paper, planning an interior staircase.

He had seen the falling gutters, the rusty roof, the plaster peeling from the walls.

He said. 'How far has the deal gone? I might be able to get you off the hook. The law is full of loopholes.'

Meanwhile Jean, who had taken such precautions to plug any possible loophole in the law, was thrown into a state of doubt by her father's response to the news. She almost lost her nerve.

'You must be mad!' he cried over the phone. 'An old house? 1814?'

'Well, only part of it. The rest is more modern.'

'Meaning?'

'1862.'

'1862? Daft, my child, daft.'

I might have been, but I did not wish to be taken off the hook and was very glad indeed that money had changed hands. Jean soon recovered her morale. Something happened which enabled her to allay her family's doubts.

The agent of Dudson Williams of Johannesburg had been the highest bidder at the auction. Williams was delighted when he heard this. Assuming that his bid of two thousand seven hundred and fifty pounds would be accepted, he went ahead with his plans, which were to clear the site and erect a block of flats. He came down to Grahamstown to get a demolition order, about which a progressive city councillor had informed him there would be no difficulty at all. (There was very little feeling for old buildings in the early 1950s. Some time after our acquisition of No. 122, a very pleasant Victorian house with a birdcage verandah in High Street was knocked down to make way for a hideous filling station.)

When Williams heard that since the sale, the place had been sold for three thousand pounds without any further reference to him, who had been the highest bidder, he hit the roof; he was as mad as a snake; he climbed the wall; in fact, he did his nut. Years later he told us so.

'Get it for me,' he instructed the penitent auctioneer. 'Go up to five thousand pounds if necessary, but get it.'

Ansley did try. First he offered us three thousand five hundred. Then a jump to four thousand five hundred. Then five thousand. But we had found what we wanted at last, a house we liked, and that is something money can't buy. There have been subsequent offers: one to use the site in order to erect a petrol station. Progressive city councillors would, no doubt, have approved.

Our plan for our property was simple. We would divide it into two by blocking off the door between the cottage and Mrs Drury's Rose Room. We would provide the cottage with a bathroom and kitchen on the old back verandah. We would have to live elsewhere until this first stage was complete; then we would move in and live in the cottage, while we altered the remainder of the building into a dwelling for ourselves. When it was complete, we would let the cottage. It would be a long and taxing programme, living among the builder's rubble and doing much of the work ourselves.

Fortunately the Deeble's house, 7 Durban Street, provided us with a base from which to complete stage one.

It is appropriate to end this chapter with a symbolic moment in the protracted conversion of 122 High Street into our home, High Corner, in which we have lived since 1952. Having turned the old 1814 cottage into a flat, we moved into it and used it as our base while we undertook the major task — the conversion of the double-storey portion of the property, the old club, into a dwelling. It was soon obvious that I had taken on an enormous task and that I would need machine tools to handle it.

After ninety years of weather and worm, the outside timber staircase was rotten and dangerous. If the four upstairs rooms 'for country members' were to be incorporated into the central living unit, we would need a new staircase and in a different position: somewhere within the masonry shell.

I drew a rough sketch of what was required and got quotations for it. The cheapest, for labour only, was six hundred pounds. I forget what the timber would have cost.

But I knew of a plentiful supply of timber. Rough, pit-sawn yellowwood boards, about ten and a half inches (27 cm) wide, had been used (in a much earlier conversion, possibly by Tom Stubbs) to line the loft of the cottage under the thatch, creating two diminutive dormer rooms. Access was by a steep, narrow set of steps which had started right in the middle of the living area of the proposed flat. Stubbs (or whoever) had used unseasoned timber which had shrunk, leaving gaps of up to half an inch between the boards. This, and the intolerable heat under the iron (which had long since replaced the thatch), persuaded me that I would not be committing a crime to strip the loft of its lining.

But how to convert the rough planks into timber?

I wrote to Ernest, asking him to lease me his thicknesser and certain other machine tools. To this he agreed, arriving a week later with them in the boot of his car. He helped me re-assemble them, and smiled as the first grey board emerged smooth and butter-yellow from the thicknesser.

'Will six weeks do?' he asked.

'I think so.'

In a careful fury of skilled physical work I spent every spare minute with those machines. For hours on end I forgot that I was a newly appointed Professor of English, or a would-be poet or playwright. Outside and inside the old building the work progressed, much of it given out to subcontractors and odd-job men. I concentrated on the staircase.

The public, I found, think they have a kind of licence to inspect any building in the process of erection or of radical alteration: any unfurnished building, with workmen going in and out, is open to the public. In my corduroys and khaki shirt, working my father's machines, with sawdust in my hair and on my eyebrows, my academic and bourgeois persona was completely camouflaged and for long periods forgotten.

All sorts of people would appear in the big room, poking about, making comments. Sometimes I made conversation difficult for them by putting a board in the thicknesser. The deafening noise obliged them to shout, shut up, or get out. They usually got out.

One day an impeccably dressed, elegant couple strolled in. Round her swan-like neck she wore a cameo on a black ribbon and she carried gloves. He, too, carried gloves and a cane, and wore a celluloid collar, the tie 'asserted by a simple pin'. Not that there was any Prufrock decadence about them, but they were Edwardians. Where on earth had they come from? They stayed a long time, talking in eager, refined undertones, until I got irritated. I was long past the thicknessing stage and had no noise on tap with which to drive them away. So I asked, with the necessary touch of ice in my courtesy: 'Can I do anything for you?'

They were just a little taken aback. Clearly the young carpenter was not quite what he seemed. Then, smiling, and as if proffering a royal charter, the fine man said, 'Young man, my wife and I sang duets in this room before you were born.'

He smiled and looked down at her, and she smiled and looked up at him; and he held out his elbow, and she put her gloved hand through it and, with an elegant wheeling motion, they turned their backs on me, leaving me crushed, to get on with the job.

I had assembled and erected the lower flight of stairs. The upper flight was also assembled on the floor, and the aperture cut in the ceiling to receive it. But to lift it to the right height and angle in order to slot the stringers into the waiting mortices would call for ropes and a squad of half a dozen student volunteers. I planned this operation for a particular Saturday afternoon.

I had borrowed a block-and-tackle from Jock West of the University Maintenance. Jean and I had a picnic lunch in the big room and then went off in search of some student power. By a rare and curious cir-

High Corner through the Drostdy gateway

cumstance, all the male students were actively engaged in either games or courting. So we returned, without manpower, a trifle crestfallen, and stared at our incomplete masterpiece.

I thought long and hard about it. Could not Jean and I do the job ourselves? I tested the weight of the flight of stairs empirically. The ratio of the tackle was such that I could lift it with comparative ease. But I would not be free to lift it as I would have to guide the tenons on the ends of the stringers into the mortices. Jean had neither the weight nor the muscle for the job – or had she? Perhaps if we both got the flight aloft, she would be able to hold it there while I did the fitting.

It was a silly thing to attempt, I suppose. Everything went as planned: then, just as I was busy fitting, the suspended flight seemed to get some extra weight from somewhere and started plunging to the floor, lifting Jean off her feet.

'Hold on!' I yelled, and, jumping to the floor, grabbed the rope and pulled her back to earth.

'All we need', I said, 'is a little more weight.'

I found a large oblong block of Witteberg quartzite in the garden, rolled it in and attached the tackle to it with a hitch which I could tighten. Sapper Butler coming into his own.

This time we won the battle against gravity. But there is always a chance, even with the most careful amateur carpenter, of a wrong measurement, or a miscalculation. Not this time.

The tenons fitted perfectly and the flight of stairs slipped into place.

During our house-warming party Bill Burnett, now in holy orders, suggested that we ask our portly bishop, Archibald Cullen and his wife Natalie, to mount the stairs together. If all went well, the safety of future users was assured.

In a simple yellowwood pediment fixed over the main entrance, which opened on to the walled garden, I incised the one word PAX.

13   1945–60

Early Poetry

According to the graduation citation for an honorary doctorate from the University of South Africa (1989), 'It is as a poet that Guy Butler is best known.' Well, my poems are there to be read and enjoyed and judged. Once in print, they have to stand or fall on their own merits. All I can do is gossip about them, when and where they were written, how they got into print, who influenced and helped me, and my many debts to other poets. From this it will be clear that I, like the general reader, am also interested in poets as people and that I would not be a poet were it not for the friendship of other poets.

During the war, having volunteered, I travelled forcibly to Egypt, North Africa, Syria, Italy from 'instep' to the Alps, and Great Britain. My mind is stocked with recollections and images, particularly of ancient and I suspect greater civilisations than our own. This travel took place during wartime, so that the scenery had a tragic atmosphere induced by an awareness of the whole human world given over to self-slaughter. The war did not only broaden my mind, it deepened and I think darkened it. My memory won't let me forget those organised madhouses called armies – where different wards, as it were, with sometimes admirable courage and skill set about murdering each other under a variety of holy banners. Little has happened in subsequent years to alter my reluctant discovery that I belong to a deeply flawed species.

Jean took the initiative in getting my poems published. She was responsible for sending one of my best early lyrics – 'Common Dawn' – to the widely read *Outspan*. Later, after listening to an SABC broadcast by Philip Burger of some of Robert Browning's shorter pieces, she wrote to him drawing attention to a young, living South African poet, Guy Butler, to whom she happened to be married. She enclosed some examples of my work. Burger responded by asking for more and gave my poems their first airing.

   Later, occasional poems appeared in army magazines, most notably *The Sable*, the magazine of the 6th S.A. Armoured Division. In 1944, after my brother had been severely wounded in Italy near Mercatale, I wrote 'To Any Young Soldier', which was published in that magazine.

I recently received a letter from a woman who had just finished reading *Bursting World*. Her husband was in Italy in 1944. So was her brother. He was 'killed by a mortar blast on 25 July 1944 near Mercatale, the action in which your brother Jeffrey was wounded. He was a super person, as popular in his regiment as your brother seems to have been'.

In a letter dated 11 February 1945, her husband had written: 'For me the main event of the day was the latest edition of *The Sable*. I quote this sonnet by F.G. Butler, 'To Any Young Soldier':

Lean your Bren against the white-washed wall
While peasants, laughing, thrust a grass-bound flask
Into your dusty hands. Smiling, bask
In their dark eyes' praise. Brief hero of them all,
Stretch your royal limbs, lean back and laugh:
You, whom last year's masters thought a fool
Have learnt from masters in another school
The meaning of a college cenotaph.

So light a fag, knock back a glass or two,
Look calmly on shell-torn terraces,
All last night's acre of especial hell;
And wonder if the years ahead of you
Will stretch like kilo-stones or cypresses
From eighteen on to eighty, or, the next shell.

Why do I quote it? Mainly because of that last line. Her brother had been hit by 'the next shell', my brother had been badly wounded by 'the next shell', and here I sit, with 'eighty' not that far ahead.

It was the editor of *The Sable*, Laurie Wale, who told me that Uys Krige was in Florence with a bunch of war correspondents and that he was sure he would be pleased to meet me.

The mere name, Uys Krige, was already magic to me. On an Information Officers' course I felt particularly lucky to find myself in the same bungalow as his brother, Arnold. To know a poet's brother was some kind of contact with a mythical man who was always cropping up in literary gossip, on the radio and in the press. Uys was the brilliant young Afrikaner poet who, in addition to English and Afrikaans, spoke Italian, Spanish, French and German. He had lived in Southern France as a professional footballer and tutored Roy Campbell's daughters in Spain. He had published powerful poems about the Spanish Civil War, such as 'Die Lied van die Fascistiese Bomwerpers'. He had returned to South Africa as an anti-fascist and supported Smuts against Nazi Germany. For this he was execrated by

Illustration by Cecil Todd for 'To Any Young Soldier', 1953

the Nationalist press and insulted and cold-shouldered by fellow Afrikaans poets. By 1944, however, the left-wing internationalist was fêted by the South African English Press as the hero–journalist who had been captured at Sidi Rezegh, escaped from a p.o.w. cage in Italy and, nothing daunted, after a brief visit to South Africa had returned as a war-correspondent to the front line in Italy.

Wale told me that I could find this paragon in the Hotel Lucchesi on the Arno upstream from the Ponte Vecchio. He told me to look him up when next on leave in Florence.

There were other journalists with Krige, such as Conrad Norton and

Jacques Malan, the radical ex-editor of a lively journal called *Trek*. Wale warned me, wide-eyed, that Uys and Jacques were brilliant and tireless talkers.

My first meeting with Uys was outside the Lucchesi. He was sitting in a jeep talking to Malan, waiting to drive to Army H.Q. for an important story. Both seemed to be talking simultaneously full spate to each other. Uys became aware of me standing patiently waiting to get a word in edgeways.

'Hullo!' he said. 'Have you seen Conrad Norton?'

Illustration by Cecil Todd for 'Cape Coloured Batman', 1953, perhaps the best-known of the author's war poems.

'My name's Butler,' I said. 'What does Norton look like?'

'Never mind,' said Malan. 'The driver will find him. As I was saying, the mistake Trotsky made was ...'

Eventually Norton was found in the loo, reading a detective story. It was the only place, he said, for a bit of quiet away from the voices of Uys and Jacques.

Coming off the cold mountains, where the liveliest intellectual exchange was over a game of poker, I found these weekend leaves in Florence in such company, which included Tony Delius at least once, quite intoxicating, both literally and figuratively. I have never recovered from them.

I left a clutch of my poems with Uys, not daring to hope for much of a response. When we next met, he said he liked them, very promising, good lyrical impulse, had I read Claudel, Lorca, Rimbaud, Rilke?

About this time, possibly stimulated by such encouraging company, I started assembling a collection. It was not easy. Writing and reading poetry while others were going on patrol or being shot at made me feel acutely my irrelevance to that particular struggle. Years later my heart gave a lift when I read 'Native's Letter' by Arthur Nortje, as brilliant a poetic talent as we have produced, written in exile, in Toronto, in May 1970. The poem ends:

for some of us must storm the castles
some define the happening.

It really is very difficult to marry the two activities. Most poets try, and quarrel among themselves and with the critics about the exact location of the castles, and the priorities to be given to the many happenings. Not all castles and happenings are political.

At Brighton, in May or June 1945, I had, as already mentioned, sent a collection off to Faber and Faber. I suppose one's first rejection slip is the most memorable. They were quite right, of course. In the first place the good poems were too few; in the second place my verse is not in the Faber key.

I wrote some very despairing lyrics after the dropping of the atomic bomb, but have never tried to work them up to publishable pitch. It is almost as though I can't allow myself to go on record as having plumbed such despairing depths.

With the end of the war and my demobilisation leave in Ireland, I found I could write poems which I thought as good as I would ever manage. Then in mid-1946, during the Oxford summer vacation, I visited South Africa. During a cold, wet June, briefly back on the Rhodes campus, I wrote two poems – 'Homecoming' and 'After Ten Years', in which I tried to suggest how my world had changed since I arrived on that campus in 1936.

About the same time I had sent a fistful of war poems off to Johannesburg to a little bilingual magazine called *Vandag*, edited by Uys Krige and Erhardt Plange. Would it be possible to meet? Perhaps Mr Krige might recall having met me in Florence in the autumn of 1944?

Meeting the same man in mid-1946 in an old-fashioned office building in the heart of Johannesburg, in the editorial office of *Vandag* was not quite the same. Civvy Street cuts young soldiers down to size, and wartime authors and poets cannot enjoy the same death-inflated fantasies when they have to find their own rations in mufti. Still, Uys radiated life and ideas. He was not plunged into the paralysing doubts that beset me. He put an enormous amount of hard work into *Vandag*, mainly in informal interviews with up-and-coming writers, journalists, culture vultures; mostly at parties where, as one of the regulars said, 'Minerva and Mercury vied with Bacchus and Venus for attention.' Jack Cope, whom I met there for the first time, talks of a 'blur of good fellowship' among a crowd of enthusiasts. Among them, bright and contained, was a slip of a girl called Nadine Gordimer. 'Watch her,' said Uys. 'A real talent.'

When not editing *Vandag*, Uys was lying on his stomach on the carpet at home, writing the story of his escape from Italy. At that period of his life, Uys wrote best while lying on his stomach. *The Way Out* was the result.

Like most South Africans who had got to know Italian villagers and farmers, Uys was full of admiration and affection for them, feelings which they reciprocated. The discovery of this sympathy and the manner in which writers like Campbell and Krige responded to the warm, bright Mediterranean rather than to the grey north of Europe made me speculate on the long-term effects of a sunny climate on the temperament of peoples. I shocked a group of fellow South Africans in Oxford, who were wondering why they did not feel more at home with English people, by saying: 'The sun is turning us all into a lot of dagoes.' Dagoes or not, Uys and I were pro-Italian, Mediterranean men.

It was in Uys's company that I first met Charles Eglington, another former Italian campaigner, born in the Western Cape, a lapsed Catholic who had been to the Diocesan College, or Bishops, with a quiet, beautifully modulated but unaffected voice. Charles was a lover of languages and ideas. He was able, but he never found a job that suited his talents nor colleagues who did not get on his highly sensitive nerves. He was, by comparison with Uys, taciturn and testy. He did not bear fools gladly, and would have scored lower than average in any goodwill or tolerance test. He set himself high standards. Poetry was an exacting craft to which he was passionately addicted. It was he rather than Uys who made me aware of the new Afrikaans poetry. He introduced me to Gerard Bakker, a Hollander who ran the Constantia bookshop. It was electrifying reading D.J. Opperman, N.P. van Wyk Louw, Ernst van Heerden and Elisabeth Eybers. Nothing vaguely comparable was happening in South African English poetry.

Uys and his friends used to meet for coffee or lunch in the old East African restaurant in Johannesburg. It was cheap, central and had a pleasant atmosphere. The black waiters were handsome, efficient and chosen for their height. The East African touch was provided by their red fezzes and by a menu in which curry and bananas figured frequently.

On two or three occasions we were joined by an odd-looking character with close-cropped hair, almost as though he had just been released from prison. His hat was too small and he pulled it down over one eye in a manner which was intended to make him look rakish I think, but instead it made him look like a rather amateur detective. His jacket was too tight across the back and the shoulders were padded. He was not voluble like Uys, but he could be very sharp, ironical and funny. His name was Herman Bosman.

One day they entered together in loud disagreement about something. Walking down Eloff Street, Herman had been outraged by the sight of a donkey cart. Not only was it overloaded, but the harness was badly patched with wire which was cutting into the poor beasts. He had stepped into the traffic, stopped the cart and started lecturing the owner-driver. Soon his lecture could not be heard for the hooting. Uys advised him to lead the cart into a parking-bay and settle the matter there. But Uys could not be heard either. A traffic cop ordered them to stop obstructing other traffic and, while they were arguing with the traffic cop, the donkey cart had continued on its way. Herman thought he would have handled the whole thing satisfactorily but for loquacious assistance from Uys.

After one of these meetings I asked Charles: 'Tell me about this chap Herman.'

'His name's Bosman. Writes quite nice folksy short stories.'

'Isn't he a little odd?'

'He borders on sanity. He spent some time on Death Row for murder.'

A year or two later members of the Wits English Department were discussing Bosman as a short-story writer and comparing him with Pauline Smith, whose work he greatly admired, and with Nadine Gordimer's early offerings.

'They are all regional writers,' I suggested. 'The Marico, the Little Karoo, the northern suburbs of Johannesburg. The country is too big and various to be evoked by one author.'

When I got back to Oxford in October 1946 Roy Macnab used to pop into 11 Wellington Square from time to time. He was in touch with the Oxford poetry scene far more closely than I. He encouraged me to submit poems to various little magazines, like *Oxford Poetry* and *The Isis*, which are so important to aspirant writers among the dreaming spires.

I remember going to hear William Plomer talk to a literary society at St Hugh's College. Roy took me along with John Barnby, another Natalian poet. We were a select enough group, about twelve. 'Fit audience find, though few.' It was the first time I had seen Plomer in the flesh and I was charmed with his urbanity: the apparently solemn cast of face, the watchful intelligence of the large eyes, the wry humour, the pleasant, deep, cultivated voice. He told us that as aspirant poets we were in for a thin time and held up for our contemplation the latest little magazine, to which he gave the name *Aceldama*. It had a certified circulation of thirteen, made up of the editor and eleven other contributing poets, who all received complimentary copies, and the editor's aunt, who did not read poetry but liked her nephew so much that she was footing the entire bill. When at a loss for literary small-talk she would volunteer that she had once met Kafka's aunt.

The moral of Plomer's story was the importance to literature, and poetry in particular, of well-disposed and affluent aunts. About a decade later, when I was English editor of *Standpunte*, I persuaded Plomer to write an article about his experience on that important little magazine called *Sjambok*, edited by Roy Campbell in Durban in 1926. *Sjambok* had come to grief because the 'affluent aunts' ceased to be well disposed after the second or third issue.

The appearance of two or three of my poems in the Oxford little magazines passed unnoticed, except by three people.

Frank Hauser took me to 'The Bird and Baby' for a beer and said I had no business to write poems. It did not fit his image of me. And what was his image of me? A healthy, somewhat thickset cowboy, cantering a bay horse across the veld. My face, he said, was a good, open, non-introspective farmer's face. Why get complicated, if one could stay simple?

Anne Welsh blew into 5 Beaumont Street, with a red scarf in one hand and a copy of a little magazine in the other. She had also been sent a copy of *Vandag*, which contained three of my war poems. She urged me to get a collection together and find a publisher. That I had already done so, and failed, was something I could not bring myself to admit. Nor could she bring herself even to admit that she wrote poetry herself. I had to wait years before I found out.

Roy Macnab came to argue about some lapse in poetic diction, and went away with more than he bargained for, a chunk of the long poem: a romantic dream section, haunted by my version of the apocalyptic horsemen who bore a startling similarity to the sinister riders in the first part of Tolkien's *Lord of the Rings*. Maybe the Jungian group-unconscious of Oxford was at that time suffering from four-or-more-horsemen-on-the-brain. In the shadow of the recent holocaust it had every right to be apocalyptic. Roy was so unenthusiastic about my poem that I showed it to no one else.

Among the most important few days in my development as a poet occurred during my ski-ing holiday in Switzerland in late 1946, recounted previously.

Having sprained my right knee and ankle, I spent the rest of the fortnight behind glass and brooded and wrote. I produced a little prose piece for *Vandag*, 'Meditations in a Ski-hut', which gives some idea of how I was trying, by contrasting Swiss and South African scenery and society, to define my place in the world.

But more important, I shook off the long poem, broke the spell of terza rima, and went into blank verse which would occasionally rise or collapse into free verse.

My recent spell in South Africa had brought about some disturbance in the depths and I found incidents and images presenting themselves, vivid and strong. It was my first essay in autobiography. As in any long poem, such as *The Prelude*, certain incidents stood out from the mass, more or less intact, like a small boulder from surrounding conglomerate. One of these was 'Myths', where portions of my cultural and geographical landscapes interpenetrate and interpret each other. It is a poem that has been misunderstood as supporting the view that the white man and his culture are irredeemably alien to Africa. It is nothing of the kind. Among other things it records a moment when Orpheus and Eurydice find partial African incarnation.

Also prophetic of a major preoccupation – the social ambience of the poet – was my indulgence in ill-informed generalities about the national character of the Swiss, or rather their lack of it, which had implications for South Africa.

'There is no great painter, poet, musician or saint whom we think of as Swiss – no doubt due to the fact that a country which speaks three different languages, Italian, French and German, must indeed find it hard to produce a distinct culture of its own. The tendency for its talent will always be to gravitate towards the centre of one of the three surrounding cultures – to Florence (or Rome); to Paris; or to Vienna (or Berlin). This is a phenomenon which affects colonies and ex-colonies as well. Plomer and Campbell are living in England. America could not hold Henry James, Eliot or Pound. How many Afrikaans poets would have stayed in South Africa if Afrikaans was still close to Dutch? I bet they'd be in Rotter-, Amster-, or some other dam.'

Back in Oxford I became obsessed once more with the long poem. It became increasingly ambitious in its scope. All my most frightening nightmares and elevating dreams, all my experiences of love and war must, with the aid of Jung's collective unconscious, find their clear or obscure affinities in myths and legends, Biblical, Greek, Germanic, Gothic, African. The vast scope of the work and its frames of reference were matched only by the superficiality of my knowledge of the myths I tried to use. I was looking for universal archetypes for a poem whose imagery would function in Africa and Europe, indeed in any culture. Hence a poem like 'Myths'.

It was probably Roy Macnab who brought to my notice an invitation for contributions to *Oxford Poetry*, to be edited by himself and Martin Starkie of Exeter. I had plenty of poems in stock but had taken to heart, perhaps too much so, the current dismissal of war poetry by critics. I remembered a sentence from an omnibus review of several first volumes: 'Mr X is still trying to get his war in order.' So I worked on more recent experiences. By the time I had finished 'Winter Solstice' (an extract from the long poem) much of the terrible winter of 1946/7 had worked its way into it: the stone-walls and bells of Oxford overlay the stone walls and bells of Florence in the winter of 1944/5.

'Winter Solstice' duly appeared, and it did attract some attention. Peter Bayley from Univ found it interesting enough to discuss it with me for at least two hours. We walked from his rooms in Univ to 11 Wellington Square and back, circumambulating the Radcliffe Camera several times en route, after midnight. All the streets of Oxford were deserted, the magical buildings looming grey above the glimmering lanes of snow.

Peter had a specific question. Why had I called Dionysus black?

I was not sure, but suggested, 'Dionysus is the opposite of Apollo, god of the Sun, of light and rationality. Also, he came from India, didn't he?'

But as we spoke I wondered whether unconsciously my white-African psyche had not projected its image of the black-African psyche on to the ancient god. The metaphor has occurred to others, most notably to Laurens van der Post in *The Dark Eye in Africa*. It was possible to see the African psyche as paralysed in the ice of white abstraction and for whites to see its liberation as a threat.

The November number of *The Oxford Viewpoint* carried an article entitled 'Oxford poetry today' devoted almost entirely to Guy Butler.

'Butler's "Winter Solstice" and "Syrian Spring" stood out from *Oxford Poetry 1947* like a stone against the trickle of that pretty Georgian stream of Drinkwater and Gibson which has meandered tiresomely into Oxford. There is no apology needed for reprinting both.' I found myself placed in surprising company. 'Like Poe, Butler has seen himself in a distorted landscape which is the mirror of his soul or of its mastering element; unlike Poe, he has set himself to record the scene exactly and whole, and it is as sufficient and singular as a Sutherland landscape.'

As someone attempting to write a long poem into which I felt I had to pour all my deepest experiences and intuitions, I needed not only an underlying mythology but an organising principle. The first I thought Jung might supply. 'That's interesting, but how?' asked Dyson, over sherry in Merton.

'Well, I find many of the people I meet in life and in books tally with his archetypes.'

'Maybe; but a myth is not a collection of characters or types, it is a story carrying a whole lot of dynamic meanings.' With which I had to agree.

With regard to the organising principle, I studied long poems and took a particular interest in Epic.

I had heard C.S. Lewis lecturing on *Paradise Lost* and on the debt of that epic to Virgil's *Aeneid*, and then on that work's debt to Homer; and I had recently learnt from C.M. Bowra's *From Virgil to Milton* (1945) that *Paradise Lost* was not the only great epic on the Virgilian model produced by the Renaissance – that *The Lusiads* of Luis de Camoens had preceded it, in 1572. The hero of this great Portuguese epic was Vasco da Gama, the discoverer of the sea route to India.

Africa appears as a gigantic obstacle which had to be circumnavigated if Europe and the East were to meet. In fact, for more than a century and a half after the route had been opened, the ships of Portugal, Spain, Holland and England hardly visited Southern Africa. The coastline was without good harbours, the poor inhabitants – hunters and gatherers and cattle keepers – had little to offer traders interested in spices, silks, gold and precious stones, and the weather, particularly at the Cape, the turning point, was notorious for its storms. Camoens embodied Africa's seeming rejection of Europe in a giant whom he created and named Adamastor – a mythical figure which has haunted the consciousness of many white South African poets during the past two centuries. Roy Campbell had named a volume of verse after Adamastor, and his poem 'Rounding the Cape' does not resonate for those who are ignorant of the myth.

Camoens kept returning to me during our voyage back to South Africa. Here was I, periodically haunted by writing a compendious poem about my experiences in Africa and Europe – and he had tried it all before. In Italy my muse

> *Had heard earth's rondure ring to Camoens' voice*
> *And felt his proud foot pound the floors of Time.*

Yes, but apart from the superb creation of Adamastor, Africa itself did not touch him into song. I read and re-read *The Lusiads* as we voyaged south along the length of Africa, but was forced to complain at his neglect of my world.

> *How few your words for Africa, how frail!*
> *In all that Unknown, nothing to uncover*
> *Except one exiled god, whom rage deforms,*
> *Old Adamastor, the sea's rejected lover,*
> *Shaking his frothy beard on the Cape of Storms,*

Still blasting with the thunder of his curse
Whatever man in Africa performs.

There was, however, one fine muted moment on African soil long after the Cape had been rounded.

So, far up the East coast, caught in a terse
Exchange with common death, your proud face winces:
All grandeur suddenly quits your verse;
Furled are the flags, dumb are the drums of princes,
Cultures and continents sink in a depth of song
Whose calm heroic irony convinces
That bones should lie in earth where their hearts belong.

He is talking of burying his countrymen without ceremony on an alien shore.

Under the palms, among the tropical shells
You left them: men who had endured their share
Of various luck since leaving Portugal:
To hide a hero from the rotting air

A common wave, or casual field, or hill
Will do as it does for the rest of men.
A man's last need is easy to fulfil.

I had been present at many funerals in Italy, some of the men I had known well and I was already busy on a long elegy for them.

I spent the next three years under the powerful influences of three very different people: Uys Krige, a freelance writer, Professor J.Y.T. Greig, head of the English Department at Wits, and Trevor Huddleston, of the Anglican monastic order, the Community of the Resurrection. The only person with whom I became really familiar was Uys.

Soon after buying 243 Jan Smuts Avenue, Parktown North in Johannesburg we found that the Kriges were living in an old building rather like a large farmhouse about a mile away in the same suburb. We liked his actress wife, Lydia Lindeque, a dark Spanish-looking beauty with a straight back and eyes that could flash and smoulder, and a wicked wit. On one of our visits to their home I went wrapped up in my Brasenose College scarf, a woollen caterpillar eight feet in length of alternate black and yellow bands. As I unwrapped myself, Lydia took the free end and progressively wrapped it round her shoulders and neck. She looked at herself in the mirror, liked what she saw, took a turn round the company, asked for corroboration, and then returned to me, saying, '*Dis myne!*' I might have demurred had she not looked so stunning in it. It did things for her it could never do for me, and brought glory to my old college!

It was distressing to their friends that Lydia and Uys did not get on better. Their troubles were complex: a chronic shortage of cash coupled with a chronic shortage of sufficiently attractive roles for Lydia to play.

So tight was money that Lydia had to ration Uys to a few shillings a day. I was not in a much better position myself. The bond payments on 243 took a big bite out of my salary. We would not have coped had Jean not gone back to work. Fortunately neither Uys nor I needed alcohol to stimulate us. We found the streets of Johannesburg endlessly intoxicating. Uys bought every paper as it came off the presses, and would descant on items that delighted or outraged him. Sitting on the hobo-laden park benches in the Library Gardens, or even in Joubert Park among a flutter of pigeons, I would listen to a man totally devoted to literature, a profoundly generous man, courageous, self-mocking, capable of eloquent anger and showers of laughter.

People said Uys was egotistical, and they were right, but Uys was also curiously innocent and endearing. His capacity to get lit up by the coruscating variety of life infected me. I envied his ability in an ironical age to cry 'hurrah', and exclaim, 'Isn't that marvellous!' Why should he limit his rejoicings and eurekas to the people or the world about him? Why not extend them to himself? Eaten up by introspection, white-anted with guilts and dreads, I was a sitting duck for Uys. He gave me a glimpse of what I or any man or Adam might have been like before the Fall into guilt. He found himself such an object of delight. The joyful surprises he sprang on himself were so unexpected, so frequent, and so original.

He was at that time translating Spanish American poets into Afrikaans. Walking down Eloff Street he was expatiating on the theory and practice of translation, about which he knew a great deal. Once so engaged, he became oblivious of time or space. He would quote a resonant phrase from Pablo Neruda, then he'd stop walking and repeat it. Then he would utter, with rhetorical ease, its Afrikaans equivalent. It sounded good to me and to him. Having rolled it round his tongue twice, he started walking once more. Then suddenly he stopped me, a hand on my forearm, looking into my face. He was radiant with a sudden discovery. How could he not have made it before? It was one of those hidden things which, once observed, are for ever obvious.

'Guy,' he said, 'I'm the world's best translator!'

I was in no position to query this discovery. The traffic lights had changed and it was necessary to evade an unleashed avalanche of automobiles.

Yet Uys was very sensitive to criticism, much of which was spiteful and vicious. Afrikaner nationalism was gaining strength, and the pressure to succumb to its in-group dynamics must have been great. Uys beheld it with a kind of prophetic grief. 'They're almost Nazis and they don't know it!' he'd cry. Then he'd say: 'No, that's not true. They do know it. Verwoerd knows it. Piet Meyer knows it. And N.P. van Wyk Louw is too good a poet not to know it.'

Uys was busy composing three plays simultaneously. We'd walk round and round Zoo Lake, or among the caged animals at the Zoo, talking about character and plot, and the power of the well-placed telling phrase; of comedy and tragedy, of Sophocles, Shakespeare, Racine, Molière, Lope de Vega, and Lorca. He'd re-read all these, excluding Sophocles, in the original; I'd try to keep abreast, with the aid of translations. Then he'd get launched into one of his plays, ringing out, for my pleasure or comment, long portions of dialogue or describing some *coup de théâtre* which had come to him in the small hours.

Uys was a great swimmer and frequented the Zoo Lake Swimming Baths. He found it perfectly possible to swim and dive while discussing one of the plays with which he was triply pregnant at that time. While I lolled on the lawn, he'd shout a question from the changing-booths, or he'd surface near me and shout, 'Blank verse is useless for comedy. Prose, flexible prose, that's what you need, prose, flexible prose.'

'Rubbish!' I said. 'What about Shakespeare?'

He dived out of sight, to reappear blowing like a porpoise.

'He only uses verse for the romantic stuff. Look at *Much Ado*. Nearly all the best exchanges between Beatrice and Benedict are in prose. Prose, flexible prose.'

This, no doubt, was what he needed for *Die Ryk Weduwee*, a charming comedy which in due course enjoyed considerable success. For his tragic play *Die Twee Lampe*, he employed prose too, but more severe and laconic if you can imagine Uys being laconic. It is a grim tale of a mean old farmer patriarch who drives both his sons to suicide, quoting the Bible to justify each disastrous step. The Afrikaans translation of the Bible rises to great heights, bringing the mountains and deserts of South Africa into that ancient apocalyptic focus. Uys's play ends with the old man receiving the news of the suicide of the second son. He opens the Bible, at the Book of Job of course, and reads a verse which sufficiently captures the desolation of that reality. Uys's problem was whether to follow the verse from Job with a fine line of his own, or place the fine line before the Job.

He recited the Krige/Job sequence in the changing-room and then, emerging in his natty trunks, asked me what I thought. I thought it sounded fine and that Job was a good note to end on. Uys then climbed on to the high diving-board and tried the Job/Krige sequence. From that elevation the words echoed impressively round the enclosure and the sunbathing teenagers wondered what was going on. Uys shouted at me:

'What do you think? Shall I try it again?'

'Yes,' I said.

This time he had a dead-quiet audience. The verse from Job rolled out, followed by Uys's punch line.

'Well?' he shouted.

'Job is better than Krige,' I said. He repeated my sentence and, overcome with laughter, ran along the diving-board and somersaulted into the water. *Jongleur de dieu.*

His Nationalist enemies said Uys talked too much and that a little more writing, in Afrikaans, would be welcome. This may have been inspired by his having written *The Way Out* in English.

'How can they say such a thing!' he cried out. 'Not work! Me? I've finished three plays in the last eighteen months!'

'Which three?' I asked.

He named them. I expressed some surprise. To me they were still on the drawing-board, as it were. Uys patted his forehead.

'*Klaar in my kop*! All I've got to do is to write them down.'

He did in due course go through the boring business of acting as his own amanuensis.

It is probably owing to the influence of Uys that I tried my hand at play-writing. True, I had written a one-act play while a student at Rhodes, but to sit down and write a three-acter, that called for passion and confidence on a different scale.

The Kriges, like ourselves, had no car. Uys, with characteristic lack of self-consciousness, used to make do for short jaunts on a girl's bicycle belonging to his daughter Eulalia. For the rest, we walked or used public transport. To get to work, I'd have to walk to the old tram terminus, and then rattle-clatter up Jan Smuts Avenue to the stop outside Wits, where I would dismount and walk to the Arts Block in some terror of the low-slung Jaguars and glossy Cadillacs driven by my students.

One autumn evening I returned in the golden blue dusk, kicking the fallen leaves of the pale-stemmed plane trees. A girl's bicycle was leaning against the jacaranda, so I knew that Uys was calling. The dusky house was in darkness.

Jean and Uys were sitting at the far end of the drawing-room in earnest conversation. Their heads were both in silhouette against the open sky of the window. Uys was looking up, appealing, gesturing with both hands. I could not hear what he was saying, but it brought a burst of delighted and incredulous laughter from Jean.

The combined effect of Jean's laugh and my appearance clearly upset him.

'Hullo, Guy. Jean, what are you laughing at? It's not funny. Guy, is she always so cruel? How do you put up with her?'

'Have a beer, Uys?'

'Hell no, I've been too long already. O.K., but only one, mind you, only one.'

We were soon deep into Proust and the nature of memory, and then Madame Bovary's fantasy life and Anna Karenina's love for Vronsky. The romantic, tragic and melancholy aspects of romantic love appealed to Uys and he was bitter, very bitter that some comic devil was always depriving him of them. From this I gathered that he and Lydia were at loggerheads again.

When he left, Jean said that he'd appeared at about four, and asked for me. She'd said that I might arrive at any time in the next two hours. Would he care for a cup of tea? No, he couldn't spare the time. An hour later Jean had said:

'Uys, I'm tired of standing, and it's getting cold. Either come inside, or get on your bicycle and scram.'

'Well, just for a few minutes.'

Ensconsed in the window seat, he confided his troubles to Jean. Lydia was being like granite, no, harder than granite, like adamant, the hardest known substance. And cold too. So cold. Ice was like fire compared to Lydia. This was hard for a man of his gentle and affectionate nature to bear. And when he told her so, do you know what the heartless beauty had said?

'No.'

'She said to me, "Uys, why don't you take a lover?" Imagine it!'

'Well, Uys,' said Jean, 'why don't you?'

He thought for a moment, and then said: 'No transport.'

That was when Jean laughed, and I entered.

It was under Uys's influence that I tried once again to learn French. The patient, gentle Harry Girling took Charles Hooper and myself for tutorials in our study at Wits. The dear fellow thought the best way to get our colonial tongues to accept the unstressed and nasal nature of French was to persuade us to sing the great classical songs of France, like 'Alouette, gentille Alouette', and 'Sur le pont d'Avignon', or 'Mademoiselle from Armentières'.

We heard subsequently that a solemn sociologist down the corridor suspected us of being three Francophile queers who periodically got high on dagga. Harry also seemed to think that the mastery of one Verlaine lyric would propel us through some otherwise impenetrable sound barrier:

Le ciel est par dessus le toit,
Si bleu, si calm!

Which was all very well, but what was it worth beside Herbert's

Sweet day, so calm, so cool, so bright,
The bridal of the earth and sky,
The dew must weep thy fall tonight
For thou must die.

Sweet rose, whose hue angry and brave
Bids the rash gazer wipe his eye ...

Yes, yes, yes. I did my best with Baudelaire and Rimbaud, struggling with cribs, poetic and prosaic, and got some dim glimmering of what French poetry must be like.

And then Charles Eglington would enter my study for his Anglo–Saxon tutorial. Here was a man, a little older than myself, who read French and loved the Portuguese poet Pessão, whom he was translating. But for the purposes of his degree Charles had to translate half of *Beowulf*. It would have been easier if I had not been a *Beowulf* devotee. It would also have been easier if I were not subject to making, and believing, such pronouncements as: 'It is worth learning Anglo–Saxon if only to be able to read "The Wanderer", a poem of a mere 120 lines.' Why did I say such things? The poem struck me as having affinities with Eliot's *The Waste Land*. It was far less pretentious. Did Eliot really expect us to know all European languages and literatures, as a kind of kindergarten preparation for the splendid finale of resonant Sanskrit, 'Datta, Dayadvham, Damyata'? Did Eliot *read* Sanskrit? Whom was he trying to bluff? Whereas this anonymous Anglo–Saxon poet, using a small vocabulary and a demanding technique, chiselled his strong torsos out of granite on the sea's edge, blow by blow, hemistich by hemistich. This was epic stuff, not Alexandrian.

That was it, I suppose. So much of my background was closer to the rigours and spatial simplicities of an epic world, so barren, so without ingrained familiarity with several literatures and languages, that I could only opt for the comparatively simple, the apparently monolithic.

But Charles could not, would not learn to decline the Anglo–Saxon nouns and never got as far as the irregular verbs in the Rev. Henry Sweet's *Anglo–Saxon Primer*. He failed his examination. In his less rational moments he held me responsible for inadequate tuition.

Some time in 1950 I was invited by the University of Natal to give two lectures on South African poetry, one in Pietermaritzburg and one in Durban. For the latter I had prepared a talk on Natal's most distinguished son, Roy Campbell, who, I thought, would be a household word in the city of his birth.

It is one of the failings of poets to think that the public at large is interested in them. But I had hoped that by 1950, a generation after

Sjambok, Durban might have got over its anger at the 'bombs of laughter' which Roy had dropped on its roofs, and grown to appreciate the man whose poems had the strong clarity of aloes in bloom on granite outcrops.

An exhausted professor of a Science had to introduce me, evidently at short notice. That is the most charitable explanation I can find for what followed.

'It gives me great pleasure this evening to introduce our speaker Guy Campbell, from the English Department of the University of the Witwatersrand. He will address us on Roy Butler, Durban's distinguished poet–son.'

I did my best to sort this out in a humorous fashion, but my chairman had fallen asleep before my first pleasantries were over. He woke up for my peroration and then rose.

'The enthusiasm of your applause, ladies and gentlemen,' he said, 'speaks volumes. I'm sure you all wish me to thank Roy Campbell for coming all the way from Johannesburg to give this lively talk on Natal's most famous poet, Guy Butler.'

During this pleasant excursion to the Garden Colony Jean and I met some of our Biggs relatives for the first time in years. Dan Biggs, married to my father's sister Josie, had deserted the dry world of the Northern Cape and bought a farm near Ixopo, which seemed to stretch from high wet uplands suitable for forestry down to bush country suitable for cattle. He was his usual independent self.

Aunt Josie was full of sparkle and took Jean and me some distance to watch the filming of a portion of *Cry, the Beloved Country*. It was my first experience of the laborious process of film-making. A rider with an urgent message had to dash through an avenue of gum-trees in a thunderstorm. The day, however, was beautifully clear. There were tractors with driving belts attached to powerful pumps employing spray-irrigation plant to create a tropical downpour. At a given signal the rain-makers started working; and at another, the rider dashed into the avenue and the cameras started rolling.

Aunt Josie introduced me to the author, Alan Paton, who was scowling and growling goodnaturedly to someone shouting the orders. The unfortunate messenger had to gallop through that artificial storm about five times before artistic consciences were satisfied. It was not a good time for literary talk, but Mr Paton did answer my question: Was he busy on another novel? Yes, he was. What was it about? About a young white policeman who interferes with a black girl, he said. In 1950 that was a conversation stopper.

Preparatory to leaving Johannesburg for Grahamstown Jean and I had held one or two farewell dinner parties. Charles Eglington ruined one of these feasts by an attack of Swiftian *saeva indignatio*, pouring vitriol in turn on all our opinions and then ourselves. We were all insufferably smug, brainless and philistine – mainly, if I recall, because we were married (he was still a bachelor). Worse, some of us actually went to Church. Charles had a Catholic background and one could never predict what would happen when religion came up. He found Anglo–Catholics particularly irritating. If one must become a God-botherer, there was only one respectable tradition in which to do it: Rome.

As each couple left, Charles speeded them on their way with a final fusillade of spluttering abuse. Jean and I were upset for all concerned, not least for Charles himself.

The next day was a Saturday and we were expecting a string of estate agents. It was my turn to show them round. In the middle of the morning, between two visitations, Charles arrived, the proudest penitent I have ever seen, with a vast bunch of roses for Jean and an anthology of Goliard poetry for me. We sat down to tea in the kitchen, where Jean was busy making a cake. The bell rang and I left to take charge of the smartest of the house agents and her even smarter client, who was dressed in superbly tailored tweeds. With her was her son, a precocious chatterbox in a Pridwin cap, a nosey-parker to boot, who felt free, and was left free, to comment loudly on the appointments of the houses through which his mother was being shown and which he might have to grace with his more permanent presence.

As the back garden was best viewed from the kitchen stoep, I led the party past Jean and Charles taking tea in the kitchen. Charles had the piteous and troubled look of a man with a stubborn hangover and Jean had placed a packet of bicarb and a glass of water in front of him.

We stood on the back stoep, looking down on to the rose garden and vegetable patch. The little horror ran down the steps, sniffing around and yapping comments like a fox-terrier after rats. The adult party was already returning when he decided to rejoin them. They were making quite appreciative noises. The house agent was in front, the prospective buyer next, and then myself. The Pridwin cap appeared in the kitchen and piped up.

'No good, Mother. Back garden's far too small for a donkey.'

At which point I heard a rasping, hissing whisper from Charles.

'Shut up, can't you, you little bastard!'

The tweed shoulders in front of me jerked as though a barbed arrow had struck the second dorsal vertebra.

No sale.

I cannot recall what impelled me to put together another collection of my own poems. Certain items which I can date, like 'The Underdogs', indicate that it was done shortly before I left Johannesburg, towards the end of 1950. I left the manuscript with Uys Krige, who was sure he'd be able to find a publisher. He mentioned two new publishers, enlightened Hollanders who valued poetry in a way the old-established South African houses did not. They also knew how to make a decent-looking book. The quality of South African book design was still abysmal. Gratefully I left him to it and turned my attention to my departure for Grahamstown. John and Tess Greig gave us a farewell tea at their home, at which my colleagues presented me with a fine book on late Medieval French painting; it still gives me pleasure.

Our move to Grahamstown in 1951 to a new job drove all creative writing out of my mind. I all but forgot that I was an embryonic poet who had entrusted a volume of poems to Uys Krige, or an embryonic dramatist who had submitted a play for a national playwriting competition. When *The Dam* was awarded a first prize, I began once more to take myself seriously as a writer. Having been asked to go to the Cape to discuss my script with the producer, I took advantage of the opportunity to visit Uys. The Kriges had moved to Cape Town because at that time there was far more of interest to a playwright and an actress in the Mother City than in Johannesburg. They were living in a large old farm-type house in Rouwkoop Road. It had a central corridor, off which were several simply furnished double rooms, sporadically occupied by any of Uys's many friends. These friends went on talking to (or rather listening to) Uys after all the transport systems of the Peninsula had gone to sleep.

It was marvellous to be with Uys again: the same intellectual artesian well, the same generosity, the same articulate critique of nationalist paranoia.

Yes, he'd found a publisher for *Stranger to Europe*, A.A. Balkema, of Amsterdam, who'd opened up a branch of his firm in Cape Town after the war. The volume would have to be shortened, a task with which Uys was quite happy to assist.

So, with both a first play and a first volume of poems in the pipeline I was in the mood to celebrate. I phoned Tony Delius, who joined us, and Jack Cope and, I think, Charles Eglington. Anyway, the car was full.

Whose car was it? I don't know, but somewhere about midnight we decided to visit an artist friend in Somerset West. We had a blow-out in a moonlit bluegum avenue. We found a village garage, and leisurely repairs with a drum of water, a rubber patch and secotine were made by a good-natured 'coloured' man while we continued our excited debate on the supreme themes of art and song. I do not recall the responses of the artist friend, whom we eventually woke up at about 2 a.m., except that he was not quite as friendly as the man who had fixed the blow-out.

About 3.30 a.m. we piled out of the car back into Uys's hospitable old house. Tony Delius grabbed my arm saying, 'Let's share a room.'

'O.K.,' I said, 'but aren't there rooms enough to go around?'
'I've been here before,' he said, 'and I need a few hours' rest.'
I went to sleep to the sound of Uys talking to someone who'd not been wise enough to fill the spare bed in his room. And I woke at first light to the sound of Uys, who had leapt out like a footpad upon someone who was on his way to the bathroom. 'What do you think about the Three Dramatic Unities of Aristotle?'

Uys had stayed with the Copes shortly before this. One of Jack's children, under 3, had asked his grandmother, 'Does Mister Krige stop talking when he's asleep?'

Long before sunrise we were in that car again, rattling down to Muizenberg for a swim. It was all so beautifully timed. Four writers, four friends, dashed into the waves together just as the sun rose.

Back in Grahamstown, having revised *The Dam* and despatched it, I turned to *Stranger to Europe*, threw out several poems and included others such as 'The Parting'. On 10 February I wrote my first letter to A.A. Balkema, expressing my pleasure at the news that Uys had given me, and asking questions as to the maximum length. He replied on the 13th, telling me how to calculate the number of lines per page. 'Each poem starts a new page.' He was anxious to get the manuscript as soon as possible. I obliged by posting it on the 18th and told him that I would be in Cape Town on 1 or 3 March for the opening night of my play. Would it be possible to meet him some time before returning to Grahamstown?

After the opening night of *The Dam*, I visited Balkema. I had a stereotyped picture in my mind of a Hollander as a substantial block of a man, with a shining bald bullet head, solemn and not given to levity. It was, therefore, a surprise to meet a slight, perpetually smiling volatile man, who seemed to find almost everything a source of fun. Even the most terrible political follies he ridiculed with a little laugh so deprecating and indulgent that there was no contempt in it. Years later, when I was reading Erasmus's *The Praise of Folly*, Balkema suddenly leapt to mind. His sense of folly was Erasmian. No human nonsense could surprise him. He'd say three or four rapid yes-yes-yeses, for every one no, lengthened into *naw*.

Our business was to discuss the format for *Stranger to Europe*. While doing this he produced examples of books of verse which he had published during the Nazi occupation of Holland. I was particularly struck by an edition of John Donne's poems, which, he explained, was one of a series of selections from English poets chosen by contemporary Netherlands poets and published underground as a kind of poetic protest against Nazi cultural pressures.

'All the best Dutch authors of the older generation, and most of the younger ones, had refused to be members of the Kultuur Kamer. I was one of the few publishers in the same position and as such was the right man for them. In retrospect nothing to be proud of. They were a kind of élite books by élite authors and artists for an élite public.' I quote this as an example of his modesty and humour.

I enjoyed that meeting. I always enjoy meeting Balkema.

I had to learn the hard way that very few people read poetry for pleasure. Outside school and university, who on earth buys and reads poetry? Particularly in English-speaking South Africa. The Afrikaans poet was indeed lucky: there were a dozen university departments devoted to encouraging the literature of the young language, and thousands of schools waiting to be fed with Afrikaans setbooks. The position was very different among the English educationists, who saw their function as essentially conservative, to keep the great tradition of English literature alive and to prevent the language from departing too far from that of the mother country. These were aims which I endorsed. But was that all that English education in Africa should be attempting to do?

When *Stranger to Europe* (1952) appeared it did not hit the headlines, nor did it fall dead from the press. The *Cape Times* sent it to Roy Campbell to review.

He began: 'The year 1952 will be remembered in the annals of South African literature for the publication of *Stranger to Europe.*'

I have not looked to see what else was published in 1952; and I wonder whether Campbell himself knew. However, it was a generous review, with some very valuable critical comment in it. It ended: 'Those poems written in Africa since the war, such as "The Underdogs", and "After Ten Years" have a brooding prophetic thundery atmosphere which is extremely impressive. This is altogether a very fine first book. Its only fault is that there is not more of it.'

What next? While not abandoning lyric, I returned with renewed determination to my fatal Cleopatra, the long poem in terza rima. Friends told me I was attempting the impossible, but I thought I knew better. They were probably right. It is still not complete. But I have hopes. *Ars longa est.* As Uys Krige used to say: 'There's lots of time, Guy. Sophocles wrote *Oedipus Rex* when he was 80.'

I worked away. By 1954 the long poem existed in thirty short cantos in terza rima – about 3 000 lines. But I found that what I had intended to be at most a shortish episode in an epic demanded more and more space. For instance, a common element in epic is serious attention devoted to dead companions: funeral games, lament, elegy. This episode grew into an independent piece, published in *Standpunte* Aug./Sept. 1955. In its final (1986) reworking, the elegy consists of fourteen sections. So also, a common enough epic episode, the battle for a city, grew over several years from a poem to a booklet of eighteen sections, published as *On First Seeing*

Florence by *New Coin* in 1968.

There it is, a kind of quarry of my experience up to the age of 36, seemingly petrified in the rough crystal of my unpolished terza rima. Apart from the two longish poems mentioned above, I have quarried smaller pieces like 'Giotto's Campanile' or 'December 1949' and from it, turned fragments into sonnets such as 'David' and 'Pieta', or into articulated lyrical meditations, like 'To a Statue of the Virgin' which I had seen on our cycle tour to the Provence in 1947.

Stranger to Europe (1939–1947) consists of twenty-three poems, the last eight of which, and 'The Parting', could not have been the volume rejected by Faber. It sold out, and there was a demand for a second edition. It was perhaps a mistake to reissue it *With Additional Poems* in 1960. I should have brought out a new volume. The twelve additional poems together with the full version of 'Elegy', not the shortened version which it printed, could easily have stood by themselves.

By 1960 I had crossed a watershed. Although I would return again and yet again to the seminal war and Oxford years, I had moved deeper and deeper into Africa – as is already apparent from several of the additional poems, from my plays, and my academic preoccupations.

14   1952–61

Apprentice Professor

I hope I have suggested just how haphazard and improvised my life had been up to the age of 33 (1951). The appointment to the Chair was decisive in determining the future use of my energies. I was now in a position of responsibility. It would be quite wrong, however, to suggest that I was clear in my own mind that this appointment was decisive or that the purchase of High Corner marked a final settling down. If the 'forties had been *wanderjahre*, the 'fifties were continuous *sturm und drang*; it was only in the 'sixties and 'seventies that I was sufficiently settled and accepted by others to play a small part in public life. This chapter will concentrate on the 'fifties.

Yet if we look back with all the advantages of hindsight, it does seem that the young Professor Butler, who was so mysteriously elevated to a Chair in 1952, was already fully formed; what followed was a putting into practice of ideas and talents which had already declared themselves in the army, at Oxford and at Wits. This being so, it is necessary to give some account of the slow maturation of my particular interests before I went public as it were – as a professor, a poet, a playwright, and in other ways.

It is clear that Guy Butler became professor with nothing on his academic record beyond M.A.s from Rhodes and Oxford: no learned articles, only a prose essay or two, a play and a few poems in little magazines and anthologies. He had done no research whatever and held no higher degree. It could never happen today. I can only assume that Rhodes and the Arts Faculty at Wits must have wanted me for my ability to get students interested and for some evidence of an energetic nature and intelligence which might in due course produce the appropriate higher research degree. This I have failed to do.

Rites of passage vary from institution to institution and from generation to generation. During the early Alty period at Rhodes the form for inaugural lectures was as follows: the initiant and his spouse, having taken what ritual precautions they saw fit, clothed themselves for a sacred meal with the Vice-Chancellor and his wife, who had invited (according to ancient laws at which I can only guess) persons fit for the occasion: such as the Dean of the initiant's faculty and his wife, and a member of the University Council and his wife. Having partaken of the ritual meal, the initiant was separated from the rest of the human race in an anteroom

Professor Guy Butler in 1954 (line drawing by Cecil Todd)

where he donned his monkish gown and hood, the only attendant being the Registrar who had to ensure that he was properly dressed, that a glass of water was available, knew in which pocket his lecture notes were, and did not run away. About the same time his colleagues, also in full academic dress, had been marshalled elsewhere, *seniores priores*, awaiting the signal to proceed to their reserved ringside seats at the place of execution. Sadistic members of the public, sensation-seeking students and cynical journalists would have taken their seats elsewhere in the auditorium.

The initiant would know that the hour had struck when the Vice-Chancellor came to join him in the condemned cell, while the Registrar would disappear to see that the gorgeously robed academic procession had stumbled into their reserved seats, again *seniores priores*. He would also check to see whether the Vice-Chancellor's wife had arrived with the initiant's wife and the ruck of the ritual dinner party. He then nodded to the Vice-Chancellor, who would invite the initiant to follow him with some such peremptory command as 'Shall we go?' On their entry the assembled body would rise, for the high priest had entered, and was leading the sacrificial victim to the slaughter.

The high priest would sit, the victim would sit, and the whole assembly would sit. The high priest would rise and try to convince the disbelieving worshippers that he and his *amapagati* had indeed secured the best beast available to offer up on this occasion in the quiet groves of academe. The victim, hearing the recitation of his meagre *curriculum vitae*, would look wildly round the audience for his spouse, hoping to exchange a reassuring glance. It was clear that she was also finding the experience taxing. They both 'looked their last on all things lovely'. Life would never be quite the same again. The high priest would end his apologia by mentioning the title of the oration with which the initiant proposed to placate the gods of learning, stepping back from the lectern and sitting down. The initiant then rose and spread his papers on the lectern, adjusted his spectacles and proceeded to give a ridiculously nervous cough. 'Then all the gods look down and smile on the unnatural scene', their hands cupped to their ears, determined not to miss a word.

Jean and I got through it all with only one major, staggering, inadvertent departure from protocol, from which we recovered as only a fit young couple who have been together on a continental cycling tour could do. We had bathed and dressed in good time, I in a fairly new dress suit and a black tie which was not of the ready-made variety, she in her little basic black. She looked absolutely smashing, as Guy Stringer would have said. We walked to the Vice-Chancellor's lodge, a fine spacious Victorian bungalow (subsequently replaced by a perfectly hideous Chemistry Block). Mrs Alty opened the door, saw Jean, and said, 'Oh my dear, you should be wearing a long frock!'

So we sprinted across the Drostdy lawns to High Corner, Jean trying to make up her mind which of her three long dresses to wear. I think she chose the one she had made out of blue curtain material but she is not sure. We strolled back to recover our composure. The tense atmosphere was eased by the presence of Steele Gray and his wife, who were friends of ours.

The ordeal itself took place in the General Lecture Theatre. I had taken the precaution of rehearsing my lecture several times, so got through it without too much stumbling and without going into injury time. The place was packed, with people sitting in the aisles.

I'm afraid I had previously read very few inaugural lectures and attended none; nor when appointed to the Chair had I spent sufficient time thinking of the ingredients that go into a good example of the genre. So I failed to preface my lecture with any reference whatever to my predecessors, Professor Stanley Kidd (1904–1932) and my own mentor, Professor Peter Haworth (1932–1951). I regret this arrogant-seeming lack of acknowledgement of the professorial (if not apostolic) succession. Nor did I take the opportunity (as is now frequently done) to offer a manifesto or declaration of intent as to how I proposed to profess my subject, nor did I attempt to remind my audience of the peculiar problems of teaching English literature and language in a bilingual country where mother-tongue speakers form less than 10 percent of the total population. As I had already in various public lectures made known my interest in South African literature in English and in the range of problems and opportunities springing from the cultural diversity of our society, it would have made good sense to pull them all together and present them on this occasion. Instead I launched straight into my topic entitled 'An Aspect of Tragedy': the moment – frequently protracted – of intense spiritual crisis and metaphysical uncertainty which is one of the distinguishing ingredients of tragedy. I went straight into the search for meaning in dramas ranging from the Greeks through to the twentieth century.

I don't think it was the right topic for that audience. Comments over coffee afterwards were vague. The only person who seemed to have the slightest idea of what I was getting at was Rob Antonissen, a Fleming in the Afrikaans/Nederlands department.

Christina van Heyningen was visiting Frank and Mavis van der Riet at the time. Our paths happened to cross the next day and I made the mistake of asking her what she thought of it. 'I liked the quotations,' she said.

When one becomes a Professor and Head of a Department one ceases in large measure to be oneself. First, you are publicly professing a subject, and the public look at you more critically, particularly if you profess a subject like English, in which they have a personal or political interest. By virtue of your elevation to a Chair, you sit in several places where you never sat before, in the Faculty of Arts and on the Senate of the University. You are a small part of a large establishment which has its rules and procedures to which you have to submit, and to whose decisions you have to conform. You sink your individuality into a corporate body.

You seldom speak for yourself alone. You find yourself drawn into debates on academic issues that are anything but academic. For instance, on 25 March 1957 the Students' Representative Council organised a symposium on university apartheid. I spoke from the floor, and here is a summary of what I said:

'Many of those who oppose university apartheid share the same basic colour prejudices as those who defend it. They think liberal, but do not feel liberal.

'The difference between the opposers and defenders lies not in their prejudices, but in their attitudes towards those prejudices. Nationalists believe that colour prejudice cannot or should not be overcome. For them it is the basis of a policy. They overrate the difficulties generated by a multiracial society. Their opponents underrate the power of prejudice and sometimes suggest that economic processes alone will lead to a solution.

'White South Africans are not, as some people overseas think, a peculiarly blind and benighted group of people. Given historical and other circumstances, it was natural enough that they should develop strong and deep colour prejudices. The history of the Afrikaner people shows them as courageous, tenacious and intelligent. They have a natural desire to survive, to be themselves. There is nothing surprising in the fact that many of them support apartheid, because, as a policy, it attempts primarily to guarantee survival, and, more important, it leaves their traditional feelings of colour unchallenged.

'Some psychologists say that human beings can operate in one of two ways: according to the pleasure principle or according to the reality principle. The former has a high regard for feelings, the second for facts. We all prefer the first, and only accept the second with reluctance. It seems to me that apartheid is a pleasure policy to protect us whites from a painful assault on our prejudices.

'Natural as it is to choose terms for survival which demand no change in our prejudices, such terms might well turn out to be the terms of suicide. I personally believe that the Afrikaner's native intelligence will show him this, and that his sense of facts, of reality, will win the day.

'We do not choose to be prejudiced. We grow up into a world of prejudice, and take our feelings from it. But it is, I take it, our Christian and moral duty to examine our prejudices, to realise what they are doing to us and to other people.

'No one can say what his grandchildren will feel about certain groups of people. People change, groups change, attitudes change. This being so, it seems shortsighted to base a national policy on a prejudice, and to legislate, year after year, to preserve so impermanent a thing.

'Recent legislation bears disturbing evidence of our preparedness to tamper with the constitution and the courts, the freedom of the subject and now of the churches and the universities, all in order to protect 'white civilisation'.

'If I believed that Man cannot overcome colour prejudice, I would be a Nationalist; I believe it will be difficult, far more difficult than most of us are prepared to acknowledge. But it is our only hope. History will not let us get away with a supreme piece of moral self-indulgence. It demands that we face the facts that we are committed or condemned to a mixed society: even the Tomlinson Report offers no escape from this. We shall have to think of Africans, speak to Africans, and meet Africans outside the master/servant relationship. It will be difficult. It will be enlightening. It may even lead to what some people believe to be that ultimate horror, a coffee-coloured race. I would prefer my descendants to be coffee-coloured and civilised, rather than to be white and barbaric. It seems to me that the more conscious of our whiteness we become, the easier we find it to pass uncivilised and uncivilising laws. Let us stop elevating prejudice into principle, and tradition into a moral commandment.

'I speak with vehemence, because two strongholds of the Truth, as I conceive it, the Church and the University, are under attack.'

The press reacted with headlines such as 'Coffee-coloured race is preferable to barbarism, professor says' (*Star*); 'Professor prefers coffee race to barbarous whites' *(Argus)*.

Dr Otto du Plessis, M.P. for Stellenbosch, held me up to the House as a horrible example of the dangers which academic liberals posed to white civilisation: 'Professor Butler has become so ultra-liberal that his colour consciousness has become blunted to the extent that he prefers a coffee-coloured race to us who are regarded as barbarians.'

Part of the trouble sprang from inaccurate reporting in some papers. In the antithesis 'coffee-coloured and civilised ... white and barbaric' the 'and civilised' was missing. I wrote to Dr Du Plessis pointing this out. '*Die Burger*, in spite of other errors, has reported this correctly ... It seems you read the *Argus* rather than *Die Burger*.' After a considerable delay he replied that he 'had spoken more in sorrow than in anger'.

As head of a department you are part of a body of students from first-years to research workers, and teaching colleagues in various established posts from temporary junior lecturers to lecturers, senior lecturers, associate professors and full professors. Being a head of a large department calls for a measure of self-denial and self-effacement which does not come easily to most of us. As my staff increased in size I had to sacrifice nearly all my preferred topics of teaching. It has been a series of farewells to all my favourites, to Conrad, Yeats, Hopkins, Keats and most of Shakespeare; but worse, one had to spend countless hours on administration, on the annual nightmare of justifying the staff you had on establishment or persuading the staffing committee of your need for more; on interviewing and selecting new staff members; on the laborious but important annual drawing-up of syllabuses and selecting set books; on the setting of examination papers and on the marking and moderation of the same. One ceases to be oneself, becoming possessed by one's staff and students.

Yet this is probably the most important work I have done in my life: trying to teach my subject as thoroughly as possible with the talents and resources available.

To tell the story of that labour would be dull for me and worse for my readers. Becoming a professor has changed the focus of this autobiography. I shall not deal with the central work by which I earned my bread, but with the peripheral, sometimes creative, activities which I shared with others from different walks of life or disciplines. This means an almost total neglect of my immediate teaching colleagues, without whom I could have achieved nothing. I regret that this should be so, and record my profound gratitude to them for years of enriching work together.

It is also essential to emphasise that an academic belongs also to an international community of teachers and scholars: a community which was once wide open, hospitable and generous to South Africans. This book cannot give any idea of the intellectual stimulus I derived from my visits overseas. I know that my teaching would have been impoverished without them. They not only widened my mental horizons but, possibly more important, my circle of friends.

Here is the briefest reference to some of these ventures abroad.

1954: Nuffield Foundation Fellowship – London, Oxford, Bristol – devoted mainly to drama. I met for the first time two rather different scholars who were to become lifelong friends – L.C. Knights then at Bristol, and Muriel Bradbrook at Cambridge.

1958: Carnegie Travelling Fellowship to Canada and U.S.A. The effect of this academic grand tour will be clear in what follows.

1960: Holland and United Kingdom. This helped to clarify my thinking on the language issue so that I took what I thought was appropriate action when I returned to South Africa.

1970: University of York, Centre for Southern African Studies, where I delivered a nettle-grasping paper entitled 'Which English? A Note on South African Literature in English'. A fashionable word at this gathering was 'alienation'. Apartheid made all South Africans alienated. At last Alan Paton objected. 'In my lifetime I have felt outraged, angry, indignant, ashamed, but alienated? Never!'

In 1952 I began the slow process of reorganising the English Department, combining the use of the three teaching tools, the lecture, the seminar, and the essay tutorial, in a manner which placed more weight on the small-group work of the seminar than on the lecture, and more emphasis on the essay than on the seminar.

While I myself enjoyed lecturing, I had doubts about its effectiveness, particularly when employed to transmit material which is already available in print or which can be duplicated. (Definition: 'A lecture is the means whereby the words in the lecturer's notebook are transferred to the notebook of the student without passing through the minds of either.')

The seminar, a group of not more than twelve students, preferably ten or less, is a far more effective teaching instrument, provided the students prepare for the meeting and the member of staff does not make a habit of misusing the time to build himself up as a great guru of some kind or another. I brought the idea of such small-group work with me from Wits.

Oxford had convinced me of the value of the essay. More than any other device it compels a student to gather information, to answer questions, and to articulate his answers in writing. It compels him to think and to communicate. A young person writing a weekly essay in a library is being compelled to think and so to educate himself. The central acts of education can only occur in the mind; and they are most likely to occur when the student is alone. They are least likely to occur in a crowded lecture theatre. Crowds are good for many things, but they are not good for thought.

Many tales are told against obtuse professors for not appreciating the genius of their students. Not all of them are true. For instance I have heard it said that Wilbur Smith took four (instead of the normal three) years to complete his B.Com. degree because the professor of English refused to give him credit for English Special, a first-year course for Commerce students; and that he only managed to pass that course when the said professor was away on sabbatical leave. Before repeating this charming legend I thought it as well to check. The records show that it contains two errors of fact. First, the course Special English was not offered at the time. Second, Wilbur Addison Smith passed English I in the third class in his first year, when Peter Haworth was still head of the department. I do, however, remember reading on request a lengthy piece of prose fiction by a student called Smith, which was certainly gripping, about a group of heroic drop-outs besieged in a seedy ruin on the outskirts of a one-horse town. The measure of conviction the story carried made me wonder what our students got up to during their vacs. I have forgotten what advice I gave him.

I was, to say the least, restive in my chair of English Language and Literature. In an application for a Carnegie Travelling Fellowship to the United States in September 1958, under 'Main Interests' I listed: (1) Modern Poetry, (2) The Nature of Poetic Drama, (3) The Writing and Production of Plays, (4) The Development of South African Literature, and finally (5) Drama Departments, their place in the university, their relationship to language departments (particularly English), the professional theatre and the public at large.

This was a *short* list made for a particular purpose.

I was quite incapable of taking a modest view of what English Language and Literature demanded of professors in the South African situation. It is possible to give only the briefest accounts of my incursions into fields which most of my colleagues at the time thought unimportant or irrelevant. These activities sprang from my growing sense of the predicament and responsibilities of the small group of mother-tongue speakers of English in my country – the English Speaking South Africans, or ESSAs. Most of my academic excursions are related in some measure to that concern: the survival of a small indigenous breed whose home language is English, and their role and responsibility in this multilingual society.

My first concern was with their language and their South African origins; secondly with their world-wide literature; thirdly with their greatest poet, Shakespeare, and the importance of the local performance of his works. The story is complicated throughout by the fact that I was not only a student of South African poetry, but a poet; not only a lover of Shakespeare's plays, but a producer of them; not only a student of drama, but a playwright.

Those who need more than the brief outlines that follow must go to my other publications, more particularly to my 'Essays on ESSAs and Their Literature' (working title) being edited by Stephen Watson.

THE ENGLISH LANGUAGE IN SOUTH AFRICAN EDUCATION

Most English departments – particularly those whose presiding genius was F.R. Leavis – believed devoutly that language studies and grammar were not essential, and indeed for the most part a waste of time. They maintained that under a good teacher the linguistic oddities of Shakespeare and Chaucer would easily be mastered, almost in passing as it were.

This struck me as nonsense. This philosophy of education came from unilingual England, which has a relatively homogeneous society in whose schools Latin was still compulsory, and from which pupils could learn the grammatical rudiments of an Indo–European tongue. But the numerical base of mother-tongue English speakers in multilingual South Africa is minuscule. At that time within the privileged white minority of five million we probably numbered one and three-quarter million, concentrated mainly in the big cities: and that white minority lived in the midst of, and was economically dependent upon, thirty-five million blacks of various shades split among some nine different language groups; to which we must add three Indian languages in Natal. South Africa is a Babel in which English is by law an official language, and therefore a second language for most South Africans.

I felt that South African school and university curricula for English should give more attention to the peculiar problems and opportunities facing (a) the small English-speaking minority in a difficult multilingual society, and (b) those for whom English was not a mother-tongue. Unilingual British, American and most Commonwealth precedents and patterns can be misleading. This society is not unilingual.

The teaching of English as Second Language was on my conscience from the start. The primary aim for most South African children should be English for practical use, to help earn one's daily bread, to fulfil the functions of *lingua franca*. It was not uncommon for me to receive letters and phone calls from headmasters and headmistresses of Afrikaans schools begging for English-speaking teachers of English. It was seldom I was able to oblige. As for the black secondary schools, of which there were very few in the 'fifties, they were still fortunate to have a fairly high percentage of mother-tongue speakers of English on their staff, a percentage which was to dwindle drastically once the Government decided to ethnicise black education.

What infuriated me was an immigration policy which discouraged English teachers from entering our country, and a bigoted insistence on bilingualism as a precondition for promotion. Our benighted educational policies have limited the entry of English teachers from the United Kingdom into educational systems in desperate need of them.

The tiny South African English-speaking community was thrown back on its own very limited resources. It was soon clear that while there might be symbolic gestures towards us from the Nationalist Party, we were to receive no real help in meeting the demands of the entire South African educational system for English school-teachers and academics. It was also very clear that few English-speaking South Africans were aware of the historical roles they ought to be playing as the possessors of the one language in the country which everybody else needed in some measure.

During my term on the Joint Matriculation Board I battled for the teaching of some grammar in schools – grammar based on modern linguistics, not old philology. Just as there were signs of an openness to this need, the academic grammarians (who should have gone full speed ahead with the production of school textbooks) were thrown into disarray by that major shift in the understanding of language associated with the name of Noam Chomsky. The literature enthusiasts had thrown the grammar baby out with the bathwater, and the grammarians had nothing but oldfashioned prescriptive clouts to swaddle it in.

I have referred elsewhere to my friendship with Professor L.W. Lanham, Professor of African Languages, and a powerful theoretical and practical linguist. His influence on me in this field is incalculable. He went on various study leaves to the U.S.A. and to Britain to keep abreast of the latest developments in linguistics and language learning. When he returned I listened, fascinated and dimly comprehending. I watched with some amazement the collapse of his belief that language is explicable on behaviourist assumptions and that miracles of language learning can be achieved with the aid of the language laboratory. I witnessed his conversion to a view of the mind as a creative, meaningful miracle rather than a push–pull behaviourist mechanism. From him I learnt something about the nature of mother-tongue interference. He also did the piece of research which answered the question which had so teased me as to the origins of the South African English accent.

In 1960 during study leave in Britain, I asked the British Council to put me in touch with someone who knew about the use of English as a *lingua franca*. This resulted in a meeting with Dr A.H. King, who had just returned from Pakistan, to which country he had gone in response to an appeal for help. English had been adopted as the language of administration, but the civil service was in danger of breaking down because letters written in English by clerks in the north could not be understood by clerks in the south and vice versa. The explanations were manifold. Dr King ended by saying: 'People who think they are helping polyglot societies by making the *lingua franca* easy or fiddling with examination results breed chaos. It is no kindness to anyone to let standards slip.'

SOUTH AFRICAN LITERATURE IN ENGLISH

My second great heresy was my interest in South African and African literature. As early as 1949 I was lecturing to Transvaal school-teachers on the difficulties of teaching a non-indigenous literature. As soon as I was in a position to do so at Rhodes, I started introducing South African works into the syllabus.

I played a leading part in helping to set up a conference, held from 10 to 12 July 1956 at Wits, of writers, publishers, editors and university teachers of English to discuss the question of South African literature in education. It was, I think, a milestone in the development of South African literature in English – certainly a gathering of writers, publishers and academics such as the country had not seen before. The proceedings were published by the University of Witwatersrand Press in 1957.

Here are two anecdotes, both of which involve Sarah Gertrude Millin, by then a grand old lady of South African letters. She felt distinctly neglected by the younger post-war generation, many of whom knew each other well, and who lapsed easily into first-name terms during discussion time. At last she could stand it no longer, and rose.

'Mr Chairman, who *is* Tony? Who *is* Guy? Who *is* Jack? Who *is* Charles? What have they published that we should be required to listen to their cosy chatter? I am an author of twenty books and I represent bulk.' She did.

Indeed, she had a point. As Professor Geoff Durrant remarked on more than one occasion: 'White South Africans all know each other, or of each other. It's an intellectual dorp.'

The other story concerns a dinner party given by the Registrar Glynn Thomas and his formidable wife. One of the distinguished guests was Mary Morison Webster. The ageing poetess had a somewhat long, sad physiognomy and had dressed her hair with a symbolical wreath of tinsel laurel leaves. The effect was quite startling, but Plomer's whispered query was bland: *'Dante redivivus?'*

The dinner party was not a success. Sarah Gertrude was determined to dominate the table in a way she had not managed to rule the afternoon session; but Mrs Glynn Thomas as hostess assumed that that was *her* right. They were both powerful and determined ladies with strong voices. As we put on our coats to leave, Plomer struggled to find a suitable comment.

'I think – yes, I'm sure – that this was the noisiest dinner party I have ever attended. The noise is what I shall remember.'

After the conference he made a sentimental journey to Pietersburg, where he had spent part of his now distant youth. What he heard there was not two shouting women but (in 'A Transvaal Morning') the 'two keen bird-notes' of 'a moss-green thrush'.

The strangeness plucked the stranger like a string.
'They say this constant sun outstares the mind,
Here in this region of the fang, the sting,
And dulls the eye to what is most defined.

'A wild bird's eye on the qui vive
Perhaps makes vagueness clear and staleness new;
If undeceived one might not then deceive;
Let me', he thought, 'attain the bird's-eye view.'

The only other head of a department at the Wits Conference who supported the cause of some South African literature in academia was Guy Haworth of U.C.T., an Australian. Unfortunately he went too far. He suggested a syllabus, which the prac. critters attacked with ill-concealed glee. I got into hot water. My concern that a child's geographical and historical environment should be present in some of the poems and stories studied at school was dismissed by one of Christina van Heyningen's young men as a passion for local colour. My riposte was uttered with a vigour which was perhaps excessive. At tea break, Christina was quivering with anger.

'I'm going to attack you!' she vowed.

She was as good as her word.

If I found it difficult to make any headway on the South African literature front with most of my professorial colleagues, I found it equally difficult to persuade my own staff to take it seriously. I managed to get occasional African items smuggled into the syllabus. Laurens van der Post's *Venture to the Interior* (1953) caused raised eyebrows, as did Joyce Cary's *Aissa Saved* (1954, '55, '56, '61) and *Mister Johnson* ('57, '58, '59). Joseph Conrad's *Heart* of *Darkness* encountered less resistance ('54,'55,'59,'62). I managed to get the following South African authors set, mainly for the first-years, during the first decade of my headship: Alan Paton's *Cry, the Beloved Country* ('60,'61); Olive Schreiner's *Story of an African Farm* ('54,'61,'62); H.C. Bosman's *Mafeking Road* ('53,'58,'59,'60); and Pauline Smith's *The Little Karoo* ('53,'62).

But it was uphill work. Even when one could advocate the inclusion of a South African work on its sheer merit, one had to persuade colleagues to provide the space and time for it by sacrificing some masterpiece from a long-established, almost sacred canon.

SPEECH AND DRAMA

My third abnormality as a Professor of English was a belief, encouraged by Professor Greig of Wits, that Elizabethan drama, and Shakespeare in particular, needed to be performed in order to be properly understood. I had no quarrel with the view that William Shakespeare was our greatest poet – that the sonnets alone can show. But when I read *Julius Caesar* as a schoolboy, I found I simply had to perform Antony rousing the Roman mob – comprised of my sulking school friends, with an equally reluctant younger brother playing Caesar's corpse, suitably provided with wounds inflicted by my big sister's lipstick. From then on I knew that Shakespeare wrote his words to be spoken by an actor doing something or other – like snatching a sheet off a wounded body, holding it up and pointing to the imaginary holes in it and crying:

See what a rent the envious Casca made:
Through this the well-beloved Brutus stabbed ...

So it is not surprising that the first Shakespeare play I produced was *Julius Caesar*. I knew it off by heart. It was performed in the open in 1951, in what is now the central quad of Rhodes University. It was my first full-scale production. I made the actors study Bertram Joseph's book on Elizabethan acting, with interesting results. The actors had to think about hand gestures and to work out sign language for themselves. While I did not ask for any great intensity or personal identification of actor and role, I did demand a clear understanding and articulation of the words, which in some cases led to a deeply felt speaking of the lines.

'A cool production', said Alan Hall, perceptive as usual. He called its action passionless, which nevertheless carried the audience along 'because the words of the best poet in the world are given priority and allowed to work on the minds of the audience without having (as so often happens) to fight against the facial or other antics of an emoting actor.'

Producers of plays in the open are sometimes rewarded with breathtaking bonuses by the weather. One night broken cloud came up, tumbling across a mysterious moon just at the right moment, and Casca and the man on the thunder-sheet could not have wished for better support during the storm scene. Things were less well-timed the next evening when it came on to drizzle while Antony was trying to rouse the fury of the Roman mob. This is difficult while the audience are putting on macs and opening umbrellas. Antony was an eloquent and bearded LL.B student. Our budget had not allowed for multiple-pleated robes and heavily draped togas. He had to make do with two threadbare sheets which the housekeeper had sold (or smuggled?) to our wardrobe mistress. The drizzle made these cling to his goose-pimpled flesh with an effect deleterious to senatorial dignity. At interval Professor Sampson (Law) demanded, through chattering teeth, whether I was determined to freeze his student to death.

I argued vehemently with critics who called Shakespeare's plays dramatic poems. They are poetic dramas, and there is a world of difference. A poem is something you read alone or recite to others in any suitable place. A play is something you watch and hear being performed by actors in public, usually in a building called a theatre. I was determined to get a proper theatre for Rhodes. Almost every year in the 'fifties and early 'sixties I produced a play – in the open, in the university's new Great Hall, or in the City Hall. I took them on tours through the Eastern Cape and Transkei from Umtata to Port Elizabeth. I was stage-struck. The fact that my own early plays never really took off was no deterrent.

By 1958 I was hovering between continuing to profess literature or switching to drama. So serious was I about this that I spent most of my Carnegie Travel Fellowship in America visiting drama schools. Subsequently I spent hours discussing drama departments with those South African pioneers, Elizabeth Sneddon of Durban, and Donald Inskip and Rosalie van der Gucht of U.C.T. When I went to Holland in 1960 I visited theatre and drama schools, and in Britain, the Bristol Drama School.

My fourth truancy from the study of the Great Tradition of English masterpieces was South African history, particularly the history of the Eastern Cape. (Some historians regarded me as trespassing.) To this I have devoted a separate, short chapter in which some attention is given to my use of history as a source for drama. That chapter will take greater liberties with time, and range to beyond the end of my teaching career.

15   1951–

High Corner

In the chapter 'A House and Two Chairs', I have given a brief description of High Corner and its history before we turned it into a home for ourselves and our four children. We adopted Patrick George (born 3 January 1953) and Charlotte Jane (11 March 1955). Within ten months of Jane's arrival Jean gave birth to a son, David Guy (10 June 1956). He was followed by Christopher Collett (3 April 1959).

This chapter will attempt to place High Corner in its setting. Then a few anecdotes might give an impression of how we lived.

Diagonally opposite to High Corner is the Drostdy Arch, a simple, unpretentious gateway built in 1842 to mark the end of the town and the start of the administrative and military headquarters of the Eastern Frontier. There are many architectural relics of the early 19th century beyond the arch – the Old Provost, a small prison with cells on a quadrant; a military graveyard; the former military hospital, now part of the Rhodes Department of Plant Sciences; a barracks for men of the garrison (the Department of Linguistics); two neat stone residences for the Commander and 2 i.c. (now Mathematics); the Headquarters of the Sappers (Political Science); and, farther west, the Old Cape Corps barracks (a students' residence). The centre piece had been the Old Drostdy, or Magistracy, built by none other than Piet Retief, on contracts which were unsatisfactory to all. It had not been well built. Most of this old area and its buildings had been acquired for Rhodes University College in 1904 and many of the early classes had been given in the old structures and in others built by the military during the Anglo–Boer War.

The master plan for the University came from the firm of Sir Herbert Baker, who had had the good sense to use the axis established by the Cathedral and the Drostdy Arch, and to place the University Tower and main block on the Old Drostdy itself. This involved demolishing the existing building, which was falling down anyway.

The area between the Drostdy and the Arch is known as the Drostdy Lawn or Grounds. This public space is owned by the University, who, however, may not build on it without the consent of the Municipality. The writ of the University runs as far as the Arch; thereafter the normal authorities that govern and misgovern our urban life take over. The Arch can suddenly become a frontier zone. It is the meeting place of Town and Gown. Through it generations of students have passed. I walk through it on average four times a day.

Before the students arrived, however, it was military terrain, and the lawns a parade ground. Old brass buttons, with regimental numbers and crests, sometimes work their way to the surface of lawns. I have picked up three in my time.

On either side of the Arch are rooms for the soldiers whose duty it was to guard the entry to the barrack area. I have a photograph of them lined up, all ten of them, their belts white with pipe clay.

The gateway is wide enough to take one vehicle only. In the 1930s it was still open to traffic. There was, however, no straight passage ahead to the tower (which was erected in 1936); instead it veered right diagonally across the lawn into Artillery Road.

It was a favourite prank of irresponsible students, secretly, silently, at dead of night, to manhandle a captured German field gun, a memento of the recent Allied triumph, from its position on the lawn hard by into the archway. Whose task was it to move it back? It belonged to the City Fathers not the University Council. (I believe the remnants of this piece have been acquired by the military museum in Johannesburg.)

On the opposite corner of High Street is 38 Somerset Street, a particularly fine old house, whose proportions seem perfect to me. It predates the double-storey portion of High Corner by half a century.

Here lived the Hobart Houghtons. He was Professor of Economics. We were sorry they had no children as we felt that, wherever our children got their bad language, they would not have got it from young Hobart Houghtons.

Desmond had acquired the place in the mid-1930s from an Advocate Starr-Stewart and his wife. Such is the reluctance of old Grahamstonians to accept new people that one is seldom known as the owner of the property one lives in; a house is often known by the name of the previous owner. So, although Desmond lived at No. 38 and the Starr-Stewarts had been absent for twenty or more years, old citizens, if asked where Professor Hobart Houghton lived, would say: 'In Advocate Starr-Stewart's house, on the corner.'

Desmond's father had been a school inspector in the old Transkei, and had had connections with both Lovedale and Fort Hare. It was through him that we met Professor Z.K. Matthews and his wife Frieda. This was the first time that Jean and I had met black people outside the master/servant relationship, apart from the Rev. James Calata of Cradock. They were exceptionally charming people who became our friends.

We were – and still are – lucky to live just across Somerset Street from the

Albany Museum, whose natural-history displays are a source of delight and enlightment to us all, but particularly to our children. And a little farther off are the Botanical Gardens to which the Governor of the day, Sir Harry Smith himself, headed the list of the contributors. (It is good to see this swashbuckling old frontier fire-eater displaying a cultivated interest for once.) 'Bots' is so close to High Corner as to serve as an extension of our garden. It also happens to be a park for the University itself. Jean and I went for our first walks together there. The other day she remarked to me, 'Do you realise that it is half a century since you first led me up this garden path?'

In the days of the directorship of Doctor Jacques Jacot-Guillarmod, there was a clump of wild banana trees in the front of the Museum, and a small fenced-in area. It contained a collection of large tortoises. The word 'collection' does not quite describe the ten tortoises, usually immobile, apparently asleep, except for one which might be seen to lift its enormous stone of a body on stiff wooden legs, and stagger a few steps before sinking to earth once more. That the remaining nine reptiles were not really dead was proved by the fact that they were in a different place each day, basking in the heat.

Our nursemaids loved the entertainment potential of those tortoises. Whenever the children were bored, they would be taken across the road with a cabbage stalk or other bit of garbage to feed the *Testudinae*. The children would squat on their hunkers perfectly content in front of a torpidity of tortoises. The maid waved the leaf like a magic wand in whose powers her belief was minimal. By some miracle a head would emerge from between scaly legs, a head that was almost like a snake's, but not so flat, with a parroty sort of a beak. At this point the children would freeze into an immobility which matched that of the remaining reptiles. No excitement can be greater at the age of 4–6 than to be holding one end of a cabbage stalk while a tortoise opens its toothless jaws and flings its head forward on to the edge of it, closes them, and cuts, or rather chops and rips, a chunk of greenness for itself.

At some time the Albany Museum decided that tortoises should not be kept in captivity. This humane step was taken without consulting the public or even informing them, let alone explaining the sudden disappearance from the lives of the people of upper High Street of these objects of interest and love.

'What has happened to our tortoises?' Suspicion and speculation took hold of the bereaved children.

Dr Jacot-Guillarmod confessed to me that he was expert at handling accusations of all sorts of misdemeanours, but he found it difficult to handle this one. As he emerged from the Museum he was confronted by three accusatory children.

'Why did you eat our tortoises?'

They were rightly suspicious of the omnivorous species to which they found they belonged.

The vacuum left by the disappearance of the tortoises was kindly filled by three bantams – two cocks and a hen – brought by Dolly Bowker to brighten our lives.

They were a nine-day wonder with the children. Well no, nine days is too long for any child's wonder to last. It is too intense a flame to live that long. But for three days, maybe four, those birds were fed and watered to excess. Then Violet Ngqia had to care for them. They took to getting through the split-pole fence. Dr Ron Wylde, of the firm that had succeeded Dr Dru Drury, said, mildly, that neither he nor his patients were fussy people but that medical examinations are best conducted without the beady-eyed participation of bantam cocks, pretty and pert as they were.

So the children were warned that the frontier had to be observed and all holes in the fence filled in. Interest in the birds flared and then flagged. Then the bantams started eating the young lettuce plants.

'Violet,' said Jean, 'will you take these birds away with you? I don't want you to eat them.'

'I will take them to my place in Peddie,' she said.

The birds vanished as if they had never been part of our lives. Or so it seemed.

It was a lovely, still autumn day, and the Wylde's gardener decided he would burn weeds in their strip of garden. The weeds were rather damp. The smell of fire was pervasive; a wisp of smoke rose into the blue from beyond the split-pole fence.

Dr Wylde's receptionist had great difficulty in persuading the children that she could not give them an appointment with the doctor and that only grown-ups could arrange appointments. Not to be defeated, they went down the lane and presented themselves at the open exit door to his consulting-room. Like the director of the Museum, he was accused:

'You killed and ate our cocks!'

'No, I did not,' said the doctor.

'Yes, you did. We saw the smoke.'

'What smoke?'

'Where you cooked them.'

The doctor left his surgery, and they pointed to the smouldering fire.

'Yes,' said Ron, 'there's the fire. But where are the feathers? You can't kill and cook a cock without leaving feathers.'

They came home only half convinced of the innocence of our neighbours. Then they forgot the mystery of the disappearance of the bantams for ever, though not the bantams themselves.

Our children's friends were drawn from a wide geographical area, so it was difficult to trace the source of some of their expressions. After overhearing the terrible language which they flung at each other during one of their not-infrequent fights, Jean and I decided that enough was enough. We lectured them on bad language. We said polite children from decent homes did not use such language, that we never did, that we were ashamed to think what our friends must think. They were to stop going to play at the police cottages down Somerset Street forthwith.

'It's too late, Ma,' said Patrick.

'What do you mean, too late?'

'They are not allowed to play with us any more.'

'Why?'

'We flook too much.'

The bad-language crisis passed and converse was resumed, but on a lesser scale. Jane reported that the gaoler was leaving, on promotion, to go to the prison at Kroonstad.

We had seen so many bad reports in the press about the treatment of prisoners that we had distanced ourselves even farther. So when Jane broke the news, Jean said, 'Well, that'll be good riddance.'

But Violet Ngqia said: 'Oh no, Mam, that gaoler, he is a good man. The location will cry when he goes.'

Suddenly we were given a glimpse of how important for the location the good running of a gaol is: it affects a far higher proportion of blacks than whites, not because blacks are less moral than whites, but because discriminatory laws and poverty inevitably increase crime.

When Jean heard Violet's testimonial for the gaoler, she asked Jane when they'd be leaving. That evening some time. Having walked into Somerset Street and seen a pantechnicon being packed with their household goods, Jean sent across a tray of tea and scones and an invitation to lunch.

I was naturally a little taken aback when I returned for lunch to find the gaoler and his entire family making themselves at home.

Jean and I both learned, fast, about the many ways in which a gaoler and his wife can make a major difference to the lives of their charges without breaking the regulations. We experienced what we had known in theory: that every necessary task in society is important and those who perform it deserve our respect; we were also touched to learn that the prison service has its pride, and its own high professional standards and goals. (In normal gaols prisoners do not slip on soap and break their necks in showers or feel obliged to jump out of high windows. These things seem to happen only when the Security Branch are in control.) And I recalled the scene in *Measure for Measure* in which the hangman refused to accept Pompey the pimp as an apprentice because he would be a disgrace to his profession.

We had expected them to leave at sunset, but they stayed on until 10.30 p.m.

Later the gaol was moved to new premises out at Waai Nek, but the cottages are still used by the police for a variety of purposes.

My most paradoxical prisoner friend was Wellington. I was restoring an old house in George Street and wrestling to uproot an ancient laurel hedge when Wellington offered his services. He was a powerful young man, ugly, cheerful, overweight (as I myself usually am) and a vigorous worker. We got on well. At the end of a week he said he would be absent on Monday because he had to appear in court. The charge? He shrugged his shoulders, and said, 'Murder.'

I had never spoken to a possible murderer before and looked at him incredulously.

'Whom did you kill?'

'My girl-friend.'

A *crime passionel*, it seemed. He had loved her and she had betrayed him.

On Monday I was naturally surprised to find him slogging away, uprooting a lantana, recently declared a noxious weed.

'Wellington, why are you not in court?'

He had decided not to go to court, because this was a matter which the white man did not understand and should leave alone. Let his own Xhosa people deal with him, let the girl's brothers and uncles come. And he grinned, relishing the prospect. I remonstrated, and explained that he was making his case worse by not going to court when summoned. Contempt of court was a serious matter.

He shrugged and said, 'The girl was my own girl, and the knife was my own knife.'

He was not at work the next day. I concluded that he had been arrested. A day later Violet Ngqia reported that Wellington's grandmother was waiting to see me under the vine – the pergola in our garden. There sat a neat, small Xhosa lady, beautifully turned out in turban and shawl, who had spent her entire working life in the kitchens of St Andrew's College. She wished to explain the case of her grandson, Wellington. He was always too clever and quick. Her other grandsons were not so smart and didn't get into so much trouble. The trouble started at school where he lost patience with the stupid teachers, and they with him. And now, this murder. His parents had long since given him up, and in any case had no money to get legal help. But she wanted a lawyer to look after him in court.

To cut a long story short, I paid for a lawyer, who eventually got the charge changed to manslaughter. He was sentenced to gaol for – was it six or was it eight years? But before the trial he was remanded in custody.

I received a letter from him – the first of many. He thanked me for the lawyer, but reported that the lawyer was no good. Would a good lawyer allow a man to spend Christmas in prison? Surely not. Moreover would I allow him, Wellington, to spend Christmas in prison? Surely not. Prison was no place in which to spend Christmas. I wrote explaining that I could not secure his release and sent him my Christmas wishes and good luck in the new year.

Stanley Xaba worked in the Rhodes Library and became a member of the old Liberal Party. We were all outraged and surprised when he was arrested and imprisoned during the first emergency.

Years later, after his release from Robben Island, he came to see us. Jean asked him which was the grimmest prison – Grahamstown or Fort Glamorgan in East London?

'No doubt; Grahamstown. So old. So cold. I could hear your children shouting from morning to night. That was the only good thing about Grahamstown prison, the sound of your children outside.'

The piece of my own handiwork of which I am most fond – our dining-room table – came to be made in this fashion.

The old Deanery – a pleasant building dating, I suspect, from the 1830s or before – was demolished to make room for the present St George's Chambers. The timber throughout had been yellowwood. The floorboards were not much use, but the ceilings – eleven-inch (28 cm) boards – were sufficiently good for the contractor to use as scaffolding. I've forgotten the stages in the negotiations but he let me have the boards for the current price of new South African pine scaffolding.

The boards were long – some twelve feet.

'Jean, what size do you want your table?'

'Big.'

'How big?'

'Long, and not too wide.'

'I need a little more detail than that.'

So I laid the boards on the lawn.

Two boards – too narrow.

Five boards – too wide.

Eventually we found the right width; about three feet.

Length was more difficult to determine. Jean wanted twelve feet. In my view this was too long. My workshop – the old converted tanning pit – could not handle twelve feet.

'Then make it somewhere else.'

'Where?'

'Where you made the staircase – the big room.'

Before sawing those planks we tried them for size on the spot, and found the optimum length, eleven feet – until Jean put the parrot cage at one end and the serving table at the other. But that is another story.

I pirated the stinkwood legs from a table I found in an auctioneer's store in Port Elizabeth. The borer-beetle had turned the yellowwood top to dust and the stringers had holes like bubbles in sponge rubber, but they had not touched the stinkwood legs. Eleven feet was a long span but I reinforced the side members with flooring on edge. I patched the nail holes as best I could, then sanded the top, but not so much that the surface lost the slight undulations left by some old craftsman wielding a block plane way back in the 1830s.

For breakfast, now, Jean and I sit in the middle of the table, opposite each other, three feet apart. For dinner parties we sit opposite each other, at the table ends, eleven feet apart, and have occasionally to shout over the heads of the eight or ten or even twelve guests who separate us.

At one of the earliest of our parties we decided to try to raise the ghost of one, William Tarrant, who had 'left the club on 30th April 1864'. We know this because he had scratched this fact with a diamond on one of the window-panes. While I was proposing a toast to Mr Tarrant, and invoking him to rise, the table started moving in an ominous way, so much so that it threatened to spill the cold consommé.

'That's enough now, Griff!' said Lou Mullins.

And Griff, the Headmaster of St Andrew's Prep., crawled out from under the table.

To revert to the old Deanery Chambers. It had a courtyard with a rose garden whose paths were tiled with old, large, yellow Grahamstown tiles and smaller reds. I asked the contractor what he wanted for them. A penny each, he said. This seemed a fair price.

The entrance to High Corner for many years was off Somerset Street, through an existing entrance in the old stone-wall, from which I laid a brick path up to the main entrance. On the left of this protruded a new addition which contained the bathrooms. Farther east, in due course, came another addition, the new kitchen which took up the width of the old verandah and a few feet of the garden. Diagonally opposite was the old stone building, reputedly the tannery, which I used as a workshop.

I decided to provide a pergola in the area defined by the bathrooms, the main building and a change of levels in line with the junction of the single and double stories, and spent many happy hours building square stone columns out of the piles of rubble which the old garden produced. When Father George Sidebottom, C.R., spent a holiday with us he made a willing apprentice. The catawba grape vine soon covered the timber superstructure with shade and sweetness in summer. This area, under and beyond the pergola, I covered with a checkerboard of old yellow and red tiles.

It has served a variety of useful purposes. In good weather we often have breakfast under the vine. I sometimes write there, or do small bits of marquetry. It is generally cooler than the workshop.

I also used to give classes, or rather tutorials, under the vine, to my own students. Some of the most memorable were with an African matriculant who asked for help with his set books. One was a work by Laurens van der Post, which gives a moving account of the sufferings of the golden San at the hands of both blacks and whites. On one occasion Abel felt compelled to utter a general preface to his answers which gave my heart a lift: his acceptance of our joint responsibility was so frank. 'Sir, I must say something. It is a terrible thing your people and my people did to these people.'

It was also a place for meeting poor people and sometimes making friends of them. They would wait under the vine until one or other of us appeared from either the front door or the kitchen, when we would listen to a variety of sad stories, most of which began, 'Sir, I have this problem.'

No day seemed to pass without its problem. Eventually it got known that we had been forced to harden our hearts and could only consider educational problems. We could not help with hire purchases, litigation, rents, marital problems, or transport to Uitenhage. On one or two special occasions I found myself paying for coffins and food for funeral feasts, and for the ceremonies that go with male initiation.

For instance, a widow of about 45, who worked in Rondebosch, somehow cast me in the role of the senior male responsible for her son who was about to come back from the bush.

'They go to the bush as boys, they come back as men,' she explained.

'Yes,' I said.

'Before they come back their old clothes must be burnt. They must meet the world as new men in new clothes.'

'Yes,' I said.

The symbolism was quite clear to both of us. Our difficulty arose over the definition of the word 'new' clothes – new to the young man, or new from the shop? She thought the latter; but I explained I had just had to buy new school clothes for three of my own sons and simply couldn't afford the complete list she had produced. And I said – and felt – that I had made a mistake in expanding my definition of education to include initiation. For her part she was disappointed in me. People had told her that I was an understanding man and would see to the needs of her son. Did I really want him to 'come out' in secondhand clothes when all the other members of the 'school' came out in new kit? I explained that the secondhand clothes I had in mind were in fair condition. Would she like to see them? She would. Her face brightened. With them she would do a deal with her brother (who ought to have been paying anyway), and make him buy the new kit for her son as a *quid pro quo*.

Sometime in August 1956, we were due to go to dinner at the Altys, the Vice-Chancellor of Rhodes and his wife. Jean came back from tennis saying she had a bad headache or a cold coming on but was prepared to go through with it. I had the good sense to insist that she go to bed.

The next morning she could not move her legs. I am slow in my reactions, but knew that we were in deep trouble. The doctors were not sure what it was – meningitis? Polio? It did not seem to matter much as the symptoms could be so similar.

The medical officer of health called and said that he wished to determine which, and to do this he would have to do a lumbar puncture – by which he could extract fluid from the spine, and get it analysed.

As a radiographer Jean knew about lumbar punctures and had described the painful operation to me. So I asked the M.O.H. to come downstairs to discuss the matter.

'Will the information you get from the lumbar puncture make any difference to the treatment of my wife?'

'No.'

'Then why do you want to do it?'

'M.O.H.'s regulations require that I should report fully on certain diseases. I need to know for the record.'

I told him as politely as I could that I would not have my wife, who was in pain enough, subjected to a lumbar puncture merely to secure a piece of information which would not affect her treatment. So he left, and the medical records of our country are incomplete. *Mea culpa.*

With Jean paralysed from the waist down, I had to run the household as best I could, and care for three children – Patrick, Jane and the baby, David. Fortunately we got the services of the excellent Sister Wigley, who took charge of the baby, and helped with Jane and Patrick.

By dint of great courage and determination, expert care and a régime of exercises, Jean gradually recovered the use of her legs. It was a very great day indeed when, a hand on the banister, an arm round my waist, she tottered down the stairs for the baptism of the baby. We invited a crowd of friends into the big room where John Hodson, the Dean, christened him David (my choice) and Guy (Jean's). Patrick sat on the landing with his legs and face between banisters, with stern instructions to keep his arms and elbows behind same.

Then, on pleasant days, Jean would venture into the garden, gradually gaining strength and confidence. At last, on sticks, accompanied by Sister Wigley, she tackled a walk as far as the bank or the post office.

Sister Wigley having left, we regularly all climbed into the car – a duck-blue, two-door Opel Rekord – and explored the minor radial roads round Grahamstown. I remember an enchanted day on the Grobler's Kloof road, stopping the car to watch – and listen to – tok-tokkie beetles. How glossy black they were, how busy darting about, pausing, banging their resonating bellies on to the hard, dry earth, listening a second and then dashing off again: high summer when the fever of life seemed both hectic and happy.

I believe that all people should have intimate experience of the three conditions through which they themselves must move – childhood, parenthood, and old age; but it is an experience which tells hardest on the youngish parent, who is between the generations with responsibility towards both and demands from both.

While Jean was recovering from polio I decided to convert the old club buttery into an American kitchen for her. It was a trying business because I had too much help from Patrick and Jane. Jane was a particularly eager *handlanger*. As soon as I picked up a hammer she regarded it as her responsibility to hand me something, anything for my free hand. To complicate matters my father visited us briefly at that time. He had taught me everything I know about handicrafts, but it was soon clear to him that I had forgotten how to do the simplest thing as it ought to be done.

I was lying on my back, trying to drill a hole in the underside of a shelf fixed to the wall. When working alone one can let off the steam of frustration by cursing aloud; but I could not behave naturally when caught between my father, in his best suit ready for church, towering above me, saying, 'You'll never get it right; you've chosen the wrong bit', and my daughter Jane, in a damp crawler, deciding that what I needed was a tomato, thrusting it in my line of vision – a leaky tomato too.

On Jean's father's death in 1962, her mother came to live with us at High Corner, in a flat which we built for her in the older dormer rooms above the oldest portion of the property, the Messenger's Cottage.

On a characteristic, generous impulse Jean handed High Corner garden over to her. With the assistance of the dignified and patient Sam Mkizi, a gentleman of the Old School, she transformed the place into a visual delight to us and to her many friends.

But, alas, small children differ from old ladies and are not capable of respecting flowers. A garden is a place for playing in; shrubs, bushes and plants are there to provide hiding-places for the setting of ambushes, for a simulated dragon's den or a tropical jungle through which explorers have to cut their way by tearing down lianas or swinging from branch to branch across imagined torrents.

Between Grannie and her grandchildren there developed a war of territorial imperatives. Jean was caught in the crossfire. Of the children, Christopher, the youngest, was the most acutely aware that the arrival of Grannie had changed his wild paradise into her tidy garden. He found a little relief behind the stockade among the stakes and on the compost heap, or in constructing, with the help of hordes of other grannie-afflicted little boys and girls, a tree house in the large flowering peach tree in the stockade. He also took to walking along the tops of the old stone boundary walls and on the roof of the workshop where Grannie's writ did not run. The sight of him aloft did nothing for his parents' nerves.

The Satchwells – Jean's brother Murray's family from Port Elizabeth –

tell a story of arriving on a visit. The eldest, Kathleen, and four brothers, got out of the car, bouncing a soccer ball, ready for a game after being cooped up for almost two hours. As they approached the Somerset Street gate they were saluted by a small boy with blond hair and blue eyes sitting astride the high boundary wall on to Somerset Street. In his best Eastern Cape accent he said:

'Be careful in the gorden or my Grennie will grouse you!'

By slow stages the war spread from the garden to the interior of the house. Mrs Satchwell was no different from other grannies in her conviction that her daughter had much to learn as a housekeeper and did not know how to bring up her children. She was, of course, very fond of them and vied with Jean in spoiling them.

Jean was working at the time at the municipal clinic as a radiographer, helping to eke out my salary. She would come home, exhausted, to be mobbed by her children with requests, complaints and mutual recriminations, then last-minute decisions about lunch for Violet Ngqia; Sam's lunch; and, of course, her mother eager to catch up with the day's events or to deliver advice about the running of the household.

Coward that I am, I tried to keep a low profile, sinking out of sight into a chair to read the *Eastern Province Herald* while Jean, Grannie, and Violet sorted out the daily crises.

I have forgotten the point at issue. Mrs Satchwell was complaining of the behaviour of the children during lunch time. Before Jean could answer the charge I heard Christopher speak with amazing authority for a small boy of 4 or 5. I looked up and he was staring straight at his tall, stooping grandparent.

'Grennie,' he said, 'you may be boss in the gorden. You're not boss in the house.'

Our neighbours on the town side, the changing constellation of doctors, were long-suffering and only once did diplomatic relations reach breaking point. This was over a question of noise; or rather what the doctors chose to call noise and what Christopher, now an undergraduate, assured me was music, the best in the world.

Both Jean and I are very fond of 'classical' music, our only differences being on questions of volume. If a genius writes for four North Country choirs, two symphony orchestras and five brass bands it is clear that many of his intended effects will be lost if played pianissimo. Such a work is Sir William Walton's 'Belshazzar's Feast'. Jean maintains that I confuse High Corner with the Royal Albert Hall. Admittedly the playing of it compels the children to leave the house, and the servants to polish the silver in the farthest corner of the garden.

Christopher cannot read music but he has an ear for rhythm, for drums. He acquired a set of these and without my permission turned my workshop

The garden gate, High Corner

– an isolated room in the middle of the garden – into a rehearsal room. Here his fellow maestros would gather, with electric guitars. To judge by the decibels they emitted, they must have used several kilowatts per session, but such is parental affection that I never even raised the question of costs, although once or twice it did occur to me to manipulate a power failure.

All would have been well if the group had kept regular rehearsal hours – after the Museum had closed up for the day, or the last patient had left the consulting-rooms. But we all know the not-to-be-denied demands of youth and musical genius.

The first sign of trouble came from the Museum across the road.

'By the way,' said one of the scientific staff to me at a cocktail party. 'Congratulations on your band.'

'My band?'

'Come off it, Professor. You're known as Grahamstown's wizard drummer.'

'That's my son, not me.'

'Well, he sure is a hot drummer! When he gets going our cleaners dance with their brooms and buckets up and down the stairs like a Marxist ballet. And the doorman swears the mummy in its case is trying to jive!'

I relayed this tale in a lighthearted way to Christopher over lunch the next day. He pretended to be amused.

'Yes, I've heard about the mummy dancing itself free of its bandages. Ha, ha, ha!'

One could laugh off the Museum and its musical mummy, but our neighbours, the doctors, were another matter. Dr Evans had inherited the rooms of Dr Wylde, who had experienced difficulty with our bantams about twelve years previously. He felt obliged to interrupt one of the rehearsals with a mild request:

'I wonder if you chaps would mind turning your guitars down a bit?'

'Okay, Doctor. Chaps, turn your guitars down a bit.'

Two patients later.

'Hi. Please turn you guitars down. I can't hear my patients and they can't hear me.' This appeal to reason resulted in a rescheduling of rehearsal times.

Once Jean and I had installed the staircase in High Corner and built on bathrooms upstairs and downstairs, and converted the billiard-room into a spare bedroom and a dining-room, and the buttery/bar into a kitchen, we found we had more space than we knew what to do with or furnish. We knew this would change once children appeared. In the meantime, we gave hospitality to clergy in need of a rest – particularly to members of the Community of the Resurrection. As an order working mainly in the townships and mission field, we saw them as the church's frontline troops in the apparently hopeless battle against the apartheid government. If they needed a little break, Jean would welcome and spoil these missionary ascetics shamelessly. Her 'priest hole' won many friends whose lives kept them in close touch with black South Africa in a rare way. Our closer friends among them were Dominic Whitnall, Martin Jarrett-Kerr, Maurice Bradshaw, George Sidebottom, and Aelred Stubbs.

For several years the Community ran a house at the ecumenical non-racial Federal Theological Seminary at Alice – until the whole property, by a shameless act of piracy, was expropriated by the Government and handed over to the University of Fort Hare, which was now confined to Xhosa speakers, whereas it had once been a university for all Africans. The fathers sometimes brought friends from the seminary staff with them, including a roly-poly lecturer with a bright eye and ready laugh called Desmond Tutu, and his wife Leah.

Before our children arrived we used the smallest of the rooms upstairs as a private chapel, where Jean and I used to say Compline regularly, sometimes joined by a visiting father who felt in duty bound to keep up with this earnest young couple. On one occasion, during provincial synod,

I think, we put up the Bishop of George, John Hunter, and his wife. He is reported to have said that he enjoyed the synod except for the extra time he had to put into devotions at High Corner – 'All that Compline!' he sighed.

When the children started arriving, the monks came less frequently, but did not disappear from the scene. A favourite was Aelred Stubbs, a charming, elongated Etonian devoted to the cause of black consciousness, and a great admirer of its leader, Steve Biko. Like many of his order, Aelred was somewhat restless within it – trying his vocation as a hermit in various places, including Masite in Basutoland. He was so disliked by our government that he was not allowed to return to South Africa at the end of a period of leave. He is now in Sunderland at a hermitage called Emmaus. Aelred had a predisposition to believe that in South Africa at least, things that were black were more likely to be beautiful than things that were white. He certainly knew far more than I did about the sufferings and indignities inflicted by the white apartheid system.

Jean loved spoiling these tired men, and Aelred in particular loved being spoiled. As the spare bedroom was upstairs, this could be quite taxing on Jean. It became clear that among the constituents most appreciated by Aelred in Jean's attentions were the domestic appointments, which no doubt satisfied, a little, his nostalgia for the elegant life he had sacrificed when becoming a monk. On one occasion he had been stopped by the police, taken to the cells, stripped and interrogated. On his release, he arrived at High Corner exhausted and said: 'I'll take a quick bath, dear, and go straight to bed. But a cup of tea would be heaven.'

Jean stopped acting as a peacekeeping force among the warring children in the garden and rushed upstairs with a tray of tea. Aelred, looking like an El Greco mystic on his deathbed, frowned slightly and said, '*Not* a kitchen teapot, dear?!'

So Jean dashed downstairs, and brought out the silver teapot. In her haste to retrieve lost time, she fell on the upstairs landing, with a great crash. 'Oh, what a *dreary* noise!' came the voice from the spare room.

Aelred, in his monk's minimal baggage, always found place for a pair of very elegant bright-red slippers, for evening wear. We delighted in his way of relaxing with a tumbler of whisky on the rocks.

In the 'sixties and 'seventies he organised what became known as holy parties of between twelve and twenty people of different races and denominations, up at St Patrick's, Hogsback, in a house left to the diocese by Hobart Houghton senior. Jean and I were invited to attend two of these. Beautiful mountain settings are good for such meetings. I count them as among the more important gatherings of my life. I have a photograph of several of us climbing Gaika's Kop – among them Michael Nuttall, Barney Pityana and W.D. Wilson. Professor Monica Wilson would come up from 'Hunterstoun' to join certain of our sessions.

High Corner in 1980, by Walter Battiss

How does one intimate the importance of such almost secret, catacomb meetings of so diverse a group in a society whose government regarded racial diversity as a principle sacred to God and whose police had to ensure that what He had separated no presumptuous man or priest should join together?

For instance, it was not permissible for a white householder to have a black guest stay more than 48 hours in his house without special permission from the magistrate. When Father Leo Rakale came to stay we conveniently forgot and broke the barbarous law. With touching care for the safety of the régime the Special Branch used to keep a kindly eye on High Corner, taking down the numbers of cars parked outside.

Jean and I are fortunate in sharing many interests and tastes, and High Corner has the wall and floor space to permit us to indulge them within the limits of our budget and the generosity of our parents. Most of our Persian carpets were gifts from Jean's mother, and a wonderful set of amari plates. From The Poplars came many 'crocks', decorative plates and vases; and from each parental home some of the best pictures we have.

We both like old yellow-wood and stinkwood country furniture, and were fortunate enough to exercise this fondness before prices rose beyond our reach. Not only did we visit the local auctioneer's sales rooms regularly, but we broke our car journeys to Cape Town or elsewhere to smouse around second-hand and antique shops in towns and dorps en route. One develops an eye for period furniture, and can pick out an old piece in a mountain of mass-produced, tasteless reproductions.

On one occasion we returned with the roofrack of our car laden with legs and backs of half a dozen broken stinkwood chairs which an auctioneer in Oudtshoorn let me have for a song, as they were 'only fit for firewood'. They presented a nice challenge. In due course, four good chairs emerged from the workshop and I still use remaining fragments of that stinkwood for marquetry. We had friends in distant villages and towns on the lookout for items we wanted. For instance we needed six chairs for the long dining-room table I had made. Marie Biggs found these for us in Graaff-Reinet – a source of other treasures.

One of the characteristics of our décor is the unashamed use of large posters, many very fine reproductions of great houses or other sites close to London, produced by London Transport, or historical collages by the British Travel and Holidays Association, or large reproductions of works of art from cities like Florence; but more especially posters of plays which I have produced myself (mainly Shakespeare) or written, or in which one or more of the family has acted; and also posters of the Grahamstown Festival.

There are three specially large posters, which were the start of the collection. They were given to me in 1960 by the director of the Rotterdamse Toneel when I was on a wonderful visit to Holland. (I was very impressed by their season of Chekhov.) I posted them to Jean; on my return I found that she had backed the one of *De Misantroop of De Verliefde Swartkyker* (Wynberg 1958) and hung it over the mantelpiece in the big room. It did not stay there for long. The staircase wall had large damp stains on it, the old lime plaster having deteriorated during a century of exposure. To hide these unsightly blemishes, large posters were ideal, and we liked the unusual effect. Even when we had the wall replastered on the outside and waterproofed, we reserved it for posters – with a bit of our personal history in each of them.

While we are very fond of collecting quite specific articles or objects, we do not claim to be collectors. We have enjoyed, at various times, keen interests in, for instance, Staffordshire figurines – particularly named figures – an infection we caught from Guy Stringer in the early 'fifties, and which we had to stop when prices rose beyond our reach. We also collected pairs of Staffordshire dogs. (My mother did not approve – they were not appropriate in a professor's house. In her girlhood in Staffordshire they were for 'the working people'.) Our neighbours, the Hobart Houghtons,

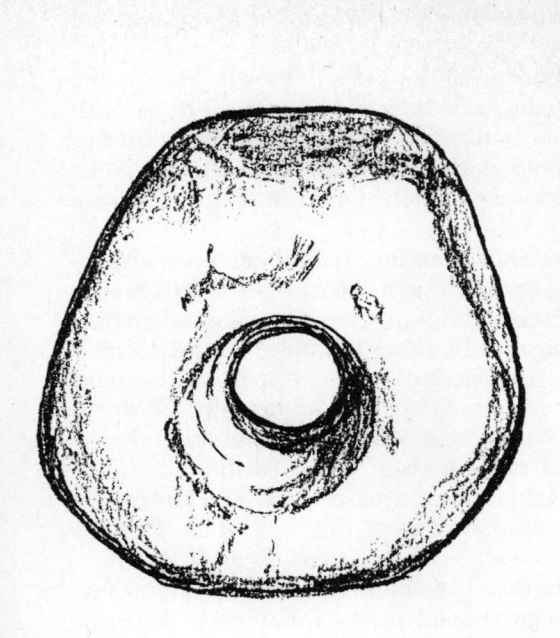

'Bushman' stones

kept golden cocker spaniels, with appropriate names like Bracken. Quite unaware of the fact that we had returned from a trip overseas with a very handsome pair of Staffordshire spaniels with lustre patches on their ears, Betty Hobart Houghton remarked on how much she wished she possessed a pair. Without a moment's hesitation, Jean gave them to her.

At the opposite extreme from brightly coloured 19th-century human figurines are my bored stones, of various sizes and sober colours – beautifully shaped by millions of years in river beds or long-since shifted shores, searched for, and found by a 'Bushman', or, more likely, Bush woman, and then patiently pierced by boring with a harder stone (they had no metals) from either side. It is generally believed that these gentle spherical forms, without a cutting edge to them, were used for digging. A fire-hardened stick is wedged into the hole, and the stone, gripped in both palms, provides both a comfortable handle and additional weight to lend power to the impact. No one can date these stones. Once made, they are indestructible. Unlike metal tools they do not rust. I hold them in my hand and wonder at the palms that first chose and bored them, and all the succeeding inheritors who used them. What bulbs and other roots, with what juices, did they unearth, for what lips talking about what? Over what distances had they migrated? Where were the bones of the hands that had handled them?

Our magpie propensities did not go unnoticed – Jeff's wife, Val, on one of their visits from the States, remarked: 'Why do you fill your house with all this jazz? You don't need it, man!' And Peggy, Jean's sister, on her annual visit from Swaziland, would say: 'My Gawd, Jean, it looks more like a junk shop every year.' Others were kinder. 'One can feel it's a house that's got people living in it.'

High Corner has been, and is, enormous fun. It has been most accommodating – initially contracting (by turning the Messenger's Cottage into a separate flat) when we were without children, then expanding when they arrived, and then contracting again when they left. Recently we decided to leave our living quarters upstairs overlooking the upper garden, oaks and jacarandas, and to move downstairs (before we actually fell down them!) into the re-incorporated Messenger's Cottage. This meant changing the entry, which had been off Somerset Street, to the old 'Club' entrance off High Street. It was while adding a master bedroom downstairs that we unearthed a rusty bridle dating from the days when Thomas Stubbs lived here.

But it is impossible to do more than provide these glimpses of how this habitation has shaped, and been shaped by, its inhabitants since we acquired it in 1951. One would need a long book to do justice to the various family gatherings and feasts in which garden and house worked beautifully together: Christmas and birthday parties for young and old; christenings; weddings; funerals; homecomings; farewells; graduations; cast parties; literary seminars; political discussions; and, most memorably, two parties to celebrate our golden wedding.

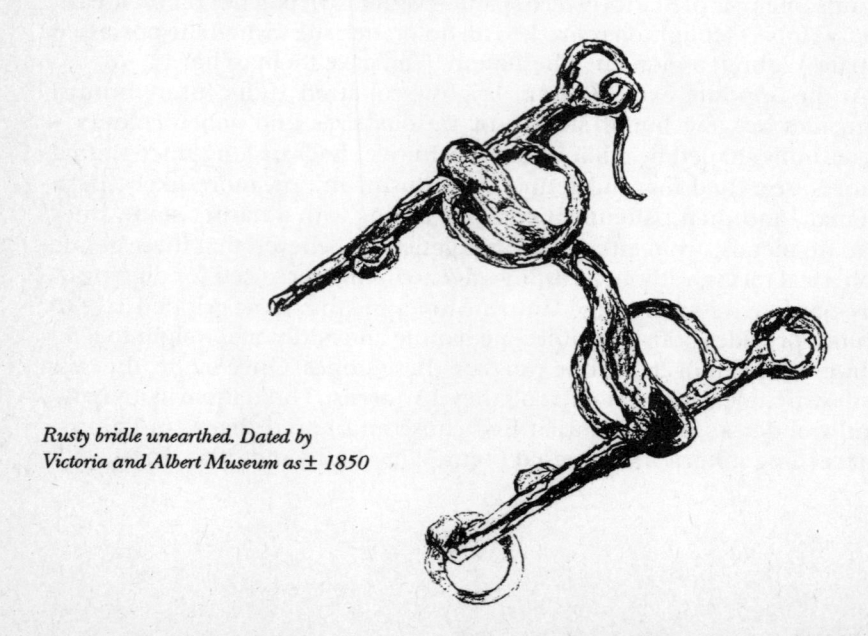

Rusty bridle unearthed. Dated by Victoria and Albert Museum as ± 1850

16 1950–60

Early Playwriting

Charles Eglington told me of competition for a play on a South African theme: the prize was to be five hundred pounds, with the possibility of a production during the forthcoming celebrations to mark the tercentenary of the landing of Jan van Riebeeck at the Cape (1652–1952). The five hundred pounds would be welcome of course, but it was the prospect of a production that attracted me. I had already grasped that one of the main snags in the path of a would-be playwright was actually to get the play performed. I had yet to learn that a bad production can be worse than no production at all.

The germ of the plot was Uncle Frank Biggs's building of the big dam on Vrede, but I changed it radically. Uncle Frank had not lived to see his dam complete and much of the final drama fell on the shoulders of his son John and Uncle Boy Vorster. I devised an entirely different ending. I altered the characters, invented others, took all the liberties I thought I needed and introduced two coloured servants. To help with the evocation of the Karoo setting of mountains and thunderstorms, I employed a lyrical chorus. I poured many of my current political and religious preoccupations into the work.

I had posted it a week before the closing date, 31 December 1950, and promptly forgot about it. The move to Grahamstown was absorbing all my attention.

At Rhodes in 1951, what I had written caught up with me. I have already mentioned that my play, *The Dam*, had won the five hundred pounds first prize in the national playwriting competition.

Early in January 1952 I flew to the Cape for consultations in Somerset West with Marda Vanne who was to produce *The Dam* for the National Theatre Organisation.

I went straight from Cape Town to Somerset West on a milk train. The coach was almost empty, so I could move from side to side to enjoy views of both the sea and the Hottentots Holland mountains. The only other passenger was one of the saddest wrecks of a man I had ever seen, middle-aged, with a shock of dirty white hair, ice-blue irises burning coldly in blood-red eyeballs and jaws without teeth, nervously chewing interminably on nothing.

The hotel at Somerset West was of the too common variety where the proprietor was interested only in its liquor licence. The hotel was run down and dirty, and the linoleum in the upstairs passage which led to my remote room was striped with little drifts of sea-sand which the south-easter had blown in through the ill-fitting doors and windows.

The ménage of Marda Vanne and Gwen Ffrangcon-Davies was everything the hotel was not; it was charming and tasteful. I was in awe of these two professionals who had spent almost a lifetime on the boards, particularly of Gwen who was volatile and imaginative. Marda was earthy and shrewd.

The teacups tinkled as we talked local theatre gossip. Gradually, via the possible casting of the play, we moved to the play itself and the points they wished to discuss. They had done their homework thoroughly and they cut me down to size by jocularly pointing out that in one place I had left a character on stage long after he ought to have left it, and that in another instance I had given a speech to a character who had not yet appeared.

'How odd,' I said. 'Must be my typist!'

'Sure,' said Marda, all charm, blowing a smoke-ring.

Then came the first big hurdle. The cast was too large. The National Theatre Organisation could not cope with so many. Ten was the outside limit. Why ten? The N.T.O. actors' bus could take ten and no more. The size of the cast could not exceed the seating capacity of the bus.

Could I not cut the chorus of two voices, male and female? suggested Gwen. It would of course be a pity, as the verse spoke well and it did evoke the Karoo setting of the farm. But, added Marda, it threw into high relief how un-Karoo-like my characters were. Karoo farmers do not speak blank verse, they don't know much about Freud and are generally reluctant to reveal their inner minds. I thought of replying that English kings did not speak blank verse, had never heard of Tudor political ideology, and would never have dreamt of opening their hearts to their barons, yet Shakespeare had made them do all of these things.

Instead I went for precedent to the Greeks and to Sartre's *The Flies*, which I suspect had encouraged me to be bloody, bold and resolute, and take on the cosmos. If the super-ego, the id, Christian ideas of love, Karoo ecology, the bitter legacy of the Anglo–Boer War, liberal idealism and black housing made odd dramatic bedfellows, they would surely shake down together in a good production. I had great confidence in the unifying power of images when launched by rhythmical speech. I was deeply indebted to T.S. Eliot for my convictions as to the transforming and subliming qualities of poetry in the theatre, but it was clear that Marda and Gwen were sceptical of dramatists (apart from Shakespeare) who wrote in verse.

Drinks were served and snacks.

Marda got us back to base, the need to cut the cast by two. What about the two coloured servants? I choked on my brandy. Couldn't they see that, although their lines were few, they were among the most important characters in the play? Apart from what they said, one should consider what they did. There was simply no play without Kaspar and Katrina. The moral of the play depended on the white hero's suicide being stopped by a simple act of human compassion, not of a rich white for a black but of a poor black for a somewhat eccentric employer. Besides, Kaspar was visually necessary to project my Karoo. I could simply not write a South African play with an all-white cast. It was a pity we couldn't employ coloured actors. At that time our immaculate white laws forbade mixed casts or mixed audiences.

Then Marda made a very practical suggestion. It struck her that, with a little re-writing, Kaspar and Katrina could double with the chorus and they could be suitably disguised in veld-coloured dominos and wear animal masks. I needed another brandy.

'Well, think about it. It is a way round your problem,' said Marda.

'The theatre', pronounced Gwen, 'lives by compromise.'

And we had a very pleasant supper with much good talk and wine.

I had given up smoking some months before but found the offer of one of Marda's cigarettes irresistible. She kindly left an open box next to me, to which I resorted frequently during the after-dinner session while the two specialist surgeons dissected my play before my eyes, revealing all the abnormalities that had escaped the loving parent's indulgent eye. My brain-child was club-footed, overweight, acromegalic and spineless. They were particularly anxious to learn from me where the spine was because once they could detect the vertebral column (by which they seemed to mean the main story line and its message), they would be able to present my play on the boards and explain to the cast what it was all about. Actors are usually rather stupid, you see, and they don't understand what they have to say, they only feel it.

It was difficult to explain the structure of *The Dam*. They were, however, keen on the religious dimension in it. What with the popularity of T.S. Eliot and Christopher Fry, religion on the stage was rather 'in' if not chic. But the religion in my play was not explicit enough. Couldn't I spell it out more, to get my message across? Audiences, you see, could be terribly stupid, even more stupid than actors.

I took another drink and lit another cigarette.

The metaphor now changed from spine to climax. Where was the main climax, where were the minor climaxes? Because once they are pinpointed, the producer and the actors have a better idea what to aim for.

I believed I knew where the high points were and we examined them. In some cases Gwen and Marda were satisfied, in others they were critical. I had not provided the actor with enough steps to reach his or her climax. You can't jump up a great hill in one leap. Perhaps I should in these cases give the actor a few more lines.

I took another drink and lit another cigarette. I thought the play was quite long enough. *More* lines?

Well, that led us to the next hurdle: the cuts. They thought cuts were essential.

Back in my sleazy hotel room I turned a dark green, a tropical sweat poured from my splitting head and I felt very ill. This was bad enough, but my mind gave way and for half an hour or more I was genuinely paranoid. I was convinced I had been poisoned, by Marda most likely. Had she not once been the wife of J.G. Strijdom, the rabid leader of the Transvaal Nats, the Lion of the North? Nearly every 'cut' proposed would have the effect of degutting the political message of the play.

After being violently ill I returned to sanity and realised that my dear old system was simply objecting to too much alcohol and, more particularly, nicotine. I took a shower and tried to sleep.

I was not the only occupant of that building. There was the man whom I'd seen on the milk train, ready-made for one of the convict roles in *Great Expectations*.

From a deep pit of desolation he groaned and sighed into the hot night. Then he'd shout with rage, 'I'll murder you, you bastard!' Then, later, he'd cry, weeping, 'Oh my darling, my darling.'

Sleep was impossible, so I re-read my play. It did seem a somewhat fabricated drama compared with the one-man show going on down the corridor. When it had run its course into oblivion I stopped puzzling over *The Dam* and slept.

I had a further brief session with Marda the next afternoon. She confided that both she and Gwen had braced themselves to deal with a bearded old professor and what a pleasant surprise it had been to meet so amenable a young man instead. It was agreed that I should rework the play in the light of our deliberations. Could I return the text in a fortnight? I promised to try.

That evening we went to a soirée in a beautiful house with a large room where Gwen gave a one-woman show of scenes from Shakespeare. She was superb. Her final readings were from a play unjustly neglected, *Henry VIII*. She gave an unforgettable portrayal of Queen Katharine.

For the opening night of *The Dam* Jean and I, still car-less, found digs in Sea Point. We had to master the mysteries of the bus services into town in order to attend various functions.

One of these was a luncheon in the Houses of Parliament hosted by my father's younger brother, James, a United Party Senator. He was, as always, charming and courteous like his wife Hilda. Both of course had anecdotes to tell of me as a 5-year-old at Louisvale.

My parents, Alice and Ernest, were there, not only to attend the opening night but to meet the mailship bringing Alice's sisters, May Daniel and

Dorothy Goddard, who had decided to visit the country in which their eldest sister had led such a difficult and interesting life. The only one of my own siblings who could attend was Dorothy. Her husband Bill Murray was stationed at Robertson, putting in the canals which have transformed that part of the world. Whenever I come across a wine from that area, I drink a toast to him. Jean's parents had come to Cape Town for the opening night and dined and wined us at the Mount Nelson Hotel where they were staying.

I cannot recall the names of the other guests, except for Abram Jonker, father of Ingrid and Anna, and his wife.

Unique of course, was my very first first night, 4 March 1952. An entire row had been allocated to the author and those relatives who were able to be present. Jean sat next to me, then Ernest, followed by Alice. Behind us, I was informed, sat a party of cabinet ministers and their wives.

As the minutes ticked by towards curtain-rise at 8.15, Jean pressed my hand. I was in need of such affectionate reassurance. With a minute to go I was overcome with unbearable panic. Here were all these people and they were going to watch my play! Suddenly it seemed to be an incredible act of vanity and exhibitionism and I could do nothing to stop it.

The lights went down in the house and the curtains parted, and there was Geoffrey Long's Karoo setting for the river-bed scene. The male and female chorus wore very effective bird masks, and started:

Listen a little to us,
Let the doors of your hearts swing open.

I was, on the whole, pleased with how Marda and her actors had lifted my words off the page.

The curtain closed for the first interval and the house lights went up. Alice, leaning eagerly across Ernest, said in a stage whisper which seemed to me to fill the house: 'Guy my son, it's absolutely marvellous! I haven't understood a single word of it!'

During the interval Uncle Jim congratulated me on having found an actor for the leading role of Douglas Long who looked so like Frank Biggs. It was in vain that I explained that my Douglas Long and Frank Biggs were not intended to be similar, and that any physical similarity was an accident. I had had no say whatever in the casting.

'Well, anyway,' said Uncle Jim, 'you've got it right.'

By the end of the play it was all too clear to me that what I had seen on the stage bore only a remote resemblance to what I had imagined before I tried to give it a local habitation and a name. And I could see many, many flaws in my part of it.

So when, to the cries of 'Author! Author!', I was hustled on to the stage, I was in a humble and apologetic mood. Nor had Marda briefed me in what to say.

I thanked her, the players and the N.T.O. for the wonderful way they had given my script flesh and blood. For the play itself, I asked the audience to bear in mind that it was a first play and that, if it served no other purpose, it had shown me that I still had to learn the A.B.C. of playwriting.

Marda was both furious and amused.

'You idiot!' she exclaimed. 'How stupid can you be? It's not for you to tell the critics how to kill your play stone dead: "Author admits ignorance of alphabet of theatre." Those hyenas will crunch your bones.'

'What should I have said?'

'Something patriotic, you dolt!'

Backstage I was introduced to Anna Neethling Pohl, a strikingly beautiful Afrikaans actress.

'Well,' she said, 'I liked it. But I suppose you'll leave now.'

'Leave?'

'Leave South Africa,' she said.

'Why?'

'Don't you all? The only city lights you English acknowledge are those of London town.'

Next morning Jean and I were up early to buy the papers hot from the street vendors. We turned to the theatre page with trembling hands. How many times has Jean been through this painful ordeal by theatre reviewers with me? That morning the critical hyenas were fairly gentle although one, sure enough, picked up the young author's reference to the A.B.C. of playwriting.

I saw Professor John Greig after the Johannesburg performance. He was furious. Why had I altered the play? I gave him an account of its metamorphosis. 'As one of the judges I felt embarrassed. What I saw on the stage was not the play to which we had awarded the prize. Never, never, never trust theatre people! They always simplify and crudify.'

When the N.T.O. company arrived in Grahamstown to perform in the packed City Hall, disaster in the form of mumps or scarlet fever struck down the junior female lead. The most experienced young actress in town, Dolores Mather-Pike, stood in for her and did remarkably well.

In this performance the storm scene, which had become more Lear-like, was so shocking that a lady in the audience lapsed into hysteria and took a week to recover, which was proof positive, said one of my fans, that *The Dam* was a powerful piece.

But I treasured a remark which I overheard in the corridor of a railway coach. People in a compartment must have been arguing the merits of the piece:

'Well,' said this East Cape voice, '*The Dam* has made me see my farm a damn site better than before.'

It has escaped the notice of some critics that the play does not end on a happy note of reconciliation between Afrikaner and English-speakers: the romance between the representatives of the next generation is frustrated by an awareness of the black misery in the townships. As for the so-called coloureds, Kaspar and Katrina, they do not accept their lot as 'serfs', as Martin Orkin calls them; and it is their anguish in the close of the play that makes Susan reject Sybrand's idyllic proposal, and opt for a life dedicated to the relief of urban misery.

While *Stranger to Europe* was still with the printers I wrote to Balkema offering him (as I was bound to by contract) *The Dam*. I was clearly delighted with the reception of the play (it had not yet reached Johannesburg) and, in my euphoric ignorance of the public's interest in poetry, wrote: 'I should imagine the success of *The Dam* will also affect the sale of the poems. Anyway I hope so. I think *Stranger* may be in a second edition before Christmas.' (The second edition – with additional poems – appeared eight years later in 1960.)

On 22 May 1952 I posted Balkema the revised version of *The Dam*, enclosing the *Rand Daily Mail* review, under the headline: 'A Prize Play Triumphs over Poor Acting':

'Mr Lefebvre alone seemed to realize that Prof. Butler has written the first important morality play in the catalogue of S.A. drama, and not a hybrid offspring of Eliot and Noel Coward; and the producer Miss Marda Vanne was certainly nodding when she allowed Gerrit Wessels and Noelle Ahrenson to burlesque the two coloured servants, for which the text gives no warrant.'

The letter enclosing this review has a postscript: '*The Star* did not have one good thing to say about the play.'

The Dam was published in 1953, dedicated to 'Father Trevor Huddleston, C.R., and the priests of the Church of Christ the King, Sophiatown, Johannesburg.

Only once have I managed to get a professional production in which my coloured characters have not been burlesqued (*Demea*, 1990). Until Fugard's *Blood Knot* (1969) actors and producers could present so-called coloureds only as comic carnival coons or parodies of whites, not as people.

In September 1952 I was invited by the Minister of Arts, Education and Science to serve on the Board of the National Theatre Organisation. I accepted and later made the time-consuming journey to Pretoria two or three times a year. On the first occasion I arrived a minute or two late and was introduced to the members round the table. There seemed to be some surprise at my appearance. When we broke for coffee I overheard the remark: 'Maar hy lyk nie soos 'n professor nie. Hy lyk ook nie soos 'n digter of 'n dramaturg nie. Hy lyk nes 'n Boer.'

I also started work on a play on the Anglo–Boer war – *The Dove Returns*

– based on a true story told me by Jean's father. A young English officer was killed in an ambush on a farm in the Western Free State and buried in the bleak veld. His parents visited his grave after the war and subsequently the Boer farmer had the remains re-interred in the shelter of the family graveyard. The parents of the dead soldier then sent a gift of a silver tea service to the family and they treasured it. This provided the germ for a tragedy with a hopeful epilogue of reconciliation. The current political crisis over the removal of the coloured voters from the common roll was echoed in the predicament of Simon, the retainer of the Boer Commandant. He refuses to be a party to the happy white ending. This was sailing right into the prevailing popular winds. Neither the Nationalist nor the English journalists were interested in finding common ground. They were looking for more hot air to fan their group prejudices. But that is another story.

I attended some of the rehearsals of *The Dove Returns* in Pretoria. I was so disappointed and alarmed at what was being done to my text that I did not stay on for the opening night. I have never seen a production of it.

It was subsequently produced by a courageous company in Manchester. The producer was so ignorant of his characters and their culture as to hang a large crucifix round the neck of the Boer mother.

Ever since seeing the *Agamemnon*, I have remained fascinated by ancient Greek drama and the power of certain of those works to speak across great historical and cultural gaps. I was particularly interested in symbolical stories which might be valid for both Europe and Africa, for blacks and for whites. This interest, combined with my growing knowledge of South Africa in the early 19th century, my reading of missionary and Settler diaries and of Xhosa and other tribal histories (most notably of the Amangwane under chief Matiwane) led me in 1959 to transpose the *Medea* of Euripides from the Aegean to the fringes of the Cape Colony in the late 1820s. Medea becomes Demea, a Tembu princess, Jason becomes Jonas, a British soldier turned trader, and Creon becomes Kroon, the leader of an (imaginary) Trek determined to establish an all-white republic on separate development lines like those of the ruling Nationalist Party. It was a prophetic allegory about the probable results of apartheid. The large cast comprised the full South African colour spectrum. This made production impossible at that time as neither casts nor audiences could be mixed. However, the apartheid taboos as they affect the theatre were sufficiently eased for *Demea* to be produced on the stage in 1990. Thirty years is a long time to wait for the possibility of seeing such an ambitious experimental work. I shall describe later in this book how it happened.

In the 1950s my interest in the theatre and performing arts grew steadily into something like an obsession. I produced *Julius Caesar* (1951), *A*

Midsummer Night's Dream (1956), *Othello* (1957), *Hamlet* (1959), *Henry IV* Part 1 (1962), *Everyman* (1963) and *Doctor Faustus* (1968).

I was incredibly lucky in my colleagues. Dennis Davison of the English Department was and has remained stagestruck and he took charge of the hempen home-spuns in *A Midsummer Night's Dream* – turning Bill Yeowart into the best Bottom I have ever seen. For some reason, still a mystery to me, Davison, an almost apolitical man, was not allowed to stay in South Africa and left us for Australia in 1957. We still correspond. It saddens and angers me to think that he should have been forced to leave.

The Professor of Fine Art, Cecil Todd, saw in the theatre an opportunity for his students to get practical experience in design and we enjoyed stimulating collaboration. The Music Department under Dr Georg Grüber also had a healthy love of performing before the public and of taking its choir on extended tours in South Africa and overseas. Our most successful early collaboration was a production of *Everyman* (1963), with appropriate medieval décor and music. Tony Voss played Everyman. A very clever sinister-looking student, whom I later cast as Iago, made a chilly Death. A good-looking Theology student with a fine voice stood in for God.

We toured this wonderfully compact and powerful allegory. Our most memorable performance was in the old church at St Matthew's, to which mission station was attached a teachers' training college.

There were other enthusiasts among the staff such as Jacques Ewer, Professor of Zoology, an excellent actor, and his wife Griff, a genius at lighting shows with very little equipment; and among the citizens, Norman Addleson of the Bar; school teachers, and so on.

While in America in 1958, I made enquiries about regional festivals with an historical taproot, of which there were several; and when in Holland early in 1960, I went to Tegelen to watch an open-air passion play. The next morning the waiter asked me whether I'd seen the play? Yes, I had. What had I thought of the centurion? He looked fine on his white horse, I said. That was me! he beamed, placing his hand on his heart.

I still hanker after a miracle play which gets the community involved as it did in medieval times, and still does here and there as at Oberammergau. A tentative start has been made at Easter time in Grahamstown.

As for my own plays, from the 'sixties on I turned to the history of the Eastern Cape for materials. Some account of these ventures, including *Demea*, will be found in the chapter 'Eastern Cape History, Diaries and Plays'.

17   1954–

More Poetry

As a South African poet, I owe an incalculable debt to Roy Campbell – from my school days onwards. In the early 'thirties our teacher, 'Pappa' Aird, remarked that this young South African had written an epic poem all about a sea turtle. I went to the library and took out *The Flaming Terrapin*. It left me drunk on new words and metaphors and rhymes, for days.

Before I met Roy Campbell in the flesh in January 1955, I had read everything of his I could lay hands on, had, in fact, written a special answer on *The Flaming Terrapin* in my Master's examination as early as 1939. I had read his first autobiography, *Broken Record*, delighting particularly in his love of animals and outrageous tall stories. He liked a good laugh – unlike most of the Romantic poets who formed our staple poetic diet. Later I'd picked up gossip and legends galore from Uys Krige, a man who had lived with the Campbells tutoring their daughters in Provence and Spain. He and Uys had taken opposite sides during the Spanish Civil War.

Roy, who had been converted to Catholicism, aligned himself with Franco. With his fascist sympathies and his feeling for traditional verse he was contemptuous of the new leftist English poets – MacNeice, Spender, Auden, Day Lewis – inventing for them the portmanteau name, MacSpaunday. On the outbreak of the war, according to Roy, MacSpaunday either fled across the Atlantic to the safety of the U.S.A., or took cushy base jobs in the British Home Front ministries, while he in due course enrolled as a ranker in the anti-Axis cause, and sweated it out in tropical Kenya as a sergeant with the King's African Rifles.

There was no end to stories of Roy's quarrels with MacSpaunday. The worst of these occurred in April 1949 when he punched Stephen Spender, who was reading his poems to the Poetry Society.

His *Talking Bronco* appeared in May 1946. I was not surprised to hear that MacSpaunday, whom he accused of having made propaganda for the Communists, were after his blood.

Roy had visited Oxford in May 1947 to address the Poetry Society – a meeting which for some reason I missed; but I soon heard various accounts of it. According to his biographer Peter Alexander (*Roy Campbell*, p. 210), Roy 'came stumping into the hall in a duffle-coat and read a number of his poems in his heavy South African accent, before explaining that he had cribbed them all from French poets'. He thought the hospitality poor, the president beforehand offering him 'nothing but tea with powdered milk'. At the conclusion he grabbed a young Australian writer, Geoffrey Dutton, and said with relief, 'Man, thank God to see another colonial amongst all these bloody Pommies. Come and let's have a drink, quick, before the pubs close.'

Other accounts have it that he wore an army greatcoat and an Australian army hat, and made the most of his lameness (the result of his war wounds, although others say rheumatism), by limping along on a heavy twisted cudgel and up the steps to the platform in Rhodes House. He spoke seated. According to David Philip, he was determinedly informal and began, 'When I came to Oxford I saw these – what you call 'em? – these dreaming spires, so I said to myself, "Giraffes," I said to myself. "Giraffes." So I wrote this poem – see what you think of it.' He then read 'Dreaming Spires', which includes the lines:

The City of Giraffes – a People
Who live between the earth and skies,
Each in his lone religious steeple,
Keeping a light-house with his eyes.

The legend says that on this or another Oxford occasion he discoursed at some length on the profound differences between the conversational prosy poetry of MacSpaunday and the lyrics of true poets like himself and his friend Dylan Thomas. He and Dylan, he maintained, still had the lyrical music of Apollo on their lips and in their ears. Now, the direct descendant of Apollo's lyre is the guitar, particularly the Spanish guitar, an instrument still beloved by those people and poets who have not abandoned the ancient elevating alliance of man and horse – the Spanish and South American caballeros, the French chevalier, the English cavaliers, even the South African Boers – the fine old equestrian traditionalists.

He argued that the real trouble with MacSpaunday was that they knew nothing about horses and the active physical life which horses symbolise. They were too cerebral. Poetry should be the celestial sweat of an active life, ideally the voice of a good tenor, perhaps, singing to a guitar strummed in the saddle. 'When MacSpaunday say nasty things about me and my poetry, I can shrug it off. I have the confidence given me by my Pegasus. None of them can ride a horse. But Dylan – Dylan is sensitive to what MacSpaunday say about him. Dylan, though a true poet, cannot ride a horse.'

Somewhere in the midst of this serio-comic turn, he had stopped in mid-sentence, transfixed apparently by the sight of something small moving across the stage in front of him from left to right. Quietly seizing his cudgel, he rose from his chair, and in spite of his lameness, stalked the creature for some distance. The cudgel came down with a wallop, sending up a cloud of dust. Campbell, examining the head of his weapon, smiled:

'Got him! I can't abide spiders!'

According to Roy Macnab 'he was an enormous success – Oxford had not seen anything like him before'.

In 1954 in Britain, Jean and I heard much sad talk about the death of the true lyric poet, Dylan, who had died in New York from some form of alcoholic poisoning. Mary and Guy Stringer, who was on leave from the army, lamented his death, but were not entirely surprised. For a time Guy had been stationed at Laugharne in Wales, and visited the pub there from time to time. The Thomases would rock up with a wheelbarrow, a practical precaution taken by Dylan's bitterly experienced wife, Caitlin. She was not strong enough to carry him back to their cottage at closing time. That is one of the saddest images I have of any poet being trundled home by his wife in a wheelbarrow, his mouth loose and open – a mouth which had intoned 'Fern Hill' from

Now as I was young and easy under the apple boughs

to

Time held me green and dying
Though I sang in my chains like the sea.

Late in 1954, when staying at Nuffield Foundation House, close to Kensington Gardens, I wrote to Campbell in Cintra, Portugal. Presuming on the favourable review he had written for the *Cape Times* of my first volume of poems, I asked him for a meeting. I was planning to return to South Africa via the Gold Coast and Nigeria, but thought of going via Portugal in order to see him. He wrote back that he would be in London in January, for treatment for his wartime injuries, and said I should phone him up then, which I did.

'It would be a pleasure to meet Stranger to Europe,' he said. 'What about 11.30, for a quick one before lunch, at "The Catherine Wheel"? It's just across the park from you.'

Having arrived a little before opening time, I watched a tall, broad and thick figure in brown tweedy untailored clothes and a highish hat approaching. The slight limp seemed to make the figure more impressive.

Roy had a natural poise and openness, an easy friendliness of manner, which struck me almost at once. 'The Catherine Wheel' was the watering-hole of other ranks from the Kensington Barracks. He hailed several of the N.C.O.s by their first names. He asked one what he thought of the short stories of Somerset Maugham which, at their last meeting, he had advised him to read. This was no patronising culture-spreading exercise, but sprang from an authentic assumption that anyone could enjoy a well-written story. Roy discussing Maugham with that corporal sprang to mind later when I read his sonnet *Luis de Camoes*.

> Camoes, alone, of all the lyric race,
> Born in the black aurora of disaster,
> Can look a common soldier in the face ...

I could not imagine any of MacSpaunday talking to a ranker with that naturalness. For one thing, their public-school voices and manner would have made it difficult for the corporals to be relaxed in their presence. A colonial with an odd accent could enjoy a kind of social neutrality in any situation where the English class system created a bristling magnetic field.

We drank beer by the quart at a fair-sized round table, Roy holding court, I presumed, from this customary throne. The circle expanded and contracted. I was introduced to many of his friends whose names escaped me, except one, a quiet, fair-haired, rather tense young man, Rob Lyle, who had founded a Catholic journal called *The Catacomb*, which he had persuaded Roy to edit. Lyle left about 12.15. Shortly afterwards a dark, harassed-looking young woman in a duffle coat appeared. Roy rose, and with a great flourish introduced his daughter Anna as La Contessa Jaime Cavero de Carondelet, making the most of the orotund Latinity. Anna hardly acknowledged my presence, but went straight into her business: to fetch her father.

'The macaroni's in the oven.'

Roy's response was to order another round of quarts. Anna left.

'You know about Dylan's death, of course?'

'A little.'

'It happened while I was on a lecture tour of Canada and the States. I was in Seattle when he died. Some nice people in Seattle. Butler, you know, if I like people I show my appreciation the best way I can. I give them something imperishable which they can enjoy for the rest of their lives. And it costs me absolutely nothing.'

He paused, clearly waiting for my question.

'And what could that be?'

'My recipe for bobotie.'

I was not sure whether this called for a laugh, but, as we were both South African exiles weeping into our beers beside the waters of Babylon, I smiled and, with my notebook and pencil at the ready, asked him for the ingredients. I wrote them down, item by item.

I lost that notebook, but four years later when we were touring the United States on a Carnegie Travelling Fellowship Jean recovered the secret. During a dinner with R.B. Heilman, whose work on *King Lear* I had enjoyed and admired, delicious bobotie was served. The recipe had been given Mrs Heilman in Seattle by a touring South African poet, Roy Campbell, and she passed it on to Jean, who still uses it regularly.

When Laurens van der Post (Roy's old associate on *Voorslag* magazine) visited Rhodes to be awarded an honorary degree, she served it at lunch.

'The best bobotie I have ever tasted!' he exclaimed.

'It's Roy Campbell's recipe,' Jean said, and, telling the table how she had come by it in Seattle, offered him the formula.

Laurens declined, saying, 'I'm afraid I don't cook.'

Here is Jean's recipe for 'Roy Campbell's Bobotie', which she generously offers to my readers:

(A) 1 level teasp. curry powder
teasp. ginger
1 dessertsp. sugar
2 large onions
(B) 2 beef stock cubes
1 tablesp. vinegar
1 handful seedless raisins
2 tablesp. chutney
1 tablesp. Worcester sauce
1 large tomato, skinned and cut up
(C) 2 slices bread damped with water and squeezed dry
1 lb. raw mince
(D) pint milk
3 eggs
1 teasp. maizena
teasp. almond essence

Method
Warm heavy pot.
Add all of A and stir until onions are clear.
Add B. Lower heat and mix well until bubbling.
Add bread and mince well mixed together.
Place in pie dish.
Beat eggs, milk, maizena and almond essence and pour over mince mixture.
Put some fresh lemon leaves (about 6 or 8) on top.
Bake in oven 350 °F until custard has set and become golden.

Roy admitted with surprising candour (we were alone for a few minutes), 'Butler, I've just been to the doctor. He says if I don't stop drinking, I'll go the way Dylan's gone.' And he ordered another round.

It was now about a quarter to one. A beautiful, tragic-looking woman entered. Roy rose, and with less flourish introduced his wife Mary. I wondered: 'Has she come to report the state of the macaroni?'

Nothing so mundane. She was very anxious about the latest news of the Pope, Pius XII, who was suffering from terrible attacks of hiccoughs.

'Roy, the latest bulletin from the Vatican ...'

But Roy was deep in converse with a new arrival, and, it seemed, deliberately ignoring her repeated attempts to get through to him with the bulletin of his Holiness's health. No doubt she hoped that talk of the Pope would penetrate Roy's brain and exorcise Bacchus sufficiently to prise him loose. Like Anna, Mary failed and quietly left. Two stricken, resigned women.

When she had gone Roy asked me what I thought of the sculptor Jacob Epstein, who had recently been knighted. I said I liked his portrait heads of Shaw and Einstein, and had a vivid recollection of a Lucifer, a powerful work, I thought. Roy then indulged in a hate session against Jacob Epstein, a hatred that went back many years to Roy's courtship of Mary in the 'twenties, and which may in part explain his anti-Semitism. Jacob, it seems, had been in love with Mary Garman's sister, Kathleen, and had become violently jealous of Roy, believing Roy was the lover of both the sisters. In due course Kathleen became Epstein's model, his mistress, and the mother of his children. But, according to Roy, he had refused to marry her – until it was suggested to him that it would be proper for a K.B.E. to tidy up his private life. I see from *Who's Who* that he married Mrs (sic) Kathleen Garman in 1955. I was right out of my depth in the dramas of Bohemia.

He introduced me to another arrival, who, hearing I was a South African, asked me a question about the Nationalist Party's racial policies. I said they did have affinities with the Nazis – that they were turning their past into a racist mystique – seeing their pioneering trek as a sort of holy exodus from an English Egypt, and the blacks as Amalekites and Jebusites to be ousted from their promised land. I referred to the hysterias which had accompanied the centenary celebrations of the Great Trek in 1938; at which point Roy interpolated – 'They all grew beards' and then 'The only crop the Boers have ever grown without a government subsidy.' (One could argue that it was the most heavily subsidised crop ever produced.)

Then back to Dylan – a friendship that had begun when Roy returned to Britain from Spain in 1941, penniless. He had got a job as an air-raid warden. The Thomases were living in the same lodgings, in a single room, cold and poor, quarrelling and madly in love. Roy shared what little money he had with them. Roy and Dylan had enough in common as poets and drinkers to become fast friends. He told with relish and no doubt some garnishing, how, when absolutely down on their beam ends, they had gone begging together – among publishers and fellow poets. Sometimes they'd confront their target in tandem, sometimes not. For instance,

Harold Nicolson (whom Roy had pilloried in *The Georgiad*) was left to Dylan *solus*, 'who came away with a quid and a lecture on the evils of drink'. And Dylan of course, had to try the stony hearts of MacSpaunday, the Ministry Poets – with minimal success. However they felt they could tackle T.S. Eliot at Faber and Faber together. 'Our Uncle, the Archbishop, received us graciously. He gave us enough for a couple of carefree days.'

Later, after the war, they had worked together on the BBC. While I was up at Oxford the Third Programme broadcast a reading of *Paradise Lost*. Dylan Thomas was cast as Satan. He was, I thought, superb: that proud voice; that necessary love of rhetoric and those words! Which reminds me of an anecdote about Roy and Dylan in a recent letter from Roy Macnab.

'I first met Campbell in Oxford in the J.C.R. at Jesus, my own college. He was reading in that high monotone of his when in walked Dylan Thomas. Campbell, in his usual disarming way, said, "Now here's a real poet," and handed the book to Dylan, who of course was a beautiful reader. What a couple, Campbell the giant with a thin voice, little Dylan with the fruity deep tones of a giant. Afterwards Campbell came round to my rooms for a drink (not tea!) and agreed to write the introduction to my South African poetry anthology (1948). It was interesting to see Campbell and Thomas together. Apart from poetry and Augustus John, drinking beer gave them something in common. Each could open his throat and down a beer in one huge gulp. I drank with them in a pub once. With Campbell and Thomas I felt I would never be a great poet because I could not get the beer down in one swallow! ...'

But now Dylan was dead.

'When I heard of it in Seattle,' said Campbell, 'I was devastated: I could hardly continue that tour. His wife, Caitlin, was left destitute. I offered to adopt one of the kids.'

There was a longish pause.

It was now 2.30. Rising heavily he said:

'Butler, I don't think we'll bother about lunch, do you?'

'Mr Campbell, I'm quite incapable of bothering about anything.'

We shook hands and went our different ways.

When the SABC phoned me on 23 April 1957 to say that Roy had died in a motor smash in Portugal and asked for comment, I had great difficulty in stringing a few lame phrases together.

I was relieved to hear that he had not been at the wheel. Mary was driving. I wrote to her, and asked if I might dedicate *A Book of South African Verse* to Roy. She agreed.

My next poetic hero – William Plomer – was Roy's opposite. They had started as great friends, turned into violent and bitter enemies (the violence coming from Roy), but achieved, I believe, some sort of mutual tolerance in the end. My initial contact with Plomer was in his capacity as reader for Jonathan Cape, to whom I sent my first attempt at a novel, upon which he wrote some encouraging and some surgical comments.

My preoccupation with South African literature in the mid-'fifties and early 'sixties emerges in my correspondence with him. I had met him in January 1955 in the Arts Theatre Club in London to discuss a play of mine called *Post Mortem* (later *The Dove Returns*), and felt that we had got on well enough for me to approach him (5 July 1955) on behalf of Professor A.C. Partridge of Wits, who 'is busy planning a symposium on The Future of English in South Africa, or some such general topic, which would act, it is hoped, as a stimulus to aspirant writers in South Africa ... We thought you might be willing to give a paper on the characteristics of South African manuscripts submitted to you ... or possibly a paper on "Provincialism, good and bad" ...' William consented to come.

On 29 October I wrote: 'I've become English editor of a bilingual literary magazine, *Standpunte*. I recently read, in *London Magazine*, a delightful article of yours on your early days in London. It occurred to me that you might be prepared to do something similar on your South African days – *Voorslag*, Campbell, yourself and van der Post?' Though William did not respond to this suggestion at this stage, he did in due course.

On 27 December 1956 I wrote expressing the hope that he had recovered from his South African trip. 'Things have warmed up since then. I've just got back from a trip to Jo'burg, where I had occasion to visit in prison Professor Z.K. Matthews of Fort Hare.'

The purpose of the letter was to get his support for 'an anthology of South African verse, to be published by the Oxford University Press. I would like to include the bulk of your South African work (Section III in *The Twofold Screen*) and several others from *Notes for Poems*.'

On 22 May 1957 I asked for permission to use the revised versions of 'The Victoria Falls' and 'Transvaal Morning' written during his recent visit. Having worked my way through countless volumes of verse in the South African Library and elsewhere, and frisked periodicals galore, I had made a selection. 'Some curiously interesting preoccupations emerge, to which I will draw attention in the Introduction. For example, nearly every poet writes about (1) the self-discovery that occurs when journeying through deserts, (2) exile, (3) the impersonality, the "otherness", of Africa. There is also a preoccupation in many with the civilising process, its losses and gains ...'

In December 1959 I wrote thanking him for his comments on a batch of poems I had sent him – comments which were 'most helpful in revising the pieces for inclusion in a new (enlarged) edition of *Stranger to Europe* which is already in proof stage'. I talk of writing 'a new novel – or the first one split down the middle. I dipped into it yesterday and find it is not as bad as I feared it might be.'

'I saw Ruth Miller in Jo'burg recently – she suffers much from the absence of an audience. Sometimes I feel like organising a sort of jamboree for all people trying to write poetry south of the Sahara.'

In 1960, during study leave in the United Kingdom, I visited him at his country cottage in Sussex. It was a lovely day, but I had come prepared for rain. At the time I was trying to learn how to wear a hat and keep it from escaping. Hats tended to give me the slip by hiding in the hatracks of planes or trains.

The current number was, I thought, extremely handsome: Tyrolean, with a longish grey silky pile, which like my hair had anarchic tendencies. As I removed it in the hallway, William exclaimed: 'What a marvellous hat! Do you give it a saucer of milk at night?'

I met David Wright in the early 'fifties, too. Neither of us knows when we first met, but we knew each other by 1954, when he was living in Great Ormonde Street. His actress wife, Pippa, was a New Zealander. He said he found their common colonial background a bond.

How many times we went to 'The George' in Tottenham Court Road I do not know, but one or two incidents float to the top of memory like bubbles on a deep tankard of beer. One could not move for poets and artists and their wives and lovers. David was a good person to be with, because his deafness necessitated the carrying of a pad and a pencil which he would thrust at any interlocutor whose lips he could not read. He himself would scrawl things down because his own toneless speech was sometimes difficult to understand, particularly in the blessed bedlam of 'The George'. It was hard to believe that he heard not a note of all that happy hubbub.

It was very different for his friend, John Heath-Stubbs, who was all but blind, and whose eyes, marbled with glaucoma, were painful to behold. He had to bring the pad right up to an eye – not in front of it, but to the side, where the vision was apparently better. What I beheld of their converse in 'The George' remains one of my pleasantest recollections of the poetic conscience at work in spite of the demons of deafness, blindness, drink and lack of room in which to move. Heath-Stubbs asked David whether he had received the poem he had sent for inclusion in a magazine he was editing. I think this message was transcribed by a friend on to David's pad as 'Got poem?' To which David nodded with such vehemence that the top of his tankard splashed on the teak counter. He should, of course, have shouted 'Yes!' The friend supplied the deficiency.

'Where?' cried Heath-Stubbs.

This David managed to lip read, and he shouted, 'Here!'

Heath-Stubbs responded, 'Give back. Comma missing.'

This presented difficulties until the friend wrote: 'Wants to add comma.'

David, who is a big man, went through his pockets – no easy feat in the crowded pub. The poem – typewritten on a single sheet of frayed foolscap

– was produced. A problem now presented itself: where to do the correcting?

The deaf poet and his blind friend secured a small piece of the bar counter, and wiped it clean of intersecting tankard rings. The blind poet felt the surface, found it to be damp, and did some further drying with his jacket cuff, then spread the typescript out slowly and very carefully, his head cocked to one side to let his minimal vision operate. He then read the poem to himself as though he were in a platonist's tower, alone – not being pushed from behind like a front-rank forward. He found the line from which the comma had been omitted and inserted it, with the care of a watchmaker adjusting a small but essential screw. David watched, beheld, and shouted and nodded 'Yes! Yes!', slapped him on the back, and ordered two more quarts while Heath-Stubbs carefully folded the poem, his fingers delicate as a man's who reads by braille.

I watched this from a little distance. I was wedged between the back of George Barker and a wall, except that between me and the wall was a large cushion of a lady in a brown-sacking smock with blotches of clay all over it; and the same substance was under the nails and cuticles of the fingers of her substantial hand embracing a tankard of beer. I am not sure whether she was talking to me or not, but her message was clear, as were the gaps in her teeth.

'People!' Gulp. And she shook her head negatively, slowly, sadly, from side to side. 'People! I've given them up.' Gulp. But, having just witnessed the miracle of the comma, I was moved to ask: 'Whatever will you put in their place?'

She looked at me balefully, gulped, and said:

'Clay.'

'Clay? Instead of people?'

'Yes, clay. You can do what you bloody well like with clay!' At which she flung her head back, and gulped down the rest of her bitter. I looked at her powerful hands, and pitied whatever clay fell into them.

My friendship with David Wright grew beyond the malty seedbed of 'The George'. David did not like the stanzaic verse I wrote in the late 'fifties, and said so, but encouraged me to write in freer, more conversational measures. This I had learnt in part to do while writing my early verse plays: in fact, some frequently anthologised pieces, like 'Isibongo of Matiwane' and 'Surveyor' are lifted from plays; the first from *Demea*, the second from an unpublished play. David went further: he found me a publisher – Abelard-Schuman – for a volume, *South of the Zambesi* (1966), entirely devoted to African subjects and almost innocent of rhyme. William Plomer wrote a generous introduction for it. The publishers suggested illustrations by John Lawrence, to which I consented, with some hesitation. They turned out to be very good. Unfortunately, *South of the Zambesi* came at a time when the publishers were undergoing a sea change, and the marketing in South Africa at least was poor.

David visited the Eastern Cape some years ago in the footsteps of his 1820 Settler forebears. I had the great pleasure of taking him to see the Fish River frontier, where we found a fink's or weaver-bird's nest, the Settler country, Manley's Flats, and the Dias Cross. Near Kwaai Hoek he sat on a large fragment of the wooden hull of an old sailing-ship, staring at the breakers whose thunder and rumble he could not hear.

Then in 1980 I visited him in Appleby-in-Westmorland with my son Christopher. Through a day of driving sleet and snow, it was his turn to show us another, older frontier – Hadrian's Roman Wall; before reaching which, vague in the smoky snow, there appeared a herd of huge grey beasts like rhino or hippo or buffalo – an uncanny evocation of Africa: the great rounded and angular sarsen stones that compose the neolithic ring known as Long Meg and Her Hundred Daughters. Some experiences escape too quickly; they are too complex, too big for words: a big-framed deaf poet in an almost blinding snowstorm, standing in an ancient circle of stones like mastodons. We correspond once or twice a year. He is a patient and frank critic of any poems I send him, some of which are very long.

From the early 'fifties my poems, my plays and my lectures began to produce some unexpected results. I started receiving letters out of the blue from quite unknown people. One came from Uitenhage from someone called Ruth Miller, enclosing two or three poems of her own. I can still recall my delight, admiration and envy as I read.

No spider struggles to create
The beautiful. His tensile arc
Knows mathematics in the dark;
A Michael Angelo of air
Who weaves a theory that states
Ultimatums on a hair.

Born to the purple of his need
He has no unsolved problems. He
Suffers no dichotomy,
But wakes to work and works to kill;
Beauty empiric in his greed,
Perfection in a villain's skill.

In due course we met in Grahamstown, in the Botanical Gardens. Who can forget those large, vulnerable eyes, and the forthright sense of the ridiculous, 'the wry sharpness of [her] mind' (Lola Watter)?

During my spell as English editor of *Standpunte* I had to sift through many poems, and find reviewers for books of poetry. Geoff Durrant was most helpful. We discovered that we agreed that the poems submitted by one, Sydney Clouts, were exceptionally original in technique and thought; so that it was a great day when Philip Segal introduced Jean and me to the Cloutses. I was on an annual pilgrimage to Cape Town – either to act as external examiner at U.C.T. or to attend meetings of the Joint Matriculation Board – in either case wading heavily through the thick kelp of academia; and here was this poet in Oranjezicht transmuting Table Mountain, the sea, the city's panorama, the political paranoia, the family sanctities into poetry – each line a poem in itself. Here is 'The Situation':

> Red Mountain, red forest.
>
> Of curious quiet the late afternoon.
>
> Is the sun setting, is it the sun?
>
> This chocolate sweetens thought.
>
> When the dung-beetle scratches the noise echoes in the house.
>
> Come wind, blow wind blow!
>
> I stand still in my garden.
>
> Let us elect a Minister from some wise stones.
>
> Set the wine on the table.
>
> Dead thought is swarming with tyrannical flies.
>
> The clouds are in Congress.
>
> Set down the fruit.
>
> Of exultant serenity shine the firm plums.
>
> Cleft rocks, torn fish in the sea.

Most writers of novels or plays start off as poets. Here is Athol Fugard on our first meeting in 1957 (taken from his dedication written for *Olive Schreiner and After : Essays on Southern African Literature in Honour of Guy Butler*, edited by Malvern van Wyk Smith and Don Maclennan, 1983):

Dear Guy
   Do you remember the words 'Fugard, this needs more work!'? They were yours and they were written at the bottom of an attempt at a poem in 1957. I was disappointed. I thought I had given it all the work it needed. Anyway,

if I remember correctly, a few more attempts followed that one but 'the man in Grahamstown' remained unsatisfied. Your criticism, while always as gentle as possible, remained firm and precise. I eventually got the message: I wasn't a poet, so I decided to imitate you in another respect and try playwriting. That was the start of a new dialogue between us – which thank God continues to this day – and which eventually led to our first meeting. How is your recall on that one? It took place in the Botanical Gardens in Grahamstown on a still autumn afternoon, and both Sheila and I recall a long and leisurely conversation, with you giving us more time and attention than we deserved. The subject was theatre and more specifically a still very suspect form of it called South African Theatre. I left that conversation with one of the major provocations of my career. I can't remember your exact words but the gist of it was something like this: 'South Africa has got more than enough of its own stories. It's time to start telling them and to stop imitating those that aren't ours.' I started to try about a year later with *No-Good Friday*. Now, twenty-four years after that, I look back gratefully on a relationship with you in which I have been on the receiving end of good advice, sincere encouragement and generous friendship.

Whenever in Cape Town, we would visit Uys Krige and Jack Cope in a cottage at Clifton which they had bought from an Afrikaans poet I greatly admired but had never met, N.P. van Wyk Louw; and these visits became more frequent after the founding of *Contrast* in 1960.

Not everyone agreed with Jack's and Uys's editorial policy. For instance, Perseus Adams persuaded himself that the receipt of rejection slips from them was not merely malicious, but proof that they were wicked men deliberately withholding good writing from the public. He would roll his eyes, glance over his shoulder, and refer to the 'Clifton Mafia'.

And Tony Delius, witty, shoulder-shrugging liberal, who sat for years in the press gallery listening to Strijdom, Verwoerd and their gang solemnly turning race prejudice into that Chinese wall of racist legislation which made us both hated and ridiculous in most of the world, and which the same Nationalist party has been forced to start demolishing. Not that Tony was that most boring of men, a self-righteous radical. In his prophetic satire, *The Last Division* (1959), he placed our local insanity in the large perspective of global folly. 'The Ethnic Anthem' demonstrates the power of satire to fix flies in amber, preserving in fossil form our crimes and follies. Here are the last two stanzas:

We've split all difference so fine –
No wider than a hair or skin –
To foil the trick of traits and needs
So shockingly the same in breeds –

For such success in our researches
We thank Thee, Lord, in separate churches.

How wondrous is our work, our way,
And thine as well, Great Separator,
Who separating night from day
Left us to sort the rest out later.

What lent my interest in South African poetry a powerful focus was a decision to produce an anthology of poems selected with more rigorous criteria than either Francis Carey Slater's or that of Gullston and Macnab. The hours spent reading slim volumes on the tops of ladders in the South African and other libraries, in writing to known poets, in discovering 'new poets', in feeling and thinking my way through masses of material and formulating my responses as clearly as I could in a compact introduction, resulted in *A Book of South African Verse*, published by the Oxford University Press, London, in 1959. It is among the most important critical tasks I performed. It was also a stage in the growth of many literary friendships.

18 1954–January 1955

West Africa

In 1954 Jean and I with our baby Patrick went to Britain on a Nuffield Foundation Fellowship. It was a very demanding time, particularly for Jean, most of whose energies were taken up with caring for the baby, while I spent my days in libraries and many of my evenings at the theatre. I was deep into my poetic drama phase. After a wintry spell in London we moved north to Oxford, where we enjoyed a beautiful spring, and made the acquaintance of the poetry of John Betjeman in such poems as 'Belbroughton road is bonny, as pinkly blooms the May'. We acquired a second-hand car in which we explored the summer countryside, and went on a long trip to Scotland and the Lakes. When he was not in the car, I carried Patrick on my shoulders.

We also renewed several friendships, before moving to a house south of Bristol in the village of Winscombe, from where I used to commute to the university, leaving Jean and Patrick in the village. It was adjacent to Sidcot, a Quaker school, which my father and his sister Mary had attended at the turn of the century. I found Bristol University stimulating, particularly the presence of L.C. Knights and the members of the Drama School. And Howard Kitto was most generous in discussing Greek drama with me.

It was also the time when I met Roy Campbell, William Plomer and David Wright as recorded in the previous chapter.

As this volume can pay little attention to my main academic interest – Elizabethan drama – my meetings with Una Ellis Fermor and Muriel Bradbrook, L.C. Knights and my old tutor J.B. Leishman can simply be mentioned with gratitude.

On 3 December Jean returned to South Africa ahead of me. After a spell back in London, I followed. I asked the British Council to arrange for me to fly back via Nigeria and the Gold Coast. I wished to look at the new African universities which were springing up in those British colonies which were moving to independence most quickly. The Council – as always – was very helpful. Before setting out I had the pleasure of meeting Peter Abrahams, one of South Africa's best-known black writers, an early example of an artist driven into exile by our society.

January 1955 was an exciting time to visit Nigeria. It seemed to be a country where a period under a colonial power might achieve some sort of vindication. Under the guiding hand of Lord Lugard some 60 million people of 250 ethnic groups had been gradually brought together under some sort of government by district officers and indigenous councils for the main regions. By 1954 this artificially created country had become a federal state. The regional councils had increased greatly in importance. Much would depend on the collaboration between these regions.

I shall have to rely heavily on recollection for this month-long visit to Nigeria and Ghana. My memory is full of vivid images and incidents, but I know enough about its vagaries to wish that I had kept a diary.

I have a clear recollection of coming in to land at Kano under a vast orange sky. The runway was not far from a huge treeless city of sunbaked mud houses. Not round huts, but houses whose characteristic form was cubic, not spherical. Space galore. And strange as it all was, the light and the smell meant home to me. It was unmistakably African – dust and powdered dung, I think.

At Lagos I was met by a driver from the University of Ibadan. He was suffering from a bad asthmatic attack and drove as though death's winged chariot were behind the old Ford V8 sedan. He was, however, determined to die at home in Ibadan. He did not steer that vehicle, he aimed it. His rivals for road space were mostly five-ton Dodge or Ford trucks adapted for passenger use: they were crowded with happy humanity, bulging in all directions, decorated in bright bandanas and prints, gourds of fruit, and unhappy chickens. These trucks were known as Mammy Wagons.

Evidence of a passion for the written word was everywhere. The city traffic had been so slow that I had time to read the legends outside the diminutive booths from which people traded or did their business. London was the reference point for Lagos:

THE MAYFAIR PARADISE LADIES HAIRDRESSING SALOON
and
MAN-ABOUT-TOWN TAILORS
(Branch Office in Bond Street, London)

Any bare space, whether fixed or mobile, was regarded as waste and lost until redeemed by the written word. So, on the tailboards of Mammy Wagons I read a succession of adverts for various goods, religious exhortations and personal messages from the driver/owner to his passengers, such as 'Hurry up, don't waste my time!'

My driver wasted no time in overtaking him and, by a miracle, dodged into a gap, almost colliding with the tailboard of the truck ahead which told me, in huge African gothic letters, 'Prepare to meet thy Maker.'

I assured my Maker that I was not ready to meet him yet and prayed for time to prepare.

The road was a bad strip of tar under enormous cottonwood trees which met overhead, creating a hazy tunnel through which we hurtled, overtaking Mammy Wagons whenever the oncoming traffic allowed the gasping driver to risk another head-on crash. I thought of Othello, 'Of hair-breadth 'scapes in th' imminent deadly breach ...'

Then the stream slowed down and one caught glimpses of a village thatched with palm leaves in the dappled shade. Fairly close to the road was a spacious rectangular meeting-place under a large pitched roof supported on poles about six feet apart, between which, except for the entrances, were mud walls about two feet high. These were used as seats and even as reclining couches for the customers, all of whom seemed to be asleep or comatose. One patron lay prone with his spine along the wall and his hands clasped across his chest. His left foot was flat on the top of the wall, with the knee raised, on which knee the right foot rested. He seemed to be dreamily admiring the silhouette of his five toes against a far, vague sky. Over the entrance to this place of peace was a large sign, in Roman capitals – THE PUB.

The stream of traffic drew to a halt. There was no oncoming traffic. My driver explained – 'Level Crossing'. I got out to stretch my legs. In the distance I could see the horizontal prohibition of the boom.

Suddenly the bush on either side of the road blossomed with white eyes and white smiles. These soon acquired heads with baskets of fruit and gourds of palm wine for sale. For half an hour the road became a market in which the villagers did a roaring trade with passengers. I bought a banana the size of a policeman's truncheon. It was coarse and tasted of nothing. Then the boom was lifted, no train having passed in the meantime. I deduced that the boom operator must be in the pay of the villagers, or that he lived under such threats that he elevated their demands above those of the Nigerian Railways.

I stayed with the principal of the emergent university, a no-nonsense ex-navy or army man who had seen enough of the worldwide empire not to be surprised by the conventions and customs of its different peoples. What should one expect? He lived simply and gave some startling answers to my questions.

'What is the most reliable way of getting a letter from Lagos to Kano? Train or bus?'

'Neither. Cleft stick.'

I was both impressed and disturbed by the campus. It seemed to bear absolutely no relation to what I had seen – and what I was soon to see – of Ibadan.

Ibadan in 1954 was a city of about a million, spread out on seven (or was it seventeen?) hills – a set of villages which had grown until they had merged. It was intersected by a spider's web of tarred main roads, along which rose occasional European-style structures, seldom more than one or two stories. Commerce seemed to be run by the Lebanese. I had been told that the heart of the place was the market, so to the market I went.

Again the small crowded booths. I needed razor blades. These I found in a booth which also stocked razors and soaps and powders, and combs and Brylcreem – everything in a Western barbershop in fact. It smelt of scented soap.

Next to it was a medicine shop with not a single patent medicine in it – not even an aspirin. Instead exotic pods and roots and seeds, and grains such as would delight my vegetarian relatives, but also a variety of medicines that would not: dead beetles and other brittle arthropods; defunct lizards; fragments of birds, and on skewers a number of dried-out rodents about the size of rats, still squinting, rather surprised at the stakes emerging from their mouths.

Next to the medicine man was a camera shop which sold not only cameras and films but nude photographs. A black adolescent was staring mesmerised at a photograph of an amply endowed white woman in the never-never, smiling in a way white women in West Africa were not expected to smile at black people. Next, brightly coloured enamelware – yellow basins and blue colanders, and scarlet tea and coffee pots and green mixing bowls – really a delight to the eye. Nearly all the owners and shopkeepers were vital and voluble women. Some said women were the financial bosses of Nigeria.

But the magic rose as the sun went down. I don't know the name of the religious sect responsible, but its followers gather at key points all round the outskirts of the city with torches and drums. Singing, they moved towards the city centre, gathering worshippers en route. I moved closer to the road along which one of the bands would pass. At my elbow a young man next to a stall was examining a mouth-organ, turning it this way and that. Then the sound of the drums must have got through to him like a current catching hold of an idling leaf in a stream. He put the mouth-organ down and floated off into the procession, his feet already obeying the beat. And this hypnotic incrementation was happening on all the main roads into the centre of the city, long irregular lines of light and song converging in the dark. It was both beautiful and magical.

What shocked my subconscious was the lack of straight lines: with few exceptions the roads of Ibadan twist and turn and writhe like unhappy worms. How people find their way is a mystery. I was also shaken by the lack of a water supply and a sewerage system. Ibadan's drains were open, the original streams and gullies of those hills, but the fluid in them looked like a thick pus.

However, the people give the overwhelming impression of abundant energy and happy-go-lucky zest. Life is for now.

The campus, some distance outside Ibadan, was beautifully planned. Its buildings employed the best insights of Western architecture. They were elegant, clean, bright shapes against the surrounding forests. But as the dusk settled down, those trees looked like praying mantises to me, hovering above delicate structures as pale as moths.

Molly Mahood arranged a cocktail party so that I could meet members of the faculty. I remember three conversations. The first was about a crisis that had developed in the play-school run for the children of faculty members – English, Scots, Yoruba, Ibo, you name it. A slender black mother was objecting, gently but firmly, to her child's literary diet of Hickory Dickory Dock, Goosey Goosey Gander and Jack and Jill. This raised the whole question of mother-tongue education in a piquant manner – a problem with which the Molteno Project of Rhodes University has had to come to terms.

The second was a crisis in the Registrar's department. Exam questions had been stolen and fed to a poor candidate, who had been sent to university by contributions from his extended family. In most of Africa one's duty to one's family takes precedence over obligations to any other body. The 'guilty' clerk was in an impossible moral dilemma: between his duty to the university, who paid his salary, and his duty to his family, who needed this particular member to qualify and become a breadwinner. The argument was interminable. Some said that, while Africa remained Africa, such things were inevitable. One African proposed, with just a ghost of a smile, that the staff of the examinations section of the Registrar's department should all be well-paid expatriates. They were unlikely to be tempted by the importunities of poor relatives in the exam hall.

The third crisis was raised by my presence, apartheid. The moral turpitude and political folly of the South African Nationalist Government was already well known: a matter then for incredulity and amazement rather than revulsion and horror. The lengths to which our racist régime would go in implementing the legislation of the early 'fifties was as yet unknown.

Towards the end of the party an earnest New Zealander, who felt that someone should question my bona fides, cleared his throat:

'Professor – you are returning to South Africa?'

'Yes.'

'In spite of Dr Malan and apartheid?'

'It is my home.'

'But are you not afraid of going back?'

'Of what?'

'Of violence, of revolution.'

'That has always been a possibility. If the Nats stay in power they will make it probable.'

'How can you contemplate living on the edge of a volcano?'

'It is better than trying to adjust to life in someone else's wasteland. It is, after all, my own volcano.'

The phrase appealed to several of the Africans who repeated it with chuckles. They were living on a volcano of their own which would erupt in the Biafran war.

At another later party – a jolly one – I got on to a very convivial wavelength with a large ebullient Yoruba in flowing robes, who looked and behaved like a Roman epicure. He admitted that he did not like the Ibo from Eastern Nigeria, small, neat, usually in European suits and probably related to the Vice-Chancellor. I had been speaking of the great variety of people, 250 ethnic groups each with its own language, that he must have to consider in his job. He spoke tolerantly enough of the Hausa, but 'as for the Ibo, we Westerners regard them as little monkeys recently fallen from the trees'. He sounded like a Transvaler from the Waterberg talking of the Venda or the Pedi.

In the event, Nigeria has proved to be quite as volcanic as South Africa: the oil-rich Ibo had to pay dearly for their hankering after independence from the Yoruba Westerners and the Muslim north. But most of the whites were optimistic – the Muslims needed the carbohydrates of the south, and the south needed the protein of the cattle-keeping north. Intelligent self-interest would ensure success.

Molly Mahood took me on two memorable expeditions: to Ife to see the ancient bronze heads, and to Oyo for arts and crafts.

The town of Ife had the same higgledy-piggledy street plan that fazes many Westerners. Many of the houses were shacks. The forest came up close to its edge, into which we walked a very short distance to see a single carved figure about as tall as a man: a very simple shape, but its vaguely human form was enough to fill the shadowy spaces round it with uneasy power. I was pleased to walk into the sun again.

The bronze heads believed to be portraits of kings dating from the 14th century are among the most beautiful objects in the world. They were then in a neat rather clinical little museum, in which one might expect to find an operating theatre or a geiger counter, not these splendid uncrowned royal heads, each a triumphantly self-contained individual. What a handsome dignified dynasty!

While we were strolling among them trying to take them in, a small boy attached himself to us, chattering incessantly. Neither of us paid much attention to him. I hoped that my concentration on the bronzes would discourage his importunity, but I was wrong in this. So I asked Molly whether he was begging for bread (he did not look like a waif) because I would happily give him something to secure the quiet which the place and occasion demanded; but she smiled and said, 'No, he is practising his English on you. He does this with all whites. He'll go far.'

'I can't understand a word,' I said.

'And I only pick up an occasional one. It's a great problem. Their own teachers find it very difficult to speak English, just as the English find Chinese. Yoruba vowels and stress patterns, let alone syntax, interfere with

*Carved calabashes from Oyo, Nigeria
(after a photograph by Sirion Robertson)*

English all the time.'

That babbling, cheerful boy was an object lesson in the curse of the African babel.

There are over six hundred languages in Africa. Teaching reading and writing is comparatively easy. Speech is far more complex.

The excursion to Oyo was wonderful in quite a different way: instead of gazing at the completed artefact in permanent bronze, we watched artists working in beautiful but perishable materials, with no ambition to achieve permanence in their work.

Crosslegged in the shade of a single tall palm sat a bright-eyed man about 40 with small mountains of gourds on one side and beautiful carved and decorated bowls on the other. The designs were mostly abstract and mathematical, sometimes relieved by bands of lettering – demonstrating once again the preoccupation with script. His equipment was the sparsest I have ever seen: no studio, merely a patch of shade under a public palm tree; and his tools – four items only that I could see. They consisted of a piece of charcoal with which he would draw his design free-hand on the calabashes, and for darkening certain portions when incised; and chalk or talc for lightening others. For cutting and carving he used old razor blades of the variety that has only one sharpened edge, and a small Joseph

Rogers pocket knife whose blade had been sharpened away to half its original width. I bought two sets of carved calabashes at five shillings each, which I still have.

Farther on at the end of a very primitive track, we came to the cloth industry, about which my memory is vague. Once again the work was done in the open air, sometimes under tree shade, or here and there under little improvised shelters which a moderate wind could blow away. There were two main work areas: the dyeing works, entirely controlled by women; and the weaving, which was the preserve of the men.

The dyeing work which I witnessed was justly famous. A large white sheet of imported cotton was taken in hand by a lady comfortably squatting with a pile of nuts beside her. These are not for eating but for creating the design; hundreds of them are tightly twisted and knotted in spirals into the cloth until the entire sheet is gathered into a ball of nuts and string. It is then allowed to soak in the dyeing vats of deep-blue indigo vegetable dye. This penetrates the knotted cloth irregularly, so that when it is spread out to dry it presents a very lively surface, somewhat puckered in places, imprinted with the silhouette of the nuts in swirls and spirals.

I had time to watch one weaver only. He was making long, narrow strips of brilliant gold material, which I gathered could be sewn together to make more useable widths. His loom was very primitive and simple. The weft was attached to a peg in the ground some ten feet away. There was no mechanism for winding the completed fabric. The weaver had to move back as his fabric grew in length. His thread was wound on a rotating frame with four arms affixed to a wooden spindle. The bearing of this axle was fixed to the earth by a mound of sundried clay. All his equipment was improvised from natural materials except the bearing itself – a Coca-Cola bottle. The ease with which Africa finds unexpected uses for European by-products is always a delight to me – such as girls with their ankles made musical by threaded crown corks. I have seen a photograph of a coruscating shoulder-to-ankle cloak, which would have filled Liberace with envy, made out of thousands of silver teaspoons cleverly linked into a sort of loose chainmail, for a chieftain.

Somewhere in me is an elementary mathematician which panics when deprived for too long of straight lines, of recognisable triangles and quadrilaterals and of simple crystalline shapes. As I have said, tropical Africa is composed of squiggles, curves, roots and leaves. Most of its towns, markets and villages seemed to be gyrating happily rather than moving in purposive lines.

One of the things that I liked about the calabash carver and the weaver was their single-minded isolation. Everybody else seemed to be engaged in communal movement amounting sometimes to an unconscious dance, as though a cosmic ballet was buried in matter and trying to fight its way through into clarity. That is what made the little scraps of dance that we witnessed quite electrifying.

In the noisy whirlpool of the markets I was arrested by the behaviour of the lonely Hausa traders. They were so quiet, so self-contained, like benign but tolerant adults among a crowd of ebullient adolescents.

I was sitting in the shade of a tree outside the principal's house when one of these gentlemen approached, looking very Biblical in his long white robe and handling a long staff with the respect that a bishop affords his crozier. He was followed in single file by a train of humble bearers on whose heads were bundles and rolls. He saluted me, so I responded. At this, without fuss or enthusiasm, he gestured to his train who spread themselves in the shade and he started to show his wares.

I had experienced this delightful method of doing business in Egypt and in the Lebanon during the war, and once again fell for the polite cunning of it, the unhurried skill, the atmosphere of trust created as between two gentlemen connoisseurs, the bland flattery. In fact, I felt compelled to make only one quite irrational purchase: a white woollen carpet, about 5 by 7 feet, with a simple geometric design of linked red rectangles. I think the clarity of it mesmerised me. It was at the other extreme of the gorgeous dark-blue spirals and whirls created by the nuts tied into the cloth. Nothing in this carpet was natural in that sense. The starved primitive Euclid in me demanded possession of it. It was a magic carpet to me.

It had one great drawback, however. It differed from normal magic carpets in that it lacked the capacity to fly. I had the greatest difficulty in getting it out of Nigeria by sea and into South Africa. It was too unwieldy to get on to a plane.

So I had to take it to the Port of Lagos, before catching my plane to Accra in the Gold Coast. None of the shipping-clerks seemed to know how to set about shipping a carpet to South Africa. I persisted, however, and in time found myself in the office of a senior export official. 'Ah yes,' he said, 'Mr X will help you.' And he handed a form in sextuplicate to be filled in by Mr X, a neat young man standing to attention at his desk.

His typing was painfully slow. His two index fingers took it in turns to peck at the keyboard like a pair of storks at irregularly scattered mealie pips. When he was half done his boss appeared again, looked over his shoulder, and reprimanded him sternly in a language I did not know, and left. The clerk removed the six sheets and started carefully interleaving a new set with the old carbon.

I looked at my watch. At this rate I would lose my flight to Accra. So I found the boss and asked if I might not expedite the process by filling in the forms myself. He consented to this, apologising for the clerk's slowness. A new man, he said, but with very good marks in the Pitman's secretarial exams. I had no time to express my scepticism on this point. In fact, I only caught my flight because it had been delayed for half an hour. (By the way, the carpet did finally arrive in Grahamstown.)

I found myself seated next to a canny North Countryman in the insurance business.

'Premiums on motor vehicles must be pretty high,' I said. 'I've never experienced such wild driving, nor seen so many road-side wrecks.'

'No insurance company in West Africa will insure any motor vehicle,' he said.

'How do you manage for clerks?' I asked.

He looked at me appreciatively. 'How long have you been in Nigeria?'

'Three weeks or so.'

'Well, old man, you've hit the nail on the head. There's no shortage of clerks with qualifications, but a qualified clerk is as rare as hen's teeth.'

'But why?'

'I'm not quite sure. But there's a story that goes like this. In 1926 a farsighted man from Lagos went to the United Kingdom and put himself through the Pitman's shorthand and typing course. In time he passed in the third class. When he got back to Lagos he opened a secretarial college and appointed himself as its principal. As he knew the difficulties his pupils would experience he could either eliminate them or skirt around them. Very few of his pupils in fact became practising clerks; they also opened secretarial colleges of their own ... all over Lagos and beyond.'

There are many such stories which one must take with a pinch of salt; but the incontrovertible fact remains of the highly qualified clerk who could not fill in a routine form.

In Accra I stayed on the Achimota campus for a few days. Professor Walton, head of the English Department, was most helpful and a Canadian called Lamb showed me the fascinating city, both by day and by night.

The manager of one of the night clubs took me to his heart for no better reason than my South African origins. He would hear no evil of South Africans, he said. And why? He'd been in the King's African Rifles during the war and they'd been sent to East Africa. He'd been the batman to a South African lieutenant for long months in a base camp. (I sometimes think base camps are worse places than front lines.) His officer quietly went to pieces when he heard that his wife had produced a baby for his best friend. The batman had to cover up for him, passing his hangovers off as headaches, and his alcoholic shakes as malaria. After a few months of this care his officer recovered. Both had unpacked their hearts and memories until there was little that they did not know about each other.

And before he left to go on to Egypt, his officer said:

'I know what you want more than anything else in the world and I'll help you to get it.'

And sure enough, when the war ended, he had sent him half his demobilisation gratuity, which was enough for his batman to buy a share in the night club.

Lamb was a marvellous guide and took me down to the busy beach to watch the fishermen with their nets and boats near the old slave fort. It was a scene that came back to me a few years later when reading Wolé Soyinka's *Brother Jero*.

There was trouble in the educational world, a head-on clash between an educationist and a politician. The matriculation examination had not produced enough candidates to fill all the vacancies at the new university. Prime Minister Nkrumah said they were to be filled with the best of the failures. It ended, I think, with the principal's resignation.

The people of Accra had much in common with those of Nigeria – the same passion for literacy, the same reverence for the Western way of life and of England in particular. The élite were nearly all Been-tos. Affluence was signalled by the epithet 'fridge-full'. To be always fridge-full was quite something. 'Jaguar' was turned into an epithet for up-to-date elegance. 'Look at that girl – she's really Jaguar.' The coastal folk were far more Westernised than the people of the interior, having been exposed to the impact of traders and missionaries for centuries. Accra had skilled men in some numbers, many of whom had been juvenile delinquents from the slums of the port. An enlightened official had arranged for them to be educated in a trade while serving time. As skills were rare, they emerged set-up for life. There is a story that one of the great ladies of Accra asked the Governor what the least offensive crime was her son had to commit in order to get sentenced and so secure a training which was not otherwise available in the Gold Coast.

Well, the emerging state of Ghana knew the importance of skills and had established an Institute of Technology in the interior among the educationally backward but wealthy and superior Ashanti, at a place called Kumasi – an institute in the process of evolving into a university.

We had to wait for our flight to Kumasi while the plane of the Prime Minister landed. Everyone stood still in their tracks to watch the new wonder of a black man walking tall, a black Head of State, that long overdue African phenomenon. Prime Minister Kwame Nkrumah looked handsome, confident and intelligent to me. The creator of the Convention People's Party whose slogan was 'self-government now' would soon be President of the first British African colony to achieve independence (1960).

The plane was familiar – a dear old Dakota – but the passengers were not. One of the most beautiful women I have ever seen was on that flight with her exquisite twin daughters, about 6 or 7. They were all dressed en suite in the same gold material, all modestly aware of their exceptional charm; and all wore earrings and necklets of the same design, in the distinctive red gold for which the Gold Coast is renowned.

There were also several simpler people laden with cloth bundles. The blight of the rectangular suitcase had not yet struck the land. They seemed quite blasé about air travel, unlike the live and bewildered chickens which they carried in or under their arms.

My hosts were Mr and Mrs Murray Carlin, who kindly spent several days driving me around. They lived outside town itself. There were road blocks everywhere. The Minister of Education's front door had been blown in during the night. The soldiers manning the road blocks waved all white drivers through. Among a host of recollections I select three.

I had seen lively wooden carvings and illustrations of chiefs and their retinues. Handsomely robed, he rides a beautiful donkey, the rest walk: the groom, who leads the ass; the herald, carrying his symbol, a cock; his champion, carrying an enormous old flintlock or 'Dane gun'; his butler, with a square gin bottle; and the bearer of his enormous ceremonial parasol. I had hoped I might be lucky to see such a procession. I was, but in process to transformation. The donkey had been replaced by a large black limousine. It drew up on the side of the road where a footpath entered the jungle. Out of it tumbled and scrambled the cock, the Dane gun, the gin bottle and the parasol. They all formed up into the appropriate sequence: but the chief without his donkey looked somewhat diminished. They were on their way to a village funeral which we subsequently watched.

The coffin had to be fetched from the mortuary in a glossy black hearse. It looked out of place on the fringe of the mud-and-thatch village where the mourners had gathered in large numbers. Instead of the black, purple, grey and white of a Western funeral, they were dressed in a variety of reds, terra-cotta predominating.

The drummers started and the chanting and the handclapping, a combination of sounds new to my ears, growing in urgency and volume, until I found it very disturbing; but what I heard was nothing to what I saw, the movement that accompanied the sound. But accompany is quite the wrong word: it suggests two activities. In this funeral rite, song, drum and dance made a single dynamic action, created by all the participants who had lost their identity in it. They did not dance the dance, the dance danced them; it seemed that the drummers' wrists, by changing their rhythm, could fling the dancers' bodies about as a juggler does his plates. Their eyes were open but there was no observant ego in them, only a glazed communal echo.

No group of Westerners could achieve that happy self-obliteration, that immolation in community. I have seen something approximating to it in a classical ballet. But the great difference is that a classical ballet is performed by highly trained artists in a theatre, before an audience seeking entertainment. We were not an audience watching a performance; we were outsiders eavesdropping on a religious rite in which the community were both performers and audience.

The power of the music was quite extraordinary. Wonderful as the experience was, I was glad when we moved away, wending through the forest to an elevated ridge which encircled a beautiful sunken lake.

The air was dead still. No birds called, not a leaf stirred. Only far below on the sunken lake, one man rowing his dugout, leaving a long, thin, silver scar on the inverted sky. It healed very slowly. After the funeral that 'silence sank like music on my heart'.

I recalled having read of an incident during the Ashanti wars which had ended with British victory in 1901. A detachment of Imperial troops was cut off in a timber fortress built on two levels in a forest clearing. The Ashanti had no artillery to demolish the white man's wooden carapace, but they did have ways of getting inside it and weakening his mind. They could drive him to distraction by the sound of drumming, ceaseless and complex. The story goes that one of their great composers for the drum orchestra produced a piece of music whose slithering rhythms were designed to induce madness. It was called 'White Man Die Upstairs'. I do not recall whether this psychological warfare was successful or not, but the music had survived among the drummers.

I asked to see something of the music department at the college and was introduced to a rather reserved African who had spent some time at the Royal School of Music in London. He kindly arranged a little concert by his students. This consisted mainly of adaptations of European music to the African mode, and a delightful traditional flute composition. I thanked him and asked for more indigenous pieces. He obliged, explaining some of the features of the drums employed – the ingenious donno, a double-headed drum shaped like an hourglass and held under the armpit like the bagpipes. The pitch of the membranes, being laced to each other, is altered by tightening or easing the upper arm's grip on the instrument. Then there was the apentemma, a single-headed open drum, rather like a top-heavy egg cup, on which the vellum is laced to six or eight pegs protruding from the upper third of the hollowed and carved trunk. They were played either with the flat of the hand or hooked drumsticks, or both.

My host's original nervousness had abated a little. So I ventured, 'What about "White Man Die Upstairs"?' His eyes narrowed a little, then he issued orders to his students. In a trice they had produced the huge talking drums which were like apentemma, only much larger and tilted at an angle of about forty-five degrees, and smaller instruments. Finally came the king of drums, a man-sized, upright giant which is inclined when it is played so that the sound can escape freely from the bottom. When this was brought, the drummers' faces all lit up. This meant serious work on eight or nine hollow trees and stretched membranes – the voice of the animal and vegetable world released by fluttering hands and striking sticks.

There was only one piece of metal in it, a little gong like a goat bell which was struck, I think, by a piece of wood and kept time for the rest.

The composition started with one drum only, but it soon drew the others in. The complexity of the rhythm was such that I was soon lost, unable to detect any regularity or variation except the click of the little metal gong. It seemed that there was no reason why the river of sound should stop its infinity of ripples and fibrillations. My white man's mind would certainly have been impaired by days and nights of it.

I was quite bewildered by West Africa. It was so utterly different from anything I had experienced before, or expected. Forests were new to me and I don't think I could ever live with them. And the forest Africans, growing cocoa and yams, were totally unlike Southern Bantu-speakers, whose culture was cattle based. Even more startling was the apparent emancipation of West African women and the extent of their commercial enterprise. Their understanding of money and the speed of their mental arithmetic were staggering.

I was also baffled by the euphoria of nearly all the white people I spoke to about the decolonisation in which they were so enthusiastically engaged. Colonies were bad in principle; in spite of which Africans were still 'unspoilt'. Given the best democratic constitutional machinery and the pattern of a tried civil service, they would soon prove themselves and move into an era in which Africa would shed the vestiges of its subjection to Europe. While I had no doubts about the rightness of granting independence, I suffered from a hunch that the effectiveness of constitutions and administrations is closely related to the societies from which they evolve. The British Constitution works for the British people. Much admired, parliamentary democracy was adopted, adapted and tried in various parts of the West, but had not proved to be a particular success among Italians, Germans, Spaniards or Russians, all of whom had opted for dictatorships of various kinds. Or had we forgotten the recent war? Why should it work in Africa among peoples whose traditions of government were so very different from Britain's? There was a rather endearing air of generous paternalism about it: 'Here, Africa, is the best we have, as a coming-out gift. We've produced this by trial and error over the centuries and we know that it works.'

I did not express this scepticism very often because I was doubtful about so unusual a judgement; but I did apparently do so to my hosts. Murray Carlin writes (11 May 1980): 'I remember you arguing – it was the time of incipient independence – that parliamentary government can't be just instituted, it has to grow. You cited English history. As liberals we were unwillingly impressed. You were right – we were wrong.'

My flight from Ghana to Johannesburg was delayed for ten hours. The magneto or some such part on the large four-propeller plane had packed up and we had to wait until a spare arrived from America on another flight. I did not go back into the city to sleep, but sat on the edge of the tarmac in a canvas chair, talking to a variety of other frustrated passengers, all chain-smoking and drinking beer after beer after beer.

One of the most picturesque of those waiting through that long night was a Dutch contractor who had gone bankrupt. He was abandoning a job on which he had hoped to make his fortune. He had put in a tender for erecting the powerline which would take electricity from the hydro-electric Volta Dam to Accra – an imaginative piece of engineering much to Nkrumah's credit. He had worked out his tender with enormous safety margins. For unskilled workmen he had paid wages better than those of skilled artisans in Europe. He had allowed for double the normal number of days which might be washed out by rain; ditto for disease; he had made provision for every conceivable eventuality.

And then he would rehearse what had gone wrong, working himself up into a rage against men who did not know how to use a pair of pliers, who lost twenty wire strainers every day. His tired too-blonde girl friend would try to calm him down. For a while he would sit there, quietly seething. Then he would start working himself up again, recounting another episode. She would put a gentling hand on his furry forearm. Responsive, he'd quieten his voice and continue to indulge himself by hissing savage sarcasms which sound so much more scathing in Dutch than in English.

I had not yet read *The Heart of Darkness*, but that sad man sprang to mind a year later when I met two characters in Conrad's prophetic work: the Accountant and the lost Russian sailor who clings to a fine manual on the technicalities of sailing in the heart of the Congo.

I had a dim feeling that the failure of this well-meaning engineer might be matched by failures of others in different spheres.

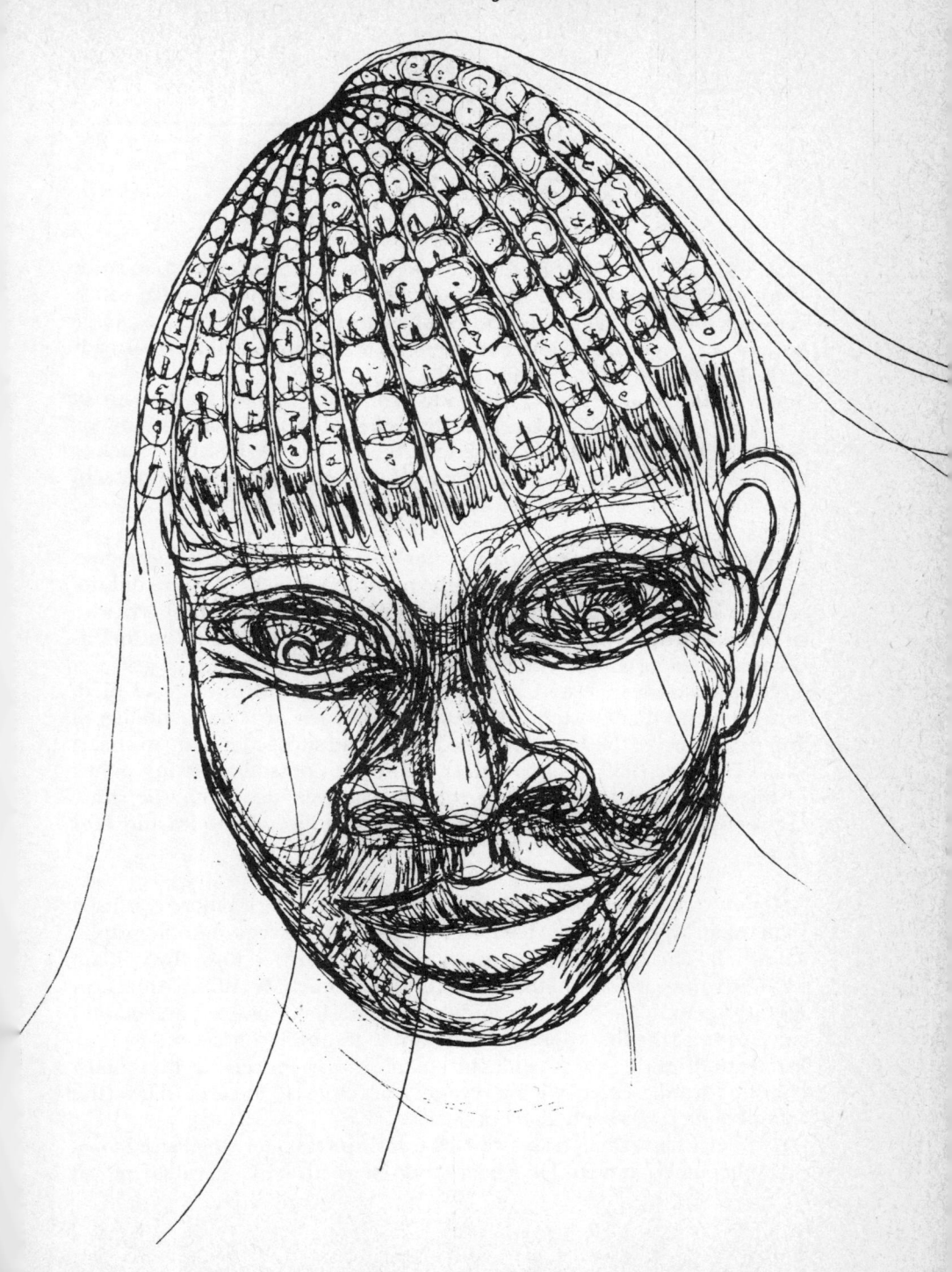

19   1958–78

Professor at Large

In 1958 Jean and I went to America on a Carnegie Fellowship, to study Drama and English Departments – a 'mind-blowing' adventure which deserves a chapter at least. It made me aware of 'a world elsewhere', a free society in a huge and various continent, in which my brother had already settled successfully and happily.

Among the many friends I made was Professor Kenneth MacGowan, of the Drama Faculty of U.C.L.A., who had worked at one time with Eugene O'Neill. One of his hobbies was Stone Age artefacts. When I got back to South Africa I sent him (having obtained the appropriate permit) half of a broken, small San digging stone.

Jean was afflicted at times by pain in her legs, which raised great anxieties in us lest they signalled a return of the polio attack of 1957. (This did not happen.) We were also grieved at the condition of my mother, who suffered a stroke which affected her speech. I tried to get to Cradock as often as possible to visit The Poplars.

While we were in America, J.G. Strijdom, Prime Minister, had died. When I heard that Dr Hendrik Verwoerd, the most articulate, intelligent and persuasive of the Apartheid politicians, had succeeded him, my heart sank. The year 1959 saw many fresh assaults on possible growing points of liberalism and the attack on the open universities by the Separate Universities Bill, which was to break the affiliation of Rhodes and Fort Hare.

As for my own career as a writer, I came back from America more confused than usual. My creative ego had taken a knock. My first very autobiographical novel, 'The Innocent Brightness', had been turned down by William Plomer, who read for Jonathan Cape, and by Monica McCall, an American literary agent. (The labour was not entirely wasted, however, and when I came to write the first volume of my autobiography in the 'seventies, 'The Innocent Brightness' was a quite invaluable source for recollections of my childhood, and written as it was, twenty years closer to the events. Like the Long Poem, it has been a sort of quarry.)

My poetry had reached an awkward transitional stage. *Stranger to Europe* had sold out. What next? I had been struggling with a demon called logical positivism. The poetic record of my battle with that benign demon had not impressed anyone, but there were other pieces, like 'Myths', dating back a decade to Switzerland in the winter of 1946–47, which I thought worth airing.

But it was my other preoccupation, plays, which I still believed ought to be written in verse, that probably took up most of my writing time. *The Dam* and *The Dove Returns* had been produced by the National Theatre Organisation – neither with much popular success. Two others had been written, and turned down – both healthy attempts to adjust to the more popular contemporary idiom, in a flexible verse which could approximate prose speech, and not bother an actor too much.

And I was almost obsessed with two major themes – an African version of the *Medea* of Euripides, which I did manage to complete as *Demea* in 1960, and an allegorical play based closely upon the wreck of the San Jão as described in that collection of Portuguese shipwrecks called *The Tragic History of the Sea*. This was to be a working out of the tragic contemporary South African scene as the result of Western capitalism's failure to listen to its Christian conscience, and indeed, to the partial corruption of that conscience itself. I never wrote it, but told Don Maclennan of the story, which he used for his own different motives some years later.

My haverings as a creative writer alternated with my academic hoverings between English Literature and Speech and Drama, and both were compounded by acute debates as to whether to attempt to leave South Africa or not. Early in 1959 I summarised my preoccupations:

1. Should we start planning to leave South Africa? No longer a situation of straws in the wind, but forests of splinters. The disastrous combination of corrupt intellectuals and the sjambok complex of the lower whites. The humiliation and ignominy of being governed by a cabinet of obscurantists and cranks.
2. What to do, as a writer, particularly with the rejected novel. Back to poetry for the present – or a new play on the groundwork of *Medea*, i.e. Medea = coloured woman, Jason = Englishman from Wellington's Army, Creon = Trekboer–patriarch.
3. Drama Department – can I press for this until (1) above is settled in my mind?

What am I? Writer? Professor of English? Or Drama? South African 'committed' to see it through? Or a possible 'intellectual' émigré?

We were inevitably influenced by our many academic friends leaving South Africa. For instance, Cecil Todd's account of his exploratory visit to the campus of the new African university at Makerere elicited this note.

'We were thrown into an agony of indecision by Cecil Todd's account (over drinks last night) of life in Kampala and conditions at Makerere (which they had just visited and to which they were moving) – an open society in Africa, where colour does not matter! Perhaps a job in an African university outside S.A. might give me what I need – an atmosphere in which to work, to get to know Africans. A place with a generous spirit, and a proper and proud view of its role. At present I feel stifled by Rhodes and Grahamstown. Something is needed to stimulate this part of the world. A Grahamstown Festival? Mentioned this to Rennie at tea on Sunday morning, who said that Hewson had written a letter proposing such a thing, to be linked with Settlers Day celebrations. Deserves a lot of thought.'

The compulsion to escape South Africa and its regime was pradoxically combined with the desire to do something to stimulate this part of the world. Periodically I would think of moving our whole family to America, particularly when my hopes of a Drama department at Rhodes receded, and I received a letter from Professor Kenneth MacGowan at U.C.L.A. saying that if I thought of leaving South Africa I should get in touch with him. I was sure that I could do well in the U.S.A.

But the emigration possibility was offset by other, more powerful considerations, which I listed as 'the attachment we both had for this house, and our love of South Africa. There is also the problem of moving four young children, and our hesitation about the American life style. And of my mother's health. How can I leave permanently while she is as she is? Nor are our other parents getting any younger.'

Then a request came from John Sutherland, editor of the *Evening Post* asking for an article 'Why I am not leaving South Africa'. The writing of it was not easy. The gist of it was simple. The headline was 'My ancestors stuck it through thick and thin'. The fact is, I felt I belonged; my family roots were deep, and strong, and so were Jean's. And I felt that my subject, English, was not merely an important practical instrument to be made available to my fellow countrymen, but that it had a creative, artistic, African future to which I was willy-nilly committed. This seemed to be corroborated by the response to *A Book of South African Verse*, which appeared in 1959, and acted as an encouraging catalyst for many.

The publication of that article 'Why I am not leaving South Africa' marked a definite stage in my finding a local habitation in South Africa, and more particularly in the Eastern Cape. From then on periods of overseas study leave, such as that to Holland and Britain in 1961, enriching as they always were, deepened my sense of commitment to this particular place, and have had wide-ranging implications for my professorial activities.

I have in the chapter 'Apprentice Professor' given some account of my interest in English as a second language or *lingua franca*. In the 'sixties this hardened into a determination to do something about it: to get language studies with a modern linguistic bias established at Rhodes. This took place in 1964, with Dr W.R.G. Branford as Senior Lecturer in charge.

In 1961 I flew a kite at an S.A.C.E.E. meeting in Cape Town, about the need to establish an Institute for the Study of English in Africa. U.C.T. had a powerful tradition of language studies; it could have provided a wonderful base from which to turn some attention away from Anglo-Saxon and Icelandic to modern English in 19th and 20th century Southern Africa. But neither of the big universities even saw my kite. So I presented it to the Rhodes Senate and they got the message. The establishment of the I.S.E.A. was announced in July 1964 during the celebrations of the sixtieth anniversary of the foundation of Rhodes University. The first director was Dr W.R.G. Branford, with myself as chairman of its board of management. The Institute has shown a talent for giving birth to other institutions.

The main interest of the first director of the Institute was lexicography – the rapidly developing English vocabulary of our country. This in time led to the establishment of the Dictionary Unit, which has produced *A Dictionary of South African English*, edited by Dr Jean Branford and now in its third edition. This project has also become a government-funded unit associated with Rhodes University.

In the late 'fifties I was approached by a charming American professor who wanted to buy manuscripts of South African authors, including my own. This made me think of the need for a local repository for such materials, which I started gathering.

In 1972 the H.S.R.C. announced the establishment in Pretoria under its auspices of a national documentation centre to cater for all major language groups. Protests from Cape Town and Grahamstown were ignored – Pretoria was to be the place. As one of my supporters said, 'Why should everything be put under Oom Paul's top hat?' This made me propose to André de Villiers (then Director of I.S.E.A.) that we should start 'a collection which would be truly representative of South African English literature, situated in a city with rather more symbolic significance for the South African English cultural heritage than Pretoria'. The materials (books and manuscripts) which I had already gathered, formed a very useful nucleus for the Thomas Pringle Collection which was cared for by the University Librarian. I wrote letters to many literary friends and secured the enthusiastic support of Stephen Gray, Jack Cope and many others. An early good omen was a gift from Meg (Bull) of Somerset East – a manuscript of Thomas Pringle's early poems in his own hand. The growth of the collection and the H.S.R.C.'s clarification of its own policy led to their funding a National Documentation Centre for English in 1974. This was declared a cultural institute in 1980, the National English Literary Museum.

The Institute's educational work in the *lingua franca* field had been limited by two constraints: money and linguistic expertise. But in 1973 the

Molteno Trust started providing the first, and Professor Lanham the second. I believe that the Molteno Project alone justifies the establishment of the Institute. Its primary-school courses, *Breakthrough to Literacy* and *Bridge to English* are revolutionising the teaching of literacy to blacks in Southern Africa, and acting as a general leaven in primary-school education. Instead of the old teacher-dominated learning-by-rote methods, which have prevailed for generations, they apply child-centred methods in the classroom with stimulating effects on both teacher and taught.

In 'Apprentice Professor' I mentioned my part in the struggle to get South African works prescribed in schools and universities. I suppose I was driven partly by a belief that children's or adults' own geographical and historical environment should occasionally be evoked in the poems, plays and novels they read in their mother tongue. There was a real danger in my childhood that English could become associated almost entirely with England, and that poetry, in particular, was about a beautiful remote land with different plants and trees and flowers, topsy-turvy seasons and upside-down moon and stars, and that one's own language was somehow foreign to the world one walked in. It was, in fact, through the Afrikaans poetry of C. Louis Leipoldt that I first realised that language and landscape could belong lovingly together. But English was already, in part at least, an African language, and I was determined that it should become more so.

As I tried to run the English department on democratic lines, I seldom invoked my power to force lecturers to do anything against their academic consciences. But from 1966 they reluctantly consented to offer African Literature as a special optional Honours subject. The sky did not fall.

From 7 to 11 July 1969 the Institute for the Study of English in Africa, whose secretary at the time was Sydney Clouts, organised a highly successful conference in Grahamstown for the English Academy of Southern Africa. It was entitled 'South African Writing in English and Its Place in School and University'.

The entire proceedings were published in *English Studies in Africa*, March 1970. *UNISA English Studies* brought out a special number in September 1970, devoted to poems by Guy Butler, Douglas Livingstone, Anne Welsh, Michael Macnamara, Perseus Adams, Sydney Clouts and Ruth Miller. With the exception of Anne Welsh who was in England, and Ruth Miller who had died, the poems were read by the poets themselves.

The debate waxed warm between those whose faces were set against making room for colonial works in literature syllabuses already overburdened with half a millennium of metropolitan riches. The most articulate and persuasive of the 'conservatives' was that brilliant lecturer and lovable man Philip Segal, then of U.C.T., and I was the chief among those who advocated introducing some African and South African works into a university syllabus. Our deep differences on this issue did not spoil our friendship. This may strike some of the present generation of English academics as evidence of a lack of proper ideological commitment, which now seems to demand a personal rejection and even hatred of any who don't agree with one's critical assumptions.

It was a wonderful gathering of literary and academic talents. Of the many fine readings and performances which remain fixed in my memory, I shall mention only two.

Alan Paton read part of his *Kontakion for You Departed*. I had always admired the eloquence of his prose, but I had no idea whatever of its cadences – particularly when read by Alan himself. It was, in fact, not so much a reading as a superbly controlled performance of that moving work. Alan was an actor of great skill. It was one of the best one-man shows I have ever attended.

Then there was the world première of Athol Fugard's *Boesman and Lena*. Here are two stories about it. The Rhodes Theatre had a wonderful cleaner and night-watchman known as Henry, a Xhosa of upright character and natural authority. Henry was proud of the theatre and was instructed to keep a sharp lookout for light-fingered vagrants who were apt to nip into the dressing-rooms to steal costumes.

Henry had been on leave and when he came on duty again he was unaware that the curtain was about to go up on the première of a play about 'coloured' or 'Hottentot' vagrants. Athol Fugard (Boesman), Yvonne Bryceland (Lena) and Glynn Day (Outa) had spent hours perfecting their make-up and rags, and had just assumed their squatting positions centre stage when Henry returned from supping and did his rounds. He could not believe his eyes: the desecration of his stage by vagrants.

'Uit! Uit!' he shouted.

Athol says they were in some danger of Henry's cudgel, but the stage manager intervened in time. The actors took comfort from this as evidence of the authenticity of their make-up.

The curtain rose.

It was an extraordinary experience. Some of us had seen earlier Fugard plays such as *The Blood Knot*, but this piece moved beyond the terrible man-made dilemma in South Africa of blood brothers who have different-coloured skins, to the desolation of the dispossessed shack-dwellers, wandering in search of a spot of earth to reassemble scraps of junk that had made their homes before the 'slum clearing' bulldozers had moved in. The play moved beyond moral indictment of forced removals into a searing exposure of spiritual dereliction in a landscape familiar to anyone who knows the Swartkops mud flats. And for me, just below that salty surface was the heath in *King Lear* and the ashheap of Job: man abandoned in a desolate universe.

The curtain came down. The applause started and swelled into a thunderclap. I went backstage to congratulate them. Boesman and Lena and Outa were still huddled there in a knot. The noise from the auditorium sounded like a hailstorm hammering on a corrugated-iron roof.

I don't know what I said. It would not have been heard.

'I couldn't believe it,' said Athol later. 'I knew I'd broken through.'

The intellectual and artistic success of this conference, which owed so much to live performances, confirmed my belief that festivals could play a creative cultural role in our society.

By 1972 we were offering South African Literature as a paper in English III, but not without trauma. At the annual departmental 'parliament' in 1971 at which this decision was taken, I am reliably informed that the following 'electrifying exchange' took place. At the time I was teaching Shakespeare and Donne, and possibly Langland. One of the ablest lecturers, a Milton and Sir Thomas Browne man, said that our students needed to realise that literature did not begin with Thomas Pringle's arrival in South Africa in 1820. He recalled, 'There was a deathly pause; you went grey, narrowed your eyes and said in slow, acid tones: 'No one needs to remind *me* that literature does not begin in 1820!'

The greatest battles I had to fight in these departmental parliaments sprang from my belief that innovatory solutions could be found once we moved beyond thinking in either/or terms, and entertained the possibility of both/and. There is much virtue in both/and. And some flexibility was already accepted at Honours level in the options offered.

On 16 August 1972 I was able to write to William Plomer:

'We have at last had the courage of our convictions, and started teaching South African literature in our B.A. English course – an optional paper in the third year, which some sixty students out of ninety chose to do.

'I am handling early diaries and South African poetry up to Campbell. Yesterday I took a seminar at which a bright 18-year-old lass gave a critical appreciation of your "Transvaal Morning". She did it extremely well. I'm sure it would have warmed your heart to hear her gay yet deferential response to the words and to the idea itself. She got the point all right.

'In the fourth year (Honours) we offer a paper called African Writing in English – a continental survey of mainly black writers, although we have included Conrad's *Heart of Darkness* and Cary's *Mister Johnson* "if only for the record".'

In 1973 African Literature in English came out of hiding as a special Honours option and was listed in the calendar. These moves caused a flutter in the literary and academic dovecotes. Writers welcomed them. 'The thin edge of the wedge,' said the Great Traditionalists. Just how thick (in both senses of the word) that wedge has proved to be is a matter of polemic into which we cannot enter here, but it is ironic that Natal, once the bastion of Leavisites, is now the most hospitable to the Africanists. Perhaps the salvation-through-literature spirit has survived there: English

Literature as moral pabulum – not for mother-tongue speakers only, but for all.

I have always felt uneasy about attempts to turn literature into politics or ethics or a substitute for religion. Literature is literature, a major human activity which should be studied in its own right, rather as we study music or painting. Of course it has moral and political dimensions, as have all human activities, but these are not its main concern.

There is the old attempt to justify poetry, drama and fiction by saying that they delight and they teach; they teach delightfully. This may be so, but no poets or dramatists or novelists really regard themselves primarily as teachers, delightful or otherwise. They are primarily artists, makers whose material, language, happens to be far more difficult to handle than pigment or sound. They write because they must, that is to please themselves, and, because they need an audience, to please others. Literature is entertainment, and people need entertainment as they need bread. There is good entertainment and bad, and entertainment for a variety of occasions. We must stop feeling guilty about it.

Is not joy the aim of life? True joy is never superficial or escapist. That's what all our profounder insights tell us. Heaven is not a place of learning or debating (that's Purgatory) but of song and dance. God is all beauty, all love, and our destiny is to enjoy him. We are told that 'for the joy that was set before him' Christ 'endured the cross, despising the shame'.

Why do we make such heavy weather of this? No musicologist apologises for Bach or Beethoven or Benjamin Britten.

As artists we derive various pleasures from our labours, for example the joy of shaping our materials; and one of the joys of studying any art is our pleasure in the well-made object, the beautifully functioning artefact, the difficult and complex task handled with elegance and grace. We also take much pleasure (inseparable from the first) in what we are embodying or incarnating. We are involved as persons in creating something other than ourselves, an object but a miraculous object which can speak to other people.

It is in this creating of 'speaking objects' that the artist differs from most people. If the field is literature, he uses language very differently from business people, mayors, journalists, sociologists, etc., who use it merely to communicate a 'prose meaning'. And unless we insist that literature's purpose, like that of all other arts, is to create pleasures and joys for mankind which the social and other sciences can't provide, we have no case at all. The social sciences are rightly concerned with caring for man's basic, predominantly physical needs. Artists are concerned with satisfying hungers other than those of the belly. We cannot live by bread alone. Artists are, all of them, non-materialists.

But – and this is a big 'but' – they must have real consciences about doing what can be done to release their fellows from bondage to their bodily needs. They must be conscientious citizens and, like everyone else, they have a responsibility towards their hungry neighbours.

The apprentice professor's theatrical interests and activities, together with his visit to drama schools in the United States, had impelled him to press for two related developments: a theatre for the university, and courses in Speech and Drama.

One of the results of the closing of the branch of Rhodes University in Port Elizabeth was the sale of the old museum in Bird Street for, I think, eighty thousand pounds. By this time there was a strong Little Theatre lobby on campus and in the city – including Rob Antonissen, Jean-Louis Cattaneo, the Ewers, Georg Grüber and Advocate Norman Addleson. Council decided to spend the Bird Street money on a Little Theatre for Rhodes.

For six months the architect Lyall Engels and I lived in each other's pockets. We did an extensive tour to the north, examining, it seemed, every building in which plays were performed in the Orange Free State and Transvaal. I wrote to several overseas theatre designers and scholars. The most important response came from Leslie Hotson. He pointed out that the theatres in which the greatest dramas had first appeared, the Greek and Elizabethan, had all been so designed as to give the audience not only a clear view of the stage but of themselves, thus emphasising the social, communal nature of the form. Tiers of boxes in a semi-circle, or a steeply raked seating on an arc, also heighten the actors' awareness of their audience. Actors and audience both go to the theatre not only to see, but to be seen. So his advice re auditorium design was to 'stack 'em up close'. This gave me the courage to go for a steep rake, which had the additional advantage of creating enough headroom for the foyer to be placed under it. To be quite sure it would work, I made a wooden scale model of it. The other main feature of the design was to soften the picture-frame effect of the proscenium arch by side boxes, and to have some playing space in front of the curtain line.

Not only had the University agreed to build a theatre, it had founded a sub-department of Speech and Drama, of which I was head, with Beth Dickerson as lecturer. She did – and still does – most of the practical teaching. All language departments collaborated to provide lectures in Dramatic Literature.

In Settlers Week, September 1966, the Theatre was duly inaugurated with performances of Mozart's *Marriage of Figaro* produced by Georg Grüber, and *Take Root or Die*, 'A Play by Guy Butler, produced by Beth Dickerson. Décor and costumes by Ken Robinson, with 70 characters based on authentic information from the letters and diaries of the 1820 Settlers, the cast including many of their direct descendants.'

We hired a railway bus and a lorry and took the circus on a grand tour through the Eastern Cape – playing at Graaff-Reinet, Somerset East, Bedford and Cradock, with visits to the Valley of Desolation, the Mountain Zebras and the Pringles of the Baviaans River valley thrown in.

It was all enormous fun, but it became increasingly clear to me that I could not do justice to the departments both of English and of Speech and Drama. I found it very difficult indeed to decide which to give up. If I should choose Speech and Drama I felt I would have to take at least a year's study leave to put myself through a crash course in voice training, mime, movement and acting, in order to have at least a rudimentary knowledge of the techniques which actors must master. At the advanced age of 50-plus, that was something I balked at doing.

So by 1966, from my chair of Eng. Lit., I had started a collection of manuscripts which provided the nucleus for the Thomas Pringle Collection which became the seed for a National English Literary Museum; launched a sub-department of English Language; founded an Institute for the Study of English in Africa (1964) and a Speech and Drama Department (1966).

It only remained to establish courses in Journalism (1970). Senate was reluctant if not truculent about this last of my projects, but accepted the subject in a special degree of Bachelor of Journalism. The sub-department was headed by Dr C.A.J. Giffard, Senior Lecturer.

By 1970, after a decade of pushing the frontiers of my subject in various directions, I found myself heading four departments, English and three sub-departments, English Language, Speech and Drama, and Journalism. The time had come for them to be independent.

In 1972 Speech and Drama became a fully-fledged department, and in 1973 Roy Sargeant was appointed as Senior Lecturer and Head. In the same year (1972) Journalism hived off. For a brief period I was Chairman of its advisory board. In 1972 Linguistics and English Language achieved the status of a separate department under the headship of Professor W.R.G. Branford.

It was a relief to get back to base, English Literature, with more time to read, and write, and try to communicate the joy and fulfilment which the arts of literature can provide.

This chapter indicates, I hope, an outline of my academic activities as Head of the Department of English between 1960 and 1973. In 1978, at my own request the University Council agreed to relieve me (aged 60) of the administrative responsibilities of running the large English Department. I would, however, continue to teach.

The new Head was Professor Malvern van Wyk Smith, who had joined the staff in 1967. Council allowed me to continue professing my subject until 1983 when I retired, aged 65. Malvern van Wyk Smith and Don Maclennan edited a festschrift, published by my friend and publisher,

David Philip: *Olive Schreiner and After: Essays on Southern African Literature in Honour of Guy Butler* – a handsome book of twenty-three items presented to me by Malvern at a function hosted by the Chairman of Rhodes University Council. The dedication was by Athol Fugard and there were poems from two special friends, fellow practitioners of the craft, Douglas Livingstone and David Wright. Lionel Abrahams came all the way from Johannesburg and spoke. My cup was full.

Nunc Dimittis? Not quite. I was appointed Research Professor until the end of 1987, and now enjoy the status of Professor Emeritus and Honorary Research Fellow. Sometimes it seems that I am busier than I have ever been.

Later Writings

My interest in history with a small *h* started not with generalities about economics or class or race, but with named individuals living in particular times. 'History is about chaps.' True, I found historiography fascinating, a sort of poetry turning people and events into symbols and metaphors. I am probably more influenced by Marx, Fraser and Toynbee than I am aware. But consciousness and conscience are irreducibly individual, and the history that interests me is the history of individuals. History is not made or experienced by Man, but by men, women and children.

For many years our family spent its holidays at Port Alfred, and wonderful times they were. I had made an early acquaintance with the coastline between Boknes and the Fish River mouth as a student during the late 'thirties; and as my knowledge of East Cape history grew, so did my interest in the landscape. I had to revise – and rejoiced in revising – my view that the African landscape was without poetic resonances.

My war years in Egypt, Syria and Italy, followed by my spell at Oxford, had made a deep and lasting impression on me; but, as I said in 'Home Thoughts', I had not 'found myself on Europe's maps':

I must go back with my five simple slaves
To soil still savage, in a sense still pure:
My loveless, shallow land of artless shapes
Where no ghosts glamorize the recent graves
And everything in Space and Time just is ...

I had to return, with a clearer love, bringing my northern Apollo with me, to encounter my own world anew.

Nervous he wanders staring-eyed among
Barbarous forms unknown to the northern muse.
Leaves, granites touch him; in ear, on tongue
New sounds and tastes, so many they suffuse
His sense with a blur of heat ...

Not only were there new sense data to be ingested; one had to learn how wrong it was to call the land loveless, shallow, artless and without ghosts:

it had merely seemed to lack these dimensions because one had been encapsulated in a language, a literature and a religion insensitive to them. One had to put oneself humbly to school, to look at the landscape wide-eyed, and to listen to its stories with less wax in one's ears.

And what stories one found along that silver succession of beaches and occasional rocky headlands, and a few miles inland! Each holiday I seemed to find another site associated with a figure who carried a weight of specific personal experience together with questions which echoed into our present and future. Within a radius of a few kilometres of Dias Cross I could visit sites which were anything but shallow, artless or without shades. Sixteen kilometres to the east were the ruins of Theopolis, City of God, ambitiously so named by the London Missionary Society, now a scattering of rubble. It had once been the base of Cobus Boesak, the great captain of the elephant and buffalo hunters, whose intervention with 130 ox-mounted crack shots on the side of the British turned the tide in the Battle of Grahamstown (1819). Twenty kilometres to the north lay Belton, or Raven Hill, the site of Wait's Party of 1820 Settlers, among whom was a young red-headed sawyer, Jeremiah Goldswain, whose semi-literate *Chronicle* is one of the most vivid accounts of life in the settlement. To the west lies Melkhoutboom, from which Karel Landman led a Trek into Natal in 1837. Closer to the coast, in a dark remnant of indigenous bush in the midst of a large ploughed field, lies the grave of Nongqawuse, the Xhosa prophetess, who, with her uncle, the diviner Umhlakaza, instigated the cattle-killing of 1856. Portuguese, Khoi, English, Xhosa, Boer, their feet weaving paths through that scrub, their mouths drinking from those streams.

Then, reading the letters of my grandfather, a 22-year-old consumptive exiled from London, I found that he had spent considerable time hard-by Boknes with the Shaws of Richmond, in 1877, during the last of the frontier wars. Like me, he had been only vaguely aware of the history of the terrain.

In 1970 I started trying to write poems about these people and their sites – a long, sporadic labour which finally appeared in 1987 as *Pilgrimage to Dias Cross*, with woodcuts by Cecil Skotnes. Far from being without 'ghosts', the poem is an indaba of shades on the headland known as Kwaai Hoek, where Dias planted his *padrão* half a millennium ago. Accepting the tragic realities of conquest and exploitation, the poem struggles to transcend them in affirming a fragile but essential awareness of universal non-material realities.

One of the more significant appointments I made to the English Department at Rhodes was Ruth Harnett. She is a devoted teacher of poetry. This I discovered very soon after she joined the staff in 1964. It was only by happy accident that I found out that she is also a fine, if somewhat

Illustration by Cecil Skotnes for Pilgrimage to Dias Cross

secretive, poet herself; and, as the poem which led to this discovery is germane to the craft and nature of poetry itself, I shall say how it happened.

I was judging a poetry competition run by an Eastern Province literary society. Among a quantity of bad, mediocre and promising work I came across a poem called 'Delos' which made me sit up and take notice: it was so beautifully assured in tone, so impeccable in its technique. I read it again and again; and, as happens when one has made a discovery, I had to show it to someone. I left my study, and found Ruth, exclaiming as I entered her office, 'Eureka! Just look at this!' She admitted almost apologetically, that she was the author.

Shortly after this the judges of a National Poetry Competition awarded me a second prize of R400. Flush with this bit of capital I decided it was time to pull down to earth a dream I had cherished from the late 'fifties onwards: to start a poetry journal. I knew from the letters that reached me from poets all over Southern Africa that there were plenty of poets around. I dreamt of organising jamborees of them, but, as poets are too poor to travel long distances, gave up the idea. They might, however, meet in print in a journal. That is what many of them needed – to see themselves in cold print: their poem all on its own, jostling for readers' attention with other poems. I knew that Bobby Willshire Jones – that rare creation, a lawyer who loved poetry – would look after the legal and business end of it. And Ruth Harnett, after some preliminary questioning, agreed to help. We decided to publish in broadsheet form and chose to call it *New Coin*. Ken Robinson designed a different cover for each issue and did the laborious business of pasting it up – early desk-top publishing.

To begin with, Ruth and I did the editing together but gradually she took over more and more of it. My contribution was sporadic, and predominantly managerial, twisting the arms of booksellers, trying to get publishers to sponsor volumes, what is called nuts and bolts work. Together we made the final selection for each number.

Looking at the first issues of *New Coin* I think that our selection was good. It would be interesting to see how it compares with other poetry outlets at that time. Of two things I am confident: we undertook to print poems of achievement and promise and we did just that. I remember our excitement at receiving a poem 'New Born Calf' from the then-unknown Oswald Mtshali – one of the first poems submitted by an African. We believed that poems didn't happen, but had to be achieved; that they had qualities which distinguished them from most spontaneous cries of self-pity, anguish and rage, although they could be piteous, anguished and very angry. And we believed that one of the things that distinguishes a poem from a piece of journalism – something written for the day – is that it moves a little beyond or above the immediate moment which generates it. You can imagine our joy at reading Clouts's 'Poetry is death cast out':

> *... Once walking*
> *amongst bushes and lizard stones I found*
> *a little further than I had thought*
> *to go, a stream with a singing sound.*

Perhaps Ruth's greatest quality is her ability to pay attention to the meanings and singing sounds generated by the words in their significant patterns and lineations on the page. She refused to give snap judgments and would always read and re-read them; and where she saw promise she would encourage and advise, sometimes at considerable length. This discriminating attention to promising talents over many years is impossible to evaluate. It has won her a wide and various circle of friends among practising poets. She has a way of reminding us not only of the rock from which a poem has to be hewn, but the patience and skill demanded. Art is costly and wasteful. Many tons of marble may be reduced to chips in order to release one caryatid. Somewhere Picasso says that a picture is the sum of many destructions. A hundred sheets of paper and as many hours may be needed to get one stanza right.

I do not know how many other poems, besides the few she has let us see, Ruth has stashed away; but if she has been reticent about sharing her own poetry with us, she has been most selfless and generous in her encouragement of any poetic talent prepared to work at the ancient and holy craft. My own debt to her is great, as it is to other poets, most notably Don Maclennan, to whom I frequently submit my efforts for comment. When he says he will read a poem, he means it, and I have benefited greatly from his scrupulous concern with the poem rather then the poet.

New Coin has changed its format several times, and has been fortunate to secure a succession of devoted editors. David Bunyan has recently edited and introduced a selection of poems from it: *25/25. Southern African Poetry – Twenty-five Themes over Twenty-five years: Selected from New Coin Poetry 1965–1989*. In his introduction to this selection, David raises the ghost of 'Butlerism', a term coined by Mike Kirkwood, then (1974) of the University of Natal, and subsequently founder of *Staffrider,* the very important magazine which Bunyan sees as 'committed to social realism, social and political prophecy, and the unproblematic embodiment of a communal voice'. He continues, 'The one noteworthy attempt to establish a poetic history and mythology for the English-speaking white community is conceded not to have survived intact following Mike Kirkwood's attack on "Butlerism" at the *Poetry '74* conference in Cape Town ... No one disputes that Butler diagnosed a need, however.'

I went to that conference totally, perhaps culpably, unaware of any pending assault by Kirkwood. At great length, employing sociological jargon I did not understand, and quoting literary theorists only some of whose names were familiar to me, he tried me at the bar of History with a capital H and found me woefully wanting. The fact must be faced that I had not kept up with theories of literature, partly because I have not the temperament or the intellectual energy, every decade, to construct and deconstruct elaborate castles of abstractions, with which all honest teachers must familiarise their students. Literary theory was soon to become more important than literature itself. In the 1970s the triumph of materialist/Marxist academics was imminent and by their standards, or Kirkwood's, there was an 'inadequate historical analysis underlying Butlerism's central thesis of the identity of the crisis'. To prove they had arrived, they needed to demolish the existing South African poetic establishment in which I was what the Australians call a 'tall poppy', and people nearer home a 'sacred cow'.

Kirkwood did a seemingly impressive hatchet job on Part II of 'Bronze Heads', but simply chose to ignore how the poem moves beyond 'a sentimental loyalty to 1820 ancestordom'. It is an act obeisance before the African dynasty or culture which produced the Ife bronzes, those portrait heads whose open, imperturbable gaze one aspired to emulate. It is true that I betrayed a colonialist wish to plant ancestral trees, and showed a paternalist willingness to share my cultural heritage; it is also true that I expressed a 'Eurocentric' belief in the need to stare, to contemplate, to count, to measure and to map; but it is also shows an acceptance of Africa as itself. In the final stanzas the poet prays for the incisive gaze of the Ife kings, and he identifies his pulse with theirs. Written shortly after a visit to Ife in 1954, these stanzas seem to have a contemporary relevance.

Few tribes chant now; and hearth-rug lions are dumb;
Most rivers and ranges are mapped and properly named;
but Africa is anything but tamed
and God alone knows what is yet to come.
In spite of city parks and private planting
there's little shade for the contemplating mind:
yet though old drums, beast cries and racial ranting
raise Cain in the thorn-scrub rising round our hearts,
the naked eye, still steady, bright, resigned
must check, cross check, each reference on its charts.

If, having made a fair and heart-felt choice
to plant ancestral, shade-endowing trees,
the back must bend, yet on rebellious knees
the heart has cause, and cannot but rejoice.
For when the tribal energies, the flames,
the golden sap and blood revive, reform,
and dance down ways the staring eye discloses;
when shapes long stifled in our sensual storm
strike free and chant their clarifying names,
who will grieve at the strain such work imposes?

O brazen heads at Ife, you who stare
over the jungle, down the cataract,
as if such staring were the first slow act
by which man masters chaos anywhere,

stare at me, you bronzes, stare, persist
till, having caught your straight, incisive gaze,
I cut the scrub with calculated glances:
stare, as I replant, on dazzling days,
ancestral trees; stare on my sweating fist
in which, this moment, your blood stream dances, dances.

I suppose it was inevitable that I should be set up as a target to be shot down in the age-old war of the generations (I was 56). I have never tried to duck my 'guilt' as an unfairly privileged white, but I knew myself to be a member of a small human sub-species called the English-speaking South African. I knew that one of my ancestors had come in 1829 as a settler, and others subsequently. I saw no reason to shed this history in the name of HISTORY. I had made it clear in and out of season that this group, which in the 19th century had for the most part been saturated with the imperial mystique and indeed had many of the colonisers' attributes as diagnosed by Kirkwood, were no longer colonists or part of an imperium, and that they had to put their alternative tradition, their quite vigorous, useable, liberal, local tradition into their politics. I saw no reason to reduce myself and others to automata dancing on the strings of Marxist economic choreographers. The ESSAs are a fact of South African society; they have been the founders and sustainers of most of the institutions which have provided small but significant bases for those who have fought against apartheid and for democracy.

My main error was to draw a distinction between English-speaking South Africans as inheritors of a South African liberal awareness which was equally opposed to Afrikaner and African nationalism. I no doubt overestimated the numbers of English-speakers who were liberally aware. Kirkwood and his kind saw this as a buck-passing ploy. As a white I was automatically a capitalist exploiter, and my only salvation was to deny my modest but real liberal South African heritage, and seek instead total immersion in the pure waters of leftist theories emanating at that time mainly from Paris. That I insisted on the political responsibility of ESSAs was not enough.

While I insisted, and still insist, that languages and cultures do differ, I also insisted that, within a given country, they influence each other, and produce common loyalties and sentiments. I said, 'English are being Afrikanerised, Afrikaners Anglicised, Africans Westernised, and everyone Africanised.'

This does not however, mean that Afrikaners or ESSAs or Zulus or Xhosas will disappear. Language is only a fraction of a culture. We can and do talk quite sensibly of European or Western culture, although Europe contains many powerful sub-cultures and dozens of different languages. African culture already is and will be something like that.

I do not accept the notion that the political triumph of an abstraction called 'the people' will produce a society with a common culture worth a row of beans – or beads. I do not believe that Xhosas are Zulus, or that either will be converted into heroic brothers in the epic working-class struggle by the waving of a Marxist wand; or that Afrikaners or ESSAs will cut their historical taproots no matter how ingeniously HISTORY is revised, deconstructed, reconstructed, etc. This is not to deny that they share in a complex economy, enjoy and suffer the same climate and landscape, aware of a process which embraces them all.

Cross-fertilisation – biological and mental – is an ongoing fact; and artists have a particularly important role to play here – as 'Bronze Heads' tries to demonstrate. Works of art can provide exchanges at depths which the sociologists and literary theorists seldom reach; they are too self-preoccupied with tight-rope balancing acts on high wires anchored on very dubious assumptions about our natures.

New Coin not only published a journal, but also longish poems in pamphlets, such as Anthony Delius's *Black South-Easter,* 1966, and my own *On First Seeing Florence,* 1968, and, with Purnell, three volumes of poetry: Sydney Clouts, *One Life,* 1966; Anne Welsh, *Set in Brightness,* 1968; and Elias Pater, *In Praise of Night,* 1969. *One Life* won the Ingrid Jonker Memorial Prize in 1967, and the Olive Schreiner Award in 1968. *In Praise of Night* won the 1971 Olive Schreiner Award.

We also published two very different poets in booklet form: Arthur Nortje, *Lonely Against the Light,* 1973; and Bruce Hewett, *The Dawn of Song,* 1984.

My own poetic activity during the 'sixties and 'seventies resulted in publications other than *Stranger to Europe with Additional Poems,* 1960. *South of the Zambesi,* 1966, marked a move away from stanzaic verse to a freer, more conversational voice. This owed much to the practice in blank verse afforded by my early verse plays and, indeed, some of the poems are speeches lifted from those plays. It also marks, I think, a further acclimitisation of my language to my land.

On First Seeing Florence followed in 1968. This grew by slow stages out of the 'long poem' to which I have referred from time to time. There are other poems, notably a long *Elegy,* which have grown from the same source. One of the major pieces of uncompleted business before me is the collection and arrangement of these substantial pieces of terza rima. In an age in which poetry – and the long poem in particular – is being 'marginalised' it tends to be put on the back-burner; but it is there.

In 1975 Stephen Gray made a selection of my poems for Ad. Donker. To my great surprise and delight *Selected Poems* won the C.N.A. Literary Award for English in 1976. *Selected Poems,* revised and enlarged, was re-issued in 1989.

Encouraged by Jack Cope, general editor of David Philip's Mantis Poets,

I assembled a small collection of short pieces, *Songs and Ballads*, which appeared in tandem with Patrick Cullinan's *Today Is Not Different* in 1978.

Pilgrimage to Dias Cross illustrated by Cecil Skotnes, about which I have already written, was published in 1987, also by David Philip.

This same period saw the production of many critical and other articles, and I edited two works on the 1820 Settlers, *When Boys Were Men* (1969) and *The 1820 Settlers* (1974), about which I write more fully in chapter 22.

In 1989 an unexpected challenge came from Pieter Struik to write the introduction of Herman Potgieter's outstanding book of photographs, mainly aerial: *South Africa: Landshapes, Landscapes, Manshapes*. I learnt a great deal about photography, landscape and conservation in the process. The book is large – too large for most coffee tables.

I am particularly concerned to keep poetry alive, and to this end have spent much time making anthologies, those important teaching instruments in which we meet poetry at school – most of us for the first and last time. While not denying the place of the general anthology (with Chris Mann I brought out *A New Book of South African Verse* in 1979), I have come to believe that one can get people who would never read poetry to do so if the poems are about something that interests them deeply. For example my son David and I made a collection of poems on South African wild animals called *Out of the African Ark* (1988), using rock art as our main source for illustrations; and Professor Jeff Opland and I have recently (1989) published *The Magic Tree*, which is a collection of South African stories in verse, depending heavily on translation in order to make the full range of our multi-inspired common heritage of narratives available in a *lingua franca*. It is time South Africans knew each other's legends and stories. I have also maintained my interest in translation, a time consuming exercise of many linguistic and poetic skills. With the aid of previous translations into English and French I translated some sixty stanzas of *The Lusiads*, the Portuguese epic about Da Gama's voyage to India. An even greater labour of love has been the translation of the whole of *Raka* from Afrikaans into English. Surely N.P. van Wyk Louw's masterpiece deserves to be more widely known than it is.

One is always surprising oneself. After my first effort at a novel had been rejected in the late 1950s, I never dreamt I would return to prose fiction again; but in 1989 was published a short novel, *A Rackety Colt* (see chapter 22) and a book of short stories, *Tales from the Old Karoo*.

It is probably the continuous writing of this autobiography that has given me a feeling for prose which I might not otherwise have developed. *Karoo Morning: An Autobiography 1918–45*, published in 1977, was followed in 1983 by *Bursting World: An Autobiography 1936–45*, and now this present volume. This substantial exercise began with a remark by David Philip towards the end of a happy anecdotal evening, 'Write your autobiography and we'll publish it.'

My known love of poetry has brought me in touch with the torn nerves of my country in unexpected ways – none more moving than my friendship with Matthew Goniwe. I shall let extracts from our correspondence tell most of the story:

Matthew to Guy: 3886/77, Prison Hospital, Umtata, 24 March 1978
   Sir,
   I am a prisoner at the above-mentioned jail.
   Will you kindly send me books on the A.B.C. of making poetry. I am sure I will find writing poetry a worthwhile exercise.
   Yours faithfully,
   Matthew Goniwe

Guy to Matthew: Rhodes University, 4 May 1978
   Dear Mr Goniwe,
   I have made some preliminary enquiries and find it difficult to select from the many possibilities available. It would help me if you could give me some idea of your educational background. Items suitable for a young man just leaving school may not be right for a university graduate with several years' teaching experience.
   There is also the question of language. Do you wish to write poetry in English only or in your mother tongue as well? Many people do both. While the two poetic traditions can affect and enrich each other, they are in many respects different. If you are interested in African poetry as well, let me know and I will see what help I can find.
   Yours sincerely,
   Guy Butler

Matthew to Guy: 11 May 1978
   Sir,
   The highest qualification I have in English is Matric. Otherwise I am in possession of the S.A.T.D. certificate, a two-year course which is offered at the University of Fort Hare. I have taught in a secondary school for two years. Much as I would love to write poetry in Xhosa, my mother tongue, I don't think I could cope. The problem is that I was born and bred in Cradock, which is a predominantly Afrikaans-speaking area; my Xhosa ... is highly affected by Afrikaans ...

Guy to Matthew: 26 May 1978 (from a letter covering the dispatch of two anthologies of verse)
   I think it important for anyone wishing to write poetry to learn a variety of poems off by heart. To *hear* a poem is very important ... Only by training our ears will we grasp the significance of pauses, phrasing and rhythm. Rhyme can be important in poetry, but it is a secondary consideration ...

I wonder whether you should not consider enrolling for one or two B.A. Courses with UNISA. A course in English might be a great help in learning to understand the nature of poetry in English, and hence help you to write it.

I was born in Cradock myself, and have written a book about my childhood there. Would you be interested in reading it?

(I sent him a copy of *Karoo Morning* and other books.)

Matthew to Guy: 30 October 1978
Thank you for the books you sent me. I am grateful to you, too grateful for words.

I am intrigued by the down-to-earth manner you came to my help.

I have started learning a few poems by heart.

I have decided to take up your suggestion to enrol for a course in English. In fact, I propose taking the following courses next year: English I, Political Science I, Communication I and Constitutional Law.

So you are also from Cradock. Doesn't this account for the well-disposed manner in which you greeted my call for help? Sounds telepathic, doesn't it? (As if you wouldn't have come to the aid of a person who does not come from Cradock!) Well, I've always wondered if you were related to the Butlers of Cradock. You have reminded me of that indefatigable lady [Mary Butler]. Also Mrs Joubert. Those two ladies did a lot for quite a number of black kids in Cradock.

(I discussed Goniwe's need of help with English setbooks amongst my staff, who between them supplied most of his wants. Some wished to know what he was in prison for, but I had never considered putting that question to him.)

Matthew to Guy, 13 November 1978
Dear Guy,
You have no idea how happy I am at this moment ... Tonight I'm going to have one of my best sleeps in years ... a wonderful sleep means a lot to us here. My dear brother, I will never forget you.

I have just received the books you sent me ...

I am sure you would like to know what puts me here. Together with other young men and women, I was detained on 19 July 1976. Five of us faced charges under the Suppression of Communism Act. Sentence was passed on 1 September 1977 ... When my time ends I will definitely come to Grahamstown to see you.
Yours sincerely,
Matthew

(He passed all his UNISA examinations well, and once again we helped him with his needs but less so since he had decided not to continue on to English II. He eventually majored in Political Science and Education. But our correspondence continued and I was still able to help him in other practical ways.)

Guy to Matthew: 25 January 1979
... It was good to know that you had been allowed to see your wife, Nyameka, and three-year-old daughter, Nobuzwe just before Christmas; and that your wife has passed her second-year B.A. Social Science exams.

Matthew to Guy: 26 April 1980
I wrote to Don [Maclennan] thanking him for the tape recorder ... To end on a pleasant note, this time next year I'll be a free man. I'll be released on 31 August 1981.

My brother Alex came to see me. At 54 he is not your junior by a large margin. As a young man he used to work selling *The Midland News* for your father. My brother helped your father, you are helping me. Well! ...

He was duly released at the end of August 1981 and I wondered when he would come and see me. What would he look like? Would the ease of our converse by mail survive a face-to-face meeting? I was seated at the big table in the sitting-room. I was working, as I often do, to background music – in this case Handel's *The Messiah*. The door was opened and there I saw a slightly built young African in jeans.

I rose, saying, 'Matthew?' and he responded, 'Guy?'

I moved towards the record player to switch off the Halleluia chorus.

'Don't!' he cried. And he started to jive forward with an elegant ease and joy, snapping his fingers, across the Persian rugs and between the upholstered chairs as if they were not there.

We embraced, thumping each other's backs. Then we sat down and talked and talked all through the music. He would hum or sing phrases, his feet gently beating the floor. He spent that weekend with us, and won the affection of us all.

He returned to teaching and was soon principal of a school in Graaff-Reinet. His intelligence and charismatic personality soon made him a leader and the incarnation of hope for much-needed improvement in black education, and, indeed, in the general lot of all blacks.

On 10 October 1981 he wrote from Cradock sending me two poems. Here is one of them.

THESE WALLS
Walls, walls, walls.
Walls all around me.

Four walls,
Four cold companions,
Four deaf and dumb.

Close, too close,
Strong, rigid, firm,
Close, too close,
They explode into my consciousness,
Big, bulking, bold.

Close, too close.
Closed.
Silence seals my soundless box.

His role in the school boycott movement and the Cradock Residents' Association led to a continuous battle with the educational authorities and with the police, during which he showed irrepressible spirit and courage. I saw him less and less frequently. In mid-1981 he spoke at a NUSAS symposium on the Rhodes campus about educational reform. We had a warm and all too brief conversation after it. I invited him to spend the night at High Corner, but he had to set out for Cradock at once – he had a meeting there next morning.

Shortly afterwards his burned and mutilated body and those of three other Cradock community leaders were found in the coastal scrub near Port Elizabeth. The perpetrators of this crime have never been discovered. In 'Ode to Dead Friends' I devoted a stanza to him:

We were born in the same small town.
You wrote from jail, for help with English verse.
Bright boy, from grim Lingelihle, you had grown
To manhood while our tyranny grew worse;
Were freed; imprisoned; freed;
Again you meet warm gatherings of friends;
Are ambushed; tortured; after four days found, dead;
And there, for Law and Order, your story ends.
But not for wife, child, brothers, comrades, these
For whom you are still magical.
We praise you! I recall
Putting on Handel at news of your release.
You blew in on the wind. 'Look! I've arrived!'
And round your room you jived
To the Halleluiah Chorus, laughing and alive.

21   1952–

Restoration of Old Houses

I am not a typical South African because I take so little interest in sport. I do not watch it and hardly know when the rugby season ends and the cricket season begins. I have a vague idea rugby is played in winter to get warm, and cricket in summer to keep cool. I do not take regular physical exercise. I am like the great American educationist, Robert Maynard Hutchings, Chancellor of the University of Chicago, who said, 'Whenever I feel like taking exercise I lie down until the temptation passes.'

My friends and my doctors tell me that this is not a joking matter, that one's body needs exercise and that one cannot expect to be healthy in mind or in body unless one's muscles have tone, and one's weight is correct for one's sex, height and age. I agree with all of this. I have, in fact, made heroic efforts, heroic but shortlived, to whip my idle body into line.

For some years I was a keen Canadian Airforce Exercise Man and punished myself for ten or fifteen minutes every morning: running on the spot, doing press-ups, knees full bend and deep breathing until I was bored out of my mind. The day held no horrors for me after doing my exercises. But I had to face the world with no will-power left for further decisions. The only advantage of doing the exercises was that children, struggling to wake up and put themselves into shape for school, would not dare to ask a bad-tempered man, running on the spot and getting nowhere, to help find their shoes or compo books.

Once, and once only, I tried to vary the routine which the Canadian health wizards had devised. Instead of running on the spot I decided to try jumping on the spot. Mrs Wyndham Kelly, who lived in the flat below our bedroom quarters (the converted billiard room) phoned Jean: 'My Dear, I'm not complaining. I'm simply curious. What is happening to the house? Have you called in the wreckers?'

In addition to tennis twice a week, Jean would take me for walks from time to time – real leg-stretching exercises, not the parental potter behind a pram round the Rhodes Great Field in the cool of the day.

But I took most of my exercise with a hammer or a saw in my hand. Whenever I produced a play in the 'fifties or 'sixties, I built the sets myself with some help from the Student Technical Staff, an engaging but erratic labour force. I also tried to establish an open-air garden for the students between the new Great Hall and Selwyn Castle (which had replaced the old student Café, or 'Kaif'). With the help of students like Bill Yeowart and Eddie Baart, we built a massive stone wall between the two, which has stood since 1957. I gave up because the Vice-Chancellor kept quibbling about the price of cement. And whenever we went down to the seaside for a holiday, I would find a bit of terracing to do. There is nothing like pick and shovel for developing the shoulders.

But the real outlet for my physical side, my chief recreation, was building. It took my mind right off literature, off the life of the intellect, and away from university affairs.

My father had been a do-it-yourself man, and was full of know-how which he had picked up by watching men at work, reading *Popular Mechanics* and using his commonsense. He would get stuck into anything, right up to his elbows. My brother and I served a long and tough apprenticeship under him. Whenever he altered The Poplars or the old outbuildings – of which there were several – we were put to work.

This side of my home education had made it natural for me to join the army as a sapper. I enjoyed the company of the artisans in the 9th Field Company, from whom I learnt a great deal. Without this do-it-yourself background we would never have offered to buy High Corner, which was falling to pieces.

But as a builder I suffered from two related handicaps: I knew very little about architectural styles or detailing. I knew that I preferred plain Georgian to Victorian Gothic, and rooms with tall ceilings and vertical timbered windows to low ceilings and horizontal steel lights. I had probably acquired the liking from Bree Street, Cradock, and the old farmhouses of my childhood, but it was quite an uneducated taste. I blush at some of the mistakes I made; but some of the worst were made on the advice of architects, very few of whom, I have learnt, have any feeling whatever for period.

The second great handicap was the lack of books on restoration of buildings in South Africa. If only Ronald Lewcock's key work, *Nineteenth-century Architecture at the Cape* (1963), had appeared ten years earlier! I was fortunate enough, however, to get to know him while he was writing it and took his advice on several occasions. Once the book appeared it became my Bible. The cavalier manner in which architects and owners have continued destroying old buildings, including many illustrated in Lewcock, is further evidence of their barbarous egocentricity.

I was, however, fortunate to have developed this interest when the epithet 'old' was the worst thing that could be said about a house in Grahamstown; and when the old portion of town – Settlers' Hill – was regarded as only fit for poor-whites, rock-spiders and an odd eccentric academic without social ambitions. The time when early small buildings would be advertised by estate agents as 'charming Settler Cottages' was still some years ahead.

And none of the work I did would have been possible with the wicked rates of interest we have to meet today. All the houses I restored were done on the never-never. Each new venture had to be financed, in part, by borrowing against the security of High Corner.

32–34 Market Street, a double storey, consists of two semi-detached houses under slates. The roof was leaky. The floors were rotten and many of the windows did not fit. Those in the front had been replaced by steel, fortunately of the correct proportions. The plumbing was very bad, W.C.s were in the gardens, and the huge cast-iron baths in the old coal sheds. Everything was in fact wrong with them except their proportions.

The tenants presented me with two very different problems: one half was occupied by a severe-looking, spick-and-span woman who kept house during term time for two or three grandchildren of the farming parents. I was reluctant to give her three months' notice. Everything about her spelt wholesome. The other half was occupied by a changing assortment of dubious 'characters'. They vacated the place almost at once without paying the rent or returning the keys. The interior doors started disappearing at night. I had to get a night-watchman to sleep in the place. They even removed the wing nuts from the catches of the casement windows.

People in the neighbourhood were relieved that a young professor had bought the place. Anything would be an improvement on the present tenants of No. 34. They trusted me with hair-raising stories about goings-on in there, which one of them did not scruple to call a house of ill repute. He had, in fact, reported it to the police and to child welfare.

Most loquacious was a pink-faced, stocky, retired farmer who had plenty of time to be philosophical about the ways of the world. It was a very good site, he observed, and a fair-sized piece of ground. The whole neighbourhood would be stimulated to renewal by clearing that slum and he congratulated me on a good and far-sighted purchase in the interests of the public.

He became worried, however, when he saw me with a tape measuring up the building in some detail. Why was I doing this? he asked.

'It's an old building, for Grahamstown. 1826 in fact. And it belonged to one of our first Doctors, Peter Campbell.'

'Well, it looks every year of its age. Give it a little longer and it will fall down of its own accord.'

'Do you think so? I can't find any major cracks in it anywhere. Most of its troubles are cosmetic.'

'What are you going to do with it?'

'Restore it.'

'No, man, no! Get a bulldozer to push it down. Clear the site, man! Put up something new. Flats. Think of flats. You can't do anything with an old ruin like this.'

He took my intention to restore the ruin as a personal affront. Maybe he felt pretty much of an old ruin himself and resented seeing that building getting a new lease of life when he knew his was running out.

At one time No. 34 had been divided into an upstairs and a downstairs flat, the upstairs being entered by a very heavy external concrete staircase which reached the first turning in the stair. This I removed and unified the building once more. In place of the door to the upstairs flat – which had opened on to the external staircase – I fitted a rather unusual large stained-glass window which I had noticed lying unloved and uncared for among the junk in Dold's yard. We were, in fact, great haunters of sales rooms and sales, looking for old furniture and joinery bargains.

One day Jean happened to pop into Dold's and found the Mills brothers in a state of hilarity over her husband's latest folly.

'We've had this church window cluttering the yard so long we don't know who brought it in. A huge window, Mrs Butler, fixed, you can't open it. Solid cast-iron. Weighs a couple of tons. I don't know what use it can be in any building. But your husband seemed surprised that we let him have it for five bob.'

This window, with a curved top, still had most of its stained glass in it, and the wooden frame round the rim was intact. Most people who see it are enchanted.

To complement the rounded top of the window, I made a curved top for the door between the main room and the stairwell; and then took out the broken fanlight from above the front door and inserted new glazing bars in a radial pattern. I was delighted a year or two later to see that it had been photographed by an architect as an example of an early Grahamstown fanlight. Indeed, house owners in the old days prided themselves on having individual designs for their fanlights and it was quite in character that those of 32 and 34 should differ. But I would not indulge in such a liberty today. My ignorance of the rules of authentic restoration would forbid it. I was only just becoming careful of taking liberties with what has survived.

15, 17 and 19 George Street was my next, and biggest, restoration undertaking.

No. 19 on the corner had a severe crack running through it from top to bottom – in the front it was very visible, between the ground-floor window and the upstairs window, and so to the roof; and in like manner through the central wall and the wall at the back of the house. I suspected that this was due to subsidence of the foundations on the Lawrence Street side caused by deep trenches dug there by the municipality to take the city sewage pipes. A consulting-engineer agreed with me, but doubted if it would be worth going to law about it. In his view there was no way of curing the cracks. No. 19 should be pulled down and rebuilt on new foundations. It would have to be done carefully because it might be providing a buttress for the wall it shared in common with No. 17. In fact, 15, 17 and 19 were on old-style foundations, which in his view were not foundations at all. Why not demolish and build a block of flats?

But I did what the old builders did on countless dwellings and wagon-houses throughout the country and the world – I had tie rods made in two sections which could be pulled together by a connecting sleeve, the threads of one half of which were lefthand, as was the corresponding half of the tie rod. Once inserted and screwed up, it meant that if the Lawrence Street wall looked like falling, it would have to pull the whole building down with it. The back wall showed a half-hearted wish to do this some time later, but the insertion of another tie rod fifteen years ago stopped that nonsense and the building seems snug and happy in its setting.

It needed considerable interior modification and a new staircase – a small job by comparison with the one at High Corner. I had my jointing bench – a six-inch Delta planer and a six-inch circular saw – set up in what was to become the kitchen, and made the stairs on the spot. It was great fun.

One Sunday after early-morning church, I went there and started sawing up some nice old yellowwood flooring remnants to make the rails for the balustrade. The saw was somewhat blunt. I was in a hurry and was not using a push stick. I had to shove fairly hard with my left hand.

I felt a hard knock on my hand and looked amazed at what the saw had done. The index finger was three-quarters severed and lying over backwards, and I caught a glimpse, just before the blood started spurting, of the section through the finger, including the shattered bone. The saw had also taken a deep slice into the ball of the thumb, but had not gone right through – the nail was still intact.

I straightened the index finger a little and wrapped my hand in my handkerchief, which was soon soaked and dripping blood at an alarming rate. I knew that I was in no condition to drive myself to the hospital, so I went into the street to look for help.

A Sunday calm was on the place. People were at church, or playing golf or at the sea or still asleep. I walked up Lawrence Street, and there in his backyard was Mr Rothman, father of Ernie Rothman, polishing his car. As usual when busy with an antique house, I was in my old clothes and no doubt looked like a hobo who didn't know that Sunday was not a good time to go begging.

'Can you take me to the hospital?' I said.

'What for?'

When I showed him the hand, he exclaimed 'Christ!', went inside and quickly returned with a large piece of cottonwool to wrap around my hand. He then drove me to the outpatients.

'Who's your doctor?'

'Doctor Muller,' I said.

Waiting for him, I had time to curse myself very thoroughly indeed. I had been guilty of two of the commonest follies of those who use circular saws: I had not had it sharpened so that one had to use far too much pressure; and I had not used a push-stick to keep my hand clear of the blade.

But what, precisely, had happened? Near the end of the old floorboard – as often in old yellowwood – was a crack or 'shake' a couple of inches long, exactly in line with the saw. Suddenly there had been no resistance and my hand had shot forward into the blade.

I lay there thinking of Robert Frost's wonderful poem 'Out, Out', about a boy who loses a whole hand while working with a saw and who dies from it. I doubted if I would die, unless I got tetanus. Perhaps the thumb could be saved, perhaps the finger –

My next concern was to keep Jean ignorant of the accident, at least until the hand was all neat and nicely bandaged. I'd also need to get a change of clothes as I was somewhat blotched with blood.

Doctor Muller took one look and said, 'We'll need an X-ray of this,' and gave me a shot to kill the pain. Although Jean was no longer on the staff of Settlers Hospital, he asked her to come and take the X-rays.

The meeting was a painful surprise for both us us. She winced at the sight.

'I'm sorry, Jean,' said Dooley Muller, 'but I need to know the extent of the splintering of the bones in the forefinger, and whether the bone in the thumb is intact. There might be a chance of saving the finger by sewing it on again.'

After two days it became quite clear that the finger beyond the cut was without blood and without feeling. Too many vessels and nerves had been cut and it had begun to putrefy. So I was sent to Dr Cathro, an orthopaedic surgeon in Port Elizabeth.

He was a Quaker, quiet, frank and efficient. He explained the state of my hand and the choices open to me.

The thumb would be all right in time, but never as sensitive as before. The index finger would have to be removed. It was, perhaps, a blessing that the effort to save it had failed because the damage was so severe that it would never have functioned properly. I would have been handicapped by a useless stiff index finger.

The question was, where to amputate? The first and obvious answer was at the cut made by the saw. But was that the best spot? Dr Cathro had a better suggestion, to remove the bones of the finger a good inch beyond the knuckle, into the palm, and then to reshape the hand so that the line between the thumb and the middle finger would approximate to the line made by thumb and index finger. He could make the middle finger take up the responsibilities of the missing index finger, most notably its opposition to the thumb – one of those evolutionary marvels in some of the primates. He could splice the muscles of the missing index finger into the middle one.

I handed over my mutilated hand to Cathro and he did a wonderful internal engineering and external cosmetic job upon it. The hand works as well as it did before, and few people notice the abnormality.

But it was almost the end of house restoration for me. Jean insisted on my selling that circular saw. Since then I have had to confine myself to furniture-making and small renovative tasks.

There were many others interested in restoring old houses – most notably Dr Eily Gledhill, who, supported by her husband Jack, was for many years the tireless genius at the centre of a company called Historic Grahamstown. We were fortunate enough to secure the practical and continuous support of Historic Homes of Africa (Dr Anton Rupert), Douglas Roberts, and Ian Mackenzie, both from Johannesburg. It is not too much to say that the restoration movement changed the visual impact of Grahamstown for the better.

35 Godfrey Collett and the millstone found on the site of the mill built by his great-grandfather.
36 Standing stone erected by Dr Tom Bowker at the old wagon drift across the Kowie River mouth.
37 High Corner staircase built by Guy.

38 *Take Root or Die*, 1966. Jeremiah Goldswain as played by his descendant Ralph Goldswain.

39 *Cape Charade or Kaatjie Kekkelbek*, 1967. Charlene Faktor as Antjie, André de Villiers as Kaspar.

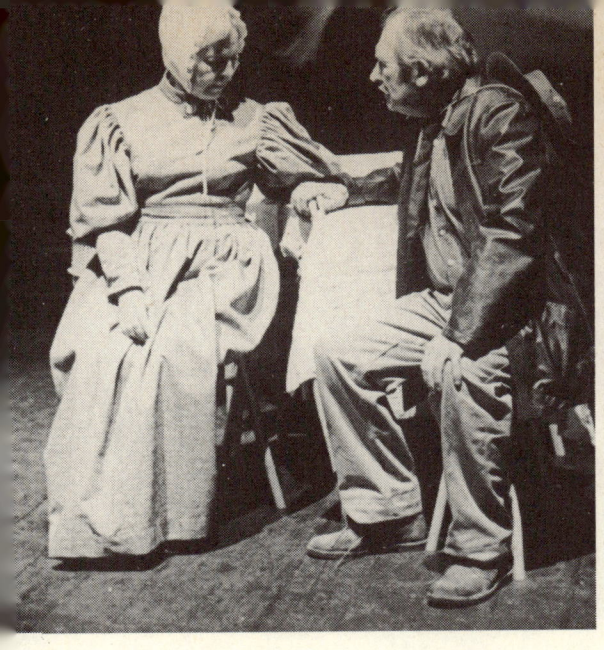

40 *Richard Gush of Salem*, 1970. Joyce Bradley as Margaret Gush, Michael Drin as George Dennison.

41 *Demea*, 1990. Graham Hopkins as Jonas, Nomse Xaba as Demea.

42 A scene from *Demea*.

43 *Noyes Fludde* by Benjamin Britten, produced by Guy Butler and George Grüber in the Cathedral of St Michael and St George during the Settler Celebrations of 1970.

44 The dedication ceremony for the 1820 Monument, 6 July 1974. Officiating were the heads of most of the Christian and Jewish denominations.

45 Dr Tom Bowker, M.P. for Albany, the originator of the 1820 Settlers Monument (bust sculpted by Ivan Mitford Barberton).

46 Dr Douglas Roberts, Vice-President of the 1820 Foundation, with Dr W.J.B. Slater, immediate past Chairman of its Council, 1979.

47 Richard Cooke, Chairman of the 1820 Foundation Council, 1979-87.

48 Dr Ian Mackenzie, President of the 1820 Foundation, 1983- .

49 A view from the Grahamstown Technical College of the 1820 Settlers Monument with the City Hall clock tower and the Cathedral steeple.

50 The Fountain Foyer, Settlers Monument, the hub of activities during festivals.

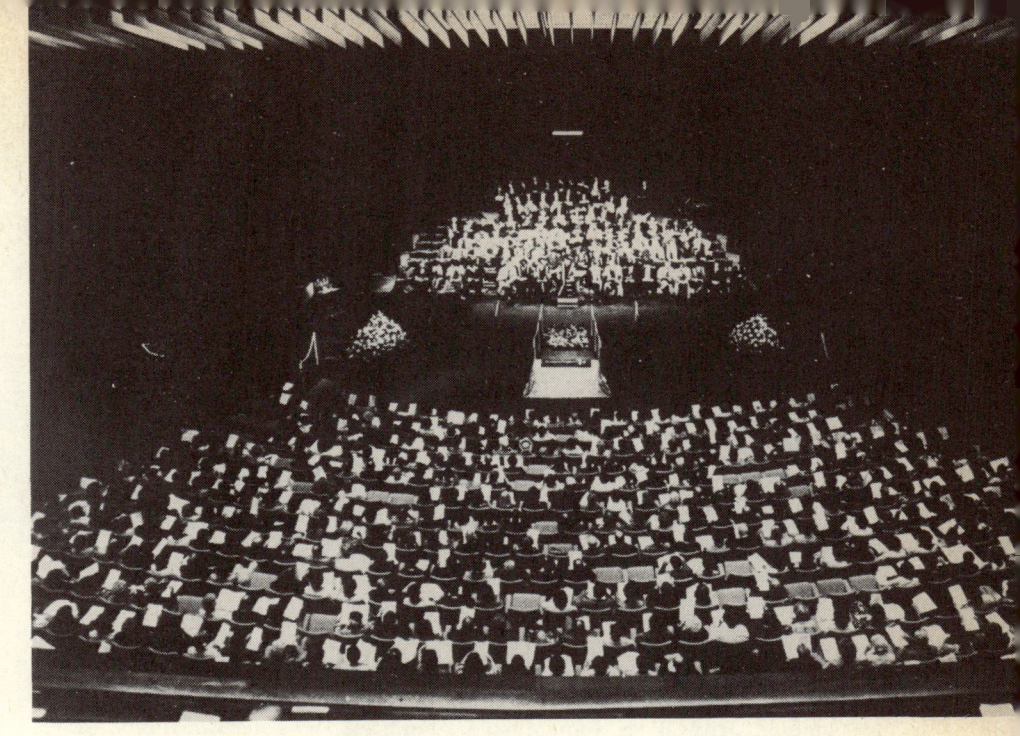

51 The Monument Theatre during a Rhodes University graduation ceremony.

52 Guy and Jean at the launch of *Bursting World*, 1983.
53 Jeffrey at the Fish River, 1974.

54 Mary Butler teaching Alice to knit after her stroke, late 1960s.

55 The Poplars, Bree Street, Cradock.

56 The family at High Corner after the memorial service for Alice Butler: (standing) Denys Biggs, John Murray, Alan Biggs, my sister Dorothy Murray, my father Ernest, my sister Christine Moys, Patricia Biggs, Senator James Butler; (sitting) David Biggs, Rex Moys, my sister Joan Butler, Alice Biggs, Mary Butler, Josie Biggs and Christine Vorster.

22   1952–

Eastern Cape History, Diaries and Plays

When I first settled into my Chair I found I could not forget that I was both a teacher and a researcher, and I started attending and organising conferences for teachers. I had a proper love of words and accents and a growing, if vague, awareness of modern linguistics. My lack of expertise did not stop me from asking questions about South African accents and usage, about bilingualism and the influence of one language upon another. In the heart of the territory settled by people from Great Britain I was conscious that they spoke in accents strange to English people elsewhere. Why?

For instance, one of my small children had a much-loved kitten that did not appreciate all the attention devoted to it. He entered the room with both hands round the animal's neck, its legs scrabbling in the air, its pink tongue protruding.

'Christopher! Put that cat down at once!'

His reply was perfect East Cape South African English.

'Wot's the metta? The ket's heppy!'

How had this vowel-shift come about?

In my boyhood I used to browse in an old diary kept for forty years by my great-great-grandfather, James Lydford Collett, who had arrived in 1821. From it I learnt how he had borrowed Afrikaans words with great freedom and certain of his spellings suggested that he spoke a dialect. I asked my colleague, Professor Winifred Maxwell of History, if she had any views on the subject; and she told me that the Settlers came from various parts of Britain and no doubt brought a variety of accents with them; and that there were many letters, diaries and reminiscences by Settlers in the Cory Library, which might help me: most notably perhaps, Jeremiah Goldswain, a lively man of little education but determined to leave a record of his life behind him. As a bad speller myself, I took my hat off to a phonetic genius who wrote 'youslis' for 'useless'. ('I have no respect', said Mark Twain, 'for a man who can spell a word in only one way.')

I had resorted to early Settler writings as a conscientious pedagogue trying to trace the origins of aberrations from the King's or Queen's

English but almost at once I found myself embroiled in the lives of the British subjects who wrote down what they felt, did and thought. (Professors are subject to going off at tangents. Who would have thought that a very efficient Professor of Chemistry, J.L.B. Smith, would get hooked on a ten-year fishing trip, chasing after the coelancanth?) I became fascinated by personal accounts, preferably still in manuscript, of life in this portion of the world in the first half of the 19th century. I found the material so absorbing that I felt impelled to find ways of making it better known. This was how I came to assemble the prose anthology of autobiographical excerpts dealing with Settler life as experienced by the writers before they reached the age of 21 – *When Boys Were Men* (O.U.P., 1969).

One unpublished item in particular gripped me – 'The Reminiscences of Thomas Stubbs'. It struck me as outrageous that it should not be in print. Why was this? Enquiries established that the Van Riebeeck Society, which had published Goldswain's *Chronicle*, was fully extended for years ahead. I made a list of some two dozen diaries relating to the Eastern Cape which might be worth publishing and, to cut a long story short, this led to the establishment of the Graham's Town Series – the first volume of which appeared in 1971. Volume 4 is *The Reminiscences of Thomas Stubbs* (1977), edited by Rob McGeogh and Winifred Maxwell. 'Winnie', who had initially looked askance at the whole proposal, dedicated her edition:

For Guy Butler
HUJUS LIBRORUM ORDINIS AUCTORI ADJUTORIQUE SUMMO

I am particularly fond of Stubbs. For over a decade he lived in the portion of the building which we have called High Corner. I have used the first part of his reminiscences as the basis of a novel, *The Rackety Colt* (1989). It was chosen as one of the five best novels for the year 1989–90 by M-Net.

This early and ongoing interest in first-person narratives by people who 'bore the battle and the breeze' in this corner of Africa has wonderful rewards. One can find the place where an event occurred, the ridge, the path, the ford, and so bring past word and present world together. Here is a moving incident from the still unpublished diary of Thomas Shone.

His wife has died. He is overcome with remorse and decides to erect a stone on her grave. We watch the progress of this tombstone, the letters being cut, surrounded by growing crops, the straying cattle, the changing weather.

'*Wednesday 3rd October, 1838.* This day I began work by finishing a pr of boots for Mary. After that I finished the day by cutting 43 letters on the tombstone. The children were weeding of the lands. Mary I was obliged to flog on account of letting the calf on the oats continually, altho' I had repeatedly warn'd her to keep him out of the land. Ann returned home this day after visiting Mrs Shone (his daughter-in-law) at Mrs Carneys, and seeing her young niece Sarah Shone. This evening we had several showers of rain with some thunder and lightning. My thoughts this day ran continually on my wife, I am very unhappy in mind for the loss of her. I hope the Lord will prepare me to follow her, to be with her, to part no more, to where trouble, grief and sorrow have an end; for this world is full of deceit, even in ones own family. Mr Newth call'd on us today and gave orders to make his wife a pr of boots.

'*Friday 5th October, 1838.* This day I began in the morning to plow lands. Which we finished and began to harrow them. Likewise I finished the cutting of my tombstone, the whole of the letters on the stone is 335. Afterwards I went and dug a piece of land. This day the wind was high and some rain fell. My thoughts this day were wandering to and fro, sometimes good, and sometimes bad; I am full of sorrow and grief on account of sin, and I can find no rest to my soul here.'

When I read the entry describing the actual placing of the stone, I packed Jean and the children into the car and paid my first visit to Clumber. Its hilltop church has one of the most charming graveyards I know. After an exciting search we found the stone. The number of letters, 335, is correct. The good 18th century couplets of the epitaph have a fine Johnsonian ring:

> *To the memory of Mrs Sarah Shone, who died Decr 20th 1837, aged 44 years*
> *Ah! Stranger had it been your lot to know*
> *The worth of her whose relics sleep below*
> *In silent sorrow o'er this grave you'd bend*
> *And mourn the wife, the Christian, and the friend.*
> *In vain are talents, wealth, or friendship's power*
> *To give support in death's tremendous hour.*
> *Learn then the Christian hopes, on these rely;*
> *Resign'd like her to suffer or to die.*

My brother Jeffrey had become Professor of History at Wesleyan University, Middletown, Conn. His special field was African History, which necessitated frequent visits to the country of his origins. He decided to examine in detail the demographic, social, political and other changes in the town of Cradock between two census years.

Our approaches to our place of birth were very different. Mine made little attempt at historical objectivity. *Karoo Morning* attempted to evoke what it was like to be me in that place at that time. Jeff was concerned to account for the changes in the nature of the town by sifting through all available archival sources and interviewing dozens of witnesses. Nevertheless at one time it seemed that we might co-author a book on our own home town, but differences in approach and the distance between our domiciles proved to be too great.

Yet the common interest gave a particular pertinence to much of our talk. Armed with maps in 1981 we followed much of the route from Cradock to Graaff-Reinet along which we had hitch-hiked in July 1946 to see our grandmother. On another occasion in 1974 with Keith Cremer as our guide, we clambered up Saltpeterskop to see the chessboard which the bored British signallers had scratched into a purple dolerite boulder. We found that we were free of the old big-brother/little-brother roles, simply two men with memories and interests in common.

More recently Jean and I have spent many happy hours in Albany and the Karoo in the company of Joan and Godfrey Collett trying to clarify the activities of a Settler ancestor, James Lydford Collett (1800–74), as set out sometimes cryptically in the diary which he kept meticulously from 1834 to 1874.

One such expedition took us deep into the mountains west of the Mountain Zebra Park towards Agtersneeuberg, to visit the farms which he had bought and developed in his best and happiest years, the 1840s. There he grew wheat and ran the merino sheep of which he was an early scientific breeder. The farm 'Waterval' was on an upper tributary of the Paul's River. It was a well-watered area which seems to have been carved out of Henningshoek and Hartbeeshoek.

The diaries made it clear that it had been necessary to fence his fields with drystone walling as in Wales. 'Old Arnot [his Welsh brother-in-law], Every and I built four miles of stone walls up there,' he recorded. So, as we went into the valley, it was exciting to ask, 'Do you see what I see?' and to get the answer, 'Stone walls!'

It was also exciting to find among masses of mountains with Afrikaans names like Blinkberg and Boesmanskrans one called Mount Snowdon, and to wonder if that was the fingerprint of old Arnot or, if not, what other Welshman?

The diary also records the building up there of a watermill to grind his corn. We asked the present owner if he knew of any likely site and he had no hesitation in directing us to it. And there, near the stream and a poplar bush, we found the shell of a substantial building and the remnants of a mill-race, with a fine millstone half buried in the alluvial soil below. This was most satisfactory and a good moment for a braai.

It was a perfect day to explore new terrain with lifelong friends in the company of an ancestral shade, one of those days which provide more pleasure than one dares to hope for. Everything conspired to make it so. After our picnic we continued up the valley, following an ancient road to Elandsfontein right up to Groenfontein, hoping to reach the Tandjiesberg watershed and to find the traces of a no-longer-used track into the upper reaches of the Vogel River which drains into the plains of Camdeboo and the Sundays River. This was the road down which James

The ruins of the water mill erected by James Lydford Collett in the Waterkloof in the 1840s (note the 'shadow' of the wheel).

Lydford Collett had sent his wool to Port Elizabeth during the War of the Axe. The surface had proved so rough that he had rolled his bales of wool to the bottom and sent the wagons down empty and undamaged, to pick up their load below.

We did not reach the watershed but near the limit of our excursion we were awarded an unforgettable sight. Suddenly, parallel to the car, golden over the green grass, a five- or six-foot cobra came sliding, combing the waving blades only slightly to either side. He posed no threat. We were all capitvated by the beauty of his colour and the smooth ease of his movements in the sparkling sun.

With delight Jean saluted him, using the words of Sydney Clouts:

'Good morning, gentle cobra, are you well?'

Among the many enthusiasts for the history of the Eastern Cape, and whose friendships made much of this work so pleasurable, are one or two I would like mention by name.

First 'Ted' Morse Jones. We had first met Edward Morse Jones in the late 'forties when he was churchwarden of St Martin's-in-the-Veld, Melrose. He had retired to Port Alfred, where he filled his tidy days with detailed researches into the fortunes and misfortunes of the 1820 Settlers. He used to come up to Grahamstown every week on Thursdays, to work in the Cory Library and the Albany Museum. His interest in the lives of the dead Settlers was complemented by his love of living birds. Both interests came together in his expeditions to particular places to find traces of Settler houses, roads, mills, graves. I recall being taken up to the top of a hill outside Bathurst to see Bailey's Beacon, erected in 1859 by a surveyor of that name. That eminence had been the point from which Colonel Cuyler, Landdrost of Albany, and his aides had supervised the wagon trains which had carried the parties of Settlers to their locations in 1820. We discussed the possibility of building a toposcope there. Ted said he would undertake to provide all the details – name of party, number of Settlers, country of origin, ship. Throughout our talk he was anxious lest my active and inquisitive boys should discover and disturb a pair of nesting dikkops! In due course I introduced Ted to Bill Slater, chairman of the 1820 Settlers Monument Committee, who accepted the toposcope idea as a proper project. It was duly erected and inaugurated by Ian Mackenzie in 1968. The Committee was also happy to publish Ted's *Roll of British Settlers in South Africa* in 1969, a great advance on previous lists and only recently (1987) superseded by M.D. Nash's *Settler Handbook*, a new list of the 1820 Settlers.

Among other Settler enthusiasts I particularly remember were Rex and Barbara Reynolds. I had known Rex as a student at Rhodes in the late 1930s. At some stage he had sold his farms in Beaufort West, tried to become a lawyer, and had then switched to photography. The Reynoldses

Poster for Cape Charade (by Jean Robinson after Frederick I'Ons)

made an excellent artistic team. In the 'sixties and early 'seventies they worked closely with me on various historical and architectural projects, providing the photographs, which we had taken on long expeditions. They also became enthusiastic restorers of old houses in Grahamstown.

When the debate as to what form the Monument to the 1820 Settlers was to take (see last chapter) was at its height, some academics suggested that it should provide a venue for festivals. One of these was the Rev. Leslie Hewson – Professor of New Testament Studies at Rhodes and a leading Methodist. A cleric is at first blush an unlikely champion of a festival. He was deeply interested in the origins of his church in South Africa, in the Rev. William Shaw and in his successors. Among these was the Rev. Henry Hare Dugmore, whose *Reminiscences of an Albany Settler* is a good introduction to Settlerdom. Edited by Hewson and Frank van der Riet, it was published in 1958.

Dugmore had delivered these *Reminiscences* as a lecture in 1870 during the celebrations held in Grahamstown to mark the 50th anniversary of the arrival of the Settlers. His epic account was so popular that it had to be repeated. The 1870 festivities had lasted a week and people came from all over the country to attend. There had been previous Settler festivals – in 1840 and 1845 – but it seems that this mammoth gathering of 1870 has a claim to be our first national festival. Had it not been for Hewson's publication of Dugmore's lecture, this very useful precedent might have escaped notice. Dugmore is remembered by a biennial lecture named after him and for one of the inscriptions in the foyer of the Monument: 'We must take root and grow, or die where we stand.'

He also provided the title of my first Settler play, *Take Root or Die* (produced in 1966, published 1970), in which I told the story of the Settlement up to its first large democratic gathering in Bathurst in 1823. I telescoped episodes from several families as recorded in their writings – Goldswain, Stubbs, 'Harry Hastings', Bertram Bowker, Pringle and others. Most of them would appear again in *When Boys Were Men*.

Take Root was followed by *Cape Charade, or Kaatjie Kekkelbek* – a play about Andrew Geddes Bain, a road-builder of genius, a pioneer geologist whose description of the Karoo system of rocks remains virtually intact, and a collector of fossils 250 million years old. He was also a satirical poet and the creator of a delightful archetype of the reckless, cheeky, charming Khoi woman, Kaatjie Kekkelbek. I staged *Cape Charade* in Grahamstown with Norman Coombes in the lead, in 1967, and Roy Sargeant produced it for CAPAB in Cape Town in 1968 at the Hofmeyr Theatre, with Frank Shelley as Bain, and Yvonne Bryceland as his long-suffering wife.

In 1968 CAPAB commissioned a play on a Settler theme to mark the 150th anniversary of the landing of the 1820 Settlers (1970). I wrote about a man dear to my heart, *Richard Gush of Salem*. CAPAB provided leading actors and the producer, Roy Sargeant. It was an exciting exercise. The play grew and changed during production with suggestions from Roy, and special music was written for it by Michael Tuffin of U.C.T. After a spell in Grahamstown, it played in the Labia Theatre in Cape Town. In 1982 Rosalie van der Gucht produced it again in Grahamstown with Deon Opperman, then a first-year student, playing Gush. He did remarkably well.

When Sargeant left his Chair of Speech and Drama at Rhodes to head the English Drama section of SATV, he decided he would produce the play for television. This meant considerable re-writing, with input from Joe Stewardson and Vincent Cox. Joe also took the part of Gush, opposite Michael McGovern, who played his opponent, Dennison. Both Rosalie van der Gucht and I thought Roy had got these two livewires crossed, which resulted in short-circuiting the drama rather than creating sparks. The piece was screened on 20 December 1984.

In 1982 the original stage version of *Richard Gush of Salem*, together with the main sources, was published by Maskew Miller. I am happy that it is occasionally set for schools. It is a true story that needs to be better known, a relevant historical precedent of the effectiveness of non-violence. I dedicated it to two Quakers, my grandfather, James Butler, and his daughter, Mary.

This concern with Settler history found its most serious expression in *The 1820 Settlers: An Illustrated Commentary* (Human & Rousseau, 1974), a work which I edited to coincide with the opening of the 1820 Settlers Monument in 1974: text by Guy Butler and John Benyon; pictures by Rex and Barbara Reynolds; captions by Eily Gledhill; and the design by Ken Robinson. While it certainly modified the traditional heroic and romantic views of the settlement, we found the subject far from exhausted, saying in our Introduction: 'We are acutely aware of gaps in our knowledge – gaps which will only be filled when, for instance, careful and detailed studies have been made of the history of each party, and of its leader and most prominent members.' This is now taking place. M.D. Nash's *Bailie's Party of 1820 Settlers* (1982) – impressive both for its scholarly detail and its acute perception – has radically changed our perspectives on that episode in South African history.

With the appearance of *When Boys Were Men* (1969) which contained material up to the discovery of diamonds in 1867, I felt I was ready to pursue my interests in the next major influx of English-speaking South Africans who had come to seek their fortunes. How different they were, this crowd from almost every land under the sun, hungry not for land to plough but for diamonds and gold, minerals related to the glamour and glitter of wealthy societies. I read a great deal about early Kimberley and the road to the North.

This interest became known. Together with my historical plays, it resulted in 1970 in a commission from a small theatrical and film consortium to research the life of Barney Barnato, and, on my findings, to outline a script for a film on this volatile and loquacious rival to the taciturn C.J. Rhodes. This brief excursion into the fringes of the film industry could do with a novella-length chapter in which the truth would certainly emerge as stranger than fiction, so fantastically different are the rituals and conventions of academics and film producers. Amazed and trying to play it cool, I found myself among a jet set who held committee meetings which came to policy decisions while driving all night at furious speed from Durban to Johannesburg; who held leisurely business discussions after delicious dinners on the edge of glimmering swimming-pools; who settled a debate about a difference of some millions of rands in a budget by asking for my sign in the Zodiac, which is Aquarius. 'Are there any other Aquarians present?' As most of the others were also Aquarians, their views prevailed.

As it was quite clear that much of the source material for Barnato was in Britain, Jean and I were flown to London for six weeks, given a free flat in Ealing near filmland, and a chauffeur-driven car on call. For the only time in our lives we enjoyed living as the affluent do.

The décor of our flat left no doubt about the continent of origin of the owner: one entire wall of the bedroom was taken up with a splendid photograph of zebras, blown up to zebra size. We went to watch films being made at Ealing Studios. During lunch in the canteen Jean said to me, 'Don't look now, but Dracula is having lunch behind you.' And there he was. Christopher Lee had removed his teeth, but not his bloodshot contact lenses. I wondered what he would look like without them.

We worked hard, chiefly at the British Library's Newspaper Archives at Collingdale. It was all great fun and we assembled a tin trunk full of source materials, anecdotes, items of scandal and a few important facts new to Barnato science.

But nothing came of the film. The principals left South Africa, presumably with the tin trunk. One of the clauses in the agreement between us was that none of the information I had gathered could be divulged until the film was made. No time limit was set for the making of that film, so my lips are still sealed. And as an SATV series has since been screened on Barnato, it is unlikely my labours will be put to use.

I have previously referred to my interest in tranforming the *Medea* of Euripides into an allegorical play for our country and our times. I wrote *Demea* in the late 1950s at the height of the Verwoerdian mania but, as the play calls for a multiracial cast (of over twenty) it could not be produced until the apartheid laws began to loosen their hold on the theatre.

The Performing Arts Council of the Transvaal (PACT) had the resources and the courage to produce it for the Grahamstown Festival in 1990. The director, Dieter Reible, spent three days in Grahamstown with me, discussing modifications and cuts. If I have one criticism of those three days it is that we did not cut enough.

David Philip published the text in time for the première. He and his wife Marie were our house guests for the festival, and sat with Jean and me in the Rhodes Theatre on the opening night. The two leads were excellent, Nomsa Xaba as Demea, and Graham Hopkins as Jonas. I was so uncertain of the audience's response that I dared not leave the auditorium at interval, but sat fixed to my seat, supported by Jean and the Philips, in the hope that some of the audience would return. To my relief, all seemed to come back for the second half, and the final applause was reassuring. Jean and I were taken backstage by Reible to meet the cast, who were quite unaffected in their appreciation of the play as we were with their performances. We had them to coffee and cake at High Corner the next morning. One of the more memorable remarks came from Peter se Puma, 'Professor, you must live another thirty years and write more plays like this. All your characters – black and white – are people. None are saints and none are devils.'

The press reports were mainly enthusiastic, but one or two were among the nastiest I have received.

23   1946–74

The Poplars

Many readers of *Karoo Morning* and *Bursting World* have asked me to give some account of the subsequent history of The Poplars, Bree Street, Cradock – the much-loved home in which Alice and Ernest brought up their five children in the 1920s and 1930s, until the processes of growth, education, jobs elsewhere, marriages and a world war scattered us to the four winds.

Ernest and Alice lived their latter years in a town increasingly controlled by Nationalist Afrikaners. They were members of a steadily diminishing English-speaking community still worshipping in 'English' churches whose congregations were shrinking in numbers and devotion.

Scattered their children may have been but The Poplars, the home they had provided, left us all with memories more durable than the bricks and mortar from which the place had been built in various stages and for various needs during the previous century. One does not obliterate or demolish a house any more easily than a human being.

The Poplars remained a family focus long after we had started establishing families of our own. It was some time before any of us really settled down in one place. Alice and Ernest stayed on in Cradock throughout the 'forties, 'fifties and part of the 'sixties and we upwardly mobile wandering children would visit them when we could. As I settled fairly early in Grahamstown I was geographically closest to them and probably saw them more frequently than any of the others.

Like most parents they 'lived for their children'; and beyond their children a circle of blood relatives – father's siblings and their children, and the great hospitable clan of Colletts and Biggses in Cradock and Graaff-Reinet, nearly all farming folk; and mother's people in England, who seldom made the journey to Africa, but whom we all visited when we went abroad.

My father was a somewhat lonely man, particularly after his children left home. He filled his spare time usefully making furniture-to-order for relatives and altering the outbuildings of The Poplars with his own hands. Once he had sold his business *The Midland News and Karoo Farmer* in 1948, he put much time into municipal affairs – the largely thankless task of sitting on committees most of whose business was to implement Nationalist social policies which were anathema to him. Their racist ideology was destroying the fairly tolerant if prejudiced spirit of the little town to which his father and he had given such devoted thought and service. Now prejudice had become law. He eventually resigned over the implementation of the Group Areas Act.

He was a shy, withdrawn man, who spoke little and took a stand on principle because 'he could do no other', not because he enjoyed public debating, and certainly not to draw attention to himself. I don't think he had an inkling of just how high-principled he was – we children may have and Alice certainly did have. She didn't agree with his teetotalism and perhaps not always with his pacifism and certainly not with his apathy towards the House of Windsor; but on his opposition to the implementation of apartheid and other racist legislation she could be more outspoken than he. We all remember her fury during the late 'twenties and 'thirties at measures taken by the school board which would, in her view, lead to the ruin of Rocklands, the school on whose staff she had served from 1911 to her marriage in 1914.

Father's religion was a mystery to me. When we held Quaker meetings in my childhood he very seldom felt moved to speak, unlike his sister Mary. Though he had been Superintendent of the Methodist Sunday School at one time, I do not recall his being very active in Methodist Church affairs; but he certainly went to evening service regularly and Alice would always accompany him. He had a pleasant singing voice, but I do not recall hearing it except when standing beside him during a church service. He would sometimes whistle while he worked and he had a keen love of classical music. He also had his favourites, like Ernest Lough singing 'O for the wings of a dove' and 'I know that my Redeemer liveth'. He was not a great reader although at one time he did belong to the Left Book Club. I do not recall him reading religious books except during Friends' reading evenings.

Alice the Anglican, on the other hand, went to St Peter's to Holy Communion or Eucharist regularly, sat on the church council, and had a kind of desperate love for all 'the poor clergy' whom the Church in its wisdom sent to look after us. She thought the boot was on the other foot. If she was short on social theory and political abstractions, she simply knew certain things: for instance, that it was wrong to object to 'natives' or 'coloureds' taking communion together with 'Europeans'. When people said it was unhygienic – that one might get an unspeakable disease from the chalice – she would observe that unspeakable diseases in Africa had all travelled the other way, from Europeans to Africans, and that anyway she was sure our Lord's blood in the chalice would prevent any nasty germs from getting out of hand.

For her there was a mystery and a power there in the sacrament, which got inside all her children in greater or less measure. Insofar as we have retained religious affiliations, we are Anglicans.

Also living in Cradock was Aunt Mary, Ernest's eldest sister. She looked after our great-Aunt Eliza at 27 Market Street until Eliza's death (1977). Then she came to live in a little flat which Ernest built for her on the old tennis court at The Poplars. It was from there that she continued her lifelong devotion to good works for the poor, and friendship to African leaders like the Rev. James Calata, the Secretary-General of the A.N.C. and one of the accused in the Treason Trial. I believe she was the first person in South Africa to approach and secure Oxfam aid for the needy – mainly in the form of clothes against the bitter Karoo winters.

She lived a very disciplined, religious life, spending some time early every morning in Bible study and prayer.

So there they were, the three most powerful influences on our lives, living at The Poplars, having their meals together, discussing world and local affairs and waiting for letters or news from the children and family and Oxfam.

If Ernest seldom joined Alice in Anglican worship, he was very happy to help the clergy at the Rectory with any odd jobs. He had a little leather attaché case which he would take with him wherever he went. Through many years of experience he had built up a kit with which he could fix all the smaller items that can go wrong with a house. Marie Biggs used to keep a list of things to be fixed 'when Uncle Ernest comes next'. But it was with some surprise that I heard he had undertaken to panel the choir of St Peter's Church. When the new side chapel of the Cathedral of St Michael and St George, Grahamstown, needed an additional ecclesiastical chair of Victorian Gothic design, I asked Ernest if he would care to make it. He did so, and very well too. I often glance at it affectionately.

While on their 1954 visit to England, Alice had, with some assistance from her family, bought a little collection of 'crocks' for her sister-in-law Uncle Jim's wife Hilda (née van Wyk) of Virginia, Louisvale. Those two had an easier, warmer relationship with each other than their brother–husbands did. Alice's letters to Hilda about those 'crocks' have survived, evidence of a shared love for pretty, old, beautiful things without which few homes are complete.

Alice's brother George of New Hall Potteries was a great help. 'His wife Frances and I went to a good place called Pidducks. I saw a lovely, graceful vase in *rouge flambé* ware and made a dive for it – Six Pounds and Six Shillings.'

Later, from Cradock, 'First of all we lost the chest containing your china and the new rugs, at least the ship did. The rugs were found in Cape Town, and have arrived safely. The crockery went to Durban but will be sent back here.' By 20 January 1955: 'All the pieces are in the old oak cabinet and nobody can knock *that* over. As for living in England again, I should love it – for half the year, summer, if we had heaps of money. I love too many people in South Africa now and the great fascination of great spaces and the hospitable people. 'East West Home's Best' is absolutely true and I don't think anything will dig Ernest out of Cradock. I would leave Cradock like a shot tomorrow and start a new life even at this age. I would love Cape Town – I don't want much, do I?! Our money won't run to it. Very steadying stuff, money! And we have spent our thousand pounds on our travels.'

On 25 February 1955: '... Last week we had an orgy of religious parties for Mary's friends the Brayshaws (Quakers) and the house is always full of people. Also my Seventh Day Adventist cook won't work on Saturdays and her baby falls sick on Mondays and Tuesdays etc. etc., so I am getting a new cook with ordinary religious convictions. And it is a great pity because Mina cooks like an Angel.'

By June of the same year, politics has taken precedence over religion. An election is in the offing.

'... At any rate if Jim gets pitched out of Parliament you can go on being successful farmers ... I tramped my feet sore doing four streets for the Women's Anti-Republic protest. I have a feeling you and Jim may find yourselves back in Parliament, but not sure how with such a set of gerrymanderers and vernookerers. Joan has joined the anti-republican league. She'd better mind her job!'

Eventually the lost and repacked crockery reached Louisvale. 14 July 1955: 'We were relieved and delighted to get your letter this morning telling us that the crocks were all safe ... What fun unpacking by the fire – like Xmas in England. It was great fun getting those things for you my dear, and they are just a beginning.'

Then the grim reaper entered on the scene.

Hilda had had an operation for cancer in 1951. It returned and further operations ensued. The Poplars couple responded according to their natures. In 1957 Alice sent a gift of more 'crocks' and Ernest made a bookrest to ease reading in bed for Hilda. She died on 8 September 1958.

A letter from Ernest to James of 30 December 1958 shows them trying to find a date when they can visit Louisvale. Would Easter 1959 do? But the letter also seeks to bridge the gap that has existed between the brothers nearly all their lives.

'It is useless', writes Ernest, 'to spend one's time on vain regrets for things that cannot be corrected, but because I am sure that one ought to try to mend or improve brotherly relationships, I shall do my best. So let me confess at once my regret for not keeping in closer touch with you after you left home (during the 1914–18 war) and consequently, as our interests differed so widely, both in character and in locality, and as neither has been very fond of letter writing, our contacts became more infrequent and less intimate; and had it not been for our dear wives who have kept up the family correspondence in their own inimitable ways, we certainly would have become more out of touch than has been the case.' And so he went up to Louisvale in April 1959, and helped Jim erect Hilda's tombstone.

Then in 1959 tragedy struck The Poplars. Alice had the first of a series of strokes which affected her left arm and her speech. It was terrible. The devil himself could not have invented a more awful ending for her life.

Alice was at her brightest in situations of talk, of dialogue, of what is now called eyeball-to-eyeball contact. She didn't need to be the centre of it, but her listening, interested face was there, the blue eyes as it were gathering all the talk, laughing, exclaiming, exploding, questioning, but never speechifying. For all her vivacity she was a good listener.

The stroke did not affect her understanding. She would hear and grasp what was being said; but whatever she wished to say came out 'scrambled' – an incomprehensible 'fruit salad' of sounds. She would launch into a sentence, her eyes alight with the old eagerness to see the response in the eyes of those to whom she was speaking, and then they'd cloud with anguish or a furious recognition that the words she was uttering came out wrong, and that the eyes in front of her were filled with bafflement, patience, pity – anything but response, the gay reciprocity which was her special gift to create. With this was an increasingly humiliating physical dependence upon others – to be clothed, to be fed, by Mary, by Ernest, by the servants.

I was absent in Holland and England for much of 1960 and sent her postcards of places which I thought she would have loved to see, travel brochures, picture books; because I knew how she sat for hours leafing through illustrated material. And Ernest made up four large albums of photographs and postcards of their 1954 visit to England and the Continent, four albums whose contents mean little to me, but which I can't quite persuade myself to throw away.

Joan reminds me of the kindness of Canon Johnson and Mrs Kathleen Johnson during this period. 'They visited Mother every day, giving Aunt Mary and Dad a break. There was a time when Dad took her to St Peter's for Holy Communion on Sundays. When this was no longer possible Canon Johnson ministered to her in her bedroom. On one occasion Dad and I joined her! It was a joy (and pain) to know that Dad, for *her* sake, had made his own kind of sacrifice. You should have witnessed Mom's wide-eyed surprise and delight, it had a jewel-like quality.'

Alice's condition gradually deteriorated until it was extremely difficult to nurse her. After a visit I got in touch with Joan, who had also seen her recently. We had both become convinced that under certain circumstances it was wrong to expect close relatives to do certain kinds of nursing. Both Mary and Ernest were gentle and considerate people, but they were old, as was their beloved patient. They dreaded having to see Alice leave

The Poplars for anywhere but Heaven. After years of patience, of literally spoonfeeding Alice, Ernest would try to *make* her take food or her pills by cajoling her as though she were a child, with baby talk. Perhaps it was my presence which caused her to explode, and with a violent gesture push his hand aside, her eyes blazing with fury. For the moment I saw what I had never seen before: a furious Alice repulsing Ernest, briefly, but it was infinitely painful to witness. Joan had witnessed this too and found it terrifying. The doctor was consulted. The pills were no longer effective. Alice now needed professional care and different medication, in a hospital.

So on 27 April 1963 we moved her to the Prince Alfred Infirmary, Grahamstown, an ancient Victorian hospital close to the campus, where I could visit her with ease.

Does one ever visit a close relative who is in hospital often enough? She was now much worse; but whenever I visited her, she would sit up, smiling and trying to make welcoming gestures with her hands. All I could do was sit beside her and hold her hand, and go over the news of the family and the children. The noises she made were impossible to interpret. These visits did little for my always wavering faith in a merciful God. Why? Why? Why?

Ernest came to live in Grahamstown to be close to her. He visited her every day. High Corner was full of children and its own dramas, so after a few weeks he moved to rooms close by. He picked up old friendships and went to 'Commem', the large Methodist church, on Sundays. Again, did one do enough for him?

One morning, 6 August 1963, I was phoned early by the P.A.I. – to come at once. I arrived at the same moment as he did and we went into the ward together.

Alice was propped up in bed, her eyes open and sightless.

'Has she gone?' asked Ernest of the nurse, who nodded.

We both sat down. Alice Eyre Stringer. The woman who had given his life its shape and who had given me my life and much else beside had changed. She was no longer the painful parody of what she had once been. Always young at heart, she was dead, blessedly dead and free at last, beyond the agony of fumbling for words and meanings in an 83-year-old body.

But Ernest could not accept it as I could. He turned to me and said again: 'Is Alice gone then?'

'Yes,' I said, and got up. He rose too and we turned to go. As I left the ward I saw the nurse pull the sheet up over her face.

But Alice was not dead. This became very clear at her funeral. All of Ernest's siblings came – Uncle Jim from Louisvale, Aunt Josie from Ixopo, Alice from Brooklyn, Aunt K from Irene, and Mary from Cradock. Of her children, all were present except Jeffrey who was in America. After a service in the Cathedral which Canon Johnson conducted with a beautiful restraint, we all gathered at High Corner. 'Once the hard part of the service is over,' says Dorothy, 'people are happy to enjoy their sense of family solidarity, and recall the past.' There was much joy and laughing reminiscence about Alice and the family.

Ernest had developed what his children regarded at the time as something of an obsession with cremation. He and Alice must be cremated and the ashes interred in the Crematorium Garden of Remembrance in Port Elizabeth. The economic and ecological arguments in favour of cremation are many, but at the time the idea was still a little odd – particularly as there was a family plot in the Cradock cemetery, with James Butler and his wife Anne Letitia lying side by side. It was quite big enough for the next generation. However, we did not wish to interfere with the final sleeping arrangements of those who had begotten and borne us; besides, not one of us was consulted on the matter. I suspect that Alice would have liked to be buried at St Peter's, but would never have suggested any arrangements that would separate her from Ernest. She was his good and faithful wife and should be beside him, no matter what.

But Dorothy was not happy with cremation. It was all so unbiblical, so artificial and mechanical, so technical. She confided her hesitations to me and we went off together to see a good Anglican priest, who made no bones about his own preference for burial, but conceded that ashes could be buried in Christian fashion. After all, did not the service for the burial of the dead contain the phrase 'Ashes to ashes, dust to dust'?

The death of Alice called for a reassessment of the life plans of Ernest and Mary.

Life at The Poplars without Alice? It was hard to imagine. But where else could Ernest live but there, in the buildings he had altered and made, among the tools in his wonderfully equipped workshop. Remarriage? At 77? Not impossible. There was at least one Cradock widow living in Grahamstown who seemed a warm, congenial soul who might have made him happy. After his five years' purgatory, watching Alice's slow deterioration, that might have been a blessing.

But what of Mary, who had given her life to the service of humankind, and her closest relatives in particular? There was never any debate in our minds as to what would happen, what ought to happen. Ernest returned to The Poplars, and Mary moved from the flat into the house, and her little flat became the spare room for visitors like ourselves from time to time.

It was a sensible, but far from ideal arrangement. Mary was no cook; and although Ernest was not a fussy man and never would descend to complaining about his sister's culinary attempts, he must have hankered for the days of Alice's régime. And as for Mary, she was not domestically inclined. Although she and Ernest could agree on many political issues, particularly as regards the steady, heartless implementation of apartheid principles in the town, Ernest did not share her interest in individual poor people. The garden flat had become a kind of 'dispensary' and 'consulting-room' for an 80-year-old white-haired lady to listen to cases of destitution, and, in true Quaker and Oxfam style, try to keep careful records of them. The main focus of practical compassion was the children, and she had some moral and practical support from the Child Welfare Society and the Red Cross. There were no indiscriminate handouts to nameless mendicants. Many could quote chapter and verse. Or try to.

But among these rejects from the farms, the families laid off by the railways, by garages and the rest, there were the inevitable con-men, the professional beggars, the thieves. It was the repeated thefts that distressed Mary and infuriated Ernest. 'Biting the hand that fed them,' was his phrase.

And there were other, subtler factors. It was one thing for the admirable Miss Butler to have done her good works in the past, from a dispensary in the location, or from her houses which she had always chosen as close to the location as possible, in that wonderful 'no man's land' – or rather, 'all persons' land' – which had existed before the Nationalist mania for racial purity mesmerised the minds of municipalities. But now, right opposite the Pastorie, next to the Manse and a stone's throw from the Rectory, the inhabitants of Bree Street had to see and smell the ragged poor for hours at a stretch, being listened to and helped by an ancient white woman of gentle speech and manners and deep convictions. It was somehow improper and inappropriate.

As far as Ernest was concerned, this was not part of the deal. Mary was living in his home; and he did not welcome The Poplars becoming an outlet for Oxfam. But there was so much more to it than that. They would have their differences and agreed to disagree; but at times there was little ease or joy in the agreement.

And Ernest was not well. He was having legal tussles with a neighbour to whom he had sold off part of the old property. In vain Mary tried to induce some Quaker calm and Christian forgiveness into his thinking, but the resentment and bitterness grew. Yet he had already started making his peace with God and Man, beginning, as we have seen, with his young brother James.

Then he went to hospital for a bladder operation in Port Elizabeth, where I visited him; and when he had recovered I drove him to Bushman's River Mouth, where he stayed for some time with his youngest sister Kathleen and her husband Boy Vorster.

And then he visited Dorothy in Pretoria, where he enjoyed the infectious company of her children. Ernest was always good with young children.

His customary reserve disappeared and he found delight in entering into their worlds, or attempting to.

At the skating-rink he was quite intoxicated by the sight of them and others gliding about at speed and with graceful ease. It brought back his own youth, skating on ice when at school in England and, later on, rollerskating in South Africa. In a trice he lost sixty years and put on a pair of skates.

When he woke up in hospital he simply could not accept that he had been so stupid, so irresponsible, so silly. At 78, still half anaesthetised, his shame also followed a childhood route. What would his big sister think? 'Don't tell Mary!' he pleaded.

While he lay in bed recovering at Dorothy's, his ankle in plaster, he opened up in a rare manner, briefly, with Joan, expressing deep religious questions raised by Alice's last years, of the suffering of innocence; and Dorothy 'found him agonising over the fact that when he had visited Alice in the Infirmary at Grahamstown she had often begged him to stay, but he would not overrun the visiting hours because he felt the nurses had to be considered. I also think that he himself could not bear to remain longer.'

And so he wandered, as I see it, trying to fill the gap left by Alice's departure.

He was blessed with a sudden end.

Early on the morning of 19 June 1965, Aunt Mary phoned from Cradock to say that Ernest had had a heart attack twenty-four hours before and was in the Cradock hospital. She thought I should come and see him. I had a heavy day of appointments and said I would set out first thing the next morning. Jean said, 'Rubbish! We're going immediately.' Which we did. The weather was bitterly cold.

As soon as we got to Cradock we went up to the hospital. I saw the doctor. Yes, it was a very severe attack and the next ten hours were crucial. Ernest was asleep at that moment, so the doctor suggested I should come back in three hours' time. Could I just look in on him? I asked.

Ernest was lying on his back, without his dentures. He was grey in colour, breathing deeply and with difficulty. What shocked me – and how often it is the little unexpected but commonplace thing that does this – was his unshaven appearance. The grey face was smudged with grey and white stubble. That was not how I remembered him. Ernest was a neat fastidious man, whom I had never seen unshaven before. I visualised him as erect, with a good colour and a spring in his step.

Jean and I walked about, talking of this and that, killing time until we went back to the hospital.

Yes, he was awake. Yes, he knew I had come. Yes, he would like to see me.

So I went in. But he was lying with his back to me, facing the wall. I don't know why. Perhaps he had to lie on his left side or perhaps he had lacked the strength to roll over. (Only those who have been really ill know how supreme an effort turning from one shoulder to another can be.) Perhaps he didn't want me to see him in his toothless, unshaven state, but I doubt if Ernest's vanity ran that far.

The sister said, 'A minute only.'

I don't know what I said. 'Hullo, Dad. I'm sorry about this. Jean said we must come at once, so here we are.' Who knows? Does it matter? What are words in such circumstances? But I remember his response, spoken with great effort. And the words seemed to me to come from deep in him.

'Thank you for coming.'

The Sister showed us out.

I was grateful to Jean for insisting on our coming immediately.

We returned through the cold air to The Poplars, the stars like magnified hoar-frost crystals overhead. Aunt Mary supplied us with hot-water bottles and we took to our beds in the little building which had been Aunt Mary's base of operations for several years.

She woke us with a tray of tea when the spire of the D.R.C. was showing very clear and black against the pale sky – but a sky still dark enough to allow a few of the brightest stars to glow.

'Ernest died shortly after midnight,' she said.

It came as little surprise. Jean had told me what to expect. But what amazed me was Mary's restraint in breaking the news. She had not wished to disturb us – we had had a terribly tiring day and would be having several more. So she had borne her brother's death alone until a new day was upon the world.

During breakfast I asked Mary whether she had had any premonition of his heart attack. Like all experienced nurses she was cautious. He had seen the doctor a few days before, who had prescribed pills. He had complained no more than usual of his increasing stiffness – how difficult he found it to pick up anything he had dropped on the workshop floor. Over the last few days he had been busy tidying up the workshop, frequently calling for the help of the gardener. No, she could not say there had been anything untoward. He had been waiting for the arrival of a little brass plate to affix to a small piece of church furniture. He had made this at Joan's suggestion, in memory of Alice. Mary handed me the keys of the workshop.

There it all was, the big familiar space, the carpenter's bench with the chisel rack behind it; all the machine tools standing to attention in their usual positions. He had always kept his workshop tidy. 'A place for everything and everything in its place.' But now more so than ever – every flat surface was swept and clean.

There was nothing surprising in this. What startled me was a neat row of four upright teak chairs along the centre of the floor. I recognised them at once. Incomplete, they had been our standing family joke against our father.

He had started making them before we came to The Poplars, in the early days of his marriage before I was 5. Although they were already glued together, he had never completed them. All that they had lacked were the riempied seats and backs. One of them had a broken leg which could easily have been fixed. They had taken up quite a lot of storage space, those four almost completed teak chairs, for a full forty years. Why had Ernest abandoned them when so near completion? I have only one, obvious answer. Alice hadn't liked them. They were neither elegant nor comfortable. They could have been the cause of an early marital confrontation. Or, as I know only too well, after much labour a project can go dead on one. We lose conviction about it and yet can't quite abandon it; we hope the enthusiasm will return, or that we will find a way to cure an inhibiting defect. I simply don't know.

Ernest had many wise saws, proverbs, pieces of encapsulated wisdom. And whenever we downed tools halfway through a job, he would say, 'Come on! Finish it! Who takes two bites to a cherry?'

I think it was Jeffrey who first retorted, 'What about those four chairs?'

Now they were complete, the second bite of the cherry taken.

But there was another surprise, small and neat, on that surface of the bench close to the vice where most of the work was done: the small piece of church furniture which he had made at Joan's suggestion.

It was a hand lectern, or missal-stand, such as is used on an altar to hold the prayer book, tilted so that the officiating priest can read the words while his hands perform those mysterious actions with the bread and the wine. Simple, functional.

The more I think about that workshop the more it seems to me that my father, knowing that he was now ready to depart, completed those two tasks. Perhaps he asked to be released and was allowed to go, leaving everything 'in apple-pie order'.

The chairs? A kind of loving, humorous reply to his children after years of joking. The tying up of loose ends.

And the lectern? That was no gesture to us. It was for Alice, for James Calata's church.

What do I recall of Ernest Butler's funeral?

I had to go to T.J. Schooling & Sons, the undertakers, to choose a coffin – a coffin which would briefly be seen during the church service and then, within twenty-four hours, incinerated in the Port Elizabeth crematorium. Ernest himself could have made a good workmanlike economical box for himself – but that would have been to create a big demonstration from the grave and draw attention to himself in an atypical manner.

Perhaps it was the pseudo-silver handles that offended me most. There was nothing pseudo about my father. I had heard that Jews insisted on a plain deal box with rope handles and I felt like asking for a Jewish coffin, there and then. But that would have been making an even more sensational objection to current Christian funeral customs.

So I chose one in which the wood still looked like wood and not like plastic, and the handles plain, not like silver paper over ornately moulded chocolate.

The family were there in strength. The Poplars was packed for the last time with Butler kin. All Ernest's siblings who had grown up in Bree Street and worshipped in the Methodist Church where the memorial service was conducted were present, except Florence who had died, and James who was ill (he died in 1966).

Josephine came through the Transkei from Murchison, Ixopo, Natal, with her son Dr David Biggs, who had boarded with us while he attended the Boys' High School.

From Graaff-Reinet came Ernest's sister Alice, and her husband Alan Biggs of Brooklyn, brought by his nephew John Biggs, Florrie's eldest son, and his wife Marie, of Vrede. His brother Denys, of Honingkrantz, came with his wife Margaret, and Billy Vorster, the eldest son of Ernest's sister Kathleen of Irene, and his wife Christine. They had had to travel over the Wapadsberg through the snow. Most of them brought flowers from the gardens of those farms.

And from all over the district people came, many of them Colletts, of the Grassridge clan from which Ernest's mother Annie Letitia had sprung, ranging from young to old.

And the townsfolk.

For pallbearers I chose someone from each of his sisters' families, and Godfrey Collett. The coffin was already in the church, covered mostly with small, white, gold-flecked flowers that appear in our winters, all highly scented, like narcissi and freesias. There were purple violets from Vrede brought by Marie Biggs. When it was over, Ernest's coffin was escorted out of the church by six of us: myself and Alan Biggs, John and David Biggs, Billy Vorster and Godfrey Collett.

I don't know how many that Methodist church can seat, but it was full to overflowing. I can't remember who sat where or who was there to shake our hands – but it was face after face from my childhood, faraway relatives who had come all the way across snow-covered mountains, and family close at hand, as well as city councillors and all the civic crowd.

But whom I had not expected – why, why had I not expected them? – were the blacks: the family retainers, gardeners and cooks, men who as boys had delivered *The Midland News and Karoo Farmer*, employees from the printing works and from Butler Bros, Booksellers. And, in spite of his banning order, the Reverend James Calata, whose birthday it was.

It would have been so appropriate to have followed Ernest's coffin to the Cradock cemetery beyond the park and the sports fields. The procession would not have been as long as his father's funeral which I had watched as a small boy, but it would also have included all races.

But Alice's ashes were already in Port Elizabeth, so to Port Elizabeth Jean and I followed the hearse. We left Aunt Mary, Joan, Dorothy and Christine at The Poplars to start sorting and labelling the furniture, the china, the cutlery, the pictures. Keith Cremer took the ladies all out to a quiet dinner, away from the house of bereavement.

There was another gathering of mourners at the crematorium, Butler and Collett relatives from Uitenhage and Port Elizabeth and a few old friends from the press. It was cold and pouring with rain. Someone pressed a button and the coffin moved out of sight to the sound of canned music to mask the noises of a high-voltage incinerator.

I had some words with an attendant about the burial of the ashes next to Alice's – a spot chosen by Dorothy and myself. I wonder if either of us could find it now?

The story of Ernest's funeral should end there, but it was followed by a memorable postscript. Jean and I still had to get back to Grahamstown from Port Elizabeth.

We ran out of petrol about 10.30 p.m. on a slight rise ten kilometres short of Seven Fountains. The night was wet, cold and windy. We had young children at home. Close to Seven Fountains is the farm Thornycroft, where James and Winifred Starke were farming at the time. After considering all the alternatives, we decided that I should try to thumb a lift to the Starkes and get them to drive me back with a gallon of petrol: or better still, for Jean to get the lift as she did not relish waiting alone in the car on the side of the road.

I tried thumbing a lift, jumping out of the car as soon as I saw the glow of approaching headlights and jumping back in again to get out of the biting wind. I played at jack-in-the-box with no result for well over an hour.

At last a huge van pulled up with two of the kindest but most piratical-looking Natal Indians in it. They spent their lives keeping Port Elizabeth supplied with bananas and other tropical fruit – a more innocuous life's work I could not imagine. But Jean thought she would prefer to look after the car, into which she locked herself, holding a hexagon spanner as protective weapon in her freezing fist.

The Starkes, who were already sound asleep, took some waking. Once they had grasped the predicament of their cousin, who had just cremated his father and whose wife was stranded alone in a car in the cold and sinister dark, they acted with speed.

The petrol was stored in drums in the dairy area of the homestead. I retain a memory of several cows looking at us with a mixture of wonder and reproach at being disturbed at that unscheduled hour.

To my great relief Jean and the car were unharmed. Her fingers were frozen stiff round the handle of the spanner and I had to prise them loose.

Joan, Dorothy and Christine stayed on to keep each other and Aunt Mary company. Sensibly led by Joan, they began turning the contents of The Poplars into lists – lists of furniture, of Alice's little collection of china, of the pictures and of the silver, preparatory to its being split five ways by the executor, me. My heart sank at the thought of it, but I knew I could rely on one thing: everyone would lean over backwards to be fair to all the others, and indeed they did. I also knew that the attorney handling all the Butler affairs, Keith Cremer, who since boyhood had been almost a member of our family, would look after the legal and financial arrangements with conscientious precision and tactful and gentle concern for us all, which he did.

One of Alice's favourite games before her stroke had been verbally to parcel out her household treasures among her children. But she made no lists and the allocations changed, and no two of us would have agreed entirely on what was 'promised' to whom. It was soon clear that there were minor clashes in expectations. It was the natural wish of each of us to secure a favourite piece of The Poplars, a precious fragment of the world Alice had created. Precious? There were no paintings by Old Masters, no heavily insured jewels, no rare collectors' pieces; and if there had been, not one of us was likely to have known the value of them. There were no price tags to anything in The Poplars. Of course Alice and Ernest discussed the price of clothes, of bread, of shoes, of milk, of petrol, of a trip to Cape Town, of what might be called our daily bread. But what Alice thought of as her treasures belonged to a sort of Heaven of beautiful things where money was incidental, accidental and irrelevant.

What member of a warm family can put a price on old vases full of flowers grown and arranged by a particular hand, or the bringing out of the best tea set? Or value a picture that has always hung in the same place?

Over the next few weeks I presided over the equitable distribution into fragments of what had been a whole, and everyone behaved perfectly. Yet such had been the love in that home that the fragments still have a sacramental power for me. A picture or a stick of furniture from The Poplars, now in one of my sisters' homes, can touch my heart.

The difficulties of dividing the contents of The Poplars, labelling them and despatching them to Johannesburg (Joan), Pretoria (Dorothy), Flagstaff (Christine), Middletown, Conn. (Jeffrey), were considerably complicated by my tearing the ligaments in my left ankle so badly that I had to live in plaster for a time, but they carried no exhausting emotional overtones.

Our problem was Aunt Mary, still living at The Poplars, still dispensing Quaker help from the garden flat. Ernest had foreseen the problem and six months before his death he had written to Joan.

'We have our names down on the waiting-lists of old people's homes and seem to be continuing our normal lives quite well considering. But I hope some more help will come along for Aunt Mary – failing which she won't be easily persuaded to leave her location sufferers helpless. Our moving from here will only take place through either of us being incapacitated or dying.'

With Ernest's death the time had come for Mary to move and she accepted this in principle. The only question was the timing.

Mary was now 80. She was hoping to report on and hand over her work to suitable people during the visit of a Quaker lady, Olive Gibson, due in Cradock on 16 August.

Then Mary phoned Joan: she had just returned from a Child Welfare meeting where she had learned that there was no one to take over her job and administer the Quaker Relief funds.

'It is all very sad for her and her clients and it will all close down at the end of August,' said Joan.

But it did not quite work out like that. Mary always had a cogent reason for not leaving just yet – in spite of an increased frequency of thefts, so much so that friends and relatives spoke to us with an urgency which amounted to an accusation of dereliction of responsibility. But move she would not. She belonged with the poor of Cradock and while she could help them she insisted on staying. She had arrangements to make and ends to tie up.

Mary's youngest sister, Kathleen, who had retired and was living at Bushman's River Mouth, went to Cradock to spend some time with her. It was agreed that Mary would be brought to High Corner with Kathleen when she returned. But once again there were difficulties.

What could be done? Owing to a leg in plaster I was incapable of going to fetch her, but Jean undertook the difficult task – a day Aunt Mary never forgot, 4 October 1965, when she had to leave Cradock much against her will. All her worldly goods had been packed in the cars and, standing in the doorway of her empty flat, she said to Jean:

'Thank you, dear. Now take it all to Grahamstown. Store it for me. I'll follow later per opportunity. When I'm ready.'

It was one of those 'crunch' moments which would have been difficult for Joan, or Dorothy, or Guy, or Christine, or Jeff, to handle. Jean does not recall what she and Aunt Kathleen said, but they brought Mary to High Corner.

She could not hide her resentment at having been moved against her will and she grieved. But not for long. She turned her attention to our children and tried to civilise them, and like Grannie Satchwell, she had little success. But she left indelible memories of a strong, no-nonsense, old lady with some very funny ideas and clothes, but full of kindness.

After a few months a vacancy occurred at the Brookshaw Home and she moved there. We expected her to fade away. But instead she blossomed. It was a marvel to behold.

For most of her life Mary had been something of a loner, a high-principled feminist ahead of her time, a pacifist, and pro-black. She had been respected but not popular. She abandoned none of her principles, but there was little call to fight for them among her fellow very senior and sometimes ailing Brookshaw companions. Many of them found her a source of comfort and strength. And it was characteristic of her to come to Jean after a few weeks and thank her for having removed her from Cradock against her will. The last years of her life were, I think, her happiest.

The most unexpected happened to Aunt Mary. She took liberties with herself as it were. She had seen enough of life, and of life at High Corner, to know that one could take a sherry or a glass of wine without becoming tiddly, silly, or going to the devil. So she would actually sip a glass of sherry, occasionally, just to be polite to her hosts. Breaking out at 90!

She was always neatly and tastefully dressed, but had absolutely no idea whatever of the world of fashion, nor of what people wore when they went out to dinner parties in the evening.

We were on the point of going off to a party, and Jean was in a silver-white kaftan, looking absolutely stunning, when the phone rang to say that Miss Butler had fallen and broken her arm.

We raced straight to Brookshaw in our glad rags. Those old folk who were still about were startled to see two youngish people in evening dress. Was Miss Butler there, or already taken to the hospital?

Miss Butler was waiting downstairs. She doubted if she ought to go to hospital. Was it sufficiently serious? Her nephew's wife, Mrs Butler, as a radiographer, would be there soon enough to settle the matter.

When she actually saw Jean, she exclaimed, 'Oh my dear, I did not intend them to get you out of bed!' The idea that Jean's kaftan was her normal night attire remained with her. As we drove her up to the hospital she refused to talk about her fall, or her pain, but shared what family news she had with us. And when we reached the X-ray department, she excused Jean's attire by saying, 'She came straight from her bed.'

Occasionally, when I was in great indecision or torment, I would visit Aunt Mary in her tiny cell and ask if she could spare half an hour just to sit with me, in silence. To sit in silence beside a holy woman for half an hour can be worth a thousand wise words. And I use the word holy advisedly.

Jean was kindness itself to my relatives and to Aunt Hilda Collett and Ruth Transvelt Keys – both denizens of the Brookshaw Home at various times. She often had them to lunch or to tea; but Aunt Mary was her favourite. She would come to lunch at least once a week, usually on Sundays. When her ninetieth birthday drew near, Jean asked her what sort of party she would like. A morning or afternoon tea? Or lunch? And whom would she like as her guests?

Aunt Mary was very touched and said she would think about it. And the more she thought about it, the more troubled in spirit she became. She could not possibly have a birthday party for only some of her friends; and it seemed that everyone in the Brookshaw Home was her friend. Everyone must be invited.

Jean organised her friends with cars to ferry the frail and aged to High Corner, where there were many tables and chairs inside the big rooms and all over the garden, laden with little manhattans of sandwiches and pagodas of cakes.

It was a logistical triumph for Jean and her friends, but we were never quite sure how successful the venture was. Many of the guests were uncertain what had happened to them. Jean remembers overhearing a *sotto voce* conversation between two of her guests who seemed too scared even to sit down and drink a cup of tea:

'Why are we here?' asked one.

'I really don't know,' came the reply. At which point Jean gently intervened.

'Aren't you happy?'

'No.'

'It's all so strange.'

'Would you like to go back to Brookshaw?'

'Yes, if you don't mind.'

And back they were taken.

But the birthday girl, Mary, was happy. She had left nobody out.

Jean and I were in Oxford in 1977. Jean felt acute reluctance about leaving not only the children but also Aunt Mary. However, we took some comfort from the fact that Jeffrey would be in South Africa and staying at High Corner for at least part of the time. Here is his account of Mary's last days and burial. I have made a mosaic of extracts from Jeffrey's letters to various people at this time.

To his daughter, 5 August, from Cradock: 'Things have been happening here, notably the rapid, mercifully rapid, decline and death of Aunt Mary. A couple of weeks ago she had a fever, seemed to recover but then had to be moved to hospital. She seemed to "stabilise", as they say in the trade, so Val and I returned to Cradock, but during the night she got rapidly weaker and early in the morning we got a call from her youngest sister Kay to say that she had died at six in the morning.

'She has been winding down for some time, particularly in losing all sense of what she had written or not written. Consequently she tended to write the same letter over several times – each one perfectly coherent and clear, but simply a repetition of one written a few days before. She and Val were very close to each other, in this situation both having "the gift of tears", as I do not. I think Val was very valuable to her, someone who did not try to hide her grief or if she tried was not able to do so. It was very sad to see how tired Mary was, the lively, clear eyes, shaded and tired. But she had some spark to the end – when Donaldson, a Presbyterian minister of whom Mary was very fond, was about to leave her the day before she died, she said, "I'd like you to kiss me."'

The Reverend Bob Donaldson arranged a memorial service at the Brookshaw, while Jeffrey notified members of the family and the Quaker community of the cremation in Port Elizabeth. Joan and Christine could not come, but Dorothy came from Pretoria; Mary's sister Alice was present, brought by John and Marie Biggs from Graaff-Reinet, and also Kathleen and Uncle Boy Vorster; and our sons David and Christopher, with Violet Ngqia.

It fell to Jeffrey to organise a service in a manner as close to Quaker practice as he could guess.

'The crematorium is not the most reassuring or dignified of places. I was a little horrified by the hierarchical structured pulpit facing the congregation with a button to be pressed at the appropriate moment. I was very bothered about how to perform an act of committal but with the help of Keith's prayer book we decided on the following. I got the man who runs the place to give me a chair so that I could face the people and after a silence I read Mary's "A Memory of Childhood". After a pause two of the Quaker ladies read short pieces, and then after a longer pause Dorothy read three pieces of scripture from the Order of Burial and when she began the Lord's Prayer I pressed the button which simply lowers the coffin out of sight. I had a rather bad moment because all this was happening behind me and as I waited, I began to be anxious that the thing might not be working. (I could have done without this piece of technology.) After a brief silence I walked out and everybody joined me.'

The letter to his daughter adds another dimension. 'Quaker meetings make powerful use of silence, and between the brief readings by various people we sat silent while the wind buffetted the building. A strange experience because Quaker meetings are usually so totally quiet and peaceful.'

It was decided to inter Mary's ashes in the Butler plot in the Cradock cemetery while Jeffrey was still in Cradock, working on the history of his home town.

On 5 September he wrote to his sister Joan.

'It's odd coming back to Cradock after all these years. So much I know so intimately – some kerbstones are even recognizable – but the Cradock of our childhood is so finally gone that I am beginning to wonder what it was really like. A happy childhood may not be the best vantage point for the urban historian.'

And on 29 October to Jean and me in Cambridge:

'On Thursday afternoon we interred Mary's ashes in the cemetery on a *hot* blustery Karoo day. I said a piece about Mary and The Poplars, Patrick Mali, a teacher, spoke on "The Florence Nightingale of the Location", and Keith about her and young people and her work in Cradock since the war. Very simple. Molly Collett, Beth Rayner, a young African she helped, a Coloured woman on the Joint Council. It's a pity you weren't there. It gave my heart a tug to realize how utterly we Butlers have left this place. Poor declining little town – it once appeared to have a life and a future even apart from the Butlers!'

The first volume of this autobiography, *Karoo Morning*, attempted to recreate the life of the Butler family at The Poplars. In this chapter I have given some account of the latter years, deaths and burials of Alice, Ernest and Mary Butler; but what of the building itself, the fabric of masonry and timber in which these people spent so much of their lives?

The floods in the Fish River Valley in 1974 reached heights that had not been exceeded in a hundred years. They destroyed The Poplars. I can do no better than use extracts from the accounts of my siblings. I start with Joan:

'I arrived at Cradock from Queenstown to be stopped at the Mill in Commissioner Street by a soldier who required to know my need to drive into Bree Street! Hardly a soul appeared. Mud and silt in the road and severely eroded pavements met my eyes all the way down to the gaol and back up to Church Street. The flood waters had reached five feet and more up the walls of most of the houses. Roofs had collapsed as interior walls built of unbaked brick turned to mud, carrying beams and roofs to floors.

'I negotiated the mud into St Peter's Church where the carpets had been removed. The font was full of chocolate-brown river water. Dad's teak-panelling round the choir, the organ manual and stalls had been scrubbed down. The water had been in the raised sanctuary – altogether a heart-rending scene. In self-defence one hardly gave a thought to the many family events that had taken place within these walls. Outside again, a "panda" bear from some home upstream, grinning from the upper branches of the pomegranate hedge leading to the rectory, and a tractor tyre crowning the marble cross teetering over a grave, presented bizarre sights.

'The Poplars, our old home on the corner of Church and Bree Streets, was my next stop. Standing still on the path leading to the front door of the last home of my parents, I listened to the silence! Not a soul around; even insects seemed dead. Aunt Mary's cottage had a watermark up to my height.

'At the cemetery, I could not lift the fallen headstone on Grandfather James Butler's grave. Many graves had sunk and headstones were all awry. Folk were weeping openly as they picked their way through the chaos there.'

My sister Dorothy describes the interior of The Poplars.

'I stood among the rubble of the flooded house which had sheltered me in childhood. The mouldering green damp patches on the walls breaking out like sores after the water had receded. The parquet flooring laid by my father lay in a heap outside the house ... The wide passage where the sun used to lie on the gleaming floor, stripped now of pictures, and in the sitting-room, incongruous but beautiful still, the peacocks strutted and preened in the frieze above the picture rail. The furrows in the garden were choked in mud, my mother's roses blooming – the stocks, chrysanthemums, narcissi flowering regardless of the human storm, the wrecked houses, the driftwood piled against the bridge ...'

About the same time, Jeff and I visited Cradock. Our impressions were much the same as our sisters'. The pergola pillars which our father had cast had been pushed over by the weight of water, and the timbers, fallen at sixes and sevens, scribbled ruin across the façade of the house – a message corroborated when we entered the hallway and saw how the interior walls of unbaked brick had collapsed.

We had both come to accept that the old Cradock of which we had such warm and happy memories had disappeared long before the flood hit it. We had to decide what to do with that ruin. We took the only possible decision – to demolish it.

But it is people, not buildings, who have a way of coming back into our lives with the most poignant force. Well after the demolition of the old house, well after the interment of Mary's ashes, Alice, Ernest and Mary sprang back to life in an unexpected manner.

I have mentioned going into the workshop, on the morning after my father's death in June 1965, and finding a missal-stand completed on the workbench.

We children had decided to contribute to a gift for St Peter's Church – a handsome prayerbook for use at the altar. Joan took the idea one stage further: to give something in our mother's memory to the Church of the Ascension in the new apartheid location called Lingelihle. Canon James Calata agreed that a missal-stand would be most welcome.

Some time after Ernest's funeral, when both Joan and I were in Cradock, Aunt Mary let it be known that Canon James Calata would like the missal-stand, in memory of Alice, to be handed over at Evensong. He would be happy to accept a gift made by Ernest Butler, a man who had proved himself to be just and a friend of the black people. For some odd reason I kept the notes of what I said.

'This little altar-desk was made by my father. It was the very last thing he made in his workshop in which he made many, many things. He left no incomplete unfinished jobs. His workshop was swept and tidy, and on the bench was his last work, this little altar-desk, this present to your Church. The message on the brass plate reads: "Presented to the Church of the Ascension in loving memory of Alice Eyre Butler 1880-1963, by her husband and children." So from this time forward my mother and father and their children will be a little part of this Church in Cradock. It is a good place to be. Also on the plate are the four letters A.M.D.G. – *Ad Majorem Dei Gloriam:* To the Greater Glory of God. That is something to remember too. Half our troubles and those of the world spring from deeds done for the greater glory of Men.'

In 1983 I was asked by Koos Roets to collaborate in the making of a four-part TV documentary on the Great Karoo. We were about to go to Teebus and Koffiebus, to take shots of the water emerging from the Orange/Fish tunnel, and it struck me that we might get some Xhosa hymn-singing from the Church of the Ascension in Cradock. I telephoned the priest-in-charge and asked him if it would be possible for his choir to sing the great hymn of Ntsikana for a TV documentary. He agreed.

The security situation at that time was tense but had eased a little. In Grahamstown one could go in and out of the location without a police permit or any official's permission.

When we arrived at the church in Lingelihle we were told we would have to wait a little while until a funeral was over. There would be another funeral in about an hour's time, so we would have to get our recording done in the pause between the burials. The choir had assembled in traditional dress: those yellow, red and ochre togas and turbans that I find both becoming and moving.

While we were waiting I sat at the back of the church. Two images leapt at me with unexpected power.

First, the organ – a small, prettily decorated Victorian instrument – was the one to which I had sung as a choirboy all my childhood in St Peter's. Here, in this utility building, it seemed incongruous but lovely. And then, the organist: the daughter of Canon James Calata himself, strikingly similar to her father. We exchanged a few words. The Canon was retired now, very old, and living in Port Elizabeth.

We had just started filming when Roets and I were summoned to the porch to speak to the Location Superintendent. Had we a permit? 'No,' I groaned and said, honestly enough, 'I thought that we were finished with all that permit crap.'

'Not in Cradock,' he said.

I came as near to creating a scene as I have ever come. I wanted to tell him to get the hell out of my church; that I had every right to be there, that it was part of my life, witness the organ; witness the missal-stand in memory of my mother. Who was he to tell me that I could not be there?

Then I recognised him. We had been to the local Boys' High School together, although he was more Jeffrey's contemporary than mine. So I said:

'Listen, man. This is a church; the choir is here to sing a hymn – the Hymn of Ntsikana.'

'You mean Nkosi Sikilel' iAfrika?'

'No. That's by Sontonga. Don't you know the great hymn of Ntsikana?'

Of course he didn't. How many white South Africans have even heard of Ntsikana, a poet and prophet more important, perhaps, than all our white missionaries taken together?

I kept my temper, mildly suggesting that it would not look good in the press if we were not allowed to record a great African hymn because of a bit of red tape.

He looked at his watch. 'I give you half an hour. The police know you are here. They are just waiting for a word from me.'

We had to rush through that recording. The coffin for the next funeral was waiting outside and the mourners gathering. Ashamed and angry, we left the church.

In my haste and confusion I forgot to go to the altar, kneel before it, and look at the missal-stand.

But there it is, in daily use, in that barn-like Church of the Ascension, Lingelihle, Cradock. It would not be there but for the love of Alice and Ernest, and the mediation of Mary Butler. It was given and accepted in a dark time when such gestures symbolised a stubborn hope that our country would grow beyond its racial obsessions.

24 1959–

Monuments and Festivals

In the 1950s there were others even more interested in the Settlers than I was, most notably Tom Bowker, United Party M.P. for Albany, affectionately known as Uncle Tom. He felt that the Settlers should have a monument. In his view they deserved one quite as much as the Voortrekkers did. To raise public interest he organised annual pilgrimages on Settlers Day (the first Monday in September) to sites important in the history of the Settlement, erecting uncut monoliths of local stone on them. I attended none of these. I was interested in the people themselves, not in making propaganda for another shrine to our ancestors, for a secular shrine was what Uncle Tom wanted, a magnificent hall with some thirty bays, one for each settler ship, with the names of the Settlers in bronze tablets on the walls, as on a war memorial.

This concept was rejected by most people. It was designated as 'dead' and 'useless'. Historians were quick to point out that the Settler lists were both incomplete and inaccurate and that known errors should not be perpetuated in bronze.

As early as 1957 three professors of Rhodes University, W.D. Maxwell, J.V.L. Rennie and Guy Butler, submitted a memorandum stressing that 'what is required is something as near to *a living memorial* as can be achieved by making the monumental structure serve some particular and appropriate purpose. The emphasis should, therefore, be upon the fundamental values of their heritage ... and upon their abiding relevance to this and future generations'. As for the site, for historical reasons and for general convenience they favoured the Drostdy Grounds, where the monument would have the opportunity 'to work in with existing cultural and educational institutions on that site (like Rhodes University and the Albany Museum), and therefore by collaboration and extension form a cultural focal point of first-rate national importance'.

To this end they proposed, not a shrine but 'an 1820 memorial chapel to serve also as a chapel for Rhodes University ... The University itself is in a position to contribute very greatly through two of its departments, the Faculty of Divinity and the School of Music ...' It would be in daily use and its sung services might in time become renowned like those of university chapels elsewhere.

The three professors had found a use for the proposed building but they had reckoned without their colleagues, most of whom rejected the chapel concept with something close to contempt. The City of Saints was already over-endowed with under-used churches, and the liberal academy did not wish its agnostic image to be obfuscated by a Shinto shrine on its front lawn. (In 1975 when the Grahamstown Training College closed its doors, the Community of the Resurrection gave Rhodes University its very fine chapel designed by Sir Herbert Baker's firm – St Mary and All Angels.)

But Uncle Tom Bowker was a persistent man, and his supporters grew in number. Some in the anti-monument or neutral camps perceived that whether they liked it or not, there was going to be a large national monument in Grahamstown, and that its nature would affect the atmosphere and 'image' of the City.

It had already been borne in on Uncle Tom that support for his dream would increase if the monument had a use or uses. 'What uses?' he asked. At this point many mere observers became participators. Long and sometimes acrimonious debates about these possible uses ensued.

Mr Bowker knew of my interest in the Eastern Cape Settlers as a various, articulate and, for their time and place, important group of people. Between sessions of parliament he would invite me to talk about his beloved project. He told me in so many words that as I was 'a man of ideas' it was my duty to get involved. I replied that a monument devoted to perpetuating a white mythology based on our nine frontier wars was something I could not touch, and that there were many like me.

A month or two later, over another pot of tea, he said: 'Butler, last night one of my supporters from Lower Albany phoned me up. He said: "Uncle Tom, I had this vision in the night. A statue, for the front of your shrine. A fine bronze horse rearing up on its hocks. Settler lad, twisted in saddle, Brown Bess into shoulder, shooting a naked savage with lifted assegai."'

There was a long pause. Eventually I asked:

'Well, Mr Bowker?'

'You know, Butler, I don't think it's such a good idea.'

'Why, Mr Bowker?'

A pause, and he leant forward a little.

'Well, you see, Butler, sooner or later – twenty, fifty, a hundred years – there will be no "Whites Only" notices anywhere. Everybody is going to be everywhere and if they don't like our monument, they'll pull it down.'

It was a turning point in my attitude to the Monument. It was quite clear that Mr Bowker was against spending money on expensive images of frontier violence. There were other Settler activities and attributes to commemorate.

Of course frontier history was a fact which could not be wished away; but one did not need to erect permanent reminders of its wars. Grass grows quickly on a battlefield but anyone who thinks, for instance, that the allocation of land in the Eastern Cape has been finally 'settled' has simply

Double Drift Fort

not been aware of the redistribution demands of the past two decades.

I have a story which illuminates how attitudes to our past conflicts undergo acceptable and surprising changes.

In the Alexandria district on the edge of a sacred grove of indigenous bush, isolated in a large field variously planted with seasonal crops, is the grave of one of our greatest and most enigmatic women, Nongqawuse, the Xhosa prophetess. As a young woman she had uttered those disastrous assurances that, provided all cattle were killed, the ancestors would return to drive the white men and their black allies the Mfengu into the sea. Thousands of cattle were killed but the ancestors did not return. Nongqawuse died an old woman in exile on the edge of the Alexandria woods.

A triangular stone of modest size has been placed at the edge of her grave, with the following inscription:

The Grave of Nongqause (sic)
The Xosa (sic) Prophetess
who lived in this vicinity
after the cattle killing in 1858
until her death in 1898.

Two cattle skulls are the only decoration. Who erected this tribute to the woman who had wished to get rid of the whites for ever? Three Settler descendants, C.L. Deacon, T.B. Bowker and I. Mitford-Barberton, had accepted her as part of their own story.

But to return to the function and siting of the monument. By 1959 the concept had evolved from a shrine or memorial chapel to an impressive multi-purpose great hall, for which Professor Thornton White of the University of Cape Town drew sketches, a handsome structure with gothic buttresses and a flat floor, with facilities for undefined cultural celebrations.

Where was this imposing structure to be sited? The mayor took Thornton White to various possible sites in the city. The city itself was prepared to donate the Botanical Gardens and Gunfire Hill to the Cape Provincial Administration as a nature reserve in which the monument could be erected. But where? Thornton White gave a talk at High Corner on Saturday evening, 13 June 1959, to representatives of Town and Gown. He favoured a 'vertical feature' on the horizon close to the existing Fort Selwyn, the great hall itself to be well below the horizon on the slopes of the hill, facing south-east – to be set in a landscape like a large 18th-century country house. This would be in easy walking distance from the campus and the city. It would also have been sheltered from the west wind.

But what I called the Rhine Castle mentality prevailed. One city councillor threatened to withdraw his blessing from the scheme unless the monument was built right on top of the hill. It was one of the many 'Settler' battles I lost. Not that the hilltop site is without its advantages, but it did pose a daunting set of problems to the architect.

I had not, however, quite given up the battle to find appropriate uses for the handsome building. I supported those who, like Professor Jack and Dr Eily Gledhill, advocated its uses as a conference centre. Conferences were in the democratic tradition dear to the British people. That excellent idea has remained on the active agenda of the Foundation.

By early 1959 Professors Rennie, Hewson and Butler had abandoned the chapel concept in favour of a festival venue. Others such as Georg Grüber and Professor Percival Kirby (who had retired to Grahamstown from Wits) supported the idea. But providing a venue for festivals struck the old guard as inappropriately frivolous for a memorial. Indeed, memorials are usually solemn places, and to this day some good people who see the fun and hear the laughter in the memorial foyer of the monument feel that they are witnessing acts of desecration.

By the early 1960s Tom Bowker's scheme was sufficiently advanced to erect a precinct stone to mark the site of the monument. This was unveiled by State President C.R. Swart, in 1961 – an event which did not pass off without incident. A tall, enterprising student acquired a Rolls Royce, dressed himself suitably in top hat and sash, and sneaked in ahead of the presidential entourage, collecting the salutes and presented-arms from the soldiers who lined the route. And there were 'stands' of staff and students up Lucas Avenue with placards to make it quite plain that the State President had not graduated in their minds from a politician to a symbolical figurehead of the entire nation. He was still 'Blackie' Swart who had brandished a sjambok in parliament as the traditional and best way of disciplining one's children and servants.

Before Tom Bowker died, however, he had been persuaded that his 'great hall' did not have as much appeal as the more complex concept of which I was one of the chief protagonists – a building which provided facilities for activities which could be seen to encourage certain aspects of the English-speaking tradition. Of many possibilities, two were chosen, neither of which is exclusively English, and both of which have long been part of South African life. First the democratic tradition; secondly the English language.

The building was to be designed as a centre for conferences, large and small. The Settlers loved debate and discussion. There is plenty of evidence of the historic British contribution to the growth of democratic institutions in our country. The conference centre would not only point to that tradition, but encourage its growth and continuance.

The building was also to be the centre for English language festivals. It would contain a large auditorium, to be the main venue for an annual festival of plays, lectures, and other items to celebrate the English language and the traditions it transmits. A balance would be kept between the classics and the encouragement of indigenous creative works. As at all festivals, music would play a great part. 'The motivation for this is clear: the English language is perhaps the greatest of the many gifts which the Settlers brought to South Africa. It is something that does not belong to us only. It is a window on the world for all our countrymen and a medium in which we think and express our feelings for our country and the world.'

Some agreed that an annual festival was a good idea, but in Grahamstown? That is a good question which is still being asked. Fortunately there were historic Settler precedents for celebrations in Grahamstown which proved useful in persuading some sceptics. But there was a general lack of enthusiasm among both Town and Gown. Indeed, many of the citizens were opposed to the whole idea, and vocal in their opposition, most notably Harold Goodwin, a blind poet whom I liked very much. 'Can any good thing come out of Nazareth?' It was as though a portion of Grahamstown, having lost the war between the wagon and the railway, wanted to be left in peace. They were descended from the 1820 Settlers and had been happily descending ever since. Who were these rowdies disturbing the even tenor of their decline? I felt it necessary to write a memorandum on the possibilities of Grahamstown as a festival city, which I submitted to the Committee on 15 January 1965:

This century has seen the growth of festivals throughout the world. Many are located in small centres. Some are annual, others less frequent; some are predominantly musical, others concentrate on drama. Starting from small beginnings many have become famous; many have a strong regional or national appeal. Those that are imaginative and well-managed have become powerful tourist attractions and sources of income to the communities which organise them.

Grahamstown has certain attributes and needs which make it worthwhile considering seriously the possibility of its becoming a festival and conference centre.

It is acknowledged to be an exceptionally charming city. One of its most powerful and least exploited assets is its historical importance as the Settler City. It holds a growing interest for South Africans, particularly those of British descent. It is the heart of the Settler country where the forebears of many South Africans first settled.

It is rich in beautiful old buildings with historical associations and the surrounding countryside has many interesting historical sites and other attractions.

As an educational centre with a University, Training College and famous Schools, it has a cultural reputation and some claim to the resources of taste, talent and experience which a festival demands.

It is on the main coastal trunk road and within easy striking distance of many coastal resorts and inland towns, and midway between the two large and expanding urban areas of Port Elizabeth and East London. Because of the Orange River Scheme the population of the Eastern Cape is bound to increase.

The location in Grahamstown of the 1820 Memorial will attract more tourists than in the past.

A festival calls for several halls and auditoria. The large auditorium which is to be part of the memorial, and the proposed Little Theatre at the University, together with the City Hall and other existing halls, will provide an adequate variety of venues.

As for the nature of the festival, I suggested:

'It should be both light-hearted and serious and while it might legitimately lay stress on the interests and traditions of English-speaking South Africans, it should never become sectional or parochial.' I then listed the elements which it might comprise:

1. Drama, including Shakespeare or other English classics, with indigenous and experimental plays.
2. Music: Choir concerts and competitions, including African choirs; opera; symphony concerts.
3. Special religious services.
4. Awards and honours to such figures as
   a) Scholars or Writers or Artists of the Year;
   b) Winners of nationwide literary competitions.
5. Lectures on a wide range of topics.
6. Exhibitions of paintings and sculpture.
7. Guided tours of the Town and of the Settler Country.

(It is gratifying, twenty-four years later, to see these pipe dreams realised in a Festival which is indeed both joyous and serious.)

About this time our bishop, Robert Selby Taylor, returned from Canada where he had attended Shakespeare productions in an out-of-the-way place near London, Ontario. He found the idea of a festival in Grahamstown appealing and supported the idea in conversation with Dr Tom Bowker.

Uncle Tom was ailing. Rumour has it that he complained to some of his old faithfuls about 'a brace of crazy professors who want us to build a music hall to our ancestors'. But before he died he gave the 'music hall' his blessing in a press statement: 'The monument will be a permanent structure, visually a monument to the 1820 Settlers, but in reality, a place for conferences, musical festivals, drama and Shakespearean works, in which maintenance of the English language will be the principal objective.'

Standing in the foyer of the Monument during one of the early Festivals I watched a group of young people near the bubbling fountain, among whom was a beautiful red-headed girl listening to a young man telling a joke. Suddenly she flung her head back and laughed, as did all the others. That glimpse of delight reminded me of a story told to me by a film producer who had wished to make a film on the frontier wars. In search of authentic information he approached Uncle Tom Bowker, in whose company he had visited the Bathurst district in the early 'fifties. There were still a few old-stagers about who could recall incidents of the last of the frontier wars (1879). The accident of the colour of the girl's hair led me to write the following lines in gratitude to Uncle Tom, without whom the incident would not have occurred.

HOW TO REMEMBER YOUR ANCESTORS

In the nineteen-fifties a gentleman from Johannesburg,
from the world of the silver screen,
decided to make a 'frontier epic'
vivid with authentic experience.
He wished to meet an old-stager or two
from the last of the frontier wars.
There were still a few about
who'd been lads in 1879.
Tom Bowker, M.P. for Albany, said,
'Let's see what we can do.'

They did the rounds of Upper and Lower Albany
but all the likelies
seemed to have died since Uncle Tom
shook hands with them last at the Bathurst Show,
— except old Isaac — Isaac What's-his-name? —
Bradfield? Timm? Tarr? or Emslie or Long,
from Salem side?
Anyway, there they sat, in 'The Pig and Whistle', Bathurst,
a living Settler Monument
in regular use since about 1830.

'Uncle Isaac,' said Uncle Tom,
'tell this gentleman from Johannesburg
how you were ambushed down at Watersmeet.'

'Ambush? Watersmeet? Let me see now ...'
His pondering pause was filled
with doves and kokkewiets.

'Yes. Four of you on horses:
you, and Tarr, and Bradfield,
and maybe a Timm or a Purdon.'

'Which Timm? Which Tarr? Which Bradfield?
Man, my life's been full of them.'

'Well, you said you were courting the sister
of one of them at the time.'

'Was I now? Well, most men had sisters then —
those days, families were large. And I,
well, I did quite a bit of courting in those days.
What was this girl's name?'

'I don't know. But I do remember
one thing you said:
"Her hair was a lovely red."'

'Red hair?'

'Yes.'

There was a long, long second of bird-haunted silence
as two pairs of old blue eyes
exchanged the secret of their delight.
Then Uncle Tom, pulling himself
back into history, swallowed and said:
'Yes; you and her brother and the others
were riding down to the drift,
down there between the fever trees,
and just when you reached the crossing at Watersmeet
it happened. Tell this gentleman what happened.'

'Of course! I remember now —
What a beauty she was! Her name?
Wait now, let's see, it'll come, it'll come ...'

'Well, you and her brother ...'

'Did she have a brother? Likely enough.
Most girls had brothers those days;
families were large.'

'You and her brother,' said Uncle Tom —

'Now what was her name! But oh,
what a peach of a girl!'

The better to remember, Uncle Isaac rose
and walked to the window, and stared
into a blue bright sky
alive with unsolicited song.

*Uncle Tom turned to the gentleman
in search of authentic frontier epic and said:
'His memory's not what it was two years ago.'
And the man from the world of the silver screen
was moved to say:
'Who wants to be bothered about an ambush
when his mind's ablaze again
with a red-headed glory of a girl?'*

With the departure of Dr Tom Bowker the monument project entered a new phase. In 1965 another Settler descendant, Dr W.J.B. Slater, recently retired Provincial Secretary of the Cape, became chairman of the 1820 Settlers National Monument Committee. He proved to be a dynamic, tireless and effective leader, making no fewer than 100 trips from Cape Town to Grahamstown on Monument affairs.

A new chapter had been opened. Many South Africans with no 1820 ancestry accepted the imaginative and unusual concept. The response on the Reef was particularly encouraging. Without the moral, practical and financial support of men like Douglas Roberts, Ian Mackenzie and Richard Cooke there would have been no living monument, no conferences, and no festivals.

In 1965 I was invited to join the Users' Committee 'to promote among other things the establishment of an annual English Language Festival and other festivals in the Great Hall'. By 1966 the Great Hall concept was replaced by one for an auditorium with raked floor to seat about a thousand people with an imaginative foyer as the monumental focus. I was appointed chairman of a Commemorative sub-committee, one of whose tasks was to plan a festival for 1970. This led to my being elected chairman of the Festivals Committee, a task which was to consume a great deal of my time for several years. I have long ceased to be chairman, but still sit on the committee which creates a festival that has become a major, if not *the* major event in the South African artistic calendar.

The year 1970 was the 150th anniversary of the landing of the 1820 Settlers. It was also the centenary of the first grand Grahamstown Festival, that of 1870, which marked the 50th anniversary of their landing.

It fell to my lot to organise an appropriate festival. It ran from 4–13 September. There was of course no Monument building as yet, and we had to use existing venues in the city. This has grown into a custom.

I persuaded the Grahamstown Amateur Dramatic Society to re-enact the highlights of the Jubilee Celebrations of 1870. 'Let's Do It Again,' or 'That's The Way It Was', devised by Kit Forbes, was performed by a large cast, many of them Settler descendants. The venue (now the Drill Hall) was the same as that in which H.H. Dugmore had delivered his mammoth lecture (see chapter 22). It was so long that in order to recover his breath he had been obliged to break it with musical interludes for which he had written both words and music. His original music having been found, it was performed by the Rhodes Chamber Choir and Albert Honey's Wind Band.

I directed *Noyes Fludde* by Benjamin Britten in the Cathedral of St Michael and St George. Dr Georg Grüber assembled, trained and conducted the ingenious combination of instruments in the orchestra. I was ably backed by Beth Dickerson on the production side and Jenny Dugmore drilled scores of scholars from the Victoria Girls' High School as animals to fill and empty the ark, singing the glorious Kyrie Eleisons and Alleluias. I did much of the set construction myself to Ken Robinson's designs, including a dazzling rainbow fan of immense proportions which unfolded behind the ark at the appropriate moment.

The Cathedral still had the old yellowwood gallery on the south wall. It provided a wonderful vantage spot from which God (Georg Grüber Junior) could give his imperious yet gentle instructions and promises to errant mankind; and also for the trumpeter, Derek Schaefer, to send thrilling cadences echoing through the building. *Noyes Fludde* is a gorgeous and complex work involving the disciplined collaboration of over a hundred bodies and voices. At one point, says Miss Dugmore, I leapt on a pew and delivered a somewhat secular sermon to them all, containing such elevating sentences as 'The only people who know their parts are the bloody animals!'

The result was worth it. I never enjoyed a production more. It was my last.

The Cape Performing Arts Board had commissioned me to write a play on a Settler theme for the occasion. I chose to dramatise one of our unsung pacifist heroes. The result was *Richard Gush of Salem*. It was directed by Roy Sargeant, whose subsequent contribution to the growth and success of the Festival was to be incalculable.

Other items on the programme were forerunners of features of future festivals. A keynote address was delivered by Sir Arthur Snelling, the British Ambassador; Professor Winifred Maxwell gave the first Dugmore Memorial Lecture; and a lecture series constituted the embryo of the Winter School. There were art, photographic and other exhibitions, a religious service and historical tours conducted by the Grahamstown and Lower Albany Historical Societies. Yellowwood trees were planted in the 1820 Settlers Memorial Nature Reserve, most of which seem to have survived almost twenty years of our erratic climate.

The mix of indigenous, experimental works and classics set a pattern which has been followed since. In 1971 Robert Selley brought his Oratorio choir from Port Elizabeth with Mozart's *Requiem Mass* and excerpts from Handel's *Messiah;* Patrick Mynhardt's Herman Charles Bosman rubbed shoulders with J.M. Synge's *The Playboy of the Western World,* and Rex and Barbara Reynolds mounted a superb exhibition of photographs of Settler architecture. The Fringe made its first appearance. There was a Ball in the City Hall, a Horse Show, and Drag Racing arranged by the Grahamstown Car Club.

In 1972 the emphasis fell on Youth, an important first step which in time would lead to the annual Schools Festival, the English Olympiad and the Eisteddfod.

Meanwhile the Monument – what Tom Bowker had called 'the musical hall to our ancestors' – was rising on Gunfire Hill. It was ready for its first conference and festival in 1974. I was deeply involved in both.

First, a Conference on 'English-speaking South Africa Today' was opened by the Hon. Mr N. Ogilvie Thompson, a Settler descendant and Chief Justice of the Republic. It fell on me to follow him with 'The Nature and Purpose of the Conference'. The table of contents of the Proceedings (Oxford University Press, 1976) shows that we had gathered an exceptional panel of authorities and that our concern was the future rather than the past. It was rounded off by 'Eleven Poems' by Sipho Sepamla. These reminded English-speaking South Africans, who might cherish the notion that the Monument was an exercise in nostalgia, that they were a highly privileged small section of a society whose laws were designed to perpetuate ethnic differences. The opening service of dedication in the foyer had been led by clerics of all major denominations and all race groups, but for years the use of the facilities of the Monument was restricted by innumerable apartheid laws. These have gradually fallen away and the Monument is now open to all sections of the South African people. The Proceedings volume ends with Sepamla's 'The Rainbow's End':

> ... *Teach me to forgive*
> *Teach me to forget the deeds of those men*
> *Who have debased me*
> *Taught me to see people as tribes.*

As for the 1974 Festival, the stage of the Monument auditorium was inaugurated in grand style by *King Lear,* the greatest play by the world's greatest playwright; by a breathtaking ballet production of the Prokofiev *Romeo and Juliet,* and Mozart's *Cosi Fan Tutte.* David Tidboald conducted a symphony concert, Alain Balegeas gave a fine recital of the piano works of Ravel, there was a sung miracle play in the Cathedral, Des and Dawn Lindberg presented 'Joseph and His Amazing Technicolour Dream Coat', the Rhodes Chamber Choir was on form, and Alan Paton lectured on 'Roy Campbell, Man and Poet'.

But there were many prophets of doom. 'The first-and-last time the auditorium will be filled,' said some. Certainly the Festival idea did not catch on immediately. To those who asked me how 'your great white elephant' was getting along, my reply was:

'The idea is good but admittedly unusual for a monument. Most people are conservative. My belief is that it will win through. It needs a little time.'

By 1984 the tide had indeed turned. It would not have done so without much devotion and generosity of time, talent, money and ideas from a host of people; and in particular, sponsors such as Five Roses, Sharp Electronics and most recently the Standard Bank. Its success has depended also on F. Lamond (Jock) Sturrock, whose design successfully integrated the commemorative and functional demands for a living monument.

Throughout the entire length of each festival Jean entertains our friends, performers, relations, V.I.P.s. and others to protracted, convivial and relaxed lunches at High Corner. They are feasts in all senses of the word. A warm hostess generates a kind of magic. Wonderful ideas blossom, friendships are made or renewed, sparks fly, oil is poured, and in the general conviviality the Festival spirit finds its fullest expression. To bring people of goodwill together to share food and wine and old and new ideas is surely the best way to celebrate.

The big rooms of High Corner are ideal for this. At one particularly memorable luncheon, someone cried, 'Where would Guy be without Jean?' Where indeed?

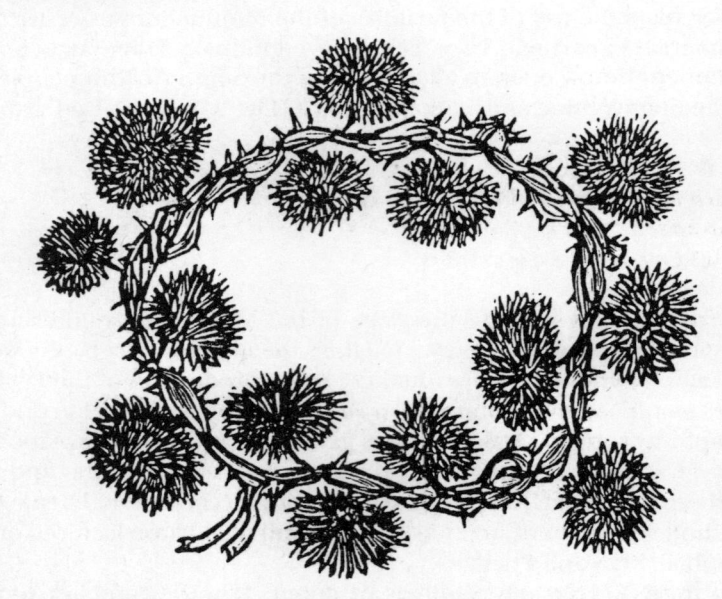

Illustration by John Lawrence for South of the Zambesi

Epilogue

Since the end of 1987 I have held the status of Professor Emeritus and Honorary Research Fellow at Rhodes University. In addition to some editing and creative work, I have enjoyed unhurried research, particularly in the Elizabethan field. This has brought me back to my first and greatest love, William Shakespeare. I have made one or two scholarly contributions which may in time contribute (via footnotes) to a clearer understanding of certain passages in the works. But as nearly always with me, I have little scruple in shelving the completion of a learned article if anything vaguely resembling a fresh idea or rhyme enters my mind.

As its national president, I devote time to the affairs of the Shakespeare Society of Southern Africa. Among its major projects is the development of editions of the plays which address the particular needs of African teachers and students.

Some educationists will question the relevance of Shakespeare in schools in contemporary South Africa – a difficult question into which I cannot enter here, but I would like to record two comments made by African teachers at a symposium. The demand that, as Shakespeare is so difficult, he ought to be dropped elicited the answer: 'That is nonsense. Mathematics is also difficult, but you don't say, Drop it. The answer is to improve the quality of teachers and textbooks.' The other comment was a blunt assertion: 'Shakespeare is acknowledged to be the best writer in English. We are entitled to make his acquaintance. Nothing but the best is good enough for us.'

In 1964, mainly as a result of the determination of Gwen Knowles-Williams of the University of Pretoria, the English Academy of Southern Africa was founded – a body which deserves far more support than it gets. I served as its second national president from 1966 to 1969. In 1970 Natal University awarded me a D.Litt (Hon.Causa); Wits followed suit in 1984; and UNISA in 1989.

In October 1989 Jean and I were invited by the English Academy of Southern Africa to attend a ceremony in Johannesburg at which the President, Angus Rose, presented me with the first of the gold medals which it had decided to award for distinguished service in the cause of English.

It was a most happy occasion for both of us. In my brief speech of thanks I mentioned that it was particularly appropriate that Jean should be with me. Since our first meeting more than half a century before, she had shared my life and supported me with love throughout my academic and artistic career.

When we had returned to our hotel room I presented the medal to her.

This book was written almost entirely under the apartheid régime. It was completed before Mr Gorbachev changed the direction of European history, and Mr F.W. de Klerk the nature and style of African politics. It is far too early to see clearly the shape of the new South Africa, but I welcome with joy the movement towards a democratic society in which the biological accident of skin-colour is not the all-determining factor in our lives. It is a great achievement to have abolished an unjust system. To replace it with a better will call not only for enormous increases in financial investment and job creation, but for the tireless practice of all the generous virtues, of tolerance, compassion and imagination. We have to break out of the critical into the creative mode. We are at an end, and also at a beginning.